Humanitarian Crises and Intervention

Humanitarian Crises and Intervention

REASSESSING THE IMPACT OF MASS MEDIA

Walter C. Soderlund, E. Donald Briggs,
Kai Hildebrandt, and Abdel Salam Sidahmed

Kumarian Press
An Imprint of Stylus Publishing

Humanitarian Crises and Intervention: Reassessing the Impact of Mass Media

Published 2008 in the United States of America by Kumarian Press
22883 Quicksilver Drive, Sterling, VA 20166 USA

Copyedit by David Johnstone
Proofread by Beth Richards
Index by Robert Swanson
Design and production by Rosanne Schloss, NY
The text of this book is set in 11/13 Adobe Sabon

Printed in the USA on acid-free paper by IBT Global

∞ The paper used in this publication meets the minimum requirements of the American National Standard for Information Sciences—Permanence of Paper for Printed Library Materials, ANSI Z39.48-1984.

Library of Congress Cataloging-in-Publication Data

Humanitarian crises and intervention : reassessing the impact of mass media /
    by Walter C. Soderlund ... [et al.].
        p.   cm.
    Includes bibliographical references and index.
    ISBN 978-1-56549-261-5 (pbk. : alk. paper) — ISBN 978-1-56549-262-2
    (cloth : alk. paper)
1. Humanitarian intervention. 2. Mass media—United States.
I. Soderlund, Walter C.
    JZ6369.H835 2008
    363.34'98560973—dc22
                                                        2008018073

This book is for the grandchildren

Ava, Jack, and Macie
Moira, Liam, and Erin

In the hope that theirs might be
a more humane world than ours has been

Contents

Tables and Maps

Tables

Maps

Preface

SINCE THE POPULARIZATION OF TELEVISION IN THE 1960S, THE ROLE OF MASS media in political processes (both international and domestic) has given rise to a significant growth area in academic research, and the research reported in this book is situated within this domain. It focuses specifically on the part played by mass media in determining which human catastrophes occurring in the post-colonial world in the period immediately following the end of the Cold War were met by "humanitarian intervention" responses by the international community—and, perhaps more importantly, which were not.

The "Post–Cold War Period" is defined as roughly the decade-long interlude between the end of the Cold War (occurring in stages between 1989 and 1991) and the cataclysmic events of September 11, 2001. The period was characterized by the convergence of a unique set of circumstances that led to a series of essentially domestic political crises in post-colonial countries, which normally would have been considered to lie outside the boundaries of UN jurisdiction. Nevertheless, given the seriousness of these crises in terms of loss of life or abuses of human rights, the dilemma of which should be addressed by the international community and in what way was a serious one.

Focusing attention specifically on crises occurring in the post-colonial world, the following chapters examine United States television and newspaper news coverage of ten such humanitarian crises with respect to (1) the volume of both newspaper and television news coverage (measuring the function of "alerting" the mass public to the existence of a crisis—a key component of the so-called CNN effect), and (2) the evaluative character of the crisis framing found in newspaper coverage—specifically whether interpretive "frames" employed in the coverage of a particular crisis in the *New York Times* tended to promote an intervention or to discourage any international response.

In examining the ten selected cases of humanitarian crisis, we have also collected data on the severity of each crisis, measured in terms of the number of deaths and refugees they caused, as well as the likelihood that the crisis might spread across national boundaries—that is, its potential for "spill-over." In addition, we judged, to the extent possible, the extent to which the "national interests" of states likely to contribute to an international intervention were involved either in the country or the area of the world where the crisis was occurring. Also assessed was the degree of risk perceived by potential intervening powers in carrying out an intervention quickly and successfully. In the overall analysis, then, five independent variables (severity of the crisis, perceived risks entailed in a successful intervention, extent of involvement of intervening powers' national interest, plus the roles of mass media in both their "alerting" and "evaluation" functions) are assessed against the actual level of the international response to the crisis. There is a huge range in the dependent variable, as crisis responses varied from only the provision of humanitarian relief, to the deployment of modest intervention forces numbering from three thousand to eight thousand, to the significant mustering of a military force numbering in the neighborhood of forty thousand troops.

The authors strongly believe that in order to understand the numbers produced by quantitative research, readers have to be aware of the historical contexts that produced them. Thus, in dealing with the various crises, we have attempted to follow the same scheme of organization—*Background, Roots of the Crisis,* and *Events Precipitating the Crisis*—in outlining the development of the situations calling for an intervention decision. Moreover, in cases where an international intervention did occur, which in some cases took place in a number of phases, we have briefly described that intervention.

Following this background information, the dependent variable, *Strength of International Response to the Crisis,* is addressed by means of a "structured focused comparison." (see George, 1979) Data dealing with five independent variables, *Crisis Severity, Perceived Risk, Involvement of National Interest,* and *Mass Media "Alerting"* and *Mass Media "Framing"* are then presented. The last is assessed through a detailed assessment of crisis coverage in the *New York Times,* focused on pro- and anti-intervention arguments that may have influenced mass publics and foreign policy decision-makers. At the end of each chapter we evaluated the *Overall Effectiveness of the International Response* in dealing with the crisis.

In the Conclusion, the comparative effects of the five independent variables are assessed both quantitatively and qualitatively. In measuring the level of international response, crisis severity, and volume of media coverage, we were able to collect data from which we could establish credible rank orders and present the Spearman Rank Order coefficients for three relationships: that between the *international response* and *crisis severity,* that between the *international response* and *volume of media coverage,* and that between *crisis severity* and *volume of media coverage.* For media framing, perceived risk, and level of national interest involvement on the part of intervening powers, the data collected unfortunately were not suitable for the constructions of rank orders but have been categorized from *low* to *medium* to *high.* Intervention framing is assessed primarily through a detailed qualitative analysis of crisis coverage in the *New York Times.*

We have a number of institutions and individuals to thank for their help in turning this book into reality. First and foremost on this list is the University of Windsor, where all the contributors have taught, and which has provided an atmosphere conducive to scholarly endeavors—for at least two of them, extending well into their post-retirement years. Our thanks go to a long list of Presidents, Vice-Presidents-Academic, Vice-Presidents-Research, Deans, Department Heads, colleagues, secretaries, and, of course, our students. Special thanks go to Kumarian Press, especially to Editor James Lance and Production Manager Erica Flock, who worked tirelessly and patiently to oversee the volume through its final phases.

We believe the conclusions arrived at in this book have clear policy implications for the present day. The adoption of the "responsibility to protect" norm by the United Nations in the fall of 2005 leaves the international community with less justification for not becoming involved in domestic crises in instances where basic human rights come under attack and states are either complicit in the violence or are unwilling or unable to stop it. Against this norm change, however, must be set the as yet undetermined effects of the seemingly endless morass in Afghanistan and the ever-deepening disaster in Iraq, which will surely serve to dampen any enthusiasm for any intervention based strictly on humanitarian grounds.

The situation is especially acute in the Darfur region of Sudan, where human rights abuses reached the level in 2004 where, as was the case with Rwanda a decade earlier, the term "genocide" was used to describe the nature of the conflict. In Haiti as well, the concept of "responsibility to protect" was invoked in 2004, but only following the international community's failure to support the elected government of President

Jean-Bertrand Aristide against a rebel insurgency in February of that year, leading to the "collapse" of the Haitian state, renewed societal violence, and need for yet another UN humanitarian intervention. Societal violence in Timor-Leste in 2006 likewise required another Australian-led intervention, followed by a UN mission. Conflict continues in Somalia as well as in the Democratic Republic of the Congo, and Northern Uganda appears to be the scene of yet another large-scale human catastrophe that has largely fallen through the cracks

The amount of information that mass media provide about impending or actual crises has been cited as critical in "alerting" mass publics in the international community to a catastrophic situation that requires attention. As well, the evaluative "frames" that media employ in their coverage have been identified as important in influencing decisions made by foreign policy elites regarding whether or not the international community will react to a humanitarian crisis with some sort of meaningful response. Just how important these components of media coverage are in the mix of factors leading to humanitarian interventions is the key question we sought to answer in the comparative research reported in the following pages. To our knowledge, no other study dealing with this topic has considered as many cases and looked at as many variables, and has done so employing both quantitative and qualitative research techniques. Moreover, in the process we believe that we have uncovered some very interesting findings to report.

—*Walter C. Soderlund*
—*E. Donald Briggs*
—*Kai Hildebrandt*
—*Abdel Salam Sidahmed*

1

Introduction:
The Problem and Research Methods

Walter C. Soderlund, E. Donald Briggs, and Kai Hildebrandt

▓ The Changing Nature of Conflict

One of the ironies associated with the end of the Cold War is that even as the collective response to Iraq's 1991 invasion of Kuwait was encouraging hope that the United Nations could begin to function according to the principles underlying the Charter, it also became evident that the world was experiencing a decisive shift from *inter-state* to *intra-state* conflict (Blechman, 1995; Bock, 2000). While Errol Henderson and David Singer (2000) have pointed out that the trend toward civil wars in former European colonies was already evident by the time the Second World War was coming to a close, during the 1960s the spread of the Cold War to the Third World intruded on and intensified these conflicts. (Soderlund, 1970) Paradoxically, however, this intrusion also forced a degree of restraint upon contending factions, as the two superpowers were able to exercise at least some influence over their chosen clients. Once the Cold War ended, however, constraints on former American and Soviet proxies were loosened or disappeared, and an environment was created in which civil wars and other less organized forms of domestic violence could flourish, leading to an increase of fragile, failing, and failed states.

Writing in 1998, Jared Chopra identified ninety-three armed conflicts that had occurred since the Cold War's end. In total, these conflicts were responsible for the deaths of 5.5 million people, 75 percent of whom were civilians. (1998, 1) Earlier, in 1995, Alan James documented that "no fewer than eighteen" of the twenty-one UN peacekeeping operations undertaken after1988 were in response to conflicts that were primarily internal in nature. (1995, 241) In their study covering the eleven-year period dating from 1989 to 1999, Peter Wallensteen and Margareta Sollenberg identified 110 distinct armed conflicts occurring in 73 locations, pointing out that of these, 94 were primarily intra-state in character, with an additional nine primarily intrastate with some foreign intervention. (2000, 635–36) Chester Crocker summarized the situation in the mid-1990s as follows:

> The post-1945 period has witnessed a rapid decline in traditional interstate conflict, and a comparable rise in internal strife: civil wars, anticolonial and anti-imperial wars, ethnic-religious conflicts, wars over regime legitimacy, wars to overthrow foreign or minority rule and other repressive systems, and wars of governmental and territorial fermentation (secession, imperial collapse, or failed states). [Moreover] . . . this trend appears to be holding. (1996, 183–84)

Thus, while the end of the Cold War unquestionably contributed to the resolution of a number of ongoing conflicts (for example, El Salvador, Nicaragua, Guatemala, and Cambodia), it also gave rise to a different set of conflicts, focused in large part on the breakup of states along ethnic lines in Eastern Europe and the former Soviet Union and on the disintegration of states in Africa, due for the most part to ethnic cleavages in post-colonial societies. (Wallensteen and Axell, 1994, 336–77; also see Brown, 1993; Mazrui, 1995; Zartman, 1995) As explained by Robert Streiter:

> The number of these small-scale but fierce conflicts escalated dramatically in the years after 1989. Relief agencies noted a nearly fivefold increase in emergencies to which they were called to give aid; almost all these were conflicts of human construction. The loosening of the bipolar grip on politics meant also that potential conflicts that had been kept in check by the Great Powers could come to the surface. Problems left over from the European colonial period also began to boil over in Africa and South Asia. (2001, xi)

▪ The State Sovereignty vs. Human Rights Debate

In the early 1990s, Secretary-General Boutros Boutros-Ghali sounded a note of optimism concerning the United Nation's ability to deal with the new situation:

> With a new-found spirit of cooperation, the members of the Security Council have begun acting decisively in recent years to take on the unresolved

problems of the past as well the emerging array of problems posed by a new era. And with new-found appeal, the international community has begun turning to the United Nations for help, not only in containing conflicts but also in resolving them—as well as preventing them in the first place. These factors, along with the outbreak of hostility in many areas around the world, have prompted the United Nations to respond with growing urgency, greater frequency and in more comprehensive form to today's crises. (1993, 66)

Direct or forceful UN intervention in political crises remained, however, complicated by the Charter's "state sovereignty" clause. Chapter 1, Article 2, paragraph 7, prohibited the world organization's uninvited intervention in situations that were considered to fall within the domestic jurisdiction of member states. (See Fromuth, 1993.) The concept of state sovereignty, which according to accepted wisdom has been evolving since the 1648 Treaty of Westphalia, has been defined by James Anderson as "the government's exclusive right to manage its internal affairs without external interference; and to conduct foreign affairs with other sovereign entities." (1992, 129) An obvious corollary to this is that "if national sovereignty is good, interference with a state's integrity must be bad." (Andrew Scott, cited in Anderson, 1992, 128)

The inclusion of this clause had been crucial in inducing states to ratify the UN Charter back in 1945, since protection for the principle of sovereignty was considered essential, especially in guarding the interests of less powerful states against those with greater military and economic capabilities. (Lyons and Mastanduno, 1995, 5–6; see also Blight and Weiss, 1992; Morales, 1994; Neack, 1995) However, as the Cold War faded into history, *human rights,* especially their abuse by states, strongly challenged the absoluteness of the *state sovereignty* principle. In the early 1990s, Christopher Greenwood posed the key question:

Does it follow . . . that when a government massacres its own people, or when the people of a state are threatened with starvation or other disaster and the government of that state refuses international aid, the international community must remain an essentially passive spectator? Although the question is an old one, recent events suggest it is ripe for reconsideration. (1993, 34)

The answer, according to Jack Donnelly, was that the old concept of state sovereignty no longer ruled unchallenged; he argued that "internationally recognized human rights have become very much like a 'standard of civilization,'" thus eroding the power of a state to do what it wishes to its population. (1998, 1) Samuel Barkin went even further, arguing specifically that a "norm change" in the area had taken place and that in the new reality if a state fails to respect its citizens' human rights, it forfeits its claim to sovereignty, thus legitimizing international intervention. (1997, 29) By the beginning of the new century, there was widespread agreement that "a normative revolution" had indeed occurred. As Andrea Talentino stated it, "The practice of intervention changed as a result and became part of conflict resolution approaches that, in extreme cases, required military force to end violence and provide support for reconstruction programs." (2005, 276; see also Bell, 2000; ICISS, 2001)

Indeed, during the decade of the 1990s, clear violations of human rights amounting to "humanitarian disasters" led in a number of cases to international interventions which either overrode or seriously infringed upon state sovereignty—Liberia, Iraq, Bosnia, Somalia, Rwanda, and Kosovo being the most noteworthy. (Abiew, 1999, 16–17) These operations gave rise to the term *humanitarian intervention,* defined by Terry Nardin as "the use of force by a state that aims to protect innocent people who are nationals of another state from *harm inflicted or allowed* by that state's government." (2006, 9, italics added)

None of these operations could be considered an unqualified success, however (see Rieff, 2002; Dallaire, 2003), and over a period of nearly two decades, the United Nations has searched for a strategy or strategies to deal with a kaleidoscope of human inhumanity but has encountered significant roadblocks along the way. The traditional concept of sovereignty may have been challenged, supplemented, or modified by the new imperatives accorded human rights, but it has by no means vanished. To most states—some more than others—it is still a jealously guarded fundamental, and hence what Jared Chopra and Thomas Weiss referred to as the "human rights-sovereignty deadlock" (1992, 95) has resurfaced to place severe restrictions on what may be attempted in the name of the international community.

Complicating the situation, the challenge to sovereignty was taking place at a time when the main perpetrators of human rights abuses were no longer "strong central governments," but rather "weak governments and failed states," thus making humanitarian intervention responses both more necessary and more difficult. (Shattuck, 1966, 169) This, of course, has meant that the practical problems associated with intervening have been far greater than they otherwise might have been, and there is consequently greater likelihood of disagreement among UN members about the appropriate response to situations of concern. When or whether, however, a consensus emerges in favor of intervening, finding a justification for doing so is clearly a lesser problem. When serious violations of human rights are occurring, in which people are being killed in numbers to constitute a genocide, or refugees are fleeing the area of conflict in sufficient numbers as to destabilize a region, it may be readily claimed that the situation constitutes a threat to international peace and security (Pease and Forsythe, 1993) or qualifies for intervention under the doctrine of "responsibility to protect," (ICISS, 2001, 32–33) thus allowing Article 2(7) to be bypassed.

In large part, the lack of success of UN-sponsored humanitarian interventions stems from an attempt to apply techniques of *peacekeeping* that had been developed and had worked reasonably well during the Cold War era, to an altered set of circumstances that required military combat operations associated with the concept of *peace enforcement.* Unfortunately, the principles underlying peacekeeping were not appropriate to these new conditions, leading to the irony that as UN-sanctioned, international intervention in domestic crises gained legitimacy, the organization's ability to deal with such crises declined.

As pointed out by Ramesh Tahkur, peacekeeping as an instrument of conflict resolution was located "in the grey zone between pacific settlement and military enforcement." (1994, 393) In most instances, the rules for these Cold War era peacekeeping operations, although developed *ad hoc,* were fairly straightforward, as outlined by Marrack Goulding:

> field operations established by the United Nations, *with the consent of the parties concerned,* to help control and resolve conflicts between them, under United Nations command and control, at the expense collectively of the member states, and with military and other personnel and equipment provided voluntarily by them; acting impartially between the parties and using force to the minimum necessary. (1993, 455, italics added)

Goulding's delineation of "Classic" or "1st generation" peacekeeping operations can be taken as definitive of that genre of operations, with the exception of the UN operation in the Congo (ONUC) in the early 1960s, which shared many of the characteristics of later post-Cold War actions.[1] (see O'Brien, 1962; Lefever, 1967; Crocker,

1996; Findlay, 1999) While the same term "peacekeeping" often has been used to refer to post–Cold War international interventions, in truth its continued use masks the complexity of military operations taken to establish peace in environments in which the combatants, for a number of reasons, are not interested in laying down their arms and are not responsive to conventional diplomatic pressures.

Many of the humanitarian crises of the 1990s were characterized by outright state failure or at least by diminished state capacity to deal with violence. In such circumstances, there is far less structure and control over the participants (often referred to as "warlords"), and as a consequence the very nature of warfare changes. Predatory military forces often operate outside the control of the state or of any recognized opposition leaders. This has led to the introduction of the term "wars of a third kind" to characterize these conflicts. As described by Yusef Bangura, these are wars where

> combatants deliberately target civilians rather than armed opponents in prosecuting goals; and atrocities are freely committed as part of strategies aimed at publicising political statements. In countries rich in natural resources, . . . the political goals of wars often interact with the multiple logics of resource appropriation . . . the looting of private property and vandalism. Such complicated outcomes have led many commentators to portray contemporary wars as being basically anarchical. (cited in Aning, 1999, 338)

The melding of the concepts of *peacekeeping* and *peace enforcement* unfortunately has led to a great deal of consequent public confusion and surprise when supposedly "easy operations" turned bloody. Nevertheless, when, and on the basis of what criteria, international humanitarian interventions should be undertaken remains a primary problem. (See Fixdal, 1998; Hoffman and Weiss, 2006.) On this point, Jean-Sébastien Rioux has argued that "an intervention—or lack thereof—is fundamentally a *political decision*. Questions of power, interests, bureaucratic, international and domestic politics undoubtedly affect whether leaders choose *to* intervene, or consciously decide to *not* intervene." (2003, 7–8) We concur fully with this assessment.

■ The Role of Mass Media

The research reported in this book examines the evolution of international responses to domestic humanitarian crises in the post-colonial world during the decade of the 1990s through an examination of ten cases, beginning with Liberia in 1990 and ending with East Timor in 1999. The range of international responses to these crises is great— from no intervention in Sudan in 1992–93 other than a relief effort, to a major military intervention involving in the neighborhood of 40,000 troops in Somalia during the same period. While other factors that enter into intervention decision-making are evaluated (namely, security and economic national interests and assessments of the perceived risks involved), the primary focus of the research is on the role of mass media in "pushing" decision makers to intervene—the so-called CNN effect, explained by Steven Livingston and Todd Eachus as "a presumed shift in power away from foreign policy machinery of government to a more diffuse array of nongovernmental actors, primarily news media organizations." (1995, 415) Proponents of a CNN effect, such as Bernard Cohen (1994), argue that governments are pressured by media-generated public opinion to undertake humanitarian interventions that they otherwise would have avoided. This phenomenon of "media push" is studied first by documenting the *amount of information* provided about a particular crisis (termed the "alerting function") and then by analyzing the *framing of the crisis,* that is, "the structures underlying the depictions that the public reads, hears and watches" (Hall Jamieson and Waldman, 2003, xii) that are contained in the information provided with respect to the wisdom of a potential intervention (termed the "evaluation-providing function").

There is no dearth of literature addressing the general role of mass media in political decision-making. Processes such as gate-keeping, agenda-setting, parameter-setting, and indexing have been studied extensively and are well-documented in the literature. (See, for example, Cohen, 1963; McCombs and Shaw, 1972; Stairs, 1977–78; Iyengar and Kinder, 1987; Rogers and Dearing, 1988; Bennett, 1990; McCombs and Shaw, 1993; Moeller, 1999; Entman, 2004.) Perhaps the most fundamental question addressed by these studies is the impact mass media make on public opinion and policy-making. In that regard, there has been an evolution in thought from Walter Lippmann (1922), who was skeptical and dismissive of media effects, to Gabriel Almond (1950), who saw the media as important in establishing a "mood" in the mass public.

In more recent years, it has been more or less taken for granted that the media, at least when sufficiently exercised on an issue and united in their portrayal of events, do indeed influence public opinion to a significant extent, including, at the extreme, the "CNN effect," which posits that decision makers can actually lose control of the policy process to powerful television images (in addition to Cohen, 1994; see Goodman, 1992, Dec. 8; Bell, 2000). While the causal links between mass media coverage, public opinion, and the policies arrived at by decision makers are complex and vary in clarity from situation to situation, media coverage is now widely acknowledged to comprise a key part of the "operational environment" in which decisions are made—this through the process of getting an issue on the "decision-making agenda," as well as by either promoting or discouraging certain policy options. (See Page and Shapiro, 1983, Robinson, 2002; Entman, 2004.) Needless to say, media influence is most likely with respect to crises in relatively remote areas of the world, where personal experience tends to be limited and where fewer alternative sources of information are available.

William Gamson defines *media-framing* as "making sense of relevant events and suggesting what is at issue." (1989, 157) As explained by Lance Bennett,

> the first important political observation about the American mass media is that to an important extent they regulate the content of public information and communication in the U.S. political system. Mass mediated messages of reality set the limits of who in the world we think we are as a people, and what in the world we think we are doing. . . . This is what the mass media do; translate the complex and multi-voiced reality of our times into another, symbolic reality of simpler messages and fewer voices. (1988, 14)

According to Robert Entman, framing involves "selecting and highlighting some facets of events or issues, and making connections among them so as to promote a particular interpretation, evaluation, and/or solution." (2004, 5) Similarly, Kathleen Hall Jamieson and Paul Waldman point out that "frames tell us what is important, what the acceptable range of debate on a topic is, and when the issue has been resolved. *By choosing a common frame to describe an event, condition, or political personage, journalists shape public opinion.*" (2003, xiii, italics added) In this sense, framing can be seen as the lens through which events are perceived and, as such, leads to certain views and understandings on the part of mass publics regarding what is going on, what is at stake for the countries involved, and how the options for dealing the problem are defined. (See also Entman, 1993; Norris, 1995; Iorio and Huxman, 1996.)

In his innovative research, Shanto Iyengar (1991) has identified two types of framing—*thematic* (placing an event in a well-established, long-term context) and *episodic* (where an event is seen as a unique and discrete occurrence). Of significance here is the concept of *thematic framing*—specifically whether a post-colonial crisis tended to be explained using the thematic frames that stressed human suffering at a level necessitating a humanitarian intervention, or cast it in terms that either discouraged or failed to promote such activity.

The role of mass media in advancing or lessening the chances that a domestic humanitarian crisis in the post-colonial world would elicit an international intervention has been the specific focus of a number of prior research efforts. Writing specifically about United States decision-making, Robert Rotberg and Thomas Weiss outline the role of mass media in the process leading to a crisis intervention:

> How well the forces of the media transmit information about overseas crises greatly influences policy-making. Whether directly, by beaming facts and interpretations directly into the offices of the president of the United States and his principal aids, or indirectly, by affecting the thinking of members of Congress, opinion-makers, or the American public, the way the media shape and package news from foreign parts is obviously critical. (1966, 1)

Nonetheless, the findings concerning the influence of media on foreign policy decision-making remain inconclusive. An early assessment claiming that "the nature and extent of the media's influence on policy generate more questions than answers" (Minear, et al., 1996, 3) was reinforced by a more recent study concluding that "scholarly and professional studies of the CNN effect present mixed, contradictory, and confusing results." (Gilboa, 2005, 34) In fact, the literature on the "CNN effect" can reasonably be divided into two schools— one stressing the importance of mass media and the other generally questioning their importance as an explanatory factor underlying intervention.

David Rieff makes the case for the importance of mass media as a factor prompting intervention by pointing out that "in reality, most of the world's horrors never get any air time at all." He adds, however, that "during the 1990s the foreign disasters the press homed in on were precisely the ones where interventions did eventually take place—Somalia, Bosnia, Rwanda, Kosovo and East Timor." (2002, 38, 40)

Bernard Cohen links the purported new-found power of mass media to the development of television news. Specifically,

> television . . . freed itself from the constraints of conventional news journalism, and has demonstrated its power to move governments. By focusing daily on the starving children in Somalia, a pictorial story tailor-made for television, TV mobilized the conscience of the nation's public institutions, compelling the government into a policy of intervention for humanitarian reasons. (1994, 9–10)

Peter Shiras also believes "the media have always been essential in shaping public opinion about mobilizing support of humanitarian crises" and highlights one of the research concerns that is addressed in our study—the "alerting" as opposed to the "evaluation-providing" function of mass media. Specifically, Shiras points to the key role of television "in alerting the public to disasters, while the print media generally play a critical role in shaping attitudes toward the nature of the disaster." (1966, 93–94)

A number of analysts have pointed to fundamental inadequacies of television news in particular to convey an adequate understanding of complex situations to mass publics. Edward Girardet suggests that we are "deluding ourselves that this massive onslaught of information is indeed providing us with the sort of quality data and insight that will enable us not only to grasp what is happening, but to deal more effectively with such crises." (1966, 45) George Kennan laments the power the media have to influence foreign policy decisions, claiming that the intervention in Somalia was an emotional response to images of suffering seen on television screens. (1993, Sept. 30) John Shattuck agrees that television news programs "have difficulty in conveying the history and texture of human rights crises." However, placing a different spin on the CNN effect, he argues that the print medium is "especially well suited to convey context and meaning and to explore ranges of options." (1966, 173–74)

The majority of scholars who have examined media effects in detail tend to adopt a minimalist view of their impact. For example, Warren Strobel attacked the issue head-on, maintaining that he

> found no evidence that news media, by themselves, force U.S. government officials to change their policies. But, under the right conditions, the news media nonetheless can have a powerful effect on the process. *And those conditions are almost always set by foreign policy makers themselves or*

by the growing number of actors on the international stage. (1997, 5, emphasis in original)

Marvin Kalb agreed, pointing out that "image in and of itself does not drive policy. . . . Image heightens existing factors." (cited in Sharkey, 1993)

Peter Jakobsen distinguishes between "national interest-driven" and "humanitarian-driven" interventions and concludes that with respect to the former "the CNN effect is irrelevant . . . because the government wants to intervene and will use the media instrumentally to mobilize domestic and international support." For humanitarian-driven operations, however,

> the CNN effect, which by definition implies that a humanitarian case for intervention exists, does appear to be a necessary . . . [but not a sufficient] condition for humanitarian enforcement. . . . In all the conflicts studied, the CNN effect put the issue of intervention on the agenda but the decision whether or not to intervene was ultimately determined by the perceived chance of success. (Jakobsen, 1996, 212)

Steven Livingston reports research dealing with two studies—one with Todd Eachus dealing with Somalia (1995) and one that compares Sudan with Somalia. (1996) Jonathan Mermin also examines the case of Somalia. (1997) Sudan is a case where there was neither extensive media coverage nor an international intervention. In that human suffering in Sudan reportedly rivaled that in Somalia, and in that both crises occurred in the same part of the world at roughly the same time, the latter case has been cited as evidence of the necessary link between media coverage and international intervention. However, with respect to Somalia, both Livingston and Eachus and Mermin argue that the time-sequence events and the newsmakers reporters turned to for information point to a case where official sources in Washington were in fact setting the media agenda for an intervention in Somalia that had been decided upon on entirely different grounds. While not dismissed, the independent impact of mass media on intervention decision-making was certainly questioned.

Along with the concept of "policy uncertainty" on the part of decision-making elites, Piers Robinson considered media framing as one of the two variables determining decisions to intervene in humanitarian crises, and he linked the two in a "policy-media interaction model." (See Robinson, 2002, Chapter 5.) He referred to a focus on the victims of human rights abuse as *empathy framing,* arguing that in such framing there is "implicit or explicit criticism of a government opposed to intervention":

> In this situation, policy-makers, uncertain of what to do and without a clearly defined policy line with which to counter critical media coverage, can be forced to intervene during a humanitarian crisis due to media-driven public pressure or the fear of potential negative public reaction to government inaction. (2000, 614; see also Robinson, 2001; and Klarevas, 2000)

On the other hand, "*distance framing* is implicitly supportive of a government opposed to intervention." (2000, 616) While we have not adopted Robinson's specific terminology, our research has examined in depth the way in which print media (specifically the *New York Times*) explicitly framed humanitarian crises in terms of either *supporting* (empathy framing) or *discouraging* (distance framing) international intervention.

■ Research Methods

It was in the hope of providing additional data to inform these media issues by comparing the international responses to a significant number of humanitarian crises within a limited time frame that we undertook this research. Our focus is on American media coverage of ten post–Cold War conflicts that were primarily *intra-state* in character and located in the post-colonial world. We examine both television and newspaper reporting, for it is clear that in the United States newspapers are able to treat events in considerable depth and may well play a critical role in setting the "agenda for serious policy discussion and fundamental changes in public thinking." (Shattuck, 1996, 174–75) Television, on the other hand, is the medium of public choice for obtaining news on a day-to-day basis. Bernard Cohen has argued that "television . . . has finally become a major force in the media-foreign policy equation," (1994, 8) and sustained visibility on television newscasts has been cited as essential to triggering the "alert" with respect to the existence of an international crisis. (Shiras, 1996, 93–94; see also Larson, 1990) Calculating the volume of coverage in newspapers and television allows for an assessment of their "alerting function" with respect to the crises under study, while the "evaluation-providing function," specifically whether international intervention was promoted or discouraged, is assessed on the basis of *New York*

Times reporting on the crises over periods of six months prior to a positive or negative decision.

We have utilized the Vanderbilt Television News Archive (http://www.tvnews.vanderbilt.edu) to determine the number of stories run on each of the ten crises by the three major American broadcast television networks (ABC, CBS, and NBC) on their premier evening newscasts during either the six months prior to the launch of a humanitarian intervention, or evidence of a decision not to intervene in crises where, based on their severity, a reasonable case for intervention could be made. In the chapters that follow, we report both the total number of stories and those appearing to contain in-depth treatment—those running two minutes in length or over as against those presented in the anchor-read, twenty- to thirty-second format of the summary of the day's news. For newspaper analysis, we have relied on the *New York Times Index* as an initial guide to content, prior to reading and coding all crisis-related items for date of publication, dateline, reporter, organizational source of material, and type of content.[2] All such items were also read specifically for framing that might be seen as explicitly promoting or discouraging an international intervention. A detailed analysis of crisis framing is presented in each chapter.

■ The Structured, Focused Comparison Approach

To the crisis case studies, we have applied the "structured, focused comparison" approach, as developed by Alexander George, to "identify the many conditions and variables that affect historical outcomes and to sort out the causal patterns associated with different historical outcomes." (1979, 44) George proposed that data be collected on specific variables in a way that (1) focuses on the key independent variables common across all cases, and (2) that the data assembled then be analyzed in a way that, while not strictly quantitative, is broadly comparable. (1979, 54–63; see also Eckstein, 1975; Mitchell and Bernaur, 1998)

Specification of the Problem

In conducting a structured, focused comparison, George outlines a number of tasks that must be accomplished in the design phase of the project. The first of these is the "specification of the research problem," which we have identified broadly as *understanding why some humanitarian crises have resulted in international interventions, while others have not*, and more specifically, *the impact of media influence on decisions to intervene.*

Variables

The second task identified by George involves the identification of the variables that will enter into the comparative case study. From the review of relevant literature, the following variables were identified as potentially important and are categorized below as to whether they are dependent or independent variables, along with guidelines for data collection.

The Dependent Variable

Strength of the International Response to the Crisis
Rank order of the crises (1–10) based on scores for the following indicators:
  A. **Did the Humanitarian Crisis Result in an International Intervention? Yes/Almost/No**
  B. **(If "Yes" or "Almost" on "A") Type of Response:**
      Led by the UN; led by a great power; led by a regional power; a combination or "hybrid" intervention response.
  C. **(If "Yes" or "Almost" on "A") Type of UN Involvement:**
      None; Chapter VI; Chapter VII; Chapter VIII
  D. **(If "Yes" or "Almost" on "A") Size of the Intervening Force:**
      Based on numbers found in documents, scholars' reports, and media coverage.

The Independent Variables

A. **Severity of the Crisis/Determinants of the International Response to the Crisis**
   Rank order (1–10) based on an assessment of numbers as found in documents, scholars' reports, and media coverage dealing with:
   i. **Estimated number of deaths** (short-term and long-term) preceding an international intervention or clear lack of international response to the crisis;

    ii. Estimated number of refugees and internally displaced persons (short-term and long-term) generated by the crisis preceding an international intervention or clear lack of international response to the crisis

    iii. Perceived likelihood of conflict spreading to other states: Five-point scale (*low* to *medium* to *high*) based on

       a. Number of shared borders;

       b. Involvement of bordering states—based on documents, scholars' reports, and media coverage regarding the potential for, as well as actual "spill-over" of conflict.

B. Pre-intervention "Assessment of Risk" on the Part of Potential Intervening Nations:
Five-point scale (*low* to *medium* to *high*) based on an assessment of documents, participants' and scholars' reports, and media coverage regarding the complexity of the crisis, as well as the type, size, and capability of forces likely to oppose the intervention.

C. Extent of "National Interest Involvement" on the Part of Potential Intervening Nations:
Five-point scale (*low* to *medium* to *high*) based on an assessment of documents, participants' and scholars' reports, and media coverage regarding strategic and economic interests of nations that were likely candidates to lead or participate in an intervention.

D. Role of Mass Media in the Six Months Prior to the Crisis Intervention or Non-intervention:

    i. "Alerting" function (volume of television and newspaper coverage)

       a. Volume of coverage on major United States TV network (ABC, CBS, NBC) prime-time evening news programs:
Rank order (1–10) as reported in the Vanderbilt Television News Archive Abstracts in the six months prior to an intervention or a clear lack of an international response to a documented humanitarian crisis.

       b. Volume of coverage in the *New York Times:*
Rank order (1–10) as reported in the *New York Times Index* in the six months prior to an intervention or a clear lack of an international response to a documented humanitarian crisis.

   ii. **"Evaluative" function (intervention framing in the *New York Times*)**
     Pro- vs. anti-intervention framing
  iii. **A detailed assessment of media coverage:** a table showing date, dateline, source, and type of content in the *New York Times*, followed by a detailed qualitative analysis of crisis framing over a six-month period as it supported or discouraged a possible international intervention.

Our assumption is that in order for a "media push" to be sufficient to prompt an international intervention response to a humanitarian crisis in the post-colonial world, two factors had to be present: (1) a significant level of media interest (as measured by the number of stories devoted to it), at least high enough to alert mass publics and decision makers to the existence of a particular crisis, and (2) a pattern of evaluative framing that was on balance supportive of an intervention, or at least not opposed to one.

Case Selection

George's third task involves case selection. Here, three conditions were necessary for a case to be included in the study. First, the time period of the crisis had to fall within the decade of the 1990s (that is, the post–Cold War period). Second, the country in which the crisis took place had to be a part of what has been referred to as the post-colonial world (defined as Africa, Latin America and the Caribbean, and Asia (minus Japan); and third, the conflict had to be primarily domestic (intra-state) in nature. The ten cases selected that fit our criteria are: Liberia (1990), Somalia (1992), Sudan (1992), Rwanda (1994), Haiti (1994), Burundi (1996), Zaire—later the Democratic Republic of the Congo—(1996), Sierra Leone (1997), Angola (1999), and East Timor—later Timor-Leste (1999).[3]

This selection obviously excludes a number of international interventions in crisis situations that occurred within or near our time frame—the Gulf War, the conflict in northern Iraq following that war, the situations in Bosnia and Kosovo, not to mention Cambodia, Guatemala, Nicaragua, and El Salvador. We have not included these because, for a variety of reasons, they do not seem wholly comparable to those we have chosen to study. The Gulf War, for example, clearly was of a quite different character and a massive operation in comparison with, say, Liberia, East Timor, or even Somalia. Equally clearly, northern Iraq was an aftermath of the Gulf War and probably does not deserve to be considered a separate operation. Cambodia, although involving a large number of international troops, better fits the "classic" type of peacekeeping operation than an attempt to staunch ethnic blood-letting such as was the case in Rwanda. The Guatemala, Nicaragua, and El Salvador situations were relatively brief in duration, and driven more by the need to disengage prior Cold War antagonists than by humanitarian considerations. We consequently felt that to include any of them would skew statistical comparisons of the crises and complicate assessments regarding media impact on decision-making with respect to them.

▪ Summary

Humanitarian intervention outcomes appear to be associated with at least one nation (usually one with a significant involvement of its own economic and/or security national interests) taking the lead role in providing funding and troops, as well as in UN decision-making leading up to an intervention.[4] Ramesh Thakur has pointed out the predominant role of the United States in the world system following the end of the Cold War: "Given that there is now only one superpower as well as one general organization, the United Nations cannot embark upon any substantial venture against the wishes of the United States. The peace of the world may well depend upon the latter's political wisdom and military power." (1994, 405)

Early on in the post–Cold War period, Thomas Friedman clarified this new responsibility for the American people: "Because the United States is now the world's only remaining superpower it cannot ignore responsibility for grave humanitarian crises in which American actions, and only American actions, could well mean the difference between life and death for thousands of people." (1992, Dec. 5, I1) It is, then, the predominant military position of the United States, including its ability to airlift the military forces of other countries to a crisis zone, plus its role in asserting political leadership (or, in a number of cases, the lack thereof) in the United Nations, that led us to focus our research on media impact on decision-making in that country. Moreover, the well-established reputation of the *New York Times* as high-priority elite reading, as well as its role as an agenda-setter for other media, established for us the importance of focusing on crisis coverage in that newspaper. (See Merrill, 1968; Talese, 1969; Berry, 1990; Malinkina and McLeod, 2000.)

We believe the findings that have emerged from this study allow us to assess the relative importance of mass media in the mix of factors that feed into decision-making processes leading to international interventions in situations of humanitarian catastrophe. Specifically, we were able to compare the extent of the international response to a crisis with its severity, perceived risks involved in a successful intervention, the role of conventional security and economic national interest in the calculations of potential intervening powers, and the extent of media interest in and framing of the crisis. On the basis of this analysis, we believe that we have been able to document the importance of media coverage (both in its alerting and evaluative roles), relative to the other factors identified in the literature as important in producing robust international intervention responses to humanitarian crises.

▪ Notes

1. Chester Crocker rightly points out that the 1960 deployment of ONUC to the Congo, "not Somalia, was the first time the international system decided to 'paint a country blue.'" He recounts that the UN deployed nearly twenty-thousand troops, plus a large number of civilians "at a cost of $2 billion (1991 dollars). The effort succeeded in holding together a vast land facing huge internal and external challenges. It checked the further intrusion of the Cold War into central Africa and warded off unknown scenarios of disorder and instability affecting much of the region. [Moreover,] . . . ONUC did these things against great odds." (1996, 192)

2. All coding of *New York Times* crisis content (963 items in total) was done by Professors Soderlund and Briggs. Based on a sample of material dealing with Somalia, Rwanda, and Haiti, intercoder reliability was established at 93 percent. (See Holsti, 1969, 140.)

As expected, most evaluative material was found in editorials, op-ed feature articles, and letters to the editor. However, evaluations of crisis situations were also contained in "hard news" pieces. These appeared mainly in quotations contained in the reporting, but sometimes in subjective judgments of reporters as well.

3. Purists may quibble with our inclusion of East Timor as one of our cases on the grounds that it was not an intra-state dispute. While technically this is true, the fact that Indonesia effectively (albeit illegally) had occupied East Timor since 1975, and that the Indonesian army, militia, and police forces were stationed within East Timor to deal with an ongoing insurgency in fact created the crisis, in our minds make it more a case of *intra-state* than *inter-state* violence. Further, that the UN sought (and finally received) Indonesian permission to intervene in the crisis, appears to reinforce our decision.

4. Bruce Jones indicates that in UN decision-making, "The conventional wisdom in New York is that to get a peacekeeping force approved one needs a major power—essentially one of the Permanent Five—to back the plan." (2001, 143)

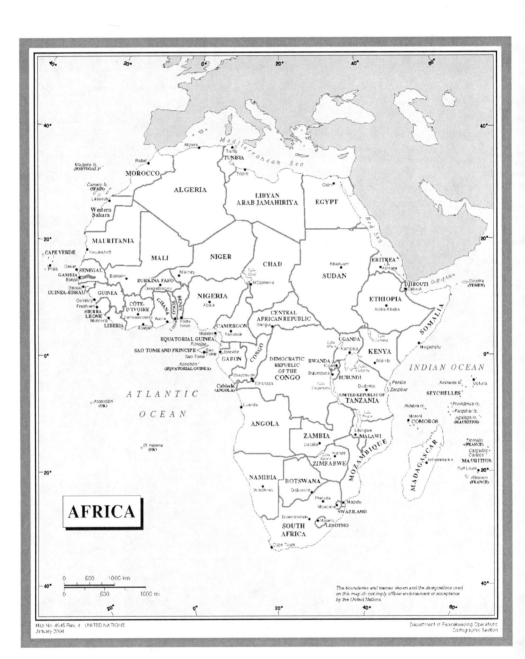

AFRICA

2

Liberia, 1990:
ECOMOG I, "Operation Liberty,"
UNOMIL

Walter C. Soderlund

■ Background

It came as somewhat of a surprise that in the early 1990s, just as the Cold War was staggering to its conclusion, Liberia was the first country to enter into a downward spiral of political and social violence, ultimately leading to state collapse. Long considered different from its African neighbors, Liberia's fairly recent history had featured "twenty-eight years of stability under one elected president, an orderly transfer of power upon his death; significant development of both central and local governmental institutions, and widening popular participation and representation in the political processes of the nation." (Lowenkopf, 1976, 1)

In a technical sense, Liberia never had been "colonized," but this characterization masked reality. The country was first established in 1822 by the American Colonization Society as a West African home for freed slaves. That organization's goals were not entirely altruistic. While there was some focus on providing opportunities not available in the United States, its major concern was to reduce the danger it felt free slaves presented to American slave owners. Freed American slaves as well as free-born Blacks were later joined by those from the Caribbean. Liberia declared itself a republic in 1847 and, as such, lays claim to be Africa's oldest European-style nation state; it was also a Charter Member of the United Nations. (Lowenkopf, 1976; Liebenow, 1987; Alao, et al., 1999; Mgbeoji, 2003)

Located on the West coast of Africa, Liberia shares borders with three countries—Sierra Leone, Guinea, and Côte d'Ivoire—and the civil war that started in Liberia in late December 1989 has affected the fortunes of all these countries, unfortunately none more so than Sierra Leone. (See Chapter 9, this volume.) With a population in 1990 estimated at between 2 and 2.5 million in a country of 442 square miles (roughly the size of Ohio), Liberia is home to sixteen indigenous African tribes (none accounting for more than 20 percent of the population), plus, of course, the all-important Americo-Liberians, who comprise less than 5 percent of the total population. (Liebenow, 1987, 35, Table 3)

Ikechi Mgbeoji argues convincingly that the circumstances of Liberia's creation in the nineteenth century are crucial to understanding its subsequent descent into violence and chaos in the 1990s:

> The emergence of Liberia as a state was not necessarily a result of the decision of its indigenous nations to constitute themselves into a state, or of its capacity to be a viable state under the Eurocentric paradigm. Rather, like many African "states," Liberia was a creation of foreign political, economic, and cultural dictates. Further, like most African states fashioned in this crucible, the inability of its elite to create an indigenous idea of or consensus about its statehood exacerbated its internal contradictions, thus paving the way for socio-political attrition and the consequent failure of the state as a collective enterprise. (2003, 2)

While it is true that Liberia was never colonized in a formal sense, the minority "Americo-Liberian" settlers proceeded to dominate the country's indigenous population (the so-called tribal people) in politics, social status, and wealth. Emmanuel Kwesi Aning has pointed out that "the history and politics of Liberia have been characterized by the complex interconnectedness of ethnicity, resources and conflict," (1999, 336) and in this complex interaction, the extent and character of the subjugation visited upon the indigenous population by the Americo-Liberians can only be described as a form of "internal colonization" that was humiliating and degrading to the historical inhabitants of the area.[1] Mgbeoji explains this apparent anachronism as follows:

> In living out their American fantasies, early "Liberians" became more American than their former masters in the United States, making a fetish of their exposure to the West. As they regarded the natives as the country's greatest problem, a state policy of political and economic exclusion of the natives was created, thus subverting the very logic behind their colonization in Africa. (2003, 5; see also Gershoni, 1985, Chapter 2)

According to S. Byron Tarr, beginning in the 1860s, "for repatriates . . . politics became 'the profession of choice.' . . . Every leading family had to have one of its members in government, for public employment alone secured agency contracts and sinecure jobs. These produced the income which financed the conspicuous consumption that guaranteed status." (1993, 74) Through their control over the True Whig Party, various Christian churches, and the Masonic Lodge, the Americo-Liberians "perpetuated themselves as a ruling class for more than a century." (Alao, et al. 1999, 12) While in 1904 the indigenous majority of Liberians gained rights to citizenship, social equality was not achieved: for example, "Christian Africans had to enter the home of an Americo-Liberian through the back door." The Americo-Liberian elite were economically dominant as well, as in the early 1970s, "4 percent of Liberians controlled 60 percent of the country's income." (Alao, et al., 1999, 15, 17) As argued by Ademola Adeleke, "ethnicity became the only index of group identification and social mobility, and the dominant ethic in the nation's collective consciousness, thereby setting the stage for political conflict." (1995, 572)

■ Roots of the Crisis

First in the 1940s under President William Tubman (through the "Unification Program"), and later in the 1970s under President William Tolbert, gradual political reforms, such as the granting of the right to vote, were introduced to increase the participation of Liberia's indigenous peoples in the country's national life. Whether in the long run these would have been successful remains an unknown; for example, Gus Liebenow claims that "the appearance of reform [was] greater than the reality." (1987, 67) At any rate, in the 1970s economic problems linked to increases in the price of oil and food (which needed to imported), combined with decreases in the prices of Liberian-produced commodities for export (iron ore and rubber), led to increased ethnic tensions. (Liebenow, 1987, 161)

In 1979, the price of a bag of rice rose by 50 percent, resulting in a mass demonstration (the "rice riot" of April 14) that saw between 40 and 140 persons killed, another 400 wounded, and widespread looting. (Liebenow, 1987, 171–72) In that it showed the fragility of the government's hold on power, the rice riot set the stage for a successful coup d'état in 1980. As explained by Liebenow, the

Tolbert government hastened its own end by applying tactics of re-pression against the groups that had organized the demonstration: "Till the bitter end . . . the central political core of the Americo-Liberian elite attempted to hold tight to the reins of power and reap a disproportionate share of the benefits of economic growth." (1987, 5)

The April 12, 1980 coup, "directed against the country's Americo-Liberian elite," was led by Master Sergeant Samuel Doe, a member of the indigenous Krahn people. (Riley, 1993, 42) The horrors that over-took Liberia in the 1990s can be traced directly to this coup, which was seen by some as "decolonization from 'Black Colonialism,'" (Dunn, 1999, 93) and which overturned the old order in a most violent man-ner. Sergeant Doe, close to illiterate, executed leading members of the Americo-Liberian elite (including the President) and over the next ten years waged a continuing ruthless campaign of repression against them. Following an unsuccessful coup against Doe's government in 1985, groups of indigenous peoples seen to be supportive of the coup-makers were targeted for brutal reprisals as well.

Adeleke explains the coup's initial acceptance and its long-term outcome as follows: "Although those who overthrew the Americo-Liberian elite were consequently proclaimed as 'heroes' and 'redeemers' by the indigenous people, this proved to be an illusion. The People's Redemption Council (PRC), as the new junta called itself, accentuated rather than transcended the ethnic contradictions which had been re-sponsible for its creation." (1995, 572–573) Eghosa Osaghe claims further that Doe and his cohorts "inherited and imitated the tenden-cies of the class it overthrew . . . [but] . . . had neither the organiza-tional skills nor the unity of the American-Liberians to perpetuate it-self." (cited in Dunn, 1999, 101)

Alexander Michael Innes describes Doe as "brutal, insecure, iso-lated, and quixotic . . . [and] . . . increasingly perceived to be connected to indigenous secret societies and witchcraft." (2004, 9) Stephen Ellis argues that "it was under Samuel Doe that Liberia for the first time came under the control of a clique more interested in plunder than in managing power to their advantage and transmitting it intact to a suc-cessor chosen by political means." (1998, 161) It was Doe's decade-long misrule, "remembered for its atrocities against Liberian citizens, which included looting, rape, arson, flogging, arbitrary arrest and sum-mary executions by the Armed Forces of Liberia," (Alao, et al., 1999, 19) that set the stage for the next act in Liberia's ultimate unraveling:

the attack against Samuel Doe's government, mounted on December 24, 1989, by Charles Taylor, the self-appointed leader of the National Patriotic Front of Liberia (NPFL).

■ Events Precipitating the Crisis

Charles Taylor, a former civil servant in the Doe government, had been charged with embezzlement, fled to the United States, was jailed there, and escaped from custody. With an initial military force numbering around one hundred and with support from Libya's Muammar Quaddafi, Taylor attacked Liberia from neighboring Côte d'Ivoire on Christmas Eve 1989 and was able quickly and effectively to exploit the widespread hatred of Doe's government. (Ellis, 1998, 166) After initially dismissing Taylor's incursion as insignificant, Doe launched a fierce counteroffensive against the native peoples (chiefly Gio and Mano) who were perceived to be sympathetic to the insurgents. This worked only to turn more of the population against Doe, and, as Taylor's forces gained control of Liberia's hinterland, the situation for Doe's government worsened very quickly. In June 1990, however, one of Taylor's military leaders, Prince Yormie Johnson, broke away from Taylor, creating his own Independent National Patriotic Front of Liberia (INPFL). This was only the first of such splintering among contenders for power (the "warlords") who, Alao et al. claim, were "the greatest obstacle to peace in Liberia," (1999, 21) and who managed to lay waste to the country over the next thirteen years in a two-phased civil war.

By August 1990, Taylor's forces controlled the majority of Liberia's rural areas and had confined Doe's government to the capital, Monrovia. Johnson, however, controlled critical approaches to the capital, denying Taylor his victory. In the fighting to that date, up to sixty thousand had lost their lives, with countless more (estimated at three hundred thousand) turned into refugees.[2] (Riley, 1993, 42) Adeleke described the situation as follows:

> To defeat Doe and occupy the Executive Mansion, Taylor would first have to eliminate Johnson, a difficult task in the circumstances. And so, the final battle for Monrovia, and the relief which Liberians expected would follow in its wake, remained a mirage. Instead, the three "armies" turned on each other, bringing their country almost to the verge of anarchy, and national suicide. Would the world watch impassively? (1995, 576)

■ The Intervention

An international intervention did materialize, but not in the form of an expected United States–led force. At the very end of July "Bush Administration officials said the United States had no intention of taking military action to stop the conflict." (Wines, 1990, July 31, A4) Rather it was a regional force led by Nigeria that took the initiative to bring peace to Liberia. The Economic Community of West African States (ECOWAS), which on August 24, 1990, launched "Operation Liberty" in the form of the Economic Community of West African States Cease-fire Monitoring Group (ECOMOG), was the first subregional organization that the UN worked with on a formal basis in carrying out peacekeeping operations. (Howe, 1996/97, 159)

"Operation Liberty" was conceived as a classic peacekeeping operation—a force to stand between those of the Doe government and those of Taylor in an attempt to end the violence. Taylor, however, opposed the intervention on the grounds that Nigeria favored the Doe government, and NPFL forces actually shelled the ECOMOG peacekeepers as they disembarked in Monrovia.[3] The worst, however, was yet to come because ECOMOG became, in effect, one of the participants in the ongoing civil war that Innes describes as "a seven-year campaign to seize control of the state." (2004, 11) Following the execution of Samuel Doe by Prince Johnson in September 1990,[4] "for the next three and a half years, ECOMOG units continued to be the main source of support for the [newly appointed] Interim Government of National Unity [IGNU]." (Gershoni, 1997, 66) The situation evolved into one where the IGNU, backed by ECOMOG, the NPFL under Charles Taylor, and various other warlords competed for power in what Aning describes as classic "war of a third kind"—"no 'fronts', no 'lines', no 'uniforms', no 'formal hierarchies.'" (1999, 338)

In this contest, it appears that the best ECOMOG could do was to ensure a military stalemate, wherein no faction was able to gain control of the county. ECOMOG's overall success in dealing with the crisis can be characterized as mixed at best, as "a pattern of alternating between peacekeeping and enforcement was to become a key aspect of the ECOMOG operation," (Alao, et al., 1999, 30) with "West African states, and indeed the international community . . . [becoming] . . . increasingly frustrated with the failure of all 12 so-called 'peace accords' . . . [signed up to 1995]." (Adeleke, 1995, 584) In fact, Yekutiel Gershoni charges that "the prolongation of the war in Liberia was in part due to the divisions within ECOWAS, and the inefficiency of ECOMOG." (1997, 57; see also Howe, 1996/97)

ECOWAS had been created in 1975 to deal with economic problems of the region, and also to counter perceived French influence, and as such was an unlikely organization to undertake a peacekeeping, much less a peace enforcement mission. The Liberian Civil War was also the organization's first such effort. (Alao, et al., 1999, 28–29) ECOWAS's membership comprised sixteen countries—nine French-speaking, five English-speaking, and two Portuguese-speaking. (Howe, 1996/97) It was also an organization deeply divided on the basis of French interests (the former colonial power, France) and English interests (the region's predominant power, Nigeria). During the conflict, for example, some French-speaking member nations, Côte d'Ivoire and Burkina Faso, provided "active support" to the insurgent forces opposing ECOMOG.[5] (Gershoni, 1997, 66) Nigeria provided the majority of troops and equipment for the ECOMOG force (about 70 percent), but command and control problems, which were evident from the beginning, continued to undermine the operation. (Howe, 1996/97, 152–60) It was noted that "the military ineffectiveness of ECOMOG was coupled with low morale and lack of discipline among its troops. ECOMOG soldiers, especially the Nigerians, it was claimed, were notorious for looting, drug dealing and harassing citizens." (Gershoni, 1997, 66; see also Tuck, 2000)

The Cotonou Peace Agreement (signed in June 1993, but one of many failed attempts to broker an end to the conflict) was to take effect August 1. It "was to be supervised by a 300-member UN Observation Mission, [UNOMIL] and led by OAU troops from Tanzania, Uganda, and Zimbabwe dispatched to reinforce an expanded ECOMOG." (Adeleke, 1995, 582) However, Howe reports that "ECOMOG cooperated, grudgingly, at best, with UNOMIL. Several UNOMIL officials complained that ECOMOG did not want UNOMIL observing activities relating to arms flows, human rights abuses, and food shipments." (1996/97, 163) To give the reader an idea of the complexity of the situation, Mgbeoji reports,

> there were six different groups fighting one another in Liberia: the NPFL, ULIMO-J, ULIMO-K, LPC, LDF, and AFL (the remnants of the Liberian Army). Fighting continued, with all the factions committing atrocities against the civilian population. . . . By [September 1994] over 200,000 Liberians had perished in the fratricidal conflict that had lasted for five years. (2003, 24–25)

Strength of the International Response: Rank order=3

  A. Did the Humanitarian Crisis Result in an International Intervention? Yes

  B. Type of Response: Combination Regional and UN-led
- **ECOMOG "Operation Liberty" 1990 ECOWAS:** led by Nigeria plus seven countries
- **UNOMIL:** 1994 Observer team led by the UN

  C. Type of UN Involvement:
- **ECOMOG:** Chapter VIII (retrospectively)

"Nor could the intervention draw on international legitimacy, since the UN did not authorize ECOMOG from the outset: the first UN political response was not until October 1992 when it retrospectively approved ECOMOG's actions under Chapter VIII of the UN Charter." (Tuck, 2000)
- **UNOMIL:** Chapter VI

  D. Size of Intervening Forces:
- **ECOMOG: 2,700 to 3,000 (initial) to 12,500 to 16,000 (maximum)**

"In mid-August 1990, the ECOMOG force of about 2,700 men arrived in Sierra Leone. Liberia's western neighbor would serve as ECOMOG's forward staging base." (Howe, 1996/1997, 154)

"ECOMOG's manpower—a maximum of about 12,500 but sometimes as low as 2,700—was too small for peace enforcement or even for effective peacekeeping." (Howe, 1996/1997, p. 168)

"The [ECOMOG] force peaked at a strength of around 16,000 in 1993 and by early 1997 consisted of around 11,000 troops." (Tuck, 2000)
- **UNOMIL: 368**

"In early 1994, 368 UN observers arrived in Monrovia. . . . Continued fighting forced the UN to reduce its observer mission drastically to about sixty in mid-1995." (Howe, 1996/97, 159)

"[It was] . . . emphasized that the United Nations Observer Mission in Liberia (UNOMIL) would only monitor implementation procedures of the Cotonou accord 'in order to verify their impartial application.' Primary responsibility for keeping the peace is ECOMOG's." (Dunn, 1999, 115)

Determinants of the International Response

  A. Severity of the Crisis: Rank order=6

    i. Number of deaths: (short-term) 5,000 up to 60,000; (long-term) 200,000 to 250,000

"More than 5,000 people are believed to have been killed in the county since the fighting began last December." (Noble, 1990, Aug. 22, A3)

"Some estimates suggest that up to 60,000 people have died after an armed insurrection against the government of President Samuel Doe was started in December 1989 by Charles Taylor, a former member of Doe's government." (Riley, 1993, 42)

"By mid-1990 Liberia had become 'a slaughterhouse.'" (Tarr, 1993, 75)

"By all accounts, the loss of life in Liberia had reached near genocidal proportions; mass starvation and widespread disease were imminent. The continued fighting posed a clear danger to the peace and security of the region, both through the creation of an enormous refugee population and through the potential (soon realized) for a direct spill-over from Liberia into neighboring states." (Wippman, 1993, 179)

"Twenty-five years of misrule and civil war left the country in ruins. Warlords fought to control our natural resources, smuggle diamonds, and traffic in arms and drugs. More than 250,000 Liberians lost their lives." (Johnson-Sirleaf, 2007, Mar. 21, A19)

ii. **Number of refugees and internally displaced persons: (short-term) 300,000 to 700,000**

"Population at risk" (1995) 2.1 million. (Weiss and Collins, 1996, 5–7, Table I.1)

". . . President Doe overresponded [to Taylor's incursion] with a scorched-earth campaign that resulted in the death of many Gio and Mano, and created over 300,000 refugees." (Adeleke, 1995, 575)

"At least 375,000 Liberians have fled the fighting into neighboring Guinea, Ivory Coast, and Sierra Leone. . . ." (UN High Commissioner for Refugees, cited in AP, 1990, July 28, I3)

"Altogether, as many as 700,000 people may have fled the country." (Ellis, 1995, 167)

iii. **Likelihood of conflict spreading to other states: 5 *high***
   a. **Number of shared borders: 3**
      Sierra Leone, Côte d'Ivoire, and Guinea
   b. **Involvement of bordering states**
"In Liberia, state failure engendered violent conflicts that, in turn, ignited combustible Sierra Leone and, for more than a

decade, set ablaze the Mano basin area of Liberia, Sierra Leone, and parts of the forest region of Guinea." (Sawyer, 2004, 437)

". . . Charles Taylor in March 1991 had launched a campaign to destabilize Sierra Leone under the leadership of Foday Sankoh and a group called the Revolutionary United Front (RUF), Taylor's aim being to punish the Sierra Leonean government for its participation in ECOMOG." (Ellis, 1995, 170)

". . . Even though the conflict started by Charles Taylor in Liberia and extended to Sierra Leone and the forest region of Guinea was fuelled by natural resources, it was not solely driven by natural resources. Taylor's ambition was also to establish a sphere of political control that transcended Liberia, and he began pursuing that ambition from the start of his onslaught on Liberia." (Sawyer, 2004, 445)

"Sierra Leonean soldiers, mostly ECOMOG veterans, fought RUF in early 1992. The war was destroying the country's economy, and the ECOMOG soldiers suffered from missing paychecks, irregular supplies, and minimal logistic support. In April 1992, these soldiers overthrew Joseph Momoh, Sierra Leone's president." (Howe, 1996/97, 157)

B. Pre-intervention "Assessment of Risk": 2 *relatively low*

"It is doubtful that the planners of ECOMOG understood the nature of the conflict they were responding to in Liberia, or the character of the conflicting parties. They simply (at least initially) relied upon the fact that the warring factions, whom they perhaps saw as seriously under-trained and under-equipped, would capitulate in the face of a West African force led by Nigeria." (Alao, et al., 1999, 29)

"The ECOMOG states clearly did not expect the war to last very long." (Howe, 1996/97, 165)

". . . It appears that the United States held back from direct intervention for other reasons [than the Gulf Crisis], which might include the possible lack of support from the West African sub-region, and the fact that military intervention might not have been a guaranteed success." (Alao, et al., 1999, 25)

C. Extent of "National Interest Involvement":
i. The international community: 2 *relatively low*

"Liberia did not offer geostrategic benefits—as it did during the Cold War—to justify the disbursements of material, political and moral costs of intervention and counterinsurgency by the international community." (Aning, 1999, 335)

"Because the [international] system's principal actors perceive no 'strategic' interest at stake, not only are their interests markedly limited (arms supply excepted), but they send signals to the protagonists that they may fight to the finish or 'work out their own solution' as best they can." (Dunn, 1999, 90)

". . . the international community had refrained from showing an interest in Liberia because its 'disintegration only minimally imperiled international security.'" (Gerald Helman and Steven Ratner, cited in Aning, 1999, 336)

"Liberia's war went largely unmarked by international actors, except for an occasional condemnation of one faction or another by the UN." (Talentino, 2005, 203)

"The situation seemed to have the makings of a higher priority crisis for both the United States and the European Union. Close historical ties—Liberians call themselves 'children of America'—led many in the West African country to expect, and to advocate, US military intervention. . . . Likewise the European Union and its member states restricted their own level of policy attention and response largely to that of providing humanitarian aid." (Minear, et al., 1996, 49)

"Not until January 1991—thirteen months after the war's start and five months after the establishment of ECOMOG—did the Security Council comment upon the war." (Howe, 1996/97, 151)

ii. **United States: 2 to 3** *relatively low* **to** *medium*

"Founded in 1822 by freed American slaves, Liberia is described as the closest the United States has ever had to a colony in Africa. Since 1946 the United States has given this country more than $800 million in aid and loans, making Liberia the largest per capita recipient of American aid in Africa south of the Sahara." (Noble, 1990, May 25, A3)

"During the Cold War, it was inconceivable that the United States would have allowed Liberia to slide into the state of anarchy that now prevailed. In addition to the historical ties, Liberia was a strategic staging post of some importance to the United States. . . . With this level of US involvement and interest in Liberia, it is difficult to dispute claims that Liberia was an ally of some importance to the United States on the African continent. . . . For these reasons, it was expected that the United

States would step in and restore order in Liberia, but this did not happen." (Alao, et al., 1999, 24–25)

"Both the Bush administration and the succeeding Clinton administration aimed to prevent direct US involvement in the two conflicts [Liberia and Sierra Leone]. Although the US had a strong interest in keeping Libya out of West Africa, the most it was prepared to do was to back peace initiatives generated by ECOWAS with diplomatic and financial assistance." (Gershoni, 1997, 63)

"No major power had expressed a desire to intervene militarily. Although the United States had vastly more ties to Liberia than did any other African country, it limited its involvement." (Howe, 1996/97, 150)

"The United States had no desire to save its former client [Samuel] Doe, and Washington disliked both [Charles] Taylor and [Prince] Johnson." (Howe, 1996/97, 151)

". . . President George Bush [declared] that Liberia was not worth the life of a single US marine." (Ellis, 1995, 168)

"We share the deep concern that others have expressed. . . . Nonetheless, it is our position that we don't intend to intervene." (Richard A. Boucher, State Department Spokesperson, cited in Wines, 1990, July 31, A2)

"Ever since World War II, the United States had viewed Liberia as having some strategic importance. Liberia allowed various US strategic installations, e.g., radio transmission stations, and strongly supported the United States in most foreign policy debates." (Howe, 1996/97, 148)

"The historical links between Liberia and the United States had raised expectations that the Bush Administration would try to end the conflict. But unlike Kuwait, Liberia posed no immediate threat to America's strategic interests, and hence 'it seemed safer from Washington to describe Liberia as an African problem, demanding African solutions.'" (Adeleke, 1995, 589)

"At a crucial point, in August 1990, something happened elsewhere in the world which took up all America's attention and definitely ruled out any possibility of US intervention in Liberia: Iraq invaded Kuwait." (Ellis, 1995, 168)

"After the Cold War ended, US policy became one of permissiveness—marginal involvement though making sizeable contributions to humanitarian assistance, but otherwise leaving the initiative for action to others." (Dunn, 1999, 106)

"The need for the USA to contain communism in Africa had evaporated. The 'special relationship' with Liberia was perhaps perceived by Liberians alone by 1990." (Tarr, 1993, 81)

"With the withdrawal of American support as the Cold War ended, the violent disintegration of the Liberian state was accelerated." (Sawyer, 2004, 444)

iii. Africa: 4 *relatively high*

"Because the OAU, the UN, and the United States were, for a variety of reasons, unwilling or unable to deal with the Liberian conflict, it was left to ECOWAS to act." (Dunn, 1999, 112)

"[In spite of lack of western interest, ECOWAS] had another perspective. It perceived the civil conflict as presenting a concrete threat to its member states. . . . As a response to [international] marginalization, this normally fractious collection of states was virtually left alone to respond to a crisis it perceived as a threat to its conception and perception of international stability and security." (Aning, 1999, 336)

". . . ECOWAS . . . emerged as the solitary initiator of a settlement of the conflict, as the United Nations and the Organization of African Unity, save for scattered homilies on the wisdom of peaceful settlement of crises, did nothing to resolve the crisis." (Mgbeoji, 2003, 20)

"It was obvious that while many were concerned about the human suffering in the war, the situation was neither sufficiently grave nor strategically important enough to deserve international intervention. But for the states in the sub-region who were entrapped by their spatial proximity to the conflict, none could escape its effects, and none could ignore its implications. Herein lies the justification for ECOWAS intervention in Liberia." (Adeleke, 1995, 589)

"The role of the OAU in the Liberian crisis has not been large. Perhaps the non-interference clause of the organization's charter spurred use of ECOWAS's defence and security protocols, or it may have been a lack of resources and any successful experience with conflict resolution. In any case, the OAU contented itself with a 'diplomatic presence' as others took the initiative." (Dunn, 1999, 107)

"Nigeria was, moreover, the only West African state with the requisite mix of motivation and resources to intervene in the war." . . . [ECOMOG] conformed with Nigeria's security and economic interests in the sub-region." (Adeleke, 1995, 578)

"What has baffled scholars is why [the Nigerian president] played such an active role in the Liberian crisis, spending well over US$8 billion of scarce Nigerian resources in a conflict that posed only a remote threat to Nigerian security and for which there was 'little solid gain for Nigeria.'" (Mgbeoji, 2003, 21)

"Liberia was the stage for a bitter struggle for dominance within the ECOWAS; the organization was fissured along Anglophone and Francophone lines. . . . Above all, Nigeria saw the war as a test of what it perceived to be its regional hegemony, for it was determined that Liberia would not succumb to the NPFL, and then join the francophone bloc inside ECOWAS." (Stuart Croft and Adrian Treacher, cited in Mgbeoji, 2003, 42–43)

"In . . . a sub-region of 16 countries where one out of three West Africans is a Nigerian, it is imperative that any regime in this country should relentlessly strive towards the prevention or avoidance of the deterioration of any crisis which threatens to jeopardize or compromise the stability, prosperity and security of the sub-region." (Nigerian President, Ibrahim Babangida, as cited in Tuck, 2000)

"The UN had not addressed the crisis in Liberia over its first two years primarily because Ethiopia and Zaire, then sitting on the Security Council, had kept the issue off the agenda. The slogan "African solutions for African problems," advanced by the OAU, reflected the continent's colonial legacy. African nations did not want to set a precedent for more intervention. That coincided with the UN's preference not to get involved." (Talentino, 2005, 223–24)

D. Mass Media: February 23 to August 22, 1990
  i. "Alerting" function (volume of television and newspaper coverage): N=132; Rank order=5
    a. Television coverage: Rank order=5
       Total (ABC, CBS, NBC): N=41
       In-depth: N=11
    b. *New York Times* coverage: N=91; Rank order=5

ii. "Evaluative" function (intervention framing in the *New York Times*)
Pro-intervention frames: N=2
Anti-intervention frames: N=1
iii. Assessment of media coverage

Herbert Howe criticizes media coverage of the conflict, claiming that "the American media—especially television—had not significantly covered Liberia's conflict and the civilian suffering." (1996/97, 150–51) Larry Minear and colleagues agree, claiming, "Despite widespread violence and suffering over more than five years, the Liberian civil war has received sparse international coverage and exhibits little media-policy interaction." (1996, 47) While these judgments may well be correct, when compared to other post-colonial humanitarian crises examined for this study, media coverage of the Liberian conflict (both by television and newspapers) is actually reasonably robust—fifth in the rank order—which suggests that if we conclude that the media failed to cover Liberia adequately, we would have to judge that they failed even more miserably in at least five other crises.

Any assessment of the contribution of media to a possible international intervention in Liberia must consider a unique factor—Charles Taylor's public relations skills, especially during the crucial early phase of the conflict. On this dimension, Stephen Ellis points to "the rebel leader's early access to the BBC to craft a public image of himself that would play a key role in his claim to NPFL leadership. 'Revealing a fine talent for public relations . . . Taylor used the media to build a national and international profile which gave him a vital advantage over other leaders of the NPFL in the early months of the war.'" (cited in Innes, 2004, 13; see also Ellis, 1998) In light of the fluidity of events in the country and Doe's unsavory reputation, a positive image of Taylor in western media certainly could have worked to influence decisions regarding the wisdom of dispatching an international force to support Doe's government. On this point, Innes argues that "Taylor's running dialogue with the BBC countered official news of the war, enhanced perceptions of rebel success, and identified Taylor as Doe's chief competitor. Access to foreign media thus provided an alternative path to legitimacy for Taylor in the first eight months of the war." (2004, 19)

Our study of *New York Times* coverage of the crisis begins in late February 1990, six months prior to the beginning of the ECOMOG intervention. Data in Table 2.1 reveal that coverage began slowly, with

Table 2.1 *New York Times* **Coverage of Liberia**

Panel 1 – Date:	N	%	Panel 2 – Dateline:	N	%
First 2 Months	2	2%	United States	22	24%
Second 2 Months	32	35%	Liberia	51	56%
Third 2 Months	57	63%	Africa (other)	18	20%
		100%	Other	0	
			Unknown	0	100%

Panel 3 – Source:	N	%	Panel 4 – Type of Content:	N	%
Local Staff	51	56%	Front-page News	4	4%
AP	14	15%	Inside-page News	76	84%
AFP	2	2%	Editorials	2	2%
Reuters	18	20%	Op-ed Features	2	2%
Other	5	6%	Photos	5	6%
Unknown	1	1%	Letters	2	2%
		100%			100%

Newspaper Coverage, by Date, Dateline, Source and Type (February 23 to August 22, 1990) N=91

only two articles appearing during the first two months of the study. The pace of coverage picked up considerably in April and June, when 35 percent of items were published, while the majority of coverage (63 percent) appeared in the two months immediately preceding the ECOMOG intervention. The vast majority of items (84 percent) consisted of inside page news. "High-impact" content (defined as front-page stories, editorials, and op-ed pieces) constituted only eight percent of total content—a comparatively low percentage. The rest of the coverage consisted of a few stand-alone photos and two letters to the editor.

Just over half the material was contributed by reporters writing for the *New York Times* (a comparatively low figure as well), with 37 percent contributed by Reuters, the Associated Press, and Agence France Presse. Over three-quarters of material originated from Africa (56 percent from Liberia alone), with *New York Times* reporter Kenneth B. Noble the largest contributor of stories. These originated primarily from Liberia, and, as the summer progressed and the fighting intensified, from neighboring states as well.

As one might expect, coverage concentrated on the civil war itself—the swift military advances by Taylor's NPFL forces; the increasingly brutal repressive tactics employed by Doe's Liberian Army; the on-again, off-again peace talks; a possible resignation by President

Doe, to be followed by new elections; the evacuation of foreigners (especially Americans by United States Marines);[6] and the split in the NPFL between Charles Taylor and Prince Johnson leading to absolute chaos in Monrovia. The situation in Liberia in mid-July was described in the first front-page story dealing with the crisis: "as close to anarchy as I could ever imagine." (a refugee, cited in Noble, 1990, July 15, I1)

Somewhat surprisingly, in spite of numerous references in stories to the "close ties" between Liberia and the United States, there was little mention about a possible United States intervention in the crisis, save for the efforts to evacuate American nationals from Liberia and conventional diplomatic efforts to get the combatants to end the fighting. On June 5, President Doe asked "'all peace-loving nations' to come to the aid of his government." (cited in Noble, 1990, June 5, A7) Obviously unhappy with the American non-response, on June 16 Doe criticized the United States directly for failing to act: "We cherish the relationship between the two countries. . . . So why don't they come to our aid?" (cited in Noble, 1990, June 16, I3)

A military intervention in Liberia on the part of the United States was clearly possible. There were four navy ships off the Liberian coast, carrying over 2,000 Marines to be used for a possible evacuation of Americans. In response to fears that the fighting could endanger United States radio and other installations in Liberia, Assistant Secretary of State for African Affairs Herman J. Cohen was asked whether the Marines "might be landed to defend the installations. . . . [Cohen] . . . responded, 'I wouldn't want to reject any option.'" (cited in Krause, 1990, June 13, A3)

This appears to be as close as the United States came to considering a military intervention. Following the massacre of a reported six hundred men, women, and children at the St. Peter's Lutheran Church in Monrovia in late July, Washington received requests from European states as well as from rebel leader Prince Johnson to send in Marines to stop the killing. (AP, 1990, July 28) This the United States was not prepared to do. According to Johnson, "I was told that our civil war was the internal affair of Liberia, as though the United States had never interfered in the affairs of other people like those of Grenada, the Philippines, or Panama." (cited in Reuters, 1990, July 31, A1) Not satisfied, Johnson announced he would arrest foreigners in Liberia, focusing on Americans, Britains, Lebanese, and Indians in order to provoke the United States into intervening militarily. (AP, 1990, Aug. 5, I19) Such arrests occurred and did indeed provoke the

United States, but only enough to send in Marines to assist in an evacuation of United States nationals and other foreigners. Johnson responded that he would launch attacks against the Marines, although there were no reports that he actually carried out his threat. (Schmitt, 1990, Aug. 8, A3)

Significantly, there was little opposition to the Bush Administration's non-intervention policy; certainly none from members of Congress, nor was any forthcoming from the *New York Times* in its editorials or op-ed pieces. Of the two editorials that focused on the crisis, one dealt exclusively with the fate of Liberians living in the United States (*NYT*, 1990, July 26), while the second applauded President Bush's prudent use of force to evacuate Americans from Liberia. It is worthy of note that this editorial considered none of the contenders for power in Liberia deserving of American support:

> Until now, Mr. Bush had proceeded with sensible caution on Liberia as rival rebel armies closed the noose on the formerly US-supported regime of Samuel Doe. By his corruption and brutality Mr. Doe had long ago forfeited all claim to American backing. Yet his rivals, Charles Taylor and Prince Johnson, are untested leaders and have yet to establish their superior legitimacy. (*NYT*, 1990, Aug. 6, A12)

The concept of "humanitarian intervention" never entered into the discussion in crisis coverage. When possible diplomatic efforts on the part of the United States were addressed, it was in terms of "ending the fighting" between the armed combatants; there was not as much as a hint of a "responsibility to protect" the Liberian population, which clearly had been targeted by "military operations" of all sides. The United States policy of non-intervention was criticized in only one piece, an unsigned, Washington-datelined inside page news story on the eve of the ECOWAS intervention focusing on feelings of betrayal on the part of Liberians living in the United States: "Though the United States has long boasted of its 'special relationship' with Liberia . . . some Liberians here feel abandoned by the Administration which has made it clear it will not intervene militarily to end the civil war." (*NYT*, 1990, Aug. 21, A10)

In late July, media attention began to focus on ECOWAS, first in terms of a diplomatic initiative to end the fighting, then on a possible military intervention, which was first reported on July 21: "[ECOWAS] . . . proposed sending a multilateral peacekeeping force to Liberia *to prevent tribal massacres*." (Reuters, 1990, July 21, I3, italics added)

While rejected immediately by Taylor, both Doe and Johnson initially favored such an intervention. However, when it became clear
to Doe that the proposed "new interim government" would not include him, he termed the proposal "unrealistic." Further, playing the
state sovereignty card, he claimed that an intervention "showed a
complete disregard for the sovereignty of Liberia." (cited in Noble,
1990, Aug. 21, A11) Taylor also opposed the ECOWAS initiative on
the ground that the rulers of both Nigeria and Guinea were personal
friends of President Doe and would use the intervening force to
maintain him in power. Taylor clearly placed the ECOWAS intervention force on notice to expect resistance: "There is no way we're
going to allow them to enter Liberia. . . . We're going to fight them
with knives, guns, cutlasses, and anything else we can find." (Senior
NPFL official, cited in Noble, 1990, Aug. 22, A3)

Among the three contenders for power, there is little doubt that
President Doe received the greatest amount of press criticism. This focused not only on his ten-year record of misrule, but also on the excessive human rights abuses carried out by his troops in their counterinsurgency campaign against Taylor. While there is mention of
Taylor's contacts with the BBC, coverage of him in the *New York
Times* was at best neutral, with a tendency toward suspicion. (See
Thomasson, 1990, July 14, I21) While Taylor did not receive press
criticism in amounts equal to Doe, he certainly was not portrayed in
coverage as the answer to Liberia's governance problems. Prince Johnson emerged late into the ongoing crisis with little advance warning.
No doubt as a consequence, commentary on him focused almost exclusively on his military operations and bizarre statements, with little
background or evaluation dealing with his leadership abilities.

■ Overall Evaluation of the Crisis Response

In the introduction to an article on Liberia, Stephen Ellis quotes a
Ghanaian businessman who had spent many years in Liberia:

> In all frankness the Liberia civil and guerrilla war topped and surpassed
> . . . [all other wars] . . . in form and character, in intensity, in depravity, in
> savagery, in barbarism and in horror. . . . As far as the men behind the
> war were concerned, one should be forewarned that the world could be
> breeding a new species of mankind with no contrite hearts, with no com-
> passion, with no regard for law and order and whose ambitions in life
> have no bounds at the peril of others. It started off in Liberia, but one

should be aware that there are many more Charles Taylors and Prince Johnsons, the new species of human kind, around, not only in Liberia, but in other places, especially in Africa. (Leonard Brehun, cited in Ellis, 1995, 165)

Mr. Brehun was correct. In addition to the estimated 200,000 to 250,000 killed over the duration of the war in Liberia, "the Office of the UN High Commissioner for Refugees claimed that 500,000 people had fled the conflict to neighboring countries—some 300,000 to Guinea, 120,000 to Côte d'Ivoire, and 80,000 to Sierra Leone. A further 1 million were believed to have been internally displaced." (Mgbeoji, 2003, 149, footnote 66) For a country with a population of at best 2.5 million, these figures are no less than staggering.

In elections held in 1997, the legitimacy of which has been questioned, Charles Taylor became Liberia's President. This, however, merely ended the first phase of the war. In 1999, fighting resumed as groups opposed to Taylor organized to bring down his government. In 2003, these forces closed in on Monrovia, where, much like Samuel Doe in 1990, the embattled president held on to remnants of power. "In June 2003, the International Criminal Court issued an indictment for war crimes against Taylor . . . [over his role in Sierra Leone] . . . and in August he resigned his presidency. However, Taylor received and subsequently accepted an offer of asylum from Nigeria." (UN Security Council, 2005) Elections were held in 2005, which resulted in the victory of Ellen Johnson-Sirleaf (previously a minister in the Tolbert government overthrown by Samuel Doe in 1980), who assumed the presidency in 2006. Also in 2006, Charles Taylor was arrested while attempting to leave Nigeria and sent to the Netherlands to stand trial for war crimes committed in Sierra Leone.

Abiodun Alao and colleagues claim that "in the worst moments of Liberia's agony there were many who sought to marginalize the importance of what was happening there. This collective failure to address the seriousness of Liberia's internal conflict was facilitated by its comparative global isolation and its proximity in time to the Gulf War." (1999, 115)

This charge certainly has validity. However, in that Liberia presented the first instance in the post–Cold War era of a "state collapse" type of crisis, where power in effect devolved to sub-state actors (the warlords), perhaps the United States should not be judged too harshly for not responding more forcefully in its early stages, especially in light of the character and record of the Doe regime and the questionable character of possible replacements. On this point, Ellis observes,

it was not clear whom the US government should support if it were to stabilize Liberia. The State Department had for years been exasperated by
Doe's corruption and brutality. But the alternative, in mid-1990, was
Charles Taylor, the leader of the NPFL, a man wanted by US law enforcement agencies for escaping from a Massachusetts jail, an ally of Libya, at
the head of an unstable revolutionary force which was committing horrible atrocities. (1998, 156)

Neither should ECOWAS be criticized unreasonably for failing to
grasp the complexities involved in establishing peace among a number
of vicious factions, or for not anticipating that a "peacekeeping" mission would in reality involve a "peace enforcement" operation. The
problems stemming from the fact that there was "no peace to keep" in
Liberia became evident only after the intervention had begun. This
said, the conflict turned into a long-term stalemate among contending
factions (with ECOMOG becoming one of these).

The international community, in this case specifically the United
States, clearly demonstrated no interest in becoming involved in any
direct way. Especially interesting is the almost total lack of debate at
the elite level in the United States on the Bush administration's non-
intervention policy. As suggested by Lance Bennett's theory of indexing
(1990), and as evidenced in *New York Times* coverage, in the absence
of elite debate the media did not take the lead in raising the issue of a
possible military intervention.[7]

The international intervention by the regional organization ECOWAS
produced what can only be judged as mixed results. The organization
was divided internally with respect to the wisdom of an intervention (with
some members actively undermining the operation), and on the ground
"Operation Liberty" was clearly deficient in areas of command and control. Besides these major impediments,

ECOMOG's manpower—a maximum of about 12,500 but sometimes as
low as 2,7000—was too small for peace enforcement or even for effective
peacekeeping. Several West African officials speculated that ECOMOG
would need 20,000 men for peace enforcement rather that the 5,000–
10,000 it usually had. . . . ECOMOG's size . . . was large enough to prevent a final battle for Monrovia, but the force was not large enough to
push the factions into successful peace talks. *Prolongation of the war was
the result.* (Howe, 1996/97, 168, italics added)

What is left unsaid in this criticism is what the results would have
been if ECOWAS had failed to take the initiative and not intervened

in Liberia. In that it was obvious that neither the UN nor any Western country was prepared to intervene, as hard as it is to imagine, the results for Liberia conceivably could have turned out even worse than they did.

▪ Notes

1. One cannot dismiss the parallels between Liberia and Haiti where, following independence in 1804, another group of previously freed slaves (the *affranchis*) morphed into a dominant ruling elite, with similar unfortunate consequences. (See Chapter 6, this volume.)

2. At the time of the intervention, the *New York Times* reported that only about five thousand people, of whom three thousand were civilians, had been killed. (Noble, 1990, Aug. 22, A3)

3. Stephen Ellis cites Taylor's opposition to the ECOMOG intervention as a critical miscalculation: "By accepting ECOMOG in 1990 Taylor could have become president with Nigerian support since he controlled most of Liberia at that juncture and already had some international backing. His failure to do this meant that, once ECOMOG had intervened to secure Monrovia and had installed a puppet government, the conflict became intractable." (1998, 162)

4. President Doe was taken captive at a meeting called by ECOMOG at its headquarters, then tortured and killed.

5. Elwood Dunn notes that "of sixteen member-states, only seven attended the summit of August 1990: the heads of state of Gambia, Ghana, Guinea, Nigeria, and Sierra Leone, and the foreign ministers of Mali and Togo. Ivory Coast and Burkina Faso did not participate and declared the creation of ECOMOG was contradictory to ECOWAS's rules." (1999, 104)

6. Vanderbilt Television News Archive Abstracts indicate that, far and away, the plight of American citizens living in Liberia and their eventual evacuation by United States Marines dominated network TV news coverage, providing the primary focus for nine of the eleven in-depth stories. This dimension of the crisis was followed by coverage of the civil war itself. United States policy with respect to a possible intervention was noted as being mentioned in one story, while the ECOWAS intervention was mentioned in two stories.

7. The author's studies of United States media coverage of the Jamaat-al-Muslimeem attempted coup in Trinidad and Tobago in 1990 and the Zapatista rebellion in Mexico in 1994 likewise point to media failing to establish a position on foreign crises in the absence of elite interest in, or disagreement over, government policy. (See Soderlund, 2003, Chapters 2 and 6.)

3

Somalia, 1992:
UNOSOM I, UNITAF,
"Operation Restore Hope," UNOSOM II

E. Donald Briggs and Walter C. Soderlund

■ Background

In some sense, the Somalia of the 1990s could be regarded as the classic example of the "failed state." But in an equally valid sense, it may also be regarded as the state that never was, except in a purely nominal fashion. At the extreme, it may even be suggested that the determination to apply established Developed World political concepts to a vastly different and little understood society contributed significantly to the turmoil that developed there.

Located in the Horn of Africa, at the beginning of the 1990s Somalia had a population estimated at between 4.5 and 6.7 million people. It is a relatively large country, about the size of Texas, and shares borders with Djibouti, Ethiopia, and Kenya. (Adam, 1999) None of these borders can be considered stable, as in each case Somalia claims people in territory over which it does not have control.

Historically, the territory of the contemporary Somalia, as well as a good deal of that of southeastern Ethiopia, northeastern Kenya, and present-day Djibouti, had been occupied for centuries largely by nomadic pastoralists who managed to survive in the harsh, arid environment without any form of centralized government. All authorities appear to agree that Somalis are culturally uniform; they speak the same language, share the same customs (including a firmly entrenched poetic tradition), and practice the same religion—close to 100 percent Muslim. Somalis are, moreover, very conscious of their uniformity, considering themselves a separate and distinct, if sometimes laughable, creation of God. The Somali tendency not to take themselves too seriously is illustrated by the well-known satirical Creation Myth, which goes as follows: "God first created the family of the Prophet Muhammad and he was very pleased with the nobility of his handiwork; then he created the rest of mankind and was modestly satisfied; then he created the Somalis and he laughed!" (cited in Samatar, 1991, 12)

One of the most difficult aspects of the Somali nation for westerners to understand is the clan system, which forms the basis upon which Somali life has traditionally been organized. On the most fundamental level, it can be said that the population is divided into a number of *clan families,* though Somalis themselves do not seem to agree on their precise number, what their names are, or at what level they operate. Said S. Samatar, for example, states positively that there are six clan families (1991, 12), while Terrence Lyons and Ahmed I. Samatar appear to suggest that there are only three (1995, 8–9) One of the Lyons/Samatar three is not mentioned by Said Samatar at all, while several that he does mention are relegated to sub-clan status by Lyons and Samatar. This is worth mentioning here only because it is a minor illustration of the confusions with which Somali society is replete, and hence the difficulties of dealing with it in terms that prevail elsewhere.

What is relatively clear, however, is that there is a complex, segmented social system, with clan families at the top, followed by clans, sub-clans, and sub-sub-sub-clans, down to the individual family (the *rer*). The relationship among the clans and sub-clans, and the responsibilities of individual Somalis to them, is governed partly by kinship, and partly by the amorphous concept of *heer,* which can perhaps be imperfectly described as a body of common wisdom that "emphasize[s] the values of interdependence and inclusiveness" and provides "acceptable and workable ways of dealing with disputes and conflicts." (Lyons and Samatar, 1995, 10) What *heer* provides for the constant inter- and intra-clan feuds that result from these cleavages is a kind of guide to determining who should be on what side, but not a form of peaceful settlement. Indeed, given the prominence accorded to "blood-payments" (in which responsibility for honoring debts and making restitution for wrongs rests on the lineage group rather than any individual wrong-doer) and the fact that clan organization is "characterized at all levels by shifting allegiances," (Samatar, 1991, 12) it could perhaps scarcely be otherwise.

▪ Roots of the Crisis

Like almost all of Africa, the territory of contemporary Somalia was divided among the European powers in the late nineteenth century.

The British gained control of the northern portion in typical fashion by entering into agreements with the elders of the various clans in that area, primarily to provide a steady supply of meat for their garrison at Aden, which was considered essential to guard the approaches to the Indian Empire. It was known as the British Somaliland Protectorate. The French, equally desirous of Red Sea possessions to protect their Indo-China colonies, but having been bested by the British at Fashoda in 1898, were forced to make do with the small enclave of Djibouti. Southern Somalia was, in turn, seized by the Italians, who saw it as a place for settlement, much as the British did the Kenyan Highlands. As a result, the Italians made much greater efforts to develop their portion of Somalia than did the British in theirs. In addition, the political chess game among the European powers resulted in Ethiopia being allowed the consolation prize of the western portion of Somali territory, what became known as the Ogaadeen (Ogaden), which is today home to more than three million Somali nationals. It should be noted that there are still significant numbers of Somalis in northern Kenya (the so-called Northern Frontier District) as well.

The Italian and British colonies were folded together into an independent Somalia in 1960. Efforts by Ethiopian and Kenyan Somalis to be included in the new state were successfully resisted by Haile Selassie and Jomo Kenyatta, despite sporadic violence against security forces in those countries and supporting agitation by Somalis "at home." The State of Somalia was consequently born in disgruntlement and dissatisfaction, which played a significant role in its short and unhappy life. It is significant that the flag adopted for the new state was deliberately chosen to represent the "dismemberment" of the Somali nation: it features a five-pointed star. Two stars represent the two joined colonies, the other three the "missing territories" in Kenya, Ethiopia, and Djibouti. The flag therefore served as a constant reminder of grievance and a perpetual distraction from the pressing needs of political and economic consolidation.

Somalia survived as an independent democracy, at least in name, for nine years. Then, on October 21, 1969, General Mohamed Siyaad (Siad) Barre seized power, following two years of political squabbling and clan-sponsored assassination. Barre proclaimed that his government would be based on the principles of "scientific socialism" and the achievement of a Greater Somalia, and would have as one of its chief aims the eradication of clan or "tribal" identities. (Lyons and Samatar, 1995, 14) Of these, the idea of the Greater Somalia had the most popular appeal, something that Barre found an increasing need for as the 1970s wore on. In August 1977, post-revolutionary conditions in Ethiopia appeared to provide an ideal opportunity. To the financial and arms support that Mogadishu had supplied to Ogaden insurgents throughout the 1960s and 1970s, Barre now added some thirty-five thousand regular, Soviet-equipped troops.

The invasion went well for the Somalis at first. They were able quickly to seize control of some 90 percent of the disputed territory. The Ethiopians, however, then appealed for Soviet assistance on the basis of being a fraternal socialist people, and Moscow, apparently considering the Ethiopians more useful as allies than the Somalis, precipitously switched sides and shipped into Ethiopia $US1.5 billion along with fifteen hundred advisors and two leading generals.[1] Some seventeen thousand Cuban troops soon joined the battle as well. The Somalis were ejected from Ethiopia within weeks, and the vision of a Greater Somalia dimmed precipitously.

More significantly in terms of subsequent events, the defeat unleashed clan divisions within Somalia itself. Scarcely a month after the withdrawal announcement, a group of army officers attempted to overthrow the Barre regime. Almost all of the coup leaders were members of the Majeerteen (Mijerteen) clan of the Daarood (Darod) clan family. Seventeen were rounded up and summarily executed by Barre. Colonel Abdullaahi Yusuf, however, escaped to Ethiopia and established there a "liberation front" (the Somali Salvation Democratic Front), which began forays into Somali territory. The government responded with vicious communal reprisals against the Mijerteen clan, including, according to Said Samatar, destruction of the water reservoirs on which clansmen as well as their livestock depended for survival. (1991, 18) Some two thousand people and more than 150,000 animals are said to have died of thirst.

It was not long before other "liberation" movements also came into being. One such was the Somali National Movement (SNM), formed by members of the Isaaq (Isaq) clan. As occupiers of the northernmost part of Somalia, the Isaqs felt that they were deprived, relative to the more developed south, and were under-represented in a government dominated by Darod and Hawiye clansmen. (Lyons and Samatar, 1995, 9) In 1988, the SNM seized control of several areas of northern Somalia, and government forces undertook reprisals against the Isaq clan as such, on the ground that its members were all potential SNM recruits. Some five thousand Isaqs are said to have been killed, and two cities, Hargeisa and Bur'o, were completely destroyed. (Samatar, 1991, 19)

Resistance to the Barre regime was not, however, confined to disaffected northern regions. In 1987 or 1988 the United Somali Congress was established by disgruntled members of the southern Hawiye clan, despite the fact that, unlike the Isaq, many of its members had been prominent in the original civilian regime and in the armed forces. The Hawiye became communal government targets as the Isaq and Mijerteen had previously. By 1989, revolt and violent repression had thus become national, rather than merely regional, and whatever small allegiance Somalis may once have felt to the state as a whole had dissolved in favor of traditional clan loyalties and clan-based defenses. By 1990, Barre's government itself, as well as the national army, were made up mainly of members of his own Marehan clan—only blood relations could really be trusted.

As Lyons and Samatar tell us, "While Siad Barre's forces terrorized much of the countryside in the waning months of the 1980s, unrest in Mogadishu increased in response to economic collapse and mounting human rights abuses." (1995, 19) There were violent clashes within the capital itself in July 1989, followed by the now-customary reprisals against clan groups. In April 1990, a group of prominent individuals (the Manifesto Group), including Aden Abdulla Osman, Somalia's first president, published a manifesto calling for the formation of a provisional government and political reconciliation with the various rebel groups. Most of the signatories were promptly arrested. By the middle of the year, Mogadishu was in chaos, with public demonstrations, riots, looting, arrests, and repression the order of every day. Barre controlled only a small sector of the city but managed to cling to the remnants of power until January 1991. However, on the 27th of that month, he fled the capital, though not the country, leaving a nightmare of anarchy behind him.

■ Events Precipitating the Crisis

Following Barre's departure from the capital, Somalia became a state without even the semblance of governmental institutions—Adam describes the situation as a "complete state collapse." (1999, 169) The Somali Salvation Democratic Front (SSDF) was more or less dominant in central and northeastern territories and was able to provide a quasi-stability that prevented widespread famine. Somewhat similarly, the Somali National Movement (SNM) gained control of the northwestern region and went so far as to declare the independent Somaliland Republic. To the south, the triangle formed by the coastal cities of Mogadishu and Kismayu and the inland one of Belet Weyn, was in total chaos. On one level, there was constant violent conflict among a variety of clan and sub-clan organizations contesting for control of territory and resources. But beneath, and acting without even the restraint of clan loyalty, armed teenage gangs known as *mooryaan* terrorized the countryside and the urban areas in continuous search for booty of whatever kind might be available.

To the extent that a main conflict could be singled out in the early months of 1991, it was between the United Somali Congress (USC), the Hawiye-based group under the leadership of General Mohamed Farah Aideed, which controlled Mogadishu and areas north of it, and the remnants of Barre's forces regrouped around Kismayu, in alliance with the Marehan-based Somali National Front. Barre's forces at one point came close to recapturing Mogadishu but were repelled by Aideed's counteroffensive. In retreat, Barre carried out a scorched-earth campaign, destroying the crops, animals, and homes of everyone in his path, to the extent that famine quickly added to the misery being suffered by the civilian population that had not already fled to Kenya or Ethiopia.

But this conveys an unrealistically "clean" image of the situation in Somalia, and especially in Mogadishu in 1991. Aideed, for instance, was not the only contender for power in the capital. In addition, there was Ali Mahdi Mohamed, who proclaimed himself interim president on Barre's flight to the south. Mahdi was nominally part of the USC faction, but once Barre's attempt to retake the capital city had been repulsed, the primary locus of conflict was the leadership struggle between the Aideed and Mahdi factions. By late 1991, the former controlled the southern part of Mogadishu, including the airport and the seaport, while the latter predominated in the north. The clashes between them succeeded in destroying the entire infrastructure of the city, while looting of private as well as public property became all-encompassing.

■ The Intervention, Phase 1 (UNOSOM I)

As is usually the case, the international community responded slowly to the growing humanitarian disaster in Somalia. Some efforts were made by the governments of Ethiopia and Eritrea to convene reconciliation conferences, but these received little support from elsewhere. Djibouti did succeed in bringing many of the Somali parties together in July 1991, but not all were represented, and Aideed in particular refused to abide by the vague and limited agreements that were worked out at the conference. The UN reportedly refused to participate in this peace effort on the grounds that the matter was too complicated. (Sahnoun, 1994, 10) According to some authorities, this was one of several missed opportunities to begin a genuine process of reconciliation and abort the downward spiral into anarchy.

It was not until December 1991 that the UN, under the prodding of Secretary-General Javier Perez de Cuellar, began slowly to take a more active role in the Somalia crisis. By this time, three hundred thousand people had died of hunger and related diseases, another five hundred thousand were in refugee camps in Ethiopia, Kenya, and Djibouti, and 70 percent of the country's livestock had been lost; in addition, three thousand people were said to be dying daily from starvation. The world organization adopted its first resolution on the matter on January 23, 1992, calling for a total arms embargo, urging the conflicting parties to agree to a ceasefire, and requesting the international community to provide increased humanitarian aid to the country. It did not, however, call for a peacekeeping mission of any kind, reportedly because the United States was opposed to such action. Talks were subsequently held in New York in February 1992, at which the parties agreed to an immediate, if vague, ceasefire. (Sahnoun, 1994, 15–16) An additional ceasefire agreement, negotiated by UN Special Envoy James Jonah, was signed by Mahdi and Aideed on March 3, under the apparent assumption that if these two could be brought into line, others would follow.

According to Jeffrey Clark's blunt appraisal, "after the cessation of hostilities UN senior diplomats foundered in the field, the Security Council dithered, and UN relief agencies squandered valuable time." (1993a, 115) A further resolution in April, however, did establish the United Nations Operation in Somalia (UNOSOM). It provided for fifty unarmed ceasefire monitors for Mogadishu, and a five-hundred-member security force to escort the delivery of humanitarian aid. However, as Mohamed Sahnoun, who was head of UNOSOM, has indicated, "UN agencies made little headway in creating distribution networks for food deliveries" and, down to July 1992, had delivered only about 26 percent of the food relief that had been promised in January. (1994, 20) Fighting frequently broke out over the delivery of such assistance as did arrive, and banditry often prevented it from reaching those areas in greatest need of it. As newly elected Secretary-General

Boutros Boutros-Ghali reported to the Security Council on August 24, the assistance provided to Somalia was "in no way adequate to meet the needs of the Somali people. Present estimates, which may be conservative, indicate that as many as 4.5 million people are in desperate need of food and other assistance." He called for a "comprehensive programme of action covering humanitarian relief, the cessation of hostilities, the reduction of organized and unorganized violence, and national reconciliation." (cited in Sahnoun, 1994, 21)

In mid-August 1992, President George Bush responded by announcing that he would supply military aircraft to transport food relief, but this failed to make any major impact due to continued looting and the inability of the five-hundred-man Pakistani security force to deploy effectively, thanks to the lack of cooperation of the Aideed faction in particular.

■ The Intervention, Phase 2 (UNITAF)

Late in November, Bush offered American troops to lead a more comprehensive attempt to stabilize the situation. On December 3, the Security Council accordingly approved the use of "all necessary means to establish as soon as possible a secure environment for humanitarian relief operations in Somalia." (Lyons and Samatar, 1995, 34) I. M. Lewis and James Mayall note that UNITAF marked "the first time that an unambiguously internal humanitarian crisis had been designated as a threat to international peace and security, thus justifying peace enforcement measures." (1996, 94) Bush emphasized, however, that the United States objective was humanitarian only, not aimed at dictating political outcomes, but merely at the creation of conditions that would permit the feeding of the starving Somali people. (Lyons and Samatar, 1995, 34) Just how the presence of a large foreign military force could avoid having a significant impact on the chaotic Somali political landscape was left unexplained.

Bush appointed Robert Oakley, former ambassador to Somalia, as his special envoy to prepare the way for the arrival of the military forces. Oakley concentrated first on trying to gain the cooperation of Farah Aideed and Ali Mahdi, under the assumption that the safe deployment of UNITAF troops required relative peace in Mogadishu. The two were induced to sign a ceasefire and truce agreement on December 11. Critics have since complained that by singling out these two leaders, Oakley conferred on them an unwarranted political legitimacy and created resentment in other parts of the country. Nevertheless, it is probably true that this approach allowed a more rapid and uneventful deployment of the twenty-eight-thousand-strong United States force than might otherwise have been the case.

UNITAF forces (twenty-eight thousand from the United States and thirteen thousand from twenty-three other countries) were concentrated in the southern third of Somali territory, leaving the remainder effectively in the hands of Somali National Movement (northwest) and the Somali Salvation Democratic Front (northeast). Precisely how UNITAF forces should operate, however, and in particular, how the prohibition on political involvement should be honored, were never clear. Secretary-General Boutros-Ghali made plain his own view that one of their chief objectives should be the disarmament of the warring militias. Washington disagreed on principle, on the ground that such action would constitute political interference, but the need to create security of some kind and allow humanitarian relief to reach those in need inevitably necessitated some confiscation and restriction of weapons, ad hoc and piecemeal though it was. It also became necessary to become involved in the inherently political tasks of establishing a civilian police force within Mogadishu, and assisting in the restoration of some of the country's destroyed infrastructure. Officially, however, UNITAF remained aloof from politics.

Two reconciliation conferences were organized by the UN in 1993, but for a number of reasons little real progress was made. First, the UN-organized gatherings focused on the clan-militia leaders to the exclusion of other community leaders. Second, the warlords disagreed among themselves as to the relative role they should be accorded. Third, United States Special Representative Robert Oakley was at the same time busily engaged in trying to rally community and religious leaders to play a larger role in the reorganization process, something that did not sit well with the warlords. Fourth, clashes between UNITAF forces and various militia groups continued in a sporadic fashion.

The second Addis Ababa conference, held in March, produced a broad-based agreement calling for a Transitional National Council (TNC), composed of one representative of each of the fifteen identified factions, plus three (including one woman) from each of eighteen regions, and five representing Mogadishu—seventy-four members in all. The TNC was to act for a two-year period until agreement could be reached on permanent institutions. In addition, there were to be regional and district councils, though the relationship between these, and between them and the central authority, was left unclear. It should be noted that the Somali National Movement, controlling the northeastern region of the country, refused to sign the agreement until such time as stability could be established in the south and appropriate negotiations entered into between the two regions.

■ The Intervention, Phase 3 (UNOSOM II)

In that from the start UNITAF had been seen as a short-term operation, on March 3, 1993, the Secretary-General submitted to the Security Council his recommendations for the transition from UNITAF to UNOSOM II. The latter would have enforcement powers under Chapter VII of the Charter and "would seek to complete, through disarmament and reconciliation, the task begun by UNITAF . . . [and] . . . provide assistance to the Somali people in rebuilding their economy and social and political life, re-establishing the country's institutional structure, achieving national political reconciliation, recreating a Somali state based on democratic governance and rehabilitating the country's economy and infrastructure." (UN, 2003a) UNOSOM II's mandate would include "preventing any resumption of violence and, if necessary, taking appropriate action against any faction that violated or threatened to violate the cessation of hostilities." (UN, 2003a) On March 5, the Secretary General appointed retired Admiral Jonathan Howe of the United States as his Special Representative for Somalia to oversee the transition, and Turkish Lieutenant-General Cevik Bir as UNOSOM II's force commander.

In the month that followed, some progress was made in the establishment of the district and regional councils, despite Admiral Howe's view that the agreement did not give sufficient emphasis to achieving a ceasefire and rehabilitating Somali civil society. In effect, everyone was in agreement that a new order had to be created in the country, but there was fundamental disagreement between those who believed that the way to accomplish that was to persuade the warlords to become statesmen, and those who thought this impossible and insisted that the only effective methodology was to create institutions which would supplant them.

It became clear by June 1993 that some militia leaders were prepared to cooperate with UNOSOM, at least for the time being, but that General Aideed was not among them. On June 5, Pakistani UN troops were ambushed at two locations on opposite sides of Mogadishu by forces thought to be allied with Aideed's Somali National Alliance. Twenty-five soldiers were killed, fifty-four were wounded, and ten went missing. The Security Council strongly condemned this unprovoked attack and authorized

UNOSOM to take all necessary measures against those responsible for it. UNOSOM accordingly conducted a series of ground and air actions in south Mogadishu on June 12 and destroyed weapons and equipment in a number of storage sites. The Secretary-General said that the object of the action was to restore peace in Mogadishu and that it should be seen "in the context of the international community's commitment to the national disarmament programme endorsed by all Somali parties at Addis Ababa on 27 March 1993." (UN, 2003a) An investigation into the June 5 incident resulted in a June 17 report that implicated SNA forces in the attack, and the UN Special Representative called on General Aideed to surrender to UNOSOM and urge his followers to lay down their arms. He directed the UNOSOM force commander to detain General Aideed, whom United States Ambassador to the United Nations Madeleine Albright now labeled a "thug." (Lyons and Samatar, 1995, 58) For all intents and purposes, political reconciliation and reconstruction now became irrelevant in UNOSOM operations. The objective, at least the immediate objective, was to apprehend the one man who was seen as standing in the way of the successful completion of the mission: Mohamed Farah Aideed.

After the events of June 1993, UNOSOM "pursued a coercive disarmament programme in south Mogadishu." (UN, 2003a) There was, in effect, more or less open warfare against Aideed's forces. In support of UNOSOM's efforts, United States Rangers and the Quick Reaction Force were also deployed to Somalia, though not under United Nations command or control. When these forces undertook an operation in south Mogadishu on October 3, they came under concentrated fire; two helicopters were shot down, eighteen American soldiers were killed, and seventy-five were wounded. Following the battle, the corpses of the American soldiers were dragged through the streets of Mogadishu, as television screens across the world clearly showed. Understandably, reactions within the United States were strong. As the *New York Times* put it, "Americans were told that their soldiers were being sent to work in a soup kitchen and they were understandably shocked to find them in house-to-house combat." (cited in Lyons and Samatar, 1995, 59) President Clinton resisted demands that American forces be immediately withdrawn, but promised that there would be a complete pull-out by March 31, 1994.

The Somali factions nevertheless met again in Addis Ababa in UN-sponsored talks in November and December 1993, despite the fact that the June and October incidents had challenged the whole concept of disarmament and reconciliation and stimulated even those factional elements that had been most receptive to UN overtures to prepare for the renewal of general conflict. Aideed refused to participate unless he were transported directly to Addis Ababa in a United States military aircraft, as a kind of public apology and token of political and personal rehabilitation. The talks were unable to reach any agreement.

Strength of the International Response
A. **Did the Humanitarian Crisis Result in an International Intervention?** Yes
B. **Type of Response:** Combination
- UNOSOM I: UN–led
- UNITAF: United States–led
- UNOSOM II: UN–led

C. **Type of UN Involvement:**
- UNOSOM I: Chapter VI
- UNITAF: Chapter VII
- UNOSOM II: Chapter VII

D. **Size of Intervening Forces: 29,000 to 45,000; Rank order=1**

"Somalia has the unique distinction of being the object of the largest humanitarian military intervention in modern history." (Samatar, 1994, 4)

"Total UNITAF forces peaked in early 1993 at 38,300." (Murphy, 1996, 225)

[Total UNITAF and UNOSOM II strength] "as of 13 November 1993 [was] 29,384." (Finnemore, 1998, 196)

- **UNOSOM I**

". . . UNOSOM I, which was established in mid-1992, failed dismally. The Security Council approved 500 troops (later increased to 3,500) for the operation, but they were not deployed, partly because of opposition from some warlords and merchants who wanted to continue looting and maintaining 'protection' rackets. Even when 500 Pakistani troops for UNOSOM I arrived in October 1992, they were kept in barracks in Mogadishu for weeks without clear instructions." (Makinda, 1993, 185)

"The task of the consolidated, 4,219-strong UNOSOM was to provide humanitarian relief, to monitor the ceasefire, to provide security, to carry out demobilization and disarmament, and to assist in national reconciliation." (Thakur, 1994, 389)

- **UNITAF**

"President George Bush ordered 36,000 troops, including 27,000 U.S. troops, to intervene under UN mandate as Operation Restore Hope . . . in December 1992." (Adam, 1999, 183)

"Approximately 28,000 American troops, combined with another 17,000 from France, Egypt, Germany, India, Canada, and Turkey occupied nearly half the country." (UN, 2003a)

"The 37,000 soldiers (26,000 of whom were from the United States and the remainder from twenty-three other countries) remained until April 1993 with a unanimous [Security Council] mandate to use force to ensure delivery of food." (Weiss, 1999, 70–71)

• UNOSOM II

"UNOSOM II was accordingly established in April [1993] with a strength of 28,000 military and 2,800 civilian staff—the largest peacekeeping force in UN history, and the first authorized under Chapter VII of the Charter." (Thakur, 1994, 396)

Determinants of the International Response
A. Severity of the Crisis: Rank order=2
i. Number of deaths: (short-term) 30,000; (long-term) 250,000 to 500,000-plus

"By midsummer 1992, the United Nations and the International Committee of the Red Cross . . . estimated that 300,000–500,000 people in Somalia had died as a consequence of war, famine, and disease. . . . It was a profound human tragedy, yet one largely ignored by American news media until late summer of 1992." (Livingston and Eachus, 1995, 417)

"By December 1992, the United Nations estimated Somali deaths at more than 300,000." (Murphy, 1996, 218)

"Whatever interpretations the reporters and authors provide, the fact remains that more than 250,000 Somali have been killed, maimed or sustained serious injuries as a result of the civil war in Somalia." (Salih and Wohlgemuth, 1994, 5)

"About 30,000 people, most of them women and children are believed to have died in the fighting that consumed Modadishu." (Perlez, 1992, July 12, I12)

"Today . . . [1993] . . . it is General Muhammad Farah Aideed, the warlord who has been most skeptical of the UN/US role and who is now blamed for the death of 350,000 Somalis last year (a figure plucked out of thin air)." (Gilkes, 1993, 23)

"By 1992, it was believed that about 400,000 people had died of famine or disease or been killed in the war." (Adam, 1999, 181)

"Red Cross officials say they believe that about one-third of Somalia's people, estimated to number anywhere from 4.5 million to

6 million, are likely to die in the next six months unless more food is pumped into the country." (Perlez, 1992, July 19, I1)

ii. **Number of refugees and displaced persons: 300,000 to 3 million**

"Population at risk" (1995) 1.1 million. (Weiss and Collins, 1996, 5–7, Table I.1)

"[By 1988] . . . the war has caused 400,000 refugees to flee, principally to Ethiopia. Another 40,000 refugees are in Djibouti, and tens of thousands have gone to stay with relatives in Mogadishu, the capital, or escaped to the United Kingdom, Holland and Canada. In addition, close to 400,000 people . . . are displaced within the Somali countryside, living without any international assistance." (Adam, 1999, 179)

"Almost 4.5 million Somalis (nearly 70 percent of the population)—including more than 1 million refugees in neighboring countries—are being kept alive through emergency assistance. . . . Almost 2 million have been displaced internally." (Samatar, 1994, 5)

"Dr. Fuchs of the Red Cross estimates that 2 million to 2.5 million Somalis—a third to a half of the population—have been displaced from their traditional land and are seeking food and shelter elsewhere." (Perlez, 1992, July 19, A8)

"Some 500,000 people were in camps in Ethiopia, Kenya, and Djibouti. . . . More than 3,000—mostly women, children, and old men—were dying daily from starvation. That was the tragic situation in Somalia at the beginning of 1992." (Sahnoun, 1994, 16)

"The tragedy was internationalized with the outflow of some 800,000 refugees into neighbouring countries." (Thakur, 1994, 388)

iii. **Likelihood of conflict spreading to other states: 5** *high*

   a. Number of shared borders: 3

     Djibouti, Ethiopia, and Kenya

   b. Involvement of bordering states

"Even though the potential for irredentism in Africa is relatively high, independent Somalia turned out to be the only consistently irredentist state." (Adam, 1999, 172)

"The Somali crises, seen in this collective study as a catastrophe, have had a ruinous impact on the Horn of Africa, and the instability within the region has complicated efforts to end the chaos in Somalia." (Lyons, 1994, 205)

"In 1992, however, the disintegration of the Somali state spilled-over into Kenya. Siyaad Barre and troops loyal to him established a stronghold north of the Kenyan border. Some, including military leaders in Mogadishu, alleged that Barre was receiving support from Nairobi. . . . The risk of clashes—and further regionalization of the conflict—increased. The issue in the 1990s may not be Pan-Somalism, but the chaos in Somalia itself may still draw Kenya into confrontation." (Lyons, 1994, 194)

"The armed resistance [to Barre] found shelter in the vast Somali-speaking population of Ethiopia. Ethiopian President Mengistu was only too happy to receive it and provide it with initial armaments and broadcast facilities. He saw this as an opportunity to take revenge against Siyad's irredentist incursion into the Ogaden in 1977." (Adam, 1999, 178)

B. Pre-intervention "Assessment of Risk": 2 to 3 *relatively low to medium*

"American military analysts do not believe that the Somali clans can muster anything more than paltry opposition to an American troop operation." (Krause, 1992, Nov. 27, A15)

"The soldiers in Somalia are essentially roving bands of poorly-trained young men and teenagers. . . . 'By its nature, it's not too significant a military operation'" (a senior Bush administration official cited in Schmitt, 1992, Dec. 1, A10)

"Somalia is not another Vietnam: America is not likely to get bogged down in a military quagmire. The Somali warlords really are little more than gangsters and should be quickly vanquished." (Bonner, 1992, Dec. 2, A23)

"Even before the United Nations approved the dispatch of U.S. forces . . . the White House was telling the world—and the thugs in Somalia—that the whole operation would be wrapped up by Jan. 20, Inauguration Day." (*NYT,* 1992a, Dec. 4, A30)

"When policy makers are asked how they can send American troops to save Somalia from its warlords but not save Bosnia from its Serbian aggressors, the reply is straightforward: Somalia is easy, Bosnia is hard." (Sciolino, 1992, Dec. 6, IV4)

"Where there are principles and no strategic interests at stake—or real opposition on the ground . . . [it is] . . . relatively easy for Washington to organize an international coalition to respond." (Friedman, 1992, Dec. 5, I4)

"The initial expectations of the American public were that Operation Restore Hope would be a low-cost and quick operation. All the polls conducted in winter 1992–93 indicate that most Americans did not expect U.S. troops to remain in Somalia for more than 1 year." (Klarevas, 2000, 537)

"In November [1992] . . . Bush adopted the risky option of sending 28,000 U.S. troops to Somalia on a humanitarian mission. . . . Bush indicated it would be a 'difficult and dangerous job' and [Secretary of State] Powell's 'best guess' was that it would take 'two to three months.'" (Brune, 1998, 19)

"Could more be done to stop the fighting and feed the famished [in Somalia]? But fearing a quagmire, the big western states have averted their gaze." (*NYT*, 1992, July 23, A22)

"[CIA analysts] . . . concluded that the anarchy in Somalia is so sweeping and the warring factions so deeply entrenched that the country will require long-term international involvement . . . [such as a formal trusteeship]." (Sciolino, 1992, Dec. 2, A18)

"Some long-time relief workers believe that there may be as many as 50,000 armed paramilitary men hidden amid the sprawling shacks and squatting in deserted villas." (Perlez, 1992, Dec. 5, I1)

". . . Somali clans are tougher and meaner than Washington thinks and will harass the American troops and inflict casualties." (views of Smith Hempstone Jr., United States Ambassador to Kenya as reported in Gordon, 1992, Dec. 6, I14)

"The White House's initial hope of wrapping up the operation before Mr. Clinton is sworn in suggests to some that President Bush did not fully appreciate the enormous logistical burdens." (Gordon, 1992, Dec. 8, A18)

C. Extent of "National Interest Involvement":
i. The international community: 2 *relatively low*

"Somalia's position on the Red Sea and the Indian Ocean has long attracted foreign interests." (Adam, 1999, 176)

"During the Cold War the strategic value of Somalia to the superpowers was inflated . . . .When the Cold War ended, the strategic value of Somalia plunged like the stock market prices on Wall Street at the start of the Great Depression. . . . No one cared enough to help prevent its disintegration." (Mazrui, 1997, 9)

[In the spring of 1992] ". . . the international community did not immediately conclude that large-scale humanitarian intervention was the appropriate response." (Lewis and Mayall, 1996, 108)

"The Somali people viewed the arrival of the UNOSOM team as a sign of outside interest in their fate. Most Somalis still could not comprehend why the world community had deserted them when they overthrew their dictator, Siad Barre, in January 1991. Above all, they could not understand why the UN and all its agencies had kept a distant and suspicious stance toward Somalis when their needs were so obvious." (Sahnoun, 1994, 16)

"By mid-summer [1992] it had become clear that, without strong support from the United States, the UN lacked the organizational resources and its members the political interest or will to fashion a coherent strategy for Somalia." (Lewis and Mayall, 1996, 109)

ii. United States: 2 *relatively low*

"The United States was the only donor to claim security interests were basic to its relationship with Somalia. The nature of U.S. security interests evolved during the 1980s. Competition with the Soviets for regional influence turned to collaboration on regional issues. . . . Facilities at Berbera and Mogadishu were still considered important but not critical to southwest Asian logistic support." (Rawson, 1994, 178)

"While Boutros-Ghali was frustrated by the intransigence of Somali warlords, [President] Bush was embarrassed by the fact that the 'New World Order,' which was identified with American leadership, was now characterized by the mass starvation of Somali children. Bush immediately offered to commit 24,000 troops to Somalia, at an estimated cost of $450m." (Makinda, 1993, 185)

"As President Bush reported in his message to Congress . . . , the rationale of the U.S. effort was humanitarian; no strategic interests were at stake." (Haass, 1999, 44)

"It is not hard to explain why the United States acted on Somalia. In addition to principled concern for the Somali people and the 'new world order.' . . . The White House figured they couldn't gain votes by acting in Somalia but their image could be tarnished if they didn't do anything." (a Bush Administration official, cited in Mermin, 1997, 396)

"By all accounts the change in the American position owed much to George Bush himself. Once he had lost the election, he was, in any case, no longer constrained by domestic considerations. Moreover, as the architect of the 'new world order' he evidently felt it incumbent on him to 'do something.'" (Lewis and Mayall, 1996, 110)

"The decision [to intervene] came too late to influence the US election results, but it fit into Bush's idea of a world in which the US can and should intervene at will. The Pentagon saw it as a way to help protect the military budget, particularly as Clinton agreed to the intervention in advance, although he may not have realized just how high the price would be. General Colin Powell, chairman of the Joint Chiefs of Staff, had some reservations, based on what he saw as the need to send sufficient numbers and the necessity of US troops to be under US command." (Gilkes, 1993, 22)

"After leaving the government, a national security aide to President Bush stated that the U.S. action was 'a good signal to the Muslim world' since Somalia was both an African and Muslim country. Moreover, since the Horn of Africa had been a major staging ground of Cold War tensions, . . . there may have been a sense that the United States was morally obligated to help states such as Somalia remain stable in a post-Cold War environment. Finally, some charge that U.S. national security interests were directly at stake; an unstable Horn of Africa could provide an opening for Iranian military and political power in the region, as well as Islamic fundamentalism, which in turn could destabilize the United States' close ally and oil supplier, Saudi Arabia." (Murphy, 1996, 237–38)

"Aside from the humanitarian issue—which admittedly is compelling . . . I fail to see where any vital U.S. interest is involved." (Smith Hempstone Jr., United States Ambassador to Kenya, cited in Gordon, 1992, Dec. 6, I14)

"George F. Kennan questioned why the American people and members of Congress had accepted President Bush's decision to send American forces to a distant land where the United States had no pressing national security issues." (Sharkey, 1993, Dec.)

iii. Italy: 3 to 4 *medium* to *relatively high*

"Long after the United States might have given up on Somalia, Italy, the World Bank, and the IMF were urging greater generosity to save the regime or keep structural adjustments on track." (Rawson, 1994, 181)

"The collapse of UN and US relations with Aideed have caused serious deterioration in the relationship with Italy, the former colonial power of southern Somalia. Italy has been a generous benefactor to Somalia over the years, while doing remarkably well itself from the association." (Gilkes, 1993, 23)

"Hence Italian irritation with the US assumption of control over UNITAF and UNOSOM2. Neither Italy (with 2,600 troops) nor France (1,090) has any representation on Admiral Howe's advisory group, or in the command structure. The Italians believed they could have achieved Aideed's disarmament through negotiations." (Gilkes, 1993, 24)

iv. Africa: *5 high*

"Nobody can suggest to me that we can invoke sovereignty and argue against a collective decision to put an end to the misery, chaos, and mayhem that, for example, is taking place in Somalia." (Salim Ahmed Salim, OAU Secretary-General, cited in Sahnoun, 1994, 50)

D. Mass Media: June 9, 1992 to December 8, 1992
    i. "Alerting" function (volume of television and newspaper coverage): N=270; Rank order=2
        a. Television coverage: Rank order=2
        Total (ABC, CBS, NBC): N=133
        In-depth: N=82
        b. *New York Times* coverage: N=137; Rank order=3
    ii. "Evaluative" function (intervention framing in the *New York Times*)
    Pro-intervention frames: N=17
    Anti-intervention frames: N=9
    iii. Assessment of media coverage

Of all the humanitarian crises of the 1990s that we have studied, with the possible exception of Rwanda, none has garnered more scholarly attention than has Somalia. While there are widely differing interpretations regarding the role of mass media in promoting the international intervention, it is acknowledged that prior to the summer of 1992, the conflict was not on the media's radar screen. As argued by Patrick Gilkes, "The power vacuum that followed the flight of Siad

Barre from Mogadishu in January 1991, and the subsequent civil war in the capital, particularly the fighting between November 1991 and March 1992, attracted little attention despite the country's collapse into anarchy." (1993, 21) However, as Lyons and Samatar note, beginning in mid-1992 that situation changed when "the tragic images broadcast by the Western media . . . captured the horrible degenerative stages of a long process of political, social, and economic disintegration in Somalia."[2] (1995, 24)

It has been established as well that once George Bush took an interest in the crisis over the summer of 1992, the situation vis-à-vis intervention changed rapidly, to the point where

> the deployment of American ground troops in Somali as part of Operation Restore Hope in December 1992 was one of the most closely followed news stories of that period. In the fall of 1992, when President Bush ordered an airlift of relief supplies—"Operation Provide Relief"—approximately one-third of the American populace began following news reports on Somalia very or fairly closely. By January 1993, the percentage of Americans closely following events in Somalia increased by two and a half times to nearly 90 percent. (Klarevas, 2000, 524)

Moreover, Americans approved the intervention: "Initial reactions in December 1992 and January 1993 were clearly favorable to the deployment, with support levels ranging—depending on question wording—anywhere from 66 to 84 percent." (Klarevas, 2000, 525–26)

New York Times coverage of the Somalia crisis was impressive: 137 items in total (third overall, following Haiti and Rwanda), with a significant percentage of high-impact content (36 percent)—front page stories (21 percent), editorials (7 percent) and op-ed articles (8 percent). A majority of coverage (53 percent) originated from Africa (35 percent from Somalia), most of it written by a *New York Times* correspondent on the ground in that part of Africa, Jane Perlez, who contributed 42 pieces, amounting to 31 percent of total crisis coverage. Material originating from the United States was high as well (42 percent), second only to that recorded for Haiti.

Coverage over the summer and fall of 1992 was both thorough and, in our opinion, of the character to have influenced the Bush administration toward initiating and then deepening the American response to the crisis. In total, framing contained in seventeen items expressly supported an intervention in Somalia, while the framing in only nine discouraged such an operation—most of the latter appearing after the decision had been made on November 26 to offer American

Table 3.1 *New York Times* Coverage of Somalia

Panel 1 – Date:	N	%	Panel 2 – Dateline:	N	%
First 2 Months	18	13%	United States	57	42%
Second 2 Months	43	31%	Somalia	48	35%
Third 2 Months	76	56%	Africa (other)	24	18%
		100%	Other	2	1%
Pre-August 14	21	15%	Unknown	6	4%
Pre-November 26	84	61%			100%
		76%			

Panel 3 – Source:	N	%	Panel 4 – Type of Content:	N	%
Local Staff	92	67%	Front-page News	29	21%
AP	23	17%	Inside-page News	85	62%
AFP	0	0%	Editorials	9	7%
Reuters	7	5%	Op-ed Features	11	8%
Other	6	4%	Photos	2	1%
Unknown	9	7%	Letters	0	0%
		100%	Other	1	.5%
					99.5%

Newspaper Coverage, by Date, Dateline, Source and Type (June 9, 1992 to December 8, 1992) N=137

troops to lead a UN intervention. Moreover, *New York Times* editorials and op-ed pieces took a decidedly pro-intervention stance, especially prior to the late November decision to commit military forces.

In the initial period of our study, the situation in Somalia was portrayed in terms that we have since come to recognize as constituting a "complex humanitarian emergency." In the first front-page story dealing with the crisis, Jane Perlez describes the "multiple catastrophes" besetting the country: ". . . the militia fighting, the drought, the countrywide lawlessness and now the terrible food shortages—have proved to be intractable problems for the United Nations and humanitarian agencies."[3] (1992, July 19, I1) Large-scale starvation was identified as the principal international concern, as a half million people were reported to be in danger of immanent death, with "as many as 2.5 million people . . . wandering around in search of food and safety." Red Cross Director Peter Fuchs termed the situation in Somalia "'a disaster . . . quantitatively' much worse than in the former Yugoslav republics." (cited in Perlez, 1992, July 12, I12) The provision of food was seen to be the primary solution to the problem; however, this solution was complicated by the fact that much of the fighting in the country was over food, thus leading to the dilemma that simply shipping in food had the likely consequence of increasing the level of violence. (Perlez, 1992, July 31, A9) In order to accomplish humanitarian relief, logically it appeared that the warlords would have to be dealt with as well.

In its first editorial appearing on the crisis, the *New York Times* took an extremely strong stand in support of international humanitarian intervention—a position that went far beyond providing humanitarian assistance. It also offered some fairly pointed criticism of President Bush for his inaction:

> Somalia's agony underscores a more basic need: an effective, mobile U.N. peacekeeping force strong enough to quell the warlords. Secretary General Boutros Boutros-Ghali has called for just such a force, consisting of volunteers, available on 48-hour call from U.N. members. But with the exception of France, the big western powers have shown little interest in his suggestion. And George Bush, the New World President, has said nothing about this proposal, or about Somalia. Meantime, a third of the country inches toward the grave. (*NYT*, 1992, July 23, A22)

In response to a report near the end of July that Somalia was "a country without central, regional or local administration," Boutros-Ghali proposed additional relief efforts by increasing the number of flights into Somalia. While this was approved by the UN, the American President was apparently not yet on-side, as the United States was criticized for being "slow in responding to Somalia." (Faison, 1992, July 25, I1)

The *New York Times* certainly did its part to prod United States decision makers into action. An August 2 editorial argued,

> Resignation in the face of such suffering is morally unthinkable. The Administration and Congress need to assure timely arrival and effective distribution of food. . . . The world is not helpless, nor are Americans wholly indifferent: All that is missing is leadership. (*NYT*, 1992, Aug. 2, IV16)

Perhaps significantly, it was on August 2 that it was reported that the State Department was forming "a special Somali task force . . . to consider whether to send airlifts of food." (Perlez, 1992, Aug. 2, IV6)

Also in early August, another factor—a comparison to what was being done in Bosnia—caught media attention and provided yet another argument in favor of a robust international response to the crisis in Somalia. Charges ranging from "Eurocentrism" at best, to "racism" at worst, were leveled against the world's major powers. In a move that was seen as highly unusual, the recently appointed Secretary-General,

Boutros Boutros-Ghali, publicly scolded the Security Council for "expanding the United Nations peacekeeping operation in Yugoslavia at the expense of urgently needed peacekeeping and relief operations in black Africa." The problem was framed by the Secretary-General in terms of "a clash between the 'colonial powers' of Europe and the desperate and often neglected developing world." (Taylor, 1992, Aug. 3, A1) The hint of racism was made explicit in a mid-August op-ed piece by Anna Quindlen: "Bosnia, with all its horrors, is at the center of public and political dialogue and Somalia, with all its horrors, is a peripheral discussion." This, she quoted the Executive Director of Amnesty International, Jack Heally, as saying, amounted to no less than "racism." (1992, Aug. 12, A19)

A number of scholars who have written on the role of media in Somalia have noted that Senator Nancy Kassebaum, a member of the Senate subcommittee on African Affairs, was critically important in raising the visibility of the crisis among American policy circles. (See for example, Livingston and Eachus, 1995; Mermin, 1997.) Anna Quindlen outlined the Senator's position as supporting "the use of an international force of soldiers to make sure food shipments get to the people. . . . [Senator Kassebaum also claimed that] . . . we lost sight of the best reason to involve ourselves in foreign affairs—because it is sometimes *the moral thing to do*." (1991, Aug. 12, A19, italics added)

On August 14, the United States announced that it would fly food into Somalia using military aircraft, and that those food deliveries would be guarded by five hundred armed UN troops. (Gordon, 1992, Aug. 15, I1) Thus the first step in a policy of humanitarian intervention had been taken and, while by no means claiming to have established a causal link between media coverage and foreign policy decision-making, it is nonetheless the case that an administration that was opposed to a UN peacekeeping operation in January, and as late as mid-July criticized for its inaction in the face of the crisis, had by mid-August adopted a policy of deploying United States military assets to provide humanitarian relief. Thanks for the decision came in a *New York Times* editorial on August 18: "President Bush, and whoever nudged his pen for ordering the . . . airlift . . . [should be given] . . . high marks." In addition to the compliment, the editorial maintained pressure on the president, as it went on to note that "the Bush administration should have done this months ago. . . . to say that nothing could be done, that Somalia was too messy and remote, would have been a shameful unthinkable abdication." (*NYT*, 1992, Aug. 18, A18)

Coverage of Somalia in the months leading up to President Bush's decision to commit troops to deal with the lawlessness affecting the delivery of food, was in large measure similar to that over the summer. An editorial on September 1 called on President Bush to take the next step and support the creation of a "permanent, multinational cavalry" to be on call for emergencies such as was occurring in Somalia: "Americans rightly wonder if they have the resources to stand alone as a global cop, yet they have a moral and security interest in responding to starvation and brutality elsewhere." (NYT, 1992, Sept. 1, A16)

Pakistani guards were slow to arrive and in mid-September it was reported that 2,400 United States Marines were going to Somalia to help guard food that continued to be looted. It was noted, however, "there was no indication of any plan to involve the American forces in combat." (AP, 1992, Sept. 16, A10) General Aideed opposed the dispatch of Marines (as he had an additional three thousand UN peacekeepers), indicating that "they would not contribute to peace in his country." (AP, 1992, Sept. 20, I10)

The first story to contain framing seen as cautionary in pursuing an international intervention appeared in a Jane Perlez "Profile" of Special UN Envoy to Somalia, Mohammed Sahnoun, who argued "against outside efforts to force a solution in a place where politics, and emotions, can be extraordinarily parochial." Sahnoun claimed that "if you try to force something on the Somalis, they think it's humiliation." (cited in Perlez, 1992, Sept. 20, IV4) Sahnoun's departure from Somalia shortly thereafter was duly noted, as was the appointment of his successor, Ismat Kittani.

A second round of editorial and op-ed opinion pushing the United States toward a further intervention in Somalia appeared beginning with an editorial in early November, again stressing the aspect of moral obligation:

> No humanitarian crisis ought to rank higher on the next American President's crowded docket. The Red Cross reckons a third of the nation may perish. *It would be morally intolerable to acquiesce in the preventable tragedy.* . . . The world's great powers, notably America and the former Soviet Union, poured weaponry into Somalia when the Horn of Africa was a strategic battleground. Now that the guns have been grabbed by warlords without heart or scruple, *the world's great powers have a moral obligation to prevent much of the nation from dying.* (NYT, 1992, Nov. 4, A30, italics added)

In mid-month, this editorial was followed by a series of three op-ed pieces—two by Anthony Lewis and one by Leslie Gelb. On November 16, Lewis canvassed the grim legacies of the Cold War, pointing out that Siad Barre had been supported by both major participants, then adding, "Somalia's present tragedy is of a dimension requiring separate discussion." (1992, Nov. 16, A17) Such a discussion was provided by Lewis in a follow-up piece on November 20, in which he argued that "no genius is required to know what has to be done to save those [starving] human beings—military force must be used to protect the relief effort from the gangs." Moreover, "this is an issue that will not wait for Bill Clinton. The Bush Administration knows that. It is a near decision on what to do next in Somalia. Americans may ask, Why us? *The answer is that being the world's only superpower carries a burden: responsibility.*" (Lewis, 1992, Nov. 20, A31, italics added) Between the two Lewis articles, Leslie Gelb offered his own strong case favoring intervention, pointing out that "legalistic scruples make no sense in Somalia, which has no government and is in a state of anarchy." (1992, Nov. 19, A27) Acknowledging that "we can't impose peace" on Somalia, Gelb advocated setting up a "security zone" in the worst drought area, where people could go to be fed. On November 26, about a week after these articles appeared, the Bush Administration announced that it had notified the UN that it was ready to send troops to Somalia to protect the distribution of food.

Once the offer of American troops had been made, the volume of crisis coverage increased dramatically, with nearly a quarter of news items appearing between the November announcement and the marine landing in Somalia on December 9. At this point, President Bush seemed sure of a "swift exit," while the Pentagon envisioned the mission lasting no more than "several months." (Gordon, 1992, Dec. 4, A1)

In terms of intervention framing, it was only after the offer of American troops had been made that the downside of the intervention was discussed. One of the earliest of such concerns was voiced by aid workers in Somalia who "feared an unwelcome outside force would unite Somali factions," leading to a shooting war with UN forces. (Perlez, 1992, Nov. 27, A14) Likewise, Amanda Barnes of British Save the Children offered that "the idea of flooding Somalia with troops amounted to a 'knee-jerk' reaction that could do more harm than good. 'If troops are to be used at all—and we accept that something needs to be done about security—it requires extreme sensitivity to the situation on the ground.'" (cited in Schmidt, 1992, Nov. 28, 16; see also Schmitt, 1992, Dec.1) Elaine Sciolino reported as well that the CIA had misgivings over the operation, indicating that agency analysts "concluded that the anarchy in Somalia is so sweeping and the warring factions so deeply entrenched that the country will require long-term international involvement . . . [along the lines of a trusteeship]." (1992, Dec. 2, A18) Jane Perlez, in a front-page News Analysis, pointed to a "mismatch" in expectations between the United States and Somali citizens, who wanted more than "the narrowly focused goal of protecting the delivery of food . . . what really interests them . . . is an end to clan violence, economic reconstruction and political reconciliation. And, they expect the Americans to deliver on all counts." (1992, Dec. 4, A1) Finally, four days prior to the landing of American forces, Smith Hempstone Jr., United States Ambassador to Kenya, questioned the operation in terms of its putting the nation's troops in harm's way at the same time as failing to serve its national interests. (Gordon, 1992, Dec. 6, I14)

While never abandoning the position that humanitarian intervention was the right route to follow in Somalia, editorial and commentary appearing in the *New York Times* began to point out the need for a more cautious approach than seemingly had been adopted by the White House; specifically problematic was the mission's "vague mandate" and the need for "a statement of short- and long-term goals." (*NYT,* 1992, Dec. 1, A24) These appeared especially important in light of Boutros-Ghali's request for a force "with the power to disarm" clan militias and American reluctance to undertake this task. (Lewis, 1992, Dec. 1, A1; Lewis, 1992, Dec. 6, I15)

Thomas Friedman pointed out in a front-page News Analysis that "Humanitarian-driven" intervention, as distinct from "National Interest-driven" intervention, was a new departure for the United States and that the grounds for entering into such operations were unclear. And he went on to warn that while initially such interventions might look relatively easy, they entailed "a moral obligation for events that last well beyond the withdrawal of American forces." (1992, Dec. 5, I4) An editorial just prior to the American landing in Somalia pointed out that such a fundamental shift in foreign policy direction needed Congressional input, if not approval (*NYT,* 1992, Dec. 4b, A30), while it was noted in another editorial appearing on the same day that President-elect Clinton, although supporting Mr. Bush's decision to intervene, reportedly had not been consulted. (*NYT,* 1992, Dec. 4a, A30) Moreover, it appeared to the *New York Times* that the United States was shouldering a disproportionate share of the burden—where, it asked, was the rest of the international community? An editorial on December 5 referred to the "Bush Doctrine" as "a recipe for endless intervention by an unwilling cop . . . [and was in need of] . . . further definition." Moreover, it was argued (prophetically, as it turned out) that "Bill Clinton . . . may well be stuck with a messy crash landing." (*NYT,* 1992, Dec. 5, I18) Elaine Sciolino's December 6 News Analysis was headlined, "Reluctant Heroes: Getting In Is the Easy Part of the Mission." (1992, Dec. 6, IV4) For his part, Leslie Gelb still believed that "Mr. Bush made the right decision on Somalia," likening the new policy to President Truman's historic 1947 decision to provide aid to Greece. (1992, Dec. 6, IV19) In its final editorial prior to the landing of American forces on December 9, attention shifted from the United States to the UN, which was seen as in need of reform, both in creating a "rapid reaction force" to deal with situations such as Somalia, and, more fundamentally, in reconstituting the membership of the Security Council. (*NYT,* 1992, Dec. 8, A24)

Did this extensive new treatment influence Bush's decision to intervene in Somalia? Richard Haass noted that following President Bush's decision to fly in food, "television picture and other eyewitness reports showed that the relief effort was not making much difference." (1999, 44) Jeffrey Clark goes further to make a very strong case for the impact of a "media push":

Public outrage at the lurid scenes from Mogadishu and Baidoa freed (or perhaps forced) the president to catapult over question of mandates and authorities to take decisive action. The "CNN factor" simply did not allow the UN and the international community to continue avoiding action as the situation deteriorated. (1993b, 213)

His judgment is backed up by Lawrence Eagleburger, who claimed,

Television had a great deal to with President Bush's decision to go in. . . . I was one of those two or three that was strongly recommending he do it, and it was very much because of television pictures of these starving kids, substantial pressures from the Congress that come from the same source, and that we could do this . . . at not too great a cost and certainly without any great danger of body bags coming home. (cited in Minear, et al., 1996, 54–55)

Our own conclusion is that the media probably did have a significant impact on the decisions to intervene in the Somali crisis. Due to his loss in the November 1992 election, President Bush was suddenly forced to consider his "legacy" four years earlier than planned. (Wines,

1992, Dec. 5; Dec. 6) In so doing, Mr. Bush's views on the appropriateness of humanitarian intervention certainly appeared to have changed from July to November 1992. In light of the volume and tone of the *New York Times* coverage of the crisis, it certainly is not unreasonable to suggest that this might well have influenced the president in the two critical decisions he made over the summer and fall of 1992. It is important to note in this respect that the reservations expressed regarding the intervention in the *New York Times* did not appear until after the second decision had been made. Our overall judgment is that following the end of the Cold War, in a world that was both complex and changing, and with a president searching for a positive role in the "new world order" that he had helped to fashion, there is *prima facie* evidence for substantial media *influence on* (certainly not *control over*) important foreign policy decisions to intervene in the Somalia crisis on humanitarian grounds.[4]

▪ Overall Evaluation of the Crisis Response

Following the October 3, 1993, incident in which eighteen American soldiers were killed and television recorded the desecration of their bodies, United States troops withdrew from Somalia as scheduled in March 1994.[5] They were, to some extent, replaced by military personnel from India, Pakistan, Egypt, and Malaysia. In May, there was a further round of talks, and again paper commitment to political reconciliation was achieved, but if anything it had still less impact on factional fighting than similar agreements concluded earlier.

By mid-1994, the situation in Mogadishu in particular had reverted to much the same state that had existed before UN intervention. The streets were generally dominated by gunmen, and looting, kidnappings for ransom, and pervasive insecurity prompted many non-governmental organizations to withdraw from the country once more. UNOSOM forces remained, but, as provided for in Security Council resolution 897 of February 4, their mandate now was mainly to protect major ports, airports, and the country's essential infrastructure, along with the personnel, installations, and equipment of the United Nations. They rarely left their bases, and had minimal impact on the overall political and security situation within the country. "Somalia," wrote Keith Richburg in the *Washington Post* of September 4, "is as unstable and devoid of hope today as at any time since it collapsed into anarchy in January 1991."[6] (cited in Lyons and Samatar, 1995, 60)

Nor was hope to be regained. There were some further efforts to persuade the factional leaders to pursue their objectives by peaceful means, and the mandate of UNOSOM II was several times renewed for a month or two—more, one suspects, because no one knew what else to do than out of any expectation of even modest progress—but in all real respects, peacekeeping in Somalia had come to an ignominious end. As Sean Murphy concluded, "The fate of the UNOSOM II operation stands as a stark warning that interventions conducted under the command and control of the United Nations are not immune to the problems that afflict interventions by individual states." (1996, 241–42) In November 1994, UNOSOM's mandate was extended for a final time, until March 31, 1995. Withdrawal took place gradually, beginning in January, and by the end of March it had been successfully completed, without incident. It had not been the most glorious chapter in the history of the United Nations.

■ Notes

1. Ethiopia, David Rawson tells us, "was bigger, it was more geopolitically significant, and its Marxism seemed more pristine, untainted by Islam as Barre's was." (1994, 152)

2. Walter Goodman claims that television news was not front and center in alerting the American public to the crisis in Somalia, pointing out that the "first live broadcast from Somalia on American television" appeared on CBS only in the last week of August, following the president's decision to use American forces to fly in food. In criticizing television news, he argues that "it is difficult to imagine a million or more white children dying in some part of the world without attracting troops of American reporters and more television pictures, no matter how difficult or dangerous a job." (1992, Sept. 2, C18)

A review of the Vanderbilt Television News Archive Abstracts tends to confirm Goodman's assessment: Only nine stories were run on network television news dealing with Somalia in the summer of 1992 prior to the president's August 14 announcement that United States military transports would be used to fly in relief supplies. Of these, four were in-depth stories, of which three were reported as showing pictures of starving people.

Prior to the November 26 presidential offer of American troops for an intervention, television coverage focused on starvation, the looting of food by rival clan-based gangs, and the plight of refugees. Once the president had committed troops, the primary focus of coverage shifted to the preparations for that intervention, with both support for, and opposition to, the announced operation reported.

In early December, both Dan Rather (CBS) and Tom Brokaw (NBC) anchored their networks' prime-time nightly news programs from Mogadishu. In total, at least 35 percent of stories featured some network personnel reporting from Somalia, while 47 percent appeared between the November 26 announcement of the intervention and the landing of the intervention force on December 9.

It appears that television news was largely reacting to decisions in Somalia rather than influencing them, although there is substantial anecdotal evidence regarding the impact of television pictures in promoting the intervention.

3. According to Steven Livingston and Todd Eachus, the July 19, 1992, *New York Times* front-page story by Jane Perlez was "the only known news item concerning Somalia thought to have affected . . . [President] Bush." (1995, 425) Livingston and Eachus do not address the possible impact of *New York Times* editorial commentary on the president's decision-making.

4. Both Steven Livingston and Todd Eachus and Jonathan Mermin stress the influence of foreign policy advisors and key politicians on the two intervention decisions. We in no way wish to dispute this emphasis, but add the editorial opinion of the *New York Times* to the mix of factors.

5. Marvin Kalb's analysis of the Mogadishu debacle is that the television "picture is 'not just an American body being dragged through the streets of Mogadishu' but 'a symbol of American power being dragged through the Third World, unable to master the challenges of the post-Cold War era.'" (cited in Sharkey, 1993, Dec.) Such views have led to the popular observation that television was responsible not only for getting the United States into Somalia, but for getting it out as well. Both assertions, while simplifying a complex situation, in our opinion contain more than a grain of truth. (For a balanced assessment, see Minear et al., 1996, 53–57.)

6. Unfortunately, the situation in Somalia does not appear to have improved over time. In the fall of 2006, the United Nations again was called upon to intervene. On December 1, "The United States circulated a draft resolution on Somalia . . . urging a regional peacekeeping force to monitor a struggle for control between the country's embattled government and its powerful Islamist foes. . . ." It was proposed that "The 8,000-member force would come from seven East African nations but not from neighboring states of Kenya, Djibouti and Ethiopia." (Hoge, 2006, Dec. 2, A7)

In early 2007, an Ethiopian military intervention on behalf of the interim government (at least tacitly supported by the United States), against an Islamic Courts Union Government, appeared to stabilize the situation. (Gordon and Mazzetti, 2007, April 8) In January 2007, the United States also initiated a series of air strikes against suspected al Qaeda fighters. These air strikes continued into June 2007.

4

Sudan, 1992:
Humanitarian Relief Efforts
Confront an Intractable Civil War

Abdel Salam Sidahmed and Walter C. Soderlund

■ Background

Located in northeast Africa, Sudan is the continent's largest country by land mass (about one-fourth the size of the United States) and shares borders with nine countries: Ethiopia, Eritrea, Egypt, Libya, Chad, the Central African Republic, the Democratic Republic of the Congo, Uganda, and Kenya. Its population is estimated at "nearly thirty million." (Johnson, 2003, 1) Sudan is generally viewed as being divided between the predominantly "Arab and Muslim north" and the predominantly "Christian and Anamist south." This categorization is, however, an oversimplification of a very complex situation in historical, socio-economic, and political terms. Sudanese society is characterized by multiple regional disparities as well as multiple ethno-religious and cultural identities at times converging, and at others diverging along these fault lines. Hence, although the conflict between the north and the south has been a conspicuous feature of contemporary Sudanese politics, other regional groups in Sudan have often expressed their grievances and discontent toward the central government, using political as well as violent means. The current conflict in Darfur (which has dominated the Sudanese political scene and media coverage since 2004) is one manifestation of the complexity of the Sudanese situation and its political dynamics.

This chapter, however, focuses on the civil war between the North and the South, which dominated the bulk of post-independence Sudanese history. In January 2005, after three years of negotiations under regional and international mediation, the Government of Sudan signed the Comprehensive Peace Agreement (CPA) with the Sudanese

Peoples Liberation Movement (SPLM) and its military wing the Sudanese Peoples Liberation Army (SPLA). (UN, 2005b, Feb. 8) The CPA put an end to over two decades of civil war between the government of Sudan and the SPLM and gave the south the right of self-determination after a transitional period of six years. The war, which started in 1983, is known in the annals of Sudanese history as the "Second Civil War." The First Civil War between the north and the south broke out in 1955, on the eve of Sudan's independence, and lasted until 1972. The bulk of Sudanese post-independence history was therefore spent in a conflict between the successive Sudanese governments, usually dominated by northern political and economic elite and southern-based rebel movements.

Sudan's Second Civil War started during the Cold War era. It was not, however, primarily a proxy war but was rather, like the First Civil War, a response to domestic problems. Yet, given the climate at the time, the new conflict soon became intertwined in the complex web of Cold War–inspired regional and international alliances. The regime of President Jaafar Nimeiri (1969–85) was a close ally of the United States and a top recipient of American military and economic support in sub-Saharan Africa. Among Sudan's neighbours, Libya and Ethiopia, both of which were Soviet allies, had developed hostile relations with the Sudanese regime for a combination of ideological and strategic reasons. Thus, when the Second Civil War broke out in 1983, the rebel movement (SPLA/M) relied on military support from Libya as well as political, logistic, and military support from Ethiopia. Following the fall of Nimeiri's regime in 1985, Libya switched assistance sides; it ceased all aid to the SPLA/M and became a supporter of Sudanese governments that assumed power after Nimeiri. However, based on its own considerations, Ethiopia continued to support the SPLA/M.

At the ideological level, the founding charter of SPLA/M pledged a commitment to socialism. (Johnson, 2003, 62–63; Sidahmed and Sidahmed, 2005, 42–43) The "socialist credentials" of the SPLA/M, which were at least partially influenced by its Ethiopian backers, gave the initial phase of the Second Civil War a semblance of a socialist rebel group fighting a right wing pro-Western regime, a feature typical of Cold War conflicts in the post-Colonial World. In fact, the SPLA/M leadership was more pragmatic than it was ideological. Its pragmatism asserted itself after 1985, when the movement sought to establish diplomatic relations with Western countries and to expand its base among wider sectors of the population, particularly in the south. With the fall of the Mengistu regime in Ethiopia in 1991, all traces of a socialist rhetoric more or less vanished from the movement's discourse.

Because the Sudanese Civil War was not a typical proxy war of the Cold War era, it did not come to a conclusion with the end of that era. It continued, with necessary adaptations dictated by the changing domestic, regional, and international circumstances. At the level of domestic politics, a military coup in June 1989 brought to power an Islamist regime with an ambitious vision of restructuring the Sudanese state and society, which adopted a policy of ruthless oppression of its opponents in the north and an extreme militarist attitude to the war in the south. In response, the SPLA/M joined a broad-based opposition umbrella known as the National Democratic Alliance (NDA), composed of all the main political groups in the country, trade union leaders, and ex-army officers. Such an alliance, which remained more or less intact throughout the 1990s, changed the political (but not necessarily the military) nature of the Sudanese Civil War, which became more an expression of conflict between the Sudanese regime and the opposition coalition than the classical north-south struggle that had characterized it at the start. At the military level, however, the war continued to be fought primarily in the south, with deleterious implications for people and land in that region.

At the regional and international levels, the policies pursued by the Sudanese regime throughout most of the 1990s cultivated the hostility of most of its neighbors and strained Sudan's relations with the key players in the international community.[1] By the mid-1990s, Sudan had joined the club of pariah states and was included on the United States list of countries that supported terrorism. Such a situation made it possible for the SPLA/M and its allies in the opposition coalition to find political, logistic, and military support among Sudan's neighbors.[2] Under the Clinton administration, the United States, which had adopted a policy of containment toward the Sudanese Islamist regime, appeared to tacitly endorse such support.[3] At the same time, due to the isolation of the Sudanese regime and its strained relations with most of the regional and international players with an interest in Sudan, it became effectively impossible to broker a peace deal to end the conflict.

■ Roots of the Conflict

Although the northern parts of Sudan bordering the Nile were home to some of the oldest states and civilizations on record, the current borders of Sudan resulted from colonial expansion and domination during the nineteenth and early twentieth centuries.[4] The country therefore became home to divergent ethno-cultural and religious groups with varying histories and levels of development. Northern Sudan, which experienced extensive processes of state formation and interaction with the outside world, also became dominated by Arabic-Islamic culture and oriented toward the Middle East and North Africa. The south, on the other hand, was largely blocked from influences of the outside world by natural barriers and geographical remoteness and did not experience a similar process of state-building. Prior to the nineteenth century, interaction between the north and south was limited to occasional hostilities or "peaceful co-existence" at the frontiers. By the beginning of the nineteenth century, the main cultural identities that characterize the Sudanese regions today were more or less formed, ranging from the Arabic-Islamic orientation of the north central region, to the strong African orientation of the south. In between, both Darfur in the far Western Sudan (which had embraced Islam) and the Nuba Mountains, in south central Sudan (most of which remained non-Muslim) retained strong regional and localized identities.

Under Turko-Egyptian rule during the nineteenth century, the south was gradually, but violently, brought into the domains of Sudan through the devastating incursions of the slave trade, the plunder of the region's natural resources, and the distortion of its social fabric. (Gray 1961) Later, under British-led Condominium rule (with Egypt), the south became subject to administrative experimentation and shifts in policy direction. Following pacification of the region during the first two decades of the twentieth century, the British administration in Sudan adopted a policy of separating the southern provinces—Bahr El-Ghazal, Equatoria, and Upper Nile—from their northern counterparts due to fear of Arab and nationalist influences spreading to the south.[5] A "southern policy," which the Sudan government formalized in 1930, sought to administer the south as a separate entity and prohibited the settlement of northern traders, officials, and educators in the region to discourage the transmission of Arab culture. The south was, however, opened to Christian missionaries, thus strengthening its non-Muslim religious orientation. Given the typical utilitarian attitude of the British colonial policy, there were hardly any projects aimed at socio-economic development in the south. The initial intention of the British colonial policy makers was apparently to annex southern Sudan to some of its other east African colonies. This policy was reversed in 1947, when a conference organized by the Sudan government at Juba, the main city in southern Sudan, and attended by representatives from both north and south, endorsed the re-integration of the two. (Beshir, 1968)

The First Civil War, 1955–1972

In August 1955, an army regiment stationed in the Equatoria province of southern Sudan mutinied and refused orders to be transferred to the north. The mutiny soon turned into a general uprising in which more than two hundred northerners, mostly civilians, were killed. (Beshir 1968, 70–73) Reasons behind the 1955 southern rebellion (the date of which subsequently marked the start of the First Civil War) were complex and focused on accumulated grievances held by the southerners toward the north and its political elite. As argued by Francis Deng:

> With the unrelenting development towards an independent united Sudan, one incident after another intensified Southern fear of domination by the North. The attitude of the Northern officials towards the Southerners, the discrediting propaganda of Northern political parties against one another in their scramble for Southern votes, the alienating strategies by which the government sought to intimidate Southerners into passivity, and above all the announcement of the results of the *Sudanisation* of 800 posts previously held by the colonial powers, out of which the South received only four minor posts, fanned southern opposition into the violent revolt of August 1955. (1973, 37, italics added)

Through concerted efforts exerted by leading persons from both north and south, as well as the British Governor General at the time, the southern revolt was subdued. The problem, however, remained dormant and later resurfaced in a civil war that lasted until 1972. Southerners could not see themselves as part of the Sudan's national politics. They were either poorly represented or absent from all the negotiations and steps that led to the country's independence, a promise that their request for a federal system would be considered was dropped at the first constitutional debate after independence, and they were normally given only insignificant ministerial portfolios in successive cabinets.

In November 1958, a military takeover led by General Ibrahim Abboud overthrew Sudan's first parliamentary regime and established a military dictatorship that ruled the country for six years. The regime pursued a policy of intensified Arabization and Islamization of the south, which led to widening support for armed struggle among the southern public. In 1963, an organization known as Anya Nya (meaning "poisonous snake") was formed to lead the rebellion against the Khartoum government. Parliamentary rule was restored in 1965, but the war continued unabated. A roundtable conference was convened in 1965 that brought together most of the political forces from the north and south (minus the Anya Nya militia), but it failed to reach an agreement on how to address the southern question. (Ruay, 1994, 114; Beshir, 1968) Subsequently the problem escalated, and the war turned into a "real civil war" as successive parliamentary governments concentrated more on a military than a political solution. The situation was aggravated further by atrocities committed by government forces that increasingly became regarded as a northern occupation force rather than a national army.

Another military coup in May 1969 brought Colonel Jaafar Nimeiri to power. The new regime recognized the historical, cultural, and economic differences that existed between the north and south and created a southern affairs ministry. In 1971, the Southern Sudan Liberation Movement (SSLM) emerged under the political and military leadership of rebel commander and former army officer Joseph Lagu. Negotiations between Nimeiri and Lagu resulted in the Addis Ababa Accord of March 1972, which gave the south autonomy within a unified Sudan. (Sidahmed and Sidahmed, 2005, 41) The Accord was subsequently incorporated into the national constitution adopted in 1973. (Khalid, 1985) As part of the agreement, some three hundred thousand southerners returned home from exile and many ex-Anya Nya soldiers were incorporated into the national army. Sudan's African neighbors and the world community at large hailed the agreement that restored peace to Sudan after seventeen years of civil war. (Johnson, 2003, 39–42)

■ Events Precipitating the Crisis

Peace prevailed in the south for about a decade, during which some progress was recorded in areas of economic development, including the expansion of infrastructure and improvements in educational and other services. For the first time in Sudan's history, the south became more explicitly integrated into national politics at various levels. By the early 1980s, however, there were visible tensions both within the southern political elite and between the regional and central governments. At the military level, there was dissatisfaction with the Addis

Ababa agreement and the way it was being implemented that manifested itself in outbursts of mutiny by ex-Anya Nya officers and enlisted men in 1975, 1976, and in early 1983. These isolated incidents culminated in the mutiny of Battalion 105 in July 1983 and in the establishment of the Sudan People's Liberation Army, SPLA, marking the effective beginning of the Second Civil War.

The direct cause of the battalion mutiny was reported to have been delayed salary payments, accusations of embezzlement from the funds allocated to the battalion, and an order from the army's general command for the battalion to relocate to the north. Yet, there were deeper reasons as well, ranging from lack of funding from the central government to support development projects in the south, to instances of interference in the affairs of the regional government, to personal and tribal rivalries among southern politicians. (Alier, 1992; Johnson, 2003)

Additionally, three significant developments effectively sealed the fate of Addis Ababa peace accord: the discovery of oil in the south; the division of the south into three smaller regions; and the incorporation of aspects of Islamic *shari'a* laws into Sudan's criminal justice system. (Verney, et al., 1995, 13–14) Oil was a problem because of disagreements and suspicion concerning revenue sharing and management of the industry. Southern fears that the north was bent on cheating it out of its fair share were seemingly confirmed by the decision to locate the oil refinery in the north. There also were attempts by the central government to redraw the border of the southern region in a way that would effectively take most of the oil fields out of the jurisdiction of the regional government. The suggestion of redividing the south actually originated among the southern politicians themselves, stemming from tribal rivalries in the region. However, it was controversial from the outset, and when it was put into effect in May 1983, the bulk of southern politicians in at least two of the provinces opposed it. (Verney, et al., 1995, 13) As for the Islamization of laws, although the decision was announced some months following the mutiny, it definitely aggravated the problem by adding a religious dimension to the conflict. This became a prominent feature of the civil war. (Johnson, 2003, 61–67)

The SPLA/SPLM and the Second Civil War

When the mutiny of Battalion 105 lingered, a southern officer, Colonel John Garang (d. July 2005), then head of the army research department in Khartoum, was sent to the region to investigate the problem. (See Johnson, 1989.) Instead of following his orders, Col. Garang—who was reported to have had links with some of the disparate rebel groups becoming active in the south—chose to join the mutinous troops. Thus, the core of the rebel movement, the Sudan People's Liberation Army (SPLA), came into existence, and it announced the establishment of its political wing, the Sudan People's Liberation Movement (SPLM), on July 13, 1983. Both the military and political wings of the SPLA/M came under the leadership of Col. Garang. The SPLA/M projected itself as a nationalist-unitary movement, rather than secessionist as the previous Anya Nya group had been. It argued that it was fighting to restructure Sudanese politics and society in a way that would tackle a wide range of historical inequalities, not just the "southern problem." (Khalid 1989) Not all southern politicians or guerrilla fighters (either inside or outside the movement) agreed with this stance, but Garang's view seemed to have prevailed at least until the early 1990s, when the issue of self-determination for the south was once again firmly put on the political agenda of the SPLA/M and eventually on the agenda of Sudan as a whole.

The SPLA/M differed from the previous Anya Nya movement in a number of ways. It was more inclusive of southern, and some non-southern, tribal and ethnic groups. Moreover, unlike former Anya Nya soldiers, SPLA/M recruits were the product of a decade-long period of peace and therefore were mostly educated, some up to university and post-university levels. The SPLA/M also appeared better armed (with tanks and portable missiles as well as the light tactical weapons typical of guerrilla movements), and it was capable of engaging the government army in significant military operations. Utilizing the animosity that existed between Nimeiri's regime and both Libya and Ethiopia, SPLA/M mobilized backing from the two neighboring countries in logistics and armament; subsequently, the rebel movement won the support of other African countries as well. Yet another feature of the SPLA/M was its effective use of media through radio transmissions, which were directed in Arabic and other languages to the entire Sudanese population. From the outset, therefore, it proved to be a serious military adversary for the Khartoum government.

During the following years, numerous peace initiatives were undertaken, but no agreement could be reached, partly because the SPLA/M took the position that an entirely new constitutional framework for Sudan had to be concluded before it was prepared to lay down its arms. Consequently, no peace agreement was reached between the successive governments and SPLA/M throughout the 1980s and 1990s. (Khalid, 1989; Alier, 1992; Beshir, 1992) As in similar situations elsewhere, despite its horrors and calamities, war proved easier to pursue than peace.

At the war front, fortunes shifted between the Sudanese army and rebel groups in an almost cyclical way. By mid-1989, the rebel movement had driven the government forces from two provincial capital towns, 14 district towns, and over 19 village councils. At that time, the movement occupied around 80 percent of the countryside in the southern region, some parts of the Nuba Mountains, and parts of the southern Blue Nile. In December 1990, the SPLA announced its control of the last governmental post between Sudan and Zaire and the Central African Republic. Thus, by the end of 1990, the SPLA/M was effectively in control of most of the south. (Sidahmed and Sidahmed 2005, 44; Johnson, 2003, 81–85)

The Salvation-NIF regime, which came to power in 1989, pursued a militarist agenda toward the civil war, aimed either at subduing the SPLA/M and ending its rebellion by force, or imposing a political solution from a position of strength. After an almost two-year period of preparation, including the receipt of arms from Iran and China, the government started its offensive against the SPLA at the beginning of the dry season in March 1992. The period of this government offensive is the focus of our media study. The SPLA/M was in a weakened position as a result of a split in its leadership and the loss of the backing provided by Ethiopia under Mengistu, who fell from power in 1991. The 1992 government offensive, code named *sayf al-'ubur* (meaning "Summer of Crossing") managed to retake fourteen garrisons and towns from SPLA control, including the two main administrative and military centers held by the SPLA/M. Douglas Johnson notes that the 1992 offensive "reintroduced fighting in areas which had been relatively free from violence for some time." (2003, 114) By 1994, the only significant presence of the SPLA was in the garrison of Nimule near the Sudanese-Ugandan border. (Sidahmed and Sidahmed, 2005, 44; Johnson, 2003, 99–100)

In spite of these advances, however, the government neither succeeded in wiping out the SPLA, nor in utilizing its military gains to reach a political settlement on its own terms. Subsequently, the SPLA managed to reassert its military position, recapturing some of the previous positions it had lost to the government army, and gradually re-establishing its control over the bulk of rural southern Sudan. In 1997, the SPLA, in cooperation with its regional allies (such as Eritrea) and northern opposition groups, took the war to the north by occupying the garrisons of Kurmuk and Gissan in eastern Sudan. By the end of the 1990s, although the SPLA never reached the formidable position it held in 1990, it had once again become a military adversary to be reckoned with. (Johnson, 2003, 100–05)

The Impact of the War

The Second Civil War, which was primarily fought in southern Sudan, caused widespread destruction and suffering to the people of that region and effectively destroyed the infrastructure and facilities that came about as a result of the Addis Ababa peace accord. By the end of the 1990s, war-related deaths probably ran into the hundreds of thousands and refugees to at least equal numbers, not to mention the many who were internally displaced and living in wretched squatters' settlements around the capital Khartoum and other places.[6]

The war affected the south in a number of other ways. There was, of course, significant disruption to the rural economy and widespread environmental damage, which systematically destroyed the livelihoods of rural civilians in particular. As early as 1986, the networks of bush shops that existed before the war had all but disappeared in the face of widespread fighting, leaving the rural population with no source for buying food and other essentials. Those who flocked to cities and towns for protection were scarcely better off because they were often hostages of one side or the other as military fortunes waxed and waned. (Verney, et al., 1995, 18)

■ The International Response

While international intervention in the Sudan Civil War appears never to have been considered as a serious option, neither was the international community totally unconcerned with the crisis. Due to the collapse of the rural economy, the disruption of the ordinary livelihoods of the southern population (in urban as well as rural areas), and the breakdown of road and river transportation networks that linked the south to other parts of the country, the situation regarding food supplies and other essentials became very desperate; in fact, the whole region came under the shadow of famine and starvation. It was in this context that in April 1989 "Operation Lifeline Sudan" (OLS) was conceived by the United Nations and other international donors. Responding to domestic and international pressures for urgent humanitarian assistance to southern Sudan, the UN launched OLS—with the consent of both government and SPLA/M—to deliver relief assistance to civilians on both sides of the conflict. The operation was divided into a "Northern Sector" with headquarters in Khartoum to access government-controlled areas, and a "Southern Sector" operating from East Africa to coordinate delivery to SPLA-held territory. (Johnson, 2003, 148–49)

The launch of OLS was welcomed both inside Sudan and internationally as a peace-enhancing effort. The operation was initially facilitated by a ceasefire, in tandem with the initiation of the first direct peace talks between the two parties.[7] However, with the rise of the Salvation-NIF regime, the continuation of the OLS program became the focus of a fierce dispute between the Sudanese government, on the one hand, and the UN and international relief agencies, on the other. We find this dispute reflected prominently in media coverage of the Sudan crisis. After a great deal of wrangling, the UN and other concerned humanitarian bodies came gradually to operate within the boundaries set forth by the Sudanese government.

The operation of the OLS Southern Sector became fraught with problems and complicated by new conditions imposed by the government. As the government gained the upper hand in the military field between 1992 and 1994, it was also able to exercise more control over delivery of relief supply to the south. The situation was further complicated by the SPLA leadership split in 1991 and subsequent fragmentation and factional fighting. As explained by Douglas Johnson,

> inter-factional fighting within the SPLA and government advances on the ground after 1992 further complicated the planning and implementation of relief, and left it increasingly open to political and military manipulation. The frequent displacement of large sections of the civilian population disrupted many attempts at the rehabilitation of the subsistence economy and local services. The presence of concentrations of displaced persons renewed the demand for the delivery of large quantities of relief supplies, while the intensification of war meant the diversion of such supplies for military use on a far greater scale than before. (2003, 150)

Because civilian populations are often under the protection or at the mercy of those who exercise military control over their areas, both the government and the various SPLA factions developed a pattern of manipulating relief provisions for their own benefit. They tended to use these relief supplies to enhance their control over the civilian population under their authority and to cultivate their loyalty, as well as to ensure the flow of food supplies to their own soldiers. Thus, outside relief became a part of the problem, as frequently happens in such cases. Peter Verney and colleagues summarized the situation as follows:

> The inefficient, costly and supposedly short-term response of external relief provision becomes a habit with its own momentum. Relief food, which rarely accounts for more than 10–15 percent of total consumption in afflicted areas, has nonetheless become a weapon of war and a source of political power. Meanwhile the stimulus towards enabling people to resume local food production and other economic activities—far more effective in overcoming famine and stabiliziing communities—is lost. (1995, 20)

Strength of the International Response: Rank order=10
   A. **Did the Humanitarian Crisis Result in an International Intervention?** No
   B. **Type of Response:** Provision of relief supplies
   C. **Type of UN Involvement:** Specialized agencies
   D. **Size of Intervening Forces:** N/A

Determinants of the International Response
   A. **Severity of the Crisis: Rank order=3**
      i. **Number of deaths:** (short-term) difficult to determine; (long-term) 1.3 million to 2 million-plus
      "The situation . . . [in Sudan] . . . is nearly as horrendous as in Somalia and is likely to get worse. (Bonner, 1992, Dec. 2, A23)
      "The civil war, re-ignited in Southern Sudan in May 1983, has been intensified by the Bashir regime's drive for a military solution, bringing the estimated death toll in Southern Sudan to over 1.3 million by May 1993." (Verney, et al., 1995, 9)
      "Since . . . [the Addis Ababa agreement of 1972] . . . the civil war, and related famines and diseases, have consumed about a million lives, displaced several million more, and dispossessed the war zone of health, educational, and other social services. Sudan has mastered its own self-destruction." (Ali and Matthews, 1999, 195)
      "Sudanese have been fighting on and off since 1955, with an estimated two million dead from war or war-induced famine." (Crocker, 1999, Aug. 6, A19)

"What is going on in Sudan, and what has been going on for the past 15 years is virtually unprecedented in terms of devastation to human lives, property and society in the south." (Jeff Drumtra, Senior Policy Analyst for the United States Committee for Refugees, cited in BBC, 1998, Dec. 11)

"It is an 18-year-old conflict that has probably killed more than two million people. Every family in southern Sudan bears scars." (Harding, 2001, April 21)

  ii. **Number of refugees and displaced persons: (short-term) 1 million; (long-term) 4 million to 5.5 million**

"Population at Risk" (1995): 3 million. (Weiss and Collins, 1996, 5–7 Table I.1)

"The United Nations said . . . that more than a million people had been forced from their homes in the last six months, joining the two million already displaced by civil war." (Perlez, 1992, Sept. 16, A1)

"In the 1990s . . . [the war in Sudan] . . . which had been more or less ongoing since the Sudan received its independence in the mid-1950s, produced a humanitarian crisis that, in numbers of persons affected, exceeded either the Kurdish or Somali emergencies." (Minear, et al., 1996, 49)

"About 5 million people have been displaced, while half a million more have fled across an international boundary. . . . By all accounts, it appears to be the worst humanitarian disaster in the world today." (Deng, 2001)

  iii. **Likelihood of conflict spreading to other states: 5** *high*
    a. **Number of shared borders: 9**
      Ethiopia, Eritrea, Egypt, Libya, Chad, the Central African Republic, the Democratic Republic of the Congo, Uganda, and Kenya.
    b. **Involvement of bordering states**

"Sudan's political boundaries with neighbouring countries have little to do with ethnic distinctions and affect numerous population groups which overlap them." (Verney, et al., 1995, 9)

"Since 1991 the number of internal civil wars has multiplied, paralleled by a deepening involvement of the Sudan government in the internal affairs of neighbouring countries, whether in pursuit of its policy of Islamic expansion or for reasons of military expediency." (Johnson, 2003, 127)

"External factors have played a role in the civil war, but their influence has tended to be felt once the fighting began. External involvement all too often strengthened the resolve of one or both parties to pursue a military option rather than seek a negotiated settlement." (Ali and Matthews, 1999, 217)

"Ethiopian and (briefly) Libyan support for the Southern guerrillas, and later for the SPLM/SPLA, brought internal Sudanese discontent into the arena of the Cold War." (Johnson, 2003, 59)

"As the SPLA presence in southwestern Ethiopia grew, it was brought increasingly into Ethiopia's internal war, and partly as an extension of the war against Khartoum's militias. . . . The Sudanese civil war only added to the political instability and insecurity of life in southern and south western Ethiopia." (Johnson, 2003, 88)

"The collapse of the Mengistu government in Ethiopia in May 1991 seriously reversed the SPLA's military momentum." (Johnson, 2003, 88)

"Ultimately, the search for allies drove Nimeiri to turn towards the south and seek a peaceful settlement of the civil war through the good offices of the World Council of Churches and Ethiopian Emperor Haile Selassie." (Ali and Matthews, 1999, 208)

". . . for many years Southern guerrillas had no choice but to seek help from regimes unsavoury to the west." (Johnson, 2003, 60)

B. Pre-intervention "Assessment of Risk": (indeterminate; as near as we can tell, no intervention was contemplated)

C. Extent of "National Interest Involvement": 2 *relatively low*
   i. The international community: 1 *low*

"In the 1990s . . . what strategic value this gigantic country possessed during the cold war has faded, while a militarized legacy remains." (Verney, et al., 1995, 9)

"Liberia was not alone in the category of ignored crises. In Sudan there was a similar lack of international resolve to address the issues raised by the protracted civil war between the secessionist Sudan People's Liberation Army (SPLA) and the Islamic government in Khartoum." (Minear, et al., 1996, 49)

"The resumption of civil war in Sudan in the context of the cold war made it subject to a number of distortions from external influence. In the early 1980s Khartoum under President Nimeiri was receiving military and economic support from a variety of allies, including the USA and Egypt, while the SPLA was supported by Ethiopia, the USSR, Cuba and Libya. A decade later there had been sweeping changes. Khartoum's supporters and friends in 1995 included Iran, Iraq, Yemen, Pakistan, Malaysia and China, with France adopting an ambiguous position." (Verney, et al., 1995, 19)

"Despite 'casualties and displacement of people by the million,' noted one commentator, the United Nations 'had chosen to regard it as a strictly internal matter.'" (Minear, et al., 1996, 49)

ii. The United States: 1 *low*

"The Sudan became important to the US as a regional counterweight to Soviet-backed Libya. The Reagan administration's high profile hostility towards Libya . . . drew the US and the Sudan into a closer military alliance." (Johnson, 2003, 57)

"Both the US and Egypt initially accepted the Bashir regime after the 1989 coup, playing down its Islamic aspect. Alarm grew when Sudan was declared an Islamic state in December 1990, and a year later, when it openly aligned itself with Iran. The US then went on to denounce Sudan as a supporter of terrorism." (Verney, et al.,1995, 19)

"Publicly, the US government emphasised Ethiopian and Libyan involvement . . . [in the civil war]. Defense Department officials were less ambivalent in their support, claiming that the Sudan was free to use US equipment to 'interdict' the infiltration of guerrillas into the Sudan. . . . Ambassador Jeanne Kirkpatrick cited US support for the Sudan as a foreign policy success." (Johnson, 2003, 67)

"In international eyes, the SPLA was tainted by its association with Mengistu, and it was soon clear than this was influencing the relief policy of the USA." (Johnson, 2003, 95)

"Initially, the Clinton administration had no policy on the Sudan, but its inauguration in January 1993 meant the departure of those figures in the Republican administrations who had defined the region in the context of the Cold War." (Johnson, 2003, 102)

"Preoccupied with the military threats to Sudan's security posed by Libya and Ethiopia and, behind them, the Soviet Union,

Cairo and Washington extended to Khartoum extensive military aid and economic support. Whether they liked it or not, they became identified with Nimeiri and his personal security." (Ali and Matthews, 1999, 209)

iii. The USSR: 1 *low*

"Having alienated both right- and left-wing forces, lacking any strong base of support at home, and cut off from his principal foreign ally, the Soviet Union, Nimeiri found himself isolated and vulnerable." (Ali and Matthews, 1999, 208)

iv. The Arab world: 2 *relatively low*

"The Gulf crisis of 1990–91 cost the Sudan some of its backers in the Arab world, as its support for Iraq alienated Saudi Arabia and other Gulf states. Iraq, a consistent supporter of the Sudanese army, was no longer in a position to supply the Sudan with arms." (Johnson, 2003, 85)

v. Africa: 4 *relatively high*

"Egypt's traditional attitude to Sudan has been proprietorial, and is conditioned by its utter dependence on the Nile for water." (Verney, et al., 1995, 19)

"With the flight of Mengistu from Addis Ababa, the SPLA had to withdraw not only all its troops, but also some 200,000 Southern Sudanese refugees from Ethiopia. The SPLA thus lost its secure bases outside of Sudan and its main source of supplies, while the government of Sudan gained the potential to outflank SPLA positions along the border by moving troops through a now-friendly Ethiopia." (Verney, et al., 1995, 16)

D. Mass Media: July 1 to December 31, 1992

   i. "Alerting" function (volume of television and newspaper coverage): N=13; Rank order=10

   a. Television coverage: Rank order=9
      Total (ABC, CBS, NBC): N=3
      In-depth: N=2

   b. *New York Times* coverage: N=10; Rank order=10

   ii. "Evaluative" function (intervention framing in the *New York Times*)
      Pro-intervention frames: N=0
      Anti-intervention frames: N=1

   iii. Assessment of media coverage

Larry Minear and colleagues noted that . . . "Sudan suffers from perennial lack of attention" . . . [and that media coverage] . . . was inhibited by access problems due to geography and logistics, poor communications, visa complications, and safety concerns." (1996, 49; see also Moeller, 1999) These factors no doubt played some role in the sparse coverage that characterized the Sudanese crisis. Raymond Bonner points to the importance of the "CNN effect" by drawing the connection between the absence of media coverage and the lack of an international response to the crisis in southern Sudan: "There isn't a demand for intervention only because photographs and stories of emaciated elders and children with distended bellies covered with flies haven't gotten out of Sudan." (1992, Dec. 2, A23)

Whatever the cause, in spite of the recognition in the *New York Times* reporting that "a huge disaster" was developing in southern Sudan (Perlez, 1992, Sept. 16, A1), as well as Raymond Bonner's assessment that "the situation . . . [in Sudan] . . . is nearly as horrendous as in Somalia and is likely to get worse," (1992, Dec. 2, A23) there was a very meager journalistic response. As seen in Table 4.1, the *New York Times,* by the volume of its coverage of the crisis, did little to alert the American public to the magnitude of that crisis, and television news did even worse. The combined total of only ten newspaper stories and three television reports placed the crisis in Sudan last in overall media coverage among the ten cases studied.

Table 4.1 *New York Times* Coverage of Sudan

Panel 1 – Date:	N	%	Panel 2 – Dateline:	N	%
First 2 Months	2	20%	United States	1	10%
Second 2 Months	7	70%	Sudan	0	0%
Third 2 Months	1	10%	Africa (other)	8	80%
		100%	Unknown	1	10%
					100%

Panel 3 – Source:	N	%	Panel 4 – Type of Content:	N	%
Local Staff	7	70%	Front-page News	1	10%
AP	3	30%	Inside-page News	7	70%
		100%	Editorials	0	0%
			Op-ed Features	2	20%
					100%

Newspaper Coverage, by Date, Dateline, Source and Type (July 1 to December 31, 1992) N=10

Most of the limited coverage in the *New York Times* originated from Africa (none, however, from Sudan) and was provided by correspondents working for the newspaper. Inside-page news dominated coverage (seven out of ten stories), while there were two op-ed pieces and one front-page story. No editorials, stand-alone photos, or letters to the editor dealing with Sudan appeared during our six-month period of study.

The Second Sudan Civil War was described in the *New York Times* reporting as having a religious component—a conflict pitting the "Government in Khartoum against a rebel army of Christians and Animists in the south." (Perlez, 1992, Aug. 19, A5) It was also noted that the intensity of violence in Sudan had increased in 1990, following the coming to power of an "Islamist Government." (Perlez, 1992, Sept. 16, A1)

The limited coverage of the crisis focused largely on two dimensions. The first was alleged misdeeds on the part of both sides in the conflict—the use of child soldiers on the part of the rebels (the SPLA), and executions (especially that of a Sudanese national working for the United States Agency for International Development) by the Sudanese Government, as well as the killing of aid workers by rebel factions. The second dimension covered was the problem (similar to that occurring at the very same time in Somalia)—of getting relief supplies, mainly food, to dislocated populations. This task was not made easier by the fact that neither side welcomed outside involvement— the Sudanese government had banned International Committee of the Red Cross (ICRC) flights in February 1992 and halted the trucking in of supplies in May. For their part, SPLA rebels routinely shot at UN relief flights. Interestingly, "Operation Lifeline Sudan" was never specifically mentioned in reporting.

The function of "alerting" the American mass public to an impending crisis in Sudan was at least attempted, as the prospects for a genuine humanitarian catastrophe were clearly outlined in one major story, in addition to the op-ed piece by Raymond Bonner. In covering the Sudan crisis for the *New York Times* from neighboring Kenya, Jane Perlez reported in mid-September in the one front-page story appearing on the crisis, that over the previous six months more than a million new refugees had been added to the two million who had been displaced previously. She warned readers that "a huge disaster, largely hidden from the world, has developed across southern Sudan." (Perlez, 1992, Sept. 16, A1)

In the context of the problems associated with providing for the needs of refugees in an extremely hostile environment, the question of a large-scale international humanitarian intervention in Sudan was addressed in only one of two op-ed pieces, that by Raymond Bonner published in early December. While the article focused primarily on Somalia (where at the time the United States was preparing to send in thirty thousand troops), it also dealt in a more limited way with both Liberia and Sudan. In all these cases, Bonner urged caution:

> The use of combat troops is premised on humanitarian objectives, as against protecting our national security, the traditional justification of deploying forces. *This is noble and a much preferable use of troops than, for example, the invasions of Grenada and Panama.* But if the humanitarian role is one that we will play in the post-cold-war world, *we should contemplate where it leads us.* (1992, Dec. 2, A23, italics added)

Bonner goes on to point out that if the United States were to adopt such a policy, it should recognize that humanitarian intervention had implications that were disquieting, if not alarming:

> Immediately we would have to send troops to Liberia, where the carnage among warring factions is taking a hundred lives a day. . . . [Further] we would have to start getting together supplies for *at least 50,000 troops that are desperately needed in southern Sudan to help provide relief. The situation there is nearly as horrendous as in Somalia and is likely to get worse,* and the Sudanese Government constantly blocks relief efforts. (1992, Dec. 2, A23, italics added)

While Bonner offers no specific advice on how to address the problems of Sudan, neither does he rule out an international intervention. However, the thrust of his argument is that while it may satisfy moral imperatives, the dispatch of a United States military force should be considered only as a last resort.

Needless to say, with a total of only ten stories appearing over a six month period—dead last in our rank ordering of newspaper crisis coverage—and three television news reports, what was happening in Sudan, much less what might or ought to be done about it, does not appear to have been first and foremost in the minds of the American media, the American public, or their foreign policy decision makers. In fact, one is left to wonder whether in the absence of the crisis in Somalia, the humanitarian catastrophe occurring in southern Sudan would have received any press coverage at all. That the *New*

York Times evaluation of an intervention for Sudan, to the limited extent that it appeared, was negative hardly seems relevant.

■ Overall Evaluation of the Crisis Response

A serious problem with the international humanitarian response to the Sudan war is that throughout the 1980s and 1990s the international community effectively remained oblivious to the question of a political settlement to the conflict. The UN and its specialized bodies, such as the World Food Program (WFP) and UNICEF, were engaged in possibly the largest relief effort ever to be primarily concerned with relief delivery, to the exclusion of peace and war issues. Likewise, the governments of the United States, countries of the European Union, and other European donors, all of which were parties to "Operation Lifeline Sudan," did not concern themselves with a peaceful resolution to the conflict, either because of their own political considerations or due to lack of interest. On the other hand, there was considerable regional involvement at various levels in the efforts to reach a peace. Ethiopia, for its own considerations (it provided the headquarters for the SPLA/M), hosted several meetings and rounds of negotiations between the rebel movement and various political groups in Khartoum, including the last parliamentary government in 1989. Other African countries, including Nigeria, which hosted two rounds of talks with the government and SPLA factions, were also involved.

Beginning in1994, the Intergovernmental Authority on Development (IGAD)—comprising Djibouti, Ethiopia, Eritrea, Kenya, Sudan, and Uganda—started a mediation effort for peace in Sudan that continued until the end of the century. The parties mediating peace negotiations were not directly or indirectly involved in providing humanitarian relief. It is noteworthy that the IGAD talks were effectively going nowhere until the Bush administration decided to actively engage itself in the process toward the end of 2001. This involvement encouraged other countries with interests in Sudan, such as the United Kingdom and Norway, to become involved under an umbrella group known as "The Friends of IGAD." It was this process that in 2005 eventually produced the Comprehensive Peace Agreement that ended the Second Civil War.

Unfortunately for the people of Sudan, just as one conflict was being resolved, another was developing momentum—this one in the western region of Darfur. While the element of religious conflict is not present in Darfur, as the population of the region is largely Muslim, the factors of race and economic marginalization that fueled the conflict in the south have again led to a humanitarian crisis of proportions where the term "genocide" has been applied to it. In January 2008, following an agreement by the Sudanese goverment in April 2007 to accept UN peacekeepers, the UN took control of the operation and began deploying an intervention force to augment the African peacekeepers already in Darfur.

■ **Notes**

1. In 1990, following Iraq's invasion of Kuwait, Sudan sided with Iraq, and its relations deteriorated with Egypt, which accused Sudan of harboring Islamic opponents. In 1991, the former Iranian President Hashmi Rafsanjani visited Sudan, a visit that signalled a Sudanese-Iranian alliance.

Throughout the first half of the 1990s, Sudan was regarded as a haven for Islamic groups and terrorism. The Sudanese government was implicated in the 1993 bombing of the World Trade Center in New York, and in 1995 it was accused of involvement in the assassination attempt against President Mubarek of Egypt in Ethiopia.

2. By 1995, the SPLA/M was receiving substantial military and logistic support from Uganda and Eritrea. It also retained a strong political and logistics presence in Kenya, which was hosting thousands of refugees from southern Sudan. Egypt had become the de facto base of northern opposition to the Khartoum government. Eritrea, as well, opened its territories to Sudanese opposition groups of all shades.

3. In 1997, United States Secretary of State Madeleine Albright met NDA leaders in Kampala, Uganda, in a gesture of American support for the Sudanese opposition.

4. Sudan was first occupied by Egypt under its autonomous and ambitious viceroy, Muhamman Ali, who established Turko-Egyptian rule over Sudan from 1821 to 1885, when it was overthrown by the Mahdist revolution. The country was once again subjected to colonial rule by an Anglo-Egyptian army that defeated the Mahdist state (1885–98) and established a condominium regime that lasted from 1898 to 1956.

5. During the period of condominium rule, Sudan was divided into nine provinces: Northern, Kassala, Blue Nile, Kordofan, Darfur, Bahr El-Ghazal, Equatoria, Upper Nile, and Khartoum.

6. Douglas Johnson, a scholar with long and first-hand experience in southern Sudan, has argued convincingly that it is indeed very difficult to trust any of the figures regularly cited regarding the number of dead as a result of the Sudanese Civil War. Commenting on Millard Burr's "Quantifying Genocide in the Southern Sudan 1983–1993" (1993), which came up with the often quoted figure of 1.3 million deaths, Johnson argues as follows:

> The first difficulty in accepting Burr's figure is the unreliability of demographic data coming out of Sudan, whether the national census, from which percentages of population growth are calculated, or documented and undocumented

reports of deaths. The multipliers then applied to extrapolate a total figure from these data present yet another problem. Since the publication of Burr's report, the figure of war-related deaths has grown with each citation, and now figures of 2.5 and even 3 million are commonly cited and accepted. (2003, 143)

7. In 1988, a Sudanese Peace Initiative was signed between the SPLA/M and the second party in the government coalition, the Democratic Unionist Party. The SPI was widely acclaimed by northern public opinion, and pressure mounted on Prime Minister Sadiq al-Mahdi's party until a broad-based government was formed in March 1989 that formally endorsed the SPI and started direct peace talks with the SPLA/M.

5

Rwanda, 1994:
UNAMIR I, UNAMIR II, and
"Operation Turquoise"

Walter C. Soderlund and E. Donald Briggs

Background

Located in the "Great Lakes" region of Africa, Rwanda is a small, land-locked country engaged primarily in subsistence agriculture. It shares borders with four countries: Burundi, Zaire (Democratic Republic of the Congo), Tanzania, and Uganda. Along with Burundi, it is the most densely populated state in sub-Saharan Africa, with a pre-genocide population estimated at 7.6 million. (Weiss, 1999, 139) Rwanda's population is composed of three broad social groups: the numerically dominant Hutu (85 percent); the Tutsi (14 percent), who have historically been socially and politically dominant; and the Twa, who make up the remaining one percent. The country has long displayed the effects of overpopulation in a predominantly agriculture society, namely land scarcity, environmental degradation, and pervasive poverty. In Peter Uvin's view, however, there is no clear link "between ecological resource scarcity and genocide in Rwanda: both are largely man-made, with deep historical, political and cultural roots." (1988, 184; see also Homer-Dixon, 1994; Uvin, 1996)

Roots of the Crisis

Ian Stewart has argued that "the Rwandan civil war had roots in the colonial period, when the Belgians had fuelled an ethnic rivalry that would ultimately erupt into the 1994 genocide." (2002, 121) Alain Destexhe goes further: "Belgium is responsible for having largely created the political antagonism between Hutus and Tutsis and then transforming it into a racial problem which sowed the seeds of the present tragedy." (1995, 71) To understand the basis for these observations, we need to briefly recall Rwanda's colonial history.

Africa in the last quarter of the nineteenth century was the world's "Final Frontier." Although Europeans had had contact with coastal regions for several hundred years (mainly for carrying on the slave trade), around 80 percent of Africa remained under indigenous rulers down to the early 1870s. (Hochschild, 1998, 42) It beckoned alluringly to those who sought adventure and wealth, and perhaps most strongly of all to those who saw it as an opportunity (or even an obligation) to gain millions of souls for their particular version of Christianity. It was thus pressures from those who felt obliged, for one reason or another, to take up the "White Man's Burden," along with fears generated by the occupation of some African territories by countries like Belgium, that inspired the well-known "Scramble for Africa" that saw the continent arbitrarily divided into spheres of influence among the major European powers.

At the Berlin Conference of 1885, Rwanda was allocated to Germany to form part of German East Africa. Following German's defeat in World War I, the League of Nations made Rwanda a Mandated Territory, and awarded its supervision to Belgium. The latter's system of colonial rule was more direct than Germany's had been, and in the long run probably more harmful. (See Melvern, 2000, 7–10.)

Scholars are agreed that the Hutu and Tutsi are culturally homogenous (Lemarchand, 1970; Newbury, 1997), but that at the time of the German conquest the minority Tutsi dominated through a feudal-like monarchical system. The Germans, for the most part, simply allowed established practices to continue, but the Belgians promoted and emphasized the difference in status between Tutsi and Hutu, on the assumption that the former were ethnically superior. Tutsis were taller, lighter-skinned, and finer of facial feature than their Hutu brethren, and the Belgians concluded that they must be the descendants of "aristocratic invaders who had come from Tibet and ancient Egypt." (Prunier, 1997, 47) A census conducted in 1933 accordingly established ethnic identity as the basis for categorizing the Rwandan population, and provided the foundation for "divisions in society becom[ing] more pronounced, with the Hutu discriminated against in all walks of life." (Melvern, 2004, 6)

When Tutsi King Mutara Rudahigua died in 1959, Belgium moved toward granting the colony independence as a republic. That meant that the majority Hutu were in control for the first time, and the transition government began the "social revolution," which promptly sought revenge against Tutsis for past abuses. As a result, 150,000 Tutsis died or fled as refugees to neighboring countries. (Olson, 1995, 219) "The new Hutu leaders . . . [targeted] . . . the entire Tutsi community—peasants, civil servants, teachers—from which the aristocracy had come." (Hatzfeld, 2005, 54) Henceforth the Tutsi population became "thoroughly marginalized, often threatened and harassed and at times killed." (Prunier, 1997, 121) In fact, additional mass killings of Tutsis in 1963, 1966, and 1973 created a "Tutsi diaspora," which ultimately led to the formation of the Rwandan Patriotic Front (RPF) led by Paul Kagame, a force that was to play a decisive role in events leading up to and eventually ending in the 1994 genocide.

In 1973, Major General Juvenal Habyarimana, also a Hutu, seized power and established a dictatorship in which, for the next three decades "Rwanda[n] political life would fall under the influence of a monstrous racist ideology that preached intolerance and hatred." (Melvern, 2004, 7) Habyarimana's rule began to disintegrate in 1990 due to a combination of economic factors (the collapse of coffee and tea prices, and the Structural Adjustments policies imposed by the World Bank) and the invasion of RPF forces from their exile in Uganda. The latter had been battle-hardened in the campaigns of Yoweri Musevini to oust Milton Obote from power in Kampala, and presented a coherent military threat of about two thousand troops. (Prunier, 1998, 125–31) They had significant success against the Rwandan army, but achieved no clear victory, and in 1991 the international community persuaded the two sides to meet in Arusha, Tanzania to hammer out a peace agreement based on the principle of power sharing. The agreement was signed in August 1993, but whatever faith the parties might have had in its basic principle was called into question two months later when the newly elected Hutu President of Burundi was overthrown and killed by the predominantly Tutsi army (see Chapter 7, this volume), and "as many as 300,000 Hutus and Tutsis died . . . and more than half a million fled, many to Rwanda." Moeller, 1999, 286)

■ Events Precipitating the Crisis

The Arusha Peace Agreement called for "a broad role for the United Nations" in supervising its implementation over a twenty-two-month transition period. (Carlson, 1999) The mission was expected to be deployed within a month of the agreement, with a daunting mandate containing several components:

[to supervise] the integration of the armed forces of the two parties . . . to guarantee the overall security of the country and verify the maintenance of law and order, ensure the security of the delivery of humanitarian assistance and to assist in catering to the security of civilians. [In addition] the force was . . . asked to assist in tracking arms caches and in the neutralization of armed gangs throughout the country, undertake mine clearance operations, assist in the recovery of all weapons distributed to or illegally acquired by civilians, and monitor the observance of the cessation of hostilities. (Carlson, 1999)

There had been reports as early as April 1993 that assaults against Tutsis in Rwanda had reached a level that might justify the use of the term *genocide*. Nonetheless, the UN, in response to "the insistence from the US and UK that any mission must be small and economical," (Melvern, 2004, 67) decided that the force of 4,260 requested by the Government/RPF negotiators could not be provided. Instead, a force of 2,548, of whom 1,428 were to be deployed by January 1994, was authorized. The United Nations Mission for Rwanda (UNAMIR) was duly established on October 5, 1993, with Canadian Lieutenant General Romeo Dallaire as force commander. UNAMIR was released from the obligation to recover weapons, but otherwise its mandate, as a classic Chapter VI Peacekeeping Force, corresponded in large part to the agenda outlined above.

General Dallaire later observed that the Arusha Accords "papered over, rather than resolved, the major problems of how to share power between formerly warring parties and how to resettle refugees in Rwanda, some of whom had left the country forty years earlier and now had children and grandchildren with a claim to Rwandan citizenship." (2003, 54) Installed as commander of a minimalist international force, he struggled constantly with impossible conditions under "Rules of Engagement" which were, in his view, rarely appropriate to conditions on the ground. He was particularly disturbed by the humanitarian abuses that continued to occur. In November 1993, he requested permission to use force "in response to crimes against humanity and other abuses." According to the Carlson Report, "Headquarters never responded formally to the Force Commander's request for approval." (1999) Moreover, the Report indicates:

Developments in Rwanda during November and December 1993 gave the new peacekeeping operation cause for concern. The political process faced a stalemate. It was also becoming increasingly clear that the political difficulties were taking place against a backdrop of more violence. According to the United Nations, about sixty people were killed in violent incidents in November and December. UNAMIR's reports from this period provide graphic descriptions of the ruthlessness with which these killings were carried out. Already at this stage, the optimistic atmosphere that had surrounded the signing at Arusha was beginning to be sobered by considerable concern about the armed activity in Rwanda, including the existence of armed militia [the Hutu Interahamwe]. (1999)

On January 10, 1994, General Dallaire received word that a trainer for the Interahamwe had revealed to UNAMIR that lists of Tutsis in various communes were being compiled "so that when the time came, the Tutsis . . . could easily be rounded up and exterminated." (Dallaire, 2003, 142) The informant also revealed a plan to maneuver UNAMIR's Belgian contingent, Dallaire's best troops, into a situation where they could be fired upon, under the apparent assumption that if even a few could be killed, the whole contingent would be withdrawn. Dallaire relayed this information to UN Headquarters along with a plan to seize known weapons caches. Kofi Annan, then Under-Secretary-General for Peacekeeping Operations, ordered the Force Commander to do no such thing, as such action would exceed UNAMIR's mandate. Dallaire was specifically instructed "'to avoid entering into a course of action that might lead to the use of force and unanticipated repercussions.'" (Carlson, 1999) Dallaire was "caught . . . completely off guard":

> The November massacres, the presence of heavily armed militias, a rabid extremist press screaming about Tutsi *Inyenzi* [Cockroaches] and demanding that blood be shed, the political impasse and the resulting tension—all were signs that we were no longer in a classic chapter-six peacekeeping situation. . . . Something had to be done to save us from catastrophe. (2003, 146)

The Carlson Independent Inquiry found it *"incomprehensible . . . that more was not done to follow-up the information provided by the informant."* (1999, italics in original)

> The security situation in Rwanda continued to deteriorate. On February 23, 1994, Dallaire reported that "information regarding weapons distribution, death squad target lists, planning of civil unrest and demonstrations abound," and "time does seem to be running out for political discussions, as any spark on the security side could have catastrophic consequences." (Carlson, 1999)

That spark, not long in coming, was the shooting-down of President Habyarimana's plane as it was landing at Kigali airport on the night of

April 6, killing the president.[1] On April 7, described by Dallaire as "the first day of a hundred-day civil war and genocide that would engulf all of us in unimaginable carnage," (2003, 262) UNAMIR had 2,538 troops in Rwanda, many of whom were poorly trained and inadequately equipped. Moreover, the nations from which many of them came suffered from what Dallaire called a "lack of will" with respect to putting their troops in harm's way in order to deal with the escalating violence.

■ The Intervention, Phase 1 (UNAMIR II)

The situation worsened rapidly both for Rwandans and for UNAMIR. Immediately following news of the President's death, well-organized military and paramilitary gangs began systematic massacres of Tutsis and moderate Hutus, starting in Kigali, but spreading quickly throughout the country. For UNAMIR, the possibility of doing anything beyond observing the mounting body count was lost on the first day of what would eventually be called genocide. On April 7, ten Belgian peacekeepers, sent to protect the Prime Minister, were beaten and killed by government troops. The Prime Minister was also killed. A week later, on April 12, "with some 20,000 Tutsis already massacred," Belgium informed the UN that it was withdrawing its remaining forces from UNAMIR and suggested "that the whole operation be suspended." (Carlson, 1999) Not surprisingly, Dallaire considered the Belgian withdrawal a devastating blow to the mission: "I mark April 12 as the day the world moved from disinterest in Rwanda to the abandonment of Rwandans to their fate." (2003, 291) The former colonial masters, he observed scornfully, "were running from this fight with their tails between their legs."[2] (2003, 310)

It is important to bear in mind that at this point the UN had to respond not only to a confused situation involving both a genocide and a renewed civil war waged by the RPF,[3] but also to the question of the very future of UNAMIR. In examining the latter, the UN considered three options: strengthening the mission, reducing it, or withdrawing it completely. Dallaire supported the first option, but he reported that "[General] Maurice [Baril] . . . simply responded that I should not expect anyone to wade into the mess in Rwanda. The reinforcement option would never see the light of day, and that was it. . . . [The Belgian Foreign Minister] put forth that the whole force needed to be evacuated before we were all massacred." (2003, 322)

On April 21, by Security Council resolution 912, the UN chose option two, "voting unanimously to reduce UNAMIR to about 270" and change the mission's mandate to that of a military observer group. Nigeria claimed that the non-aligned movement favored option one, but "could not support it because of the lack of political will. . . . The United Kingdom responded by stating that option one was not feasible because of the lessons drawn from Somalia that conditions on the ground could evolve rapidly and dangerously." (Carlson, 1999) The decision resulted in the withdrawal of one thousand of UNAMIR's troops to Nairobi at the height of the slaughter. (2003, 333) Then, as the situation in Rwanda had begun to be openly called genocide by the end of April, the Secretary-General recommended a reversal of the decision to reduce the force.

The UN debated the precise terms of the mandate of a renewed force during the early weeks of May. What was eventually agreed upon remained "vague on the genocide and the role the force should play in stopping it," but UNAMIR II was created by Security Council resolution 918 on May 17. It called for the deployment of 5,500 troops within thirty-one days. (Dallaire, 2003, 374) "The two primary tasks of UNAMIR II were described as (a) To attempt to assure the security of as many assemblies as possible of civilians who are under threat, and (b) To provide security, as required, to humanitarian relief operations." (Carlson, 1999) However,

> by 25 July, over two months after resolution 918 was adopted, UNAMIR still had only 550 troops, a tenth of its authorized strength. Thus the lack of political will to react firmly against the genocide when it began was compounded by a lack of commitment by the broader membership of the United Nations to provide the necessary troops in order to permit the United Nations to try to stop the killing. (Carlson, 1999)

General Dallaire noted the final futility of the UN initiative: "UNAMIR 2 did not complete its deployment until December 1994, fully six months after the genocide and the civil war were over and when it was no longer needed." (2003, 433, footnote 2)

▪ The Intervention, Phase 2: "Operation Turquoise"

The role of France in the Rwandan crisis is both unclear and controversial. France had supported Habyarimana's government against the RPF by providing both arms and military training. It, along with other developed countries, had quickly withdrawn its own nationals from Rwanda in the first days of the genocide without offering a modicum of assistance to beleaguered Rwandans, and, most curious of all, it maintained a "para-battalion" of troops in Kigali that provided no assistance to UNAMIR and was "closed-mouthed about its strength and true mission in Rwanda."[4] (2003, 71; see also 47, 62)

On June 19,

> the secretary-general wrote to the president of the Security Council . . . to say that the phase-one deployment was about to go ahead, but that because no nation had provided a fully equipped and trained battalion, UNAMIR would not be operational for at least three more months. In these circumstances—combined with the exponential increase in humanitarian problems and the fact that UNAMIR was taking casualties as it attempted to provide a modicum of support for Rwanda—Butros-Ghali suggested that the Security Council consider a French-commanded multinational operation under a *chapter seven mandate* to assure the security and protection of displaced persons and civilians at risk in Rwanda. (Dallaire, 2003, 432–3, italics added)

The French intervention, which began a scant five days later, took the code name "Operation Turquoise." Dallaire was not alone in failing to understand why the French, if they were genuinely, if belatedly, interested in aiding Rwandans, did not simply bolster his minimal forces. He ultimately concluded that "Operation Turquoise" was little more than "a humanitarian cloak to intervene in Rwanda, thus enabling the RGF to hold on to a sliver of the country and retain a slice of legitimacy in the face of certain defeat." "I could not believe," he added, "the effrontery of the French."[5] (2003, 425)

The presence of the French force not only did not help, but actually complicated Dallaire's work, as "the genocidaires believed the French were coming to save them and that they now had carte blanche to finish their gruesome work." (2003, 426) The Independent Inquiry headed by Prime Minister Carlson found:

> *It was unfortunate that the resources committed by France and other countries to Operation Turquoise could not instead have been put at the disposal of UNAMIR II. . . . [Further] [t]o have two operations present in the same conflict with the authorization of the Security Council but with diverging powers was problematic.* (1999, italics in original)

The French force in Rwanda numbered 2,174 troops on the ground, with another 340 available in air support roles. (Vaccaro, 386)

Over the summer of 1994, the situation in Rwanda was further complicated by the fact that the successful RPF offensive had created another massive flow of refugees, mainly Hutus this time, who, by July, "overwhelmed the real story of the genocide." (Chaon, 2007, 164) By mid-July, some three hundred thousand people had fled into neighboring Zaire. (Dallaire, 2003, 469) Operation Turquoise's primary contribution was to establish a "Humanitarian Protection Zone" for refugees along the border with Zaire. Ironically, though possibly not unintentionally, the protection provided was mainly to Hutus, many of whom had participated in the massacre of their neighbors and were fleeing retribution at the hands of the advancing RPF army.[6] The French intervention ended in August, a month following the RPF victory in the civil war. Thus, in the final analysis, neither UNAMIR II nor Operation Turquoise ended the slaughter of the Tutsis; this came about as a result of the RPF military victory. As the Carlson Report concluded, "About a hundred days after it began, the horrific genocide in Rwanda ended, leaving deep and bitter wounds behind."

Strength of the International Response to the Crisis: Rank order=6
    A. Did the Humanitarian Crisis Result in an International Intervention? Yes
    B. Type of Response: Combination
       • UNAMIR I 1993: led by the UN
        "Operation Turquoise" 1994: led by France, authorized by the UN
       • UNAMIR I 1994: led by the UN
    C. Type of UN Involvement:
       • UNAMIR I: Chapter VI
        "Operation Turquoise": Chapter VII
       • UNAMIR II: Chapter VI
    D. Size of Intervening Force: 3,610
       • UNAMIR I: 2,538 deployed in January 1994, reduced to 220 on April 21
        "Operation Turquoise": 3,060
        "At its height on 13 July, the multinational coalition comprised 2,552 French troops and 508 African troops from 7 states [totaling 3,060]." (Vaccaro, 1996, 385)
       • UNAMIR II: on May 17, 5,500 troops were authorized within thirty-one days; however, as of July 25, only 550 troops had actually been deployed

Determinants of the International Response
A. Severity of the Crisis: Rank order=1
i. Number of deaths (short-term): 500,000 to 1,000,000; (long-term): 1 million-plus

"The death toll, which was estimated at 200,000 by the end of April, reached 500,000 by the end of May and 800,00 by the last day of June." (Dallaire, 2003, 375)

"In the course of a few terrible months in 1994, 1 million people were killed in Rwanda." (Melvern, 2000, 4)

"Approximately 800,000 people were killed in the 1994 genocide in Rwanda." (Carlson, et al., 1999)

"The final death toll from the genocide would be measured at almost one million." (Jones, 1999, 77)

"Statistics comparing Rwandan population figures before and after the genocide indicate that 1.1 million Rwandans appear to have died or gone missing between April 1994 and Spring 1995." (Kuperman, 2001, 21)

ii. Number of refugees and displaced persons: (short-term) 2 million to 4.7 million

"Population at Risk" (1995) 4 million. (Weiss and Collins, 1996, 5–7, Table I.1)

"[In late May 1994 the RPF] . . . advance was also . . . creating a new humanitarian catastrophe of displaced persons and refugees. Hutus, scared to death by hate radio accounts of RPF atrocities, were moving ahead of the withdrawing RGF—vast numbers of them, at least two million." (Dallaire, 2003, 388)

"By July 1994, the Hutu government . . . was clearly at risk of collapsing to advancing [Tutsi] rebels. Fearing reprisals at home, more than a million Hutus fled across the borders to Zaïre, Uganda, Tanzania, and elsewhere." (Stewart, 2002, 121)

"On 14–15 July [1994], 1.2 million refugees poured across the border into the Goma region of Zaire in just under 24 hours." (Jones, 2001, 138)

". . . 4.7 million people were forced to flee." (Vaccaro, 1996, 367)

"At the end of the war, rough figures suggest 2.2 million refugees in Tanzania, Burundi, and Zaire, with an additional 1.7 million internally displaced persons throughout southern and southwestern Rwanda." (Jones, 2001,137)

iii. Likelihood of conflict spreading to other states: 5 *high*
a. Number of shared borders: 4

Burundi, Zaire (the Democratic Republic of the Congo), Tanzania, and Uganda

b. Involvement of bordering states

(Tutsi/Hutu ethnic conflicts in Burundi, Zaire, and Uganda)

"Rwanda, along with Burundi, whose fate is intimately linked to that of Rwanda, forms a barrier between Zaire, Uganda, Kenya, and Tanzania. . . . Historically, conflict in one state has generated interference from others. . . . [Yoweri] Museveni's eventual victory over Obote [in Uganda's civil war] was greatly aided by Rwandan refugees in Uganda, who later became members of the RPF." (Jones, 1999, 56)

"I warned that if the millions of Rwandans on the move to the west pushed into Zaire and Burundi, the world would end up with a cataclysmic regional problem, not a Rwandan problem." (Dallaire, 2003, 399)

B. Pre-intervention "Assessment of Risk": *5 high*

". . . no member of the UN with an army strong enough to make a difference is willing to risk the lives of its troops for a failed African nation-state with a centuries-old history of tribal warfare and a deep distrust of outside intervention." (Sciolino, 1994, Apr. 15, A3)

"We will recommend to our government not to intervene as the risks are high and all that is here are humans." (Comment of a UN Assessment Team, during the first weeks of the genocide, as cited in Dallaire, 2003, 6)

"Focused on building institutions of peaceful transition, the UN and the moderate forces in Rwanda underestimated the potency and deadly seriousness of both the propaganda and the planning [leading to the genocide]." (Jones, 1999, 75)

"But even though Kigali was crawling with elite foreign forces, no nation was interested in reinforcing us except the Belgians and a few non-aligned Third world states. By [April 11] there were five hundred French para-commandos working out of the airport, and a thousand Belgian paras staging in Nairobi. To that I could add 250 U.S. marines in Bujumbura. A force of that size, well-trained and well-equipped, could possibly bring an end to the killings. But such an option wasn't even being considered." (Dallaire, 2003, 284)

"As to the value of 800,000 lives in the balance books of Washington . . . we received a shocking call from an American staffer. . . . He wanted to know how many Rwandans had died, how many were refugees, and how many were internally displaced. He told me that his estimates indicated that it would take the deaths of 85,000 Rwandans to justify risking the life of one American soldier." (Dallaire, 2003, 499)

"I also do not contend that the physical impediments to timely intervention—the speed of the killing, the lack of accurate information, the difficulty of airlifting sufficient forces to Africa—are the sole reasons the international community failed to intervene effectively during Rwanda's 1994 genocide. Lack of political will also contributed." (Kuperman, 2001, viii)

C. Extent of "National Interest Involvement"
i. The international community: 2 *relatively low*

"Rwanda had little intrinsic strategic value to outsiders, and few countries identified their national interests with the country or its people." (Vaccaro, 1996, 374)

"The international community stood by while a half million Rwandans were butchered in political and intertribal violence. With Rwanda, the major powers junked the doctrine of humanitarian intervention. And because they did not define the conflict in Rwanda as a threat to their respective national security interests, they failed—with the too-late exception of France—to intervene on conventional grounds." (Muldoon, 1995, 61)

"The international community did nothing to stop the Rwandan genocide." (Holzgrefe, 2003, 17)

"[The Rwandan hard-liners] had already concluded that the West did not have the will, as it had demonstrated in Bosnia, Croatia and Somalia, to police the world, to expend the resources or to take the necessary casualties. They had calculated the West would deploy a token force and when threatened would duck or run. They knew us better than we knew ourselves." (Dallaire, 2003, 79)

"On April 29 . . . Boutros Boutros-Ghali urged the deployment of additional, all African UN peacekeeping forces to Rwanda, and submitted a plan . . . that called for sending 5,500 soldiers to Kigali under an expanded UNAMIR mandate. . . . However, the United States . . . pointed out that . . . no state had made a firm offer to send their forces to Rwanda and that the Rwandan factions had not given unconditional consent to the UN operation." (Murphy, 1996, 245)

"In Rwanda's relationship with the international community before 1990, its almost total economic dependence contrasted with its minimal relevance in strategic and political terms." (Jones, 1999, 55)

ii. United States, Britain, and Canada: 2 *relatively low*

"Unfortunately, Rwanda had never been of more than marginal concern to Washington's most influential planners." (Power, 2003, 330)

"The great humanitarians in the U.S. administration wanted no part of anything inside Rwanda that could lead to American casualties." (Dallaire, 2003, 490)

"With reference to the Rwandan civil war, as one American diplomat said, 'We didn't have a dog in that fight.'" (Jones, 1999, 64)

"The United States can be accused of not taking up its moral responsibility as the major world power, blocking the initiative of UN Secretary-General Boutros Boutros-Ghali and preventing US officials from using the word genocide to sidestep the international obligation to intervene that recognition of the crime would have imposed." (Destexhe, 1995, 71)

". . . guidelines issued by the . . . Clinton Administration during the crisis . . . [PDD-25] . . . called for the deployment of U.S. forces for UN peacekeeping only when U.S. national interests were at stake, and Rwanda did not present such a situation." (Murphy, 1996, 258)

"The Americans were unwilling to engage in what appeared to be yet another bloody, internecine tribal war, and without American backing other members of the Security Council were reluctant to act." (Jones, 1999, 77)

"In Britain, public concern over the violence is increasing, but as in most of the rest of Europe, there is no strong move to send troops to join the UN peacekeeping force." (Kinzer, 1994, May 25, A1)

"As permanent members of the UN Security Council, the UK and the US could have taken action in accordance with the 1948 Convention on the Prevention and the Punishment of the Crime of Genocide, a legally binding treaty. . . . In 1994 the US and the UK undermined international law over Rwanda. While these states resisted even using the word genocide, this would appear to indicate that they were aware that it carried some form of obligation to act." (Melvern, 2004, 272)

"[In the summer of 1993] Canada's defence department was unconvinced that the Great Lakes region of central Africa was a priority." (Dallaire, 2003, 53)

iii. Belgium: 3 *medium*

"The trouble was, as I was bluntly told on a few occasions, no one but the French and possibly the Belgians had any interest in that part of the world." (Dallaire, 2003, 50–51)

"Belgium supported the Hutu government until 1990 when apparently wary of the government's corruption and human rights abuses, Brussels threw its political support to the newly resurgent RPF. Subsequently, the RPF set up its European headquarters there. . . . The extent of Belgian material support to the RPF is unclear." (Vaccaro, 1996, 374–75)

"Prior to the death of 10 Belgian peacekeepers on 7 April 1994, and the subsequent Belgian decision to withdraw its peacekeepers, Belgium had engaged in a flurry of activities in an effort to warn the international community about the possibility of the resumption of the conflict as well as the prospect of a massacre of a large number of civilians. Belgium had also tried to get the Security Council to strengthen the peacekeeping force. Belgian's warnings and the proposal for an enhanced peacekeeping force largely fell on deaf ears." (Adelman, n.d., 5)

"[Following the death of its peacekeepers,] . . . just as Belgium had once lobbied strenuously for an enhanced UNAMIR presence, it now advocated that the entire UNAMIR force be withdrawn and lobbied strenuously to that end. Further, contrary to the promise . . . made to General Dallaire, Belgium also ordered its troops to bring all their equipment and weapons with them upon withdrawal." (Adelman, n.d., 5)

iv. France: 4 *relatively high*

"Following the initial invasion by the RPF, both Zaire and France sent troops to help bolster Habyarimana's government, though because Mobutu's troops seemed more interested in looting new territory than protecting it, they were quickly asked to leave. French troops, ostensibly in Rwanda to train the Rwandan Armed forces and to protect French nationals and other foreigners, have been accused of playing a far more active role in the war with the RPF. Following the 1993 RPF offensive, the size of the French contingent grew to 680 troops, which were deployed north of Kigali, where there were no

French nationals. Moreover, French troops were reported to have played a direct role in the fighting, and French trainers advised Rwandan officers in tactical combat situations." (Reed, 1998, 137)

"The willingness of France to take the lead in such an intervention . . . ["Operation Turquoise"] . . . was met by other states with some misgivings; France had played a major role in arming and training the Hutu-dominated Rwandan government forces, which were responsible for many of the killings in Rwanda." (Murphy, 1996, 247–48)

"Traditionally, French policy in Africa was driven by two dominant goals—the preservation and enhancement of France's historical position in Africa largely through the promotion of *francophonie,* and, secondly, the promotion of French economic supremacy in francophone Africa." (Adelman, n.d., 6)

"France closed its eyes to the growing racism at the heart of the system and the increasing number of massacres over the past four years and continued to support the former [Habyarimana] regime to the bitter end." (Destexhe, 1995, 71)

"The French had a relationship with the Habyarimana regime that stretched back to the mid-seventies. The French government had made a significant investment in French-speaking Rwanda, supplying it with arms and military expertise, support that had escalated to outright intervention against the RPF insurgent force in October 1990 and again in February 1993." (Dallaire, 2003, 62)

"The [Tutsi] rebels assert that the French are afraid that the victory of English-speaking Tutsis schooled in Uganda would erode a francophone sphere of influence." (Jean Pierre Cot, cited in Rouvez, 1994, 76)

"From the end of the Arusha process, France was not the active supporter of Rwanda, but its passive supporter. . . . Though clearly supporting the peace process and the effort to install a multi-party regime, France was still obsessed with its own perception. The 'Anglophone' invaders were the principal beneficiaries of the agreement and France remained very sensitive to the Uncivil War being waged by the extremists against the Tutsi population. When France recovered some degree of concern, it was more to protect its own sense of honour than to protect the Tutsi or ensure that the perpetrators of the genocide were totally stopped and caught to be tried for their crimes." (Adelman, n.d., 12)

"France alone took a more assertive approach, deploying military forces in southwest Rwanda in late June. Rather than reflecting pressure from French or European media, however, Opération Turquoise was more the product of French political interests in Francophone Africa." (Minear, et al., 1996, 65)

"Paris newspapers have criticized the UN for not acting sooner, but there have been few calls for direct French intervention." (Kinzer, 1994, May 25, A1)

v. Africa: 5 *high*

"At the continental level, the context for the civil war was provided by the change in the political realities in Africa in the post-Cold War era, marked by a decline in Western intervention and superpower competition. Among the results was growing emphasis on finding 'African solutions to African problems.'" (Jones, 1999, 56)

"The states with most at stake in Rwanda were its immediate neighbors: Burundi, Tanzania, Uganda, and Zaire. Stability and economic development in Rwanda would clearly serve their interests, but they had little capability themselves to influence either variable constructively." (Vaccaro, 1996, 374)

"Another important link in the arms trading business was the Rwanda embassy in Cairo, where a first deal had been concluded only weeks after the October 1990 [RPF] invasion with the help of Egypt's deputy foreign minister, Dr Boutros Boutros-Ghali . . . .The initial deal with Egypt was for a total of $US5.8 million and included 60,000 grenades, . . . some two million rounds of ammunition, mortar bombs, 4,200 assault rifles, rockets and rocket launchers. . . . A series of other deals followed, with thousands of landmines, grenades and Kalashnikov assault rifles sent from Cairo to Kigali over the years 1990 to 1993." (Melvern, 2004, 58)

"At the least, Western diplomats and African specialists say, there is a special relationship between the Ugandan leader (Yoweri Musevini) and the RPF." (Schmidt, 1994, Apr. 18, A6)

". . . the self-interest [of Tanzania] had largely to do with its knowledge that conflicts in either Rwanda or Burundi would result—as it had previously—in large refugee flows into Tanzania, with which it was ill-equipped to deal." (Jones, 1999, 67)

"The sense of urgency that pervaded the sub-region and continental levels [in February 1994] was lost at the international level where Rwanda was of marginal importance." (Jones, 1999, 75)

"According to Zairian newspapers, Zaire provides arms to the Hutu-dominated Rwandan army-in-exile that is preparing for a reinvasion of Rwanda." (Smith, 1966)

D. Mass Media: December 25, 1993 to June 24, 1994
    i. "Alerting" function (volume of television and newspaper coverage): N= 242; Rank order=3
    a. Television coverage: Rank order=3
        Total: (ABC, CBS, NBC) N=103
        In-depth: N=48
    b. *New York Times* coverage: N=139; Rank order=5
    ii. "Evaluative" function (intervention framing in tbe *New York Times*)
    Pro-intervention frames: N=12
    Anti-intervention frames: N=15
    iii. Assessment of media coverage

The role of the mass media in alerting the American public to the Rwandan crisis has engaged the interest of scholars as did the case of Somalia. Such an alert was certainly necessary as this personal episode recounted by Rene Lemarchand points out:

> For all intents and purposes the American public discovered Rwanda in April 1994 when television brought into our living rooms scenes of bloodshed right out of the Apocalypse. Until then reports of ethnic violence went largely unnoticed. . . . Days after the invasion of Rwanda by the Rwanda Patriotic Front (RPF) in October of 1990, Rwanda's ambassador invited me to accompany him to the Washington bureau of *Time* magazine to explain the very dangerous situation then developing. The bureau chief received us with some embarrassment. He did not know exactly where Rwanda was. After glancing at the map, he expressed doubt that the story would interest his readers. *Time*, like most of the print media, gave hardly any coverage to what some would not hesitate to identify as the root cause of the 1994 genocide. (1998a, 41)

Our study of media coverage of the Rwanda crisis begins December 25, 1993, six months prior to France's Operation Turquoise. Bruce Jones describes the media environment during that period as follows:

> In November 1993, an article about the civil war in Rwanda referred to it
> as the "Forgotten War." Five months later, the world's media flooded to
> the nation to cover the savage killings of 1994, in which up to one million
> Rwandans were butchered in three months. As a result of this uneven cov-
> erage, perception of conflict in Rwanda is dominated by images of geno-
> cide. The civil war that preceded it dating from October 1990 remains lit-
> tle known and less explained. (1999, 53; see also Livingston, 2007)

And media coverage was what General Dallaire wanted. From very
early on in the tragedy, he was convinced that the media were the
most effective instrument available to shame the world into action to
stop unbelievable butchery.[7] A passage from *Shake Hands with the
Devil* illustrates this:

> With the Belgian departure, it appeared that Mark Doyle of the BBC
> might also leave. I called him into my office and made him an offer he
> could not refuse. He could live with us, be protected by us, be fed and
> sustained by us, and I would guarantee him a story a day and the means
> (my satellite phone) to get that story to the world. I did not care if his
> story was positive or negative about UNAMIR as long as it was accurate
> and truthful. The key was for him to become the voice of what was hap-
> pening in Rwanda. (2003, 332)

It would probably be excessive to claim that Dallaire's efforts were by
themselves responsible for the heavy newspaper coverage of the genocide, but they probably were of significant help in that regard. Overall, Rwanda was second only to Haiti in volume of newspaper coverage and third when television coverage is added.

As Table 5.1 indicates, there were only three stories about Rwanda
in the *New York Times* prior to the start of the genocide. That meant
that the American public had little opportunity to realize the gravity
of the situation before it was already a frenzy of blood-letting.[8] Just
over fifty percent of stories originated in Africa (twenty-three percent
from Rwanda), while about a third came from the United States, either
from the UN or from Washington. Nearly sixty percent of stories were
written by *New York Times* correspondents, chief among them Donatella Lorch and William Schmidt in Africa and Paul Lewis at the
UN, while another quarter originated with the Associated Press and
Reuters. Inside-page news dominated coverage (69 percent), while
"high impact" content (front-page stories, editorials, and op-ed articles) stood at a respectable 22 percent. There were also a number of
stand-alone photos and two letters to the editor.

Table 5.1 *New York Times* **Coverage of Rwanda**

Panel 1 – Date:	N	%	Panel 2 – Dateline:	N	%
First 2 Months	2	1%	United States	45	32%
Second 2 Months	43	31%	Rwanda	32	23%
Third 2 Months	94	68%	Africa (other)	42	30%
		100%	Other	9	6%
Pre-April 7	3	2%	Unknown	11	8%
April 7 and after	136	98%			99%
		100%			

Panel 3 – Source:	N	%	Panel 4 – Type of Content:	N	%
Local Staff	80	58%	Front-page News	21	15%
AP	20	14%	Inside-page News	94	68%
AFP	0	0%	Editorials	6	4%
Reuters	16	12%	Op-ed features	4	3%
Other	14	10%	Photos	7	5%
Unknown	9	6%	Letters	3	2%
		100%	Other	4	3%
					100%

Newspaper Coverage, by Date, Dateline, Source and Type (December 25, 1993 to June 24, 1994) N=139

Pre-genocide coverage dealt with the ongoing violence and the possibility of doubling the UN force. On the day following the president's death, a front-page article by William Schmidt reported that "the Rwandan capital . . . dissolved into terror and chaos . . . as disparate army and police forces went on a rampage, reportedly killing the country's interim Prime Minister and at least ten Belgian peacekeeping soldiers." It was also noted that under its rules of engagement the UN peacekeeping contingent was restricted from using force to rescue the besieged Prime Minister. (1994, April 8, A1) Subsequent coverage continued to focus on the rapidly mounting death toll, efforts to negotiate a ceasefire between the Government and RPF, and efforts by western countries to evacuate their nationals—a process that began with the French seizure of the airport in Kigali two days after the president's assassination. There were also some "backgrounders" that sought to explain the origin, history, and intensity of Hutu-Tutsi animosity. (See, for example, Wharton, 1994, April 9.)

The first *New York Times* editorial on the crisis appeared on April 10. In apparent reflection of the general state of confusion that existed at the time, it assigned "presumptive blame for the orgy of slaughter . . . to Tutsi warriors seeking to reimpose their past dominance."

Hutus were blamed as well for "radio broadcasts . . . just as bloody as those of the Tutsi." While the editorial did not argue that an international intervention might be in order, it did suggest that "neighboring states, the OAU and the UN all have a primary responsibility to provide emergency relief and keep the doors open for peacekeeping." (1994, April 10, IV18) An April 14 op-ed piece by Frank Smyth of Human Rights Watch blamed the French for the crisis, claiming that "the horror in Rwanda should serve as a grisly lesson in the dangers of imperial reach" and accusing France of having supported and armed the Habyarimana government, as well as condoning its anti-Tutsi policies (1994, April 14, A12)

In the early days of the genocide, with twenty thousand or more Rwandans reported killed and the UN considering evacuating its entire force from the country, there seemed to be little motivation for international action. As Elaine Sciolino wrote from Washington, "The disintegration of Rwanda into chaos and anarchy has evoked expressions of horror and sympathy from the international community—and a firm pledge to stay away." She went on to argue that "even with the political will, the financial resources and the military might, the US and its allies have decided it would be difficult to maintain . . . [peace] . . . without transforming the country into a UN trusteeship or a colonial-style administration." Such a hands-off approach, she concluded, would have "no political costs at home." (1994, April 15, A3) Donatella Lorch added on April 21 that "the Security Council, preoccupied with Bosnia, has taken no decision on Rwanda since the killings began two weeks ago." (1994, A3)

As April progressed and the killing continued, questions about the plight of refugees and the impact of the crisis on neighboring countries joined the mix of issues noted in reports filed from Rwanda and surrounding countries. (Schmidt, 1994, April 18) Spokesmen for international aid agencies also began to be heard.[9] Jean-Luc Thevoz of the International Committee of the Red Cross called the situation across the country "catastrophic," (cited in AP, 1994, April 19, A3) and on April 20, in a letter to the editor, Jeri Laber, Executive Director of Human Rights Watch, advanced the idea of an international intervention: "The UN and the international community should find the means to protect the innocent and bring the carnage to an end." (1994, April 20, A18) When it was announced that the UN would actually reduce, rather than enhance, its presence in Rwanda, despite protests from human rights groups that the move would only increase the carnage, Paul Lewis observed simply that "diplomats said there was no willingness to send another big peacekeeping force, like the one that had been sent to Somalia." (1994, April 22, A1)

In its second editorial on the crisis, the *New York Times* agreed with the UN's decision to downsize its Rwandan mission, pointing out that "Somalia provides ample warning against plunging open-endedly into a 'humanitarian' mission." Acknowledging that "the world has few ways of responding effectively when violence within a nation leads to massacres and . . . breakdown of civil order," the editorial went on to call for "considering whether a mobile, quick response force under UN aegis is needed to deal with such calamities" and concluded that in the absence of such a force, *"the world has little choice but to stand aside and hope for the best."* (1994, April 23, A24, italics added)

Boutros Boutros-Ghali became convinced late in April that "the scale of human suffering in Rwanda and its implications for the stability of neighboring countries leaves the Security Council with no alternative but to examine [the] possibility [of taking] forceful action to restore law and order and end the massacres." (cited in Lewis, 1994, May 1, A1) In response, the Clinton administration was reported to be "examining the idea of helping to organize and pay for military intervention in Rwanda by neighboring African countries." (Lewis, May 1, A1) On May 3, Boutros-Ghali asked African heads of state to commit troops to an "all-African" peacekeeping force. The RPF, however, indicated its opposition to any UN intervention, a position it continued to hold throughout the summer. (Lewis, 1994, May 3, A3) A May 3 editorial held out little hope for UN success in quelling the violence, noting that "the bitter truth is that the Security Council has no arrows in its quiver and that in these matters the 'international community' is a nebulous phantom. Ending the massacres is beyond the capacity of lightly armed peacekeepers." (1994, May 3, A23)

Human rights groups continued to press for an intervention. In a May 11 op-ed piece appearing roughly five weeks into the slaughter, "genocide" was referred to as "a fact in Rwanda." The author, Alison Des Forges of Human Rights Watch, called upon President Clinton to appeal to French President Mitterrand "to demand that the killing stop." She also supported a UN force "to save civilians from military attack, starvation and disease." She asked the pointed question: "Can we do anything less?" (1994, May 11, A25)

In spite of the endorsement of an African peacekeeping force by Nelson Mandela (AP, 1994, May 11), the United States continued to move very slowly. Madeleine Albright indicated that the idea of the

UN sending five thousand troops to Rwanda was "more than the organization can handle," and as an alternative she broached the idea of establishing a "protection zone" along the Rwandan border for fleeing refugees. (Lewis, 1994, May 12, A9) The United States did not, however, block approval of a plan to deploy the five thousand Africans, who were to "enter Rwanda by land . . . and establish protected zones along its borders, which would draw displaced persons from the interior. The force would then slowly work its way deeper into the country." It was noted, however, that "not a single African country has come forward with a firm offer [of troops.]" (Lewis, 1994, May 14, A1)

The Clinton administration remained concerned about a possible "overreach" in Rwanda. An unnamed administrative official commented that "we all recognize that we really should get involved here—that the humanitarian stakes are high. . . . But the question is how do we do it in a smart way? How can we best use 5,000 troops? We want some very clear answers." (cited in Jehl, 1994, May 18, A1) An editorial appearing on May 18 endorsed President Clinton's cautious approach. "The Clinton Administration has rightly resisted a clamor for instantly expanding a minuscule UN peacekeeping force to halt the human carnage in Rwanda. . . . It is simple prudence for the UN not to leap into an empty swimming pool. However agonizing the slaughter, there is now no effective international force for ending it." (NYT, 1994, May 18, A22; see also Lewis, 1994, May 17)

The Vatican lent its voice to those criticizing international inaction, comparing "the killing of thousands of children in Rwanda to the biblical 'slaughter of the innocents' by King Herod." (Reuters, 1994, May 24, A3)[10] European governments took positions similar to that of the United States, deploring the slaughter but "not willing to take the risks inherent in trying to stop it." (Kinzer, 1994, May 25, A1) Finally, on May 26, Boutros-Ghali "called out" the international community: he openly referred to what was going on in Rwanda as "'genocide' and said it was a 'scandal' that the world had not acted speedily to end the blood-letting." (Lewis, 1994, May 26, A1)

President Clinton responded by listing "Rwanda among the world's many bloody conflicts where the interests at stake did not justify the use of America's military power." (Lewis, 1994, May 26, A1) He promised, however, "to help in recruiting more peacekeepers for Rwanda," and pledged fifty armored personnel carriers to the mission, while indicating as well that the United States was prepared "to airlift troops if necessary." (Reuters, 1994, May 28, A5) But, significantly, he

also issued instructions that government spokespersons should "not
. . . describe the deaths . . . as genocide, even though some senior officials believe that is exactly what they represent." (Jehl, 1994, June 10,
A8) This stemmed from the obligation under the 1948 Convention on
Genocide to "do something" when genocide occurs. This "no speak"
dictum finally provoked some criticism of American policy from the
New York Times. It its editorial of June 15 it observed:

> One can stipulate that the US has no vital interests or historical ties in
> Rwanda that might justify sending troops to this tormented Central
> African country. That said, the Clinton Administration chose an awful
> time to delay logistical aid to the UN peacekeepers, and a worse time to
> apply a semantic sponge to crimes against humanity. (1994, A24)

Interestingly, the administration reversed itself on the very next day,
deciding that genocide was occurring in Rwanda after all, and promising that the personnel carriers could be delivered in less than a
month's time, and agreeing, moreover, that the cost of their "rental"
would be $10 million rather than the $15 million originally requested.
(Gordon, 1994, June 16, A12)

It was also on June 16 that France announced its plans for Operation Turquoise, describing it as "a ground intervention to protect
groups threatened with extinction." (Foreign Minister Alain Juppe,
cited in Reuters, 1994, June 16, A12) The *New York Times* did not
comment editorially on the French operation prior to its launch, but
in a June 20 story from Paris, Marlise Simons reported that the foreign minister had indicated that "the intervention would be strictly
humanitarian and the reaction of African countries had been 'unanimously favourable.'" (1994, June 20, A7) A special report from Kenya
questioned at least the last of this, however: "The French military intervention has attracted only limited international support, and a
highly sceptical response from diplomats and relief workers." (*NYT,*
1994, June 24a, A8) An editorial the same day labelled the French
plan "risky" and noted that a "swift transition from the mostly French
to an all-African operation in Rwanda seems the safest and wisest
course." (1994, June 24b, A26)

The general explanation for the failure of the international community to take any decisive action in Rwanda, and for the equal failure of the media to mount any sustained pressure for it to do so, was
that everyone was overtaken by the ferocity and pace of the killings.
Douglas Anglin offers perhaps the most persuasive argument:

The speed of developments in Rwanda meant that, initially, public opinion was not as crucial a factor as in Somalia, Ethiopia, and earlier humanitarian crises, especially as the television cameras were tied up in
Bosnia, South Africa (for the 27 April elections), Haiti and elsewhere. . . .
Even when the full horror of the genocide was projected in the media and
public attitudes began to change, the policy of most Security Council
members appeared to be to do as little as they could get away with, and
still retain a modicum of international respectability. (2002, 30)

Larry Minear and colleagues add to this that "the conflict had elements involving both civil war and ethnic strife . . . [and that] . . . had
the media been clear from the outset in identifying its genocidal core,
coverage might have reduced the convenient excuse that governments
enjoyed [for not acting]." (1996, 64)

Given the unique circumstances in Rwanda, however, it may be
questioned whether even a rapid and forceful international intervention
would have avoided the genocide. Alan Kuperman is of that opinion:

A realistic US military intervention launched as soon as President Clinton
could have determined that genocide was being attempted in Rwanda
could not have averted the genocide. It could, however, have saved an estimated 75,000 to 125,000 Tutsi from death, from 15 to 25 percent of
those who ultimately lost their lives, in addition to tens of thousands of
Hutu. (2001, 109)

That surely would have been worth doing. But despite the urging of
the Secretary-General, the Vatican, and various human right groups,
the world felt, in the phrase quoted earlier, that there was "little
choice but to stand aside and hope for the best."

■ Overall Evaluation of the Crisis Response

As the Carlson Report emphasizes, the international community should
have done better. In trying to understand why it did not, some analyses
of the worst case of deliberate inhumanity to man in living memory have
fallen back on searching for the generic roots of genocide. Claudine
Kayitesi, for example, finds botanical allusions helpful: "A genocide is
a poisonous bush, that grows not from two or three roots but from a
tangle of roots that has moldered underground where no one notices it."
(cited in Hatzfeld, 2005, 90) Gerard Prunier explains the particular tangle pertinent to Rwanda: "In Rwanda all the preconditions for genocide
were present: a well organized civil service, a small tightly controlled land

area, a disciplined and orderly population, reasonably good communications, and a coherent ideology containing the necessary lethal potential." (1995, 238) Such analyses may be close to the truth, and are certainly not without academic interest, but they help little when it comes to the "Responsibility to Protect" a population in the process of being exterminated.

If Somalia was "not the most glorious chapter in UN history," Rwanda must be judged to have been its worst. Yet, to say that it failed egregiously and to stop there is to imply that it had a chance of success. It is arguable that that might have been the case had it not been for Somalia. But that seems far from certain. A less disillusioned and embittered United States might have been willing and able to goad fellow members of the UN to action, but given suspicions about peacekeeping and the UN generally that prevailed in Washington even prior to Somalia, it is by no means sure that there would have been any such willingness, or that others would have responded positively had there been. Then again, the sad truth is that even with a favorable political climate in New York, the slow-moving UN machinery probably could have managed little more than a face-saving operation by the time the Rwandan tragedy had already played to its bloody end. The fact is that the UN, as presently constituted, will never be able to respond satisfactorily to blitzkrieg-like events such as occurred in Rwanda in 1994.

As a final footnote to the genocide, it should be noted that the RPF victory that brought it to an end was responsible in turn for further conditions of instability and hardship in the region. The return of Tutsi control in Kigali (albeit with a coalition government) caused the flight of some two million, mainly Hutu, refugees to Burundi and Zaire. (Lautze, et al., 1998, 25) Not a few of these were participants in the killing frenzy of the previous months, and it was of course often impossible to distinguish these from "true" refugees. (See Rosenblatt, *NYT*, 1994, June 5, VI38.) In providing humanitarian assistance to these refugees, therefore, the world was in the ironic position of aiding the perpetrators of the genocide.

■ Notes

1. The circumstances surrounding the shooting-down of President Habyarimana's plane are still a matter of controversy. "The generally accepted explanation had been that extremists among Rwanda's Hutu majority had killed Mr. Habyarimana . . . because he was about to share power with the Tutsi in a bid to end the

civil war." However, a French investigation into the incident has "suggested that Mr. Kagame, then head of the mainly-Tutsi . . . rebel army, ordered the assassination. Mr. Kagame's office has dismissed the allegation." (Edwards, 2004, March 11, A13) In November 2006, based on the fact that the plane had a French crew, a French judge issued "arrest warrants for nine aides of Paul Kagame, Rwanda's President . . . for the destruction of the aircraft, leading Rwanda to recall its ambassador to France." It was pointed out that the UN had rejected a full-scale inquiry into the shooting-down of the aircraft in 1997. Steven Edwards's article ended with the observation "only an independent international investigation has any chance of solving the mystery. Why the resistance?" (2006, November 27, A12)

2. General Dallaire's rebuke of Belgium was deep-seated, as the following account attests: "[In WWII] [a]s Canadian soldiers fought tooth and nail against the Germans, King Baudouin of Belgium and his ruthless lackeys kept millions of black Africans in Rwanda and all of the Great Lakes region of Central Africa under subjugation, raping these countries of their natural resources. And here I was, in the heart of one of King Baudouin's former colonies, watching Belgian troops abandon us in the midst of one of the worst slaughters of the century because they have lost some of their professional soldiers to soldierly duties." (2003, 318)

3. The Carlson Report found that efforts carried out by the UN and UNAMIR to re-establish a ceasefire between the warring parties, rather than dealing with the new circumstances of the genocide, had been "a costly error in judgment." (1999) Journalists as well were confused by the chaotic situation that confronted them. As pointed out by Anne Chaon, "Most journalists are not experts in genocide. Many of them . . . arrived in Rwanda with very little knowledge of the country. So it was tempting, especially in the beginning, to speak of the civil war, and to link these massacres to previous massacres since 1959. We failed to understand that the killing was something totally new, that this was not a continuation of what had happened before." (2007, 162)

4. In March 2004, Paul Kagame laid the blame for the 1994 massacre on the French, claiming that "the French government supplied weapons, logistical support and even senior military planners to the regime of militant ethnic Hutus responsible for the slaughter of 800,000 ethnic Tutsis and moderate Hutus." While acknowledging that the charges were not new, the report characterized Kagame's accusation as "the most explicit statement of the allegations" of French complicity in the genocide. (*Windsor Star,* 2004, March 17, B2) Alain Rouvez cites a "semi-permanent French deployment" of five hundred troops in Rwanda at the time of the genocide. (1994, 186; see also Reed, 1998, 137)

5. Sean Murphy disagrees, concluding that "on balance . . . the actions of the French forces ultimately confirmed an overall humanitarian motivation. France was appalled by the atrocities being committed and believed it was in a position to assist in ending the bloodshed. As such, the French intervention fits the concept of humanitarian intervention." (1996, 257)

6. A recent research study by American academics disputes "the commonly held view that most of the million or so victims were Tutsis targeted by the Hutu majority." Rather, it says as many Hutus may have died as Tutsis. By this analysis, as the rule of law broke down, many Rwandans felt free to engage in an orgy of political assassinations and settling of scores that accompanied, and perhaps

exceeded, the genocidal rampages against the Tutsis. Based on census figures and the arithmetic of death, researchers Christian Davenport and Allan Stam argue that "if the frequently used figure of 800,000 is taken as approximating the total number of dead, about 300,000 Hutu and the tiny Twa would have been among the victims." (Edwards, 2004, April 7, A10) Moreover, if one uses the Rwandan government's figure of one million killed, "the number of Hutu and Twa deaths would have equalled or exceeded the number of Tutsi deaths." According to Davenport, "All this complexity and nuance is exactly what we've been trying to address. It directly challenges the very simplistic understanding that one particular group went after another particular group and eliminated them." (cited in Edwards, 2004, April 7, A10) Stam points out that their analysis complicates the options that were open to UNAMIR: *"If there are two bad guys that are both behaving bestially, then there is not one side you can prop up. . . . That means that the UN had to have been prepared to run the country after an intervention, and nobody was prepared to do that."* (cited in Edwards, 2004, April 7, A10, italics added)

7. The index to Dallaire's book gives another indication of the importance of mass media to the UNAMIR force commander. There are twenty distinct entries under "Media Coverage" and "Media Relations" as well as an additional twelve entries under "RTLM" (Radio Television Libres des Mille Collines), the hard-line Hutu radio station, while BBC reporter Mark Doyle is mentioned on four separate occasions.

8. The Vanderbilt Television News Archive Abstracts tell us that prime time news coverage of Rwanda by ABC, CBS, and NBC was concentrated entirely in the genocide period. By April 11, all three networks had reporters in Africa working the story. Reports dealt chiefly with tribal murder, as well as chaos and fighting related to the civil war, with many videos of dead bodies in the street. The term "genocide" first appeared on April 25, about the same time General Dallaire began using it. Other themes covered in reporting were the evacuation of western nationals, the plight of refugees, and possible international intervention—both the UN and French missions. In our opinion, given the difficult circumstances of a rapidly unfolding and complex situation, TV news did a reasonable job in alerting the US population to the enormity of what was occurring. Moreover, in that Susan Moeller reports that public opinion in the United States was opposed to an intervention in Rwanda by a margin of 34 to 51 percent (1999, 290), and that Linda Melvern reports that the "vast majority" of killings took place within the first six weeks of the genocide (2007, 199), it is unlikely that even massive media attention would have led to a stronger international response. As Michael Salwen has demonstrated, agenda-setting by mass media does not occur instantaneously; up to six months of continuous media coverage may be necessary to affect public perceptions regarding the salience of an event. (1998) Thus, in the case of Rwanda, the pace and scale of the killing simply exceeded any reasonable expectation that public opinion might be mobilized in time to influence government policy.

9. Lindsey Hilsum provides an excellent analysis of the media strategies pursued by NGOs in Rwanda, stressing the symbiotic relationship between aid agencies and journalists. (2007)

10. The headline of a front-page story by Donatella Lorch appeared to say it all: "Thousands of Rwandans Wash Down to Lake Victoria." (May 21, A1)

CENTRAL AMERICA AND THE CARIBBEAN

6

Haiti, 1994:
"Operation Restore (Uphold) Democracy," UNMIH

Walter C. Soderlund and E. Donald Briggs

▓ Background[1]

Located in the Caribbean between Cuba and Puerto Rico, Haiti shares the island of Hispaniola with the Dominican Republic. In the mid-1990s, it had a population variously estimated at between seven and eight million people. Originally conquered and colonized by Spain, over time the western third of the island fell under French rule, and during the eighteenth century St. Domingue, as it was then known, became the wealthiest colony in the French empire—that wealth was generated by a brutal, slave-based plantation system of sugar cultivation. Beginning in 1791, and continuing for thirteen years, a slave revolt led by Toussaint L'Ouverture turned back French, English, and Spanish attempts to regain control of the colony. The ultimate result in 1804 was Haitian independence and one of the greatest acts of human liberation ever recorded. (See James, 1963)

The path by which the richest colony in the Caribbean in 1791 became transformed by 1994 into the poorest nation in the Western Hemisphere is long and torturous, with blame falling both on domestic leadership and international undermining, including a neo-colonial venture on the part of the United States in the early decades of the twentieth century. It is possible to trace the origins of problems with the Haitian state back literally two hundred years to circumstances surrounding its independence. In any case, few would argue with the assertion that Haitian history has been marked more by crisis than by stability—certainly any stability brought about by other than dictatorial governments.

In attempting to understand the problems facing Haiti during the mid-1990s, an appreciation of its history is essential. The country is significantly less developed, and a great deal poorer, than most countries in the western hemisphere, and, although it has been independent for two hundred years, it has had literally no experience with democratic governance.

In similar fashion to Liberia (see Chapter 2, this volume), in Haiti the end of slavery did not eliminate the effects of that institution. As Alex Dupuy explains, prior to the revolution there had been a group of freed slaves and free-born Africans in Haiti (the *affrichis,* some of whom owned slaves), and following independence this group, although itself divided by color, asserted its dominance over the mass of newly freed slaves:

> With the whites out of the way, the acrimonious prejudices between mulattoes and Blacks would resurface as a principal division that would underline much of the struggle for power between the two factions of the dominant class in post-independent Haiti. As this occurred, the "color" question replaced the "race" question in the ideological battle ground between black and mulatto elites. In that context, the racist ideology developed during the colonial period to defend white supremacy became refined and transformed into ideologies of "color" that undergirded the struggles between the two factions of the dominant class and the broader cultural struggles to define the meaning of nationhood and peoplehood in the new Haiti. (Dupuy, 2004, 18)

Adding to Haiti's problems was "a militaristic pattern or behavior and a hierarchical social structure," necessitated by the pressing need to re-establish an economy that had been devastated by years of warfare. (Fatton, 2006, 15–16)

It is also important to understand that an independent Haiti, created as it was by a rebellion of slaves, did not sit well with the "international community" of the time. Hence its legitimacy as a state was challenged, and political obstacles to success were placed in the country's path. The net result was, as Peter Hallward argues, that

> much of Haiti's subsequent history has been shaped by efforts, both internal and external, to stifle . . . [independence] . . . and to preserve the essential legacy of slavery and colonialism—the spectacularly unjust distribution of labor, wealth and power that has characterized the whole of the island's post-Columbian history. (2004)

The United States was initially torn between its fear that condoning a slave revolt in Haiti would encourage similar uprisings in the

Southern states on the one hand, and its antipathy to French colonialism in what it considered its own backyard on the other. Until 1806, the latter appears to have weighed slightly more heavily than the former, for limited assistance was reluctantly provided to the Haitian rebels. However, a *rapprochement* with France then tipped the balance the other way, and produced a trade embargo of Haiti which began a process of Haitian isolation from the world economic system. (Abbott, 1988) The United States refused to extend diplomatic recognition to the Haitian government until 1862, when it was embroiled in its own civil war, fought largely over the issue of slavery.

The twentieth century would bring a quantum increase in United States involvement in Haitian affairs. Few, however, would argue that the overall results were beneficial to the country. As the European world moved into the new round of imperialism and colonial expansion toward the end of the nineteenth century that had a major impact on Africa, the United States also came of age as a world power. And it was, not surprisingly, the Caribbean Basin—America's so-called "backyard"—that caught the attention of American imperial thinkers. Haiti's strategic position within the Caribbean, combined with acute political instability and German interest in acquiring a naval coaling station on the island, led to an American military occupation of the country in 1915 that lasted formally until 1934. (Plummer, 1988) A summary judgment on this formative period in United States-Haitian relations is that whatever gains might be attributed to the colonial occupation, in terms of the creation of economic infrastructure and improving health, were at least off-set by the importation of American-style racism and a failure on the part of Washington to give any substantive meaning to the concept of democracy. The result was that the occupation served to solidify the power of the mulatto economic, social, and political elite vis-à-vis the mass of Black Haitians. (Bellegarde-Smith, 2004; see also Millspaugh, 1931; Nicholls, 1996; Schmidt, 1971)

▪ Roots of the Crisis

The event that set in motion the United States-led 1994 intervention in Haiti can be fixed fairly precisely—the February 1986 "assist" given to the removal of the dictator Jean-Claude ("Baby Doc") Duvalier. The nearly thirty years of Duvalier family rule, characterized by extraordinary greed, combined with brutal political repression carried out by the feared Tontons Macoutes, proved catastrophic for

Haiti. (Fauriol, 1988) The dictatorship led to some of the most talented members of Haitian society (the mulatto elite) being forced into exile; wealth was transferred out of the country as well. (Maingot, 1986–87) Accordingly, when Haiti finally rid itself of the Duvaliers in 1986, the country was gripped by poverty, illness, and misery, with a huge gap existing between the few who were very rich and the vast majority who were very poor. (Hector, 1988) In that the United States carried considerable colonial and quasi-colonial baggage with respect to Haiti, any direct military intervention in the affairs of the country was problematic.

■ Events Precipitating the Crisis

The widespread hope that things would be different in the post-Duvalier period was short-lived. While a new Constitution was enacted, the first and second elections held under its auspices were marred by violence and fraud. (Bellegarde-Smith, 2004; Nelson and Soderlund, 1992) Free and meaningful elections were not held until December 1990, when a controversial Catholic parish priest, an exponent of Liberation Theology, anti-American ideology, and a champion of Haiti's poor, Jean-Bertrand Aristide, swept to victory with just over two-thirds of the popular vote. (Ives, 1995a; Stotzky, 1997) Father Aristide was genuinely viewed as a political savior by Haiti's masses, just as he was seen as a menace by Haiti's elite and more conservative elements in the United States.

This democratic decision on the part of the Haitian people was not allowed to stand. Less than seven months after taking office as the popularly elected president, Aristide was overthrown in a military coup on September 30, 1991. The coup was carried out under the leadership of Lt. Gen. Raoul Cédras, the Aristide-appointed army chief (Farmer, 1994).[2] This coup set in motion the crisis that preoccupied United States foreign policy decision makers over the summer of 1994 and led to the September negotiated intervention that restored President Aristide to power a month later.

Immediately following the 1991 coup, the Bush administration gave strong, verbal support to the restoration of the elected Haitian president. However, Bush stipulated that military force would not be used to achieve such a restoration, stating, "I am disinclined to use military force. . . . We've got a big history of American force in this hemisphere, and so we've got to be very careful about that." (cited in Friedman, 1991, Oct. 3, A8) Once it became clear that the Haitian military would not surrender power voluntarily, the policy adopted by the United States to force the junta to give up power was a commercial embargo, organized and implemented by the Organization of American States (OAS), later joined by the United Nations.

In hindsight, it is obvious that there was a major disconnect between United States rhetorical and operational policy regarding the wisdom of returning Aristide to power. In fact, Kim Ives charges that the American policy of support for Aristide was deceptive, in that the "slow strangulation of Haiti's first democratically elected president and his nationalist program had begun" within a week of the coup. (1995b, 66; see also Morely and McGillion, 1997; Jefferies, 2001)

While the American rhetorical policy of returning Aristide to power continued, the embargo that was to accomplish it failed to achieve its objective—not surprising, given the less-than-forceful stance of Washington and lax enforcement by the Dominican Republic, which was not sympathetic to Aristide. Moreover, as early as November 1991, the Bush administration had to contend with an important consequence of the coup and the policy of economic sanctions put in place to reverse it—namely, the growing numbers of Haitians leaving the island by sea to get to the United States. On the ground that many of the boats that were used to leave Haiti were unseaworthy, Haitians were interdicted at sea and taken to the United States naval base at Guantanamo Bay, Cuba, for processing and detention.

James Helis provides the following description of the situation in Haiti confronting the United States at the end of 1992:

> In addition to the refugee problem, Bush had to confront the dilemma of restoring democracy to Haiti through supporting the often anti-American and less than desirable Jean-Bertrand Aristide. The latter was every bit as determined to have his way as were the Haitian military. Political discussions between Aristide's supporters and his opponents typically went nowhere. . . . Within the US government, a campaign to discredit Aristide included leaks to the press alleging mental instability and drug addiction. While military intervention could have ended the crisis, there was no stomach in the US for another occupation of Haiti or for the use of American force to restore Aristide. (2001, 120)

When the Clinton administration came to power in early 1993, an estimated three thousand political killings had taken place in Haiti since the 1991 coup, and American intelligence agencies estimated that large numbers of Haitians were ready to take to the seas to get to the United States. During the 1992 presidential campaign, Bill Clinton had called for the return of Aristide on the grounds of "restoration of democracy" and had criticized Bush's policy of forced repatriation of refugees. However, when he assumed office, Clinton found himself faced with the prospect of a truly massive flow of "boat people" from the unhappy island, and he quickly changed course. He was influenced, according to Morris Morley and Chris McGillion, by memories of the 1980 exodus of Cuban refugees from the port of Mariel.

> Within days of his inauguration . . . Clinton backtracked on his position [on Haitian refugees] following warnings that the United States might soon be confronted by a new wave of at least 200,000 Haitians fleeing the brutality of military rule. Sensitive to the electoral damage suffered by the Carter administration in the wake of the 1980 Mariel boat lift of over 125,000 Cuban refugees to Florida, Clinton tumbled from the high moral ground of the election campaign and announced that the existing policy would remain in place. (1997, 367)

Clinton faced other difficulties in attempting to restore Aristide to the presidency. Not only did he have to persuade the Haitian military to give up power, he had to contend with serious divisions within both governmental ranks and the American public at large. More than a few members of his own administration had strong doubts about restoring the less-than-cooperative priest to power. Many members of Congress (mainly Republicans, but some Democrats as well) opposed the President's policy. (von Hippel, 1995)

In the summer of 1993, the United States and the UN (through an arms and oil embargo) pressured President Aristide and the Haitian generals to arrive at a compromise that would remove the military government and restore the elected President. The resulting Governor's Island Agreement, signed in July, set out a series of steps through which this would be accomplished by the end of October 1993. Toward the end of September 1993, following further atrocities against Aristide's supporters in Port-au-Prince, the UN Security Council established the UN Mission in Haiti (UNMIH) composed of just under thirteen hundred military trainers and construction specialists. (Helis, 2001, 125) The purpose of the mission was to stabilize the country before Aristide's return, which was scheduled for October 30.

What followed in the wake of the Governor's Island Agreement was a near-textbook case of the principles of "bureaucratic politics" as enunciated by Graham Allison. (See Allison and Zelikow, 1999.) Each of the major segments of the American governmental apparatus involved with foreign affairs appears to have had a position of it own with respect to the Haitian situation, and to have been prepared not only to argue strenuously in its support, but also to act on its position regardless of presidential orders or negotiated agreements. In general, the State Department seems to have favored the policy outlined in the Governor's Island Agreement, while the CIA and the Pentagon had serious reservations about Aristide and/or the wisdom of returning him to power. (Morley and McGillion, 1997; Stotzky, 1997; Shacochis, 1999; Helis, 2001)

In the fall of 1993, the USS *Harlan County* headed for Port-au-Prince laden with construction equipment, medical specialists, and military trainers from Canada and the United States. When it tried to dock at the Haitian capital on October 11, it was met by an unruly "crowd of about 100 persons, . . . with open police support, chanting anti-US slogans." (Perusse, 1995, 55) In addition, a ship blocked access to the dock. After only the briefest of hesitations, no doubt based largely on worries over the possibility of American casualties following the recent peacemaking debacle in Somalia, the *Harlan County* was ordered to leave Haitian waters, and the UNMIH advance team left shortly thereafter.

These extraordinary events constituted not only a humiliating setback for the United States/OAS/UN Haitian policy, but it was also seen as a major blow to the credibility of American foreign policy generally, with ABC news anchor Peter Jennings calling it "the single most humiliating moment in the entire Haiti crisis." (cited in Goodman, 1994, July 27, C14) Yet, according to Allan Nairn, the CIA was instrumental in organizing and supporting the Front for the Advancement and Progress of Haiti (FRAPH), the group that orchestrated the dock-side demonstrations. (1994, Oct. 24, 461; see also Doyle, 1994, 55–56) Nor does opposition to Aristide appear to have been limited to the CIA. As informants later told Bob Shacochis, people within the U.S. embassy in Haiti worked "'openly to subvert U.S. policy' . . . throughout 1993 and 1994." (1999, 33; see also Bogdanish and Nordberg, 2006, Jan. 29)

In any case, with the retreat of the *Harlan County,* the Governor's Island Agreement was dead, and economic sanctions, which had been lifted in August, were reimposed. Yet, the basic contradiction underlying United States Haitian policy remained. As explained by Lawrence Eagleburger in early 1992: "We are on horns of a dilemma. Once you tighten the embargo, it begins to hurt and you increase the refugees." (cited in French, 1992, May 18, A1) Thus, it was back to square one, except that, if anything, the pressure on the Clinton administration to resolve the Haitian dilemma once and for all was now greater than ever. (Ives, 1995c, 110)

▪ The Intervention

By January 1994, it was becoming painfully clear that the only way to remove General Cédras and his junta from power was by means of a military invasion. On May 8, the administration's decision "to stop the automatic return of the boat people to Haiti effectively put US policy on a one-way street towards intervention because it led to a dramatic increase in the number of refugees which only an intervention could stop quickly." (Jakobsen, 1996, 211) Indeed, by June, the Coast Guard was "rescuing" two thousand to three thousand Haitians per day from the waters of the Caribbean. (Berman and Goldman, 1996, 310)

At the end of July, the military option was placed on the front burner when the UN Security Council, acting on a United States request, passed Resolution 940 authorizing the creation of a Chapter VII–based "U.S.-led multinational force . . . empowered 'to use all necessary means' to restore the democratically elected government of Haiti." (Niblack, 1995, 5; von Hippel, 2000) With the passage of this resolution the justification for a humanitarian intervention was in place. The military option, however, was unpopular among politicians outside of the White House as well as with the American public. Even within the Congressional Black Caucus there was division, and influential lawmakers in both Republican and Democratic parties voiced opposition to, or at least skepticism regarding, the wisdom of an American military intervention. The president took the position that while he would surely welcome congressional support for an intervention, its absence would not deter him from acting, as such authority fell within presidential powers.

As the summer of 1994 was coming to an end, the administration ordered a full-scale military invasion of Haiti to proceed, and a force in the neighborhood of twenty thousand strong, representing over twenty nations, was marshaled for what was referred to as a "hard entry" into Haiti. However, a last-ditch attempt to talk the generals out of Haiti was commissioned in the form of a mission to Haiti led by former President Jimmy Carter, Senator Sam Nunn, and retired General Colin Powell. The "Carter Mission," as it came to be known, late in the evening of September 17, at a time when American troops were literally in the air on their way to begin the invasion, succeeded in reaching an eleventh-hour agreement with General Cédras to leave Haiti. (Shacochis, 1999, 53–77) Thus, a hostile invasion was transformed into a negotiated intervention, and the operation changed from "restoring" democracy to "upholding" it. In truth, neither term reflected the true nature of the task that lay ahead.

The agreement negotiated with the Haitian generals was not without certain ambiguities, which, as Bob Shacochis reports, became painfully apparent once American forces were present in Haiti. Especially troublesome were "Rules of Engagement," specifically with respect to what was called "Haitian on Haitian violence" and more generally regarding relations with the previously identified and vilified enemy—the Haitian army. (Farmer, 1994) A major task of the intervention force was to send the generals leading the junta into exile once they had been granted amnesty. Once the status of the junta leaders had been dealt with, the actual restoration of Aristide took place on October 15.

Significant to understanding why the intervention failed to have a lasting impact on Haitian political stability, Sean Murphy points out that

> the United States saw its mission in Haiti as narrowly defined: to return Aristide to power and to give Haitians a short period of time to begin rebuilding their nation. With memories of Somalia still fresh, the United States did not engage in systematic disarming of Haitian civilian paramilitary groups, or pursue extensive infrastructure rebuilding, or anything else that suggested "nation-building." (1996, 276)

Thus, following Aristide's restoration, the majority of American troops were quickly removed, while order was maintained by UN forces until a new Haitian police force was put in place. On January 30, 1995, the UN declared that "a secure and stable environment" existed in Haiti, and on March 31, the United States transferred responsibility for policing Haiti to the UN, although Murphy argues that "conditions in Haiti . . . were far from stable throughout 1995." (1996, 276) Also important in light of future developments, on April 28, 1995, President Aristide disbanded the Haitian army. (See Niblack, 1995; Stotzky, 1997.) The mandate of the UN mission to Haiti (UNMIH) was scheduled to end in June 1996. However, at the request of the Haitian government, UNMIH's presence was extended twice, and it finally left the country in July 1997. A Canadian police-training mission remained in Haiti until March 2000. (Helis, 2001, 140)

Strength of the International Response to the Crisis: Rank order=2
   A. **Did the Humanitarian Crisis Result in an International Intervention?** Yes
   B. **Type of Response:** Combination

- **"Operation Restore Democracy," July 1994:** a multi-national force led by the United States/UN-Sanctioned under Security Council Resolution 940.
- **UNMIH**
  [UN Security Council Security Resolution 940] ". . . also provided for the deployment of UNMIH once a 'secure and stable' environment had been established, and it increased the UNMIH's authorized strength to six thousand." (Helis, 2001, 133)

C. **Type of UN Involvement:**
  - **Operation Restore Democracy:** Chapter VII
  - **UNMIH:** Chapter VII

D. **Size of Intervening Forces: 20,000 to 28,000**
  "Operation Restore (Uphold) Democracy":
  "The 20,000-troop intervention should have been called Operation Restore (Uphold) Aristide" (Jonas, 2004, Feb. 13, A6)
  "Total Personnel . . . 28,800." (U.S. Department of Defense, 1994, Sept. 15, A8)
  - **UNMIH: 6,900**
  "The Security Council . . . [authorized] . . . the buildup of UNMIH to a strength of six thousand and nine hundred police monitors and trainers. The MNF [Multi-National Force] stood down and turned over the peacekeeping mission in Haiti to UNMIH at the end of March 1995." (Helis, 2001, 136)

Determinants of the International Response

A. **Severity of the Crisis: Rank order=10**
  i. **Number of deaths (short-term): 4,000 to 5,000**
  "During its tenure, the Cedras regime was responsible for various acts of barbarity including the arrest, torture, rape, murder, and destruction of property of thousands of ordinary Haitians and many prominent Aristide supporters. Five thousand Haitians were killed." (von Hippel, 2000, 98)
  ". . . the military government has killed nearly 4,000 Haitians." (State Department Report, cited in Sciolino, 1994, Sept. 13, A13)
  "Hundreds of supporters of Rev. Jean-Bertrand Aristide and other civilians have been killed in Haiti in recent months in the bloodiest wave of political terror since the army overthrew Father Aristide as President two and a half years ago." (French, 1994, Apr. 2, I1)

"Haiti is distinguished from every other case study . . . by the fact that very little actually happened in the country. There was no full-fledged civil violence." (Talentino, 2005, 136)

"[Based on justifications for intervention established by the International Commission on Intervention and State Sovereignty] . . . 'large scale loss of life' and 'large scale ethnic cleansing,' . . . it is debatable whether the decisions to intervene militarily in Haiti, either in the mid-1990s or mid-2000s, would have met such a formidable test." (Shamsie and Thompson, 2006, 5)

ii. **Number of refugees and displaced persons (short-term): 50,000-plus to 800,000**

"Population at Risk" (1995) 1.3 million. (Weiss and Collins, 1996, 5–7, Table I.1)

"One month after the September 1991 military coup ousted President Jean-Bertrand Aristide, over 6,000 Haitians fled the country. Numbers continued to rise through May 1992, reaching a monthly high of 13,053." (Berman and Goldman, 1996, 309)

"In February 1992 the United Nations HRC reported that more than twenty thousand refugees had fled the 'violence, torture and military coercion of the FRAPH.'" (Thompson, 2006, 57)

"Tens of thousands [of Haitians] fled the country, while an estimated 300,000 were unable to live at home for fear of persecution, and therefore internally displaced." (von Hippel, 2000, 98)

"While during all of 1993 there had been but 2,000 Haitians intercepted at sea, in June 1994 there were 5,603, and almost 6,000 in the period from 1 to 4 July." (Helis, 2001, 131)

"Currently some 15,000 Haitians have applied for refugee status. About 3,000 have been admitted while 55,000 more are thought to be interested in applying but have not yet done so." (Lewis, 1994, Apr. 29, A13)

"CARE, the relief organization that now feeds about 477,000 Haitians daily, said in a recent report that the country is deteriorating daily." (French, 1994, May 4, A11)

"As many as 800,000 Haitians—5 percent of the population—have been driven into hiding by the climate of fear." (State Department Report, cited in Sciolino, 1994, Sept. 13, A13)

iii. **Likelihood of conflict spreading to other states: 1** *low*

a. **Number of shared borders: 1**

The Dominican Republic

b. Involvement of bordering states

Relations between Haiti and the Dominican Republic have long been strained. The Dominican Republic was accused of lax border security, nullifying the impact of OAS sanctions. Moreover, due to their likely hostile reception in the Dominican Republic, Haitians refugees opted for the sea route to the United States. Further, the remoteness of the border region and animosity between Haiti and the Dominican Republic would make it unlikely that domestic Haitian violence would spread to the Dominican Republic.

"Haiti did not present a threat to peace (regional or international) or a particularly grave threat to its own citizens." (Talentino, 2005, 140)

B. Pre-intervention "Assessment of Risk": 1 to 2 *low to relatively low*

"The only really clear points were that Haiti was indeed nearby and that the military mission was certainly achievable." (von Hippel, 2000, 103)

"There is every reason to think an international invasion would succeed. Haiti's 7,000-man military is hardly a formidable opponent." (Senator John Kerry, 1994, May 16, A17)

"Unlike Somalia, which was awash in arms and run by violent, closely knit clans, the Haitian military is not expected to offer much resistance." (Gordon and Schmitt, 1994, May 30, I1)

"As Haiti readies itself for a possible American invasion, it does so without any recent experience in war or the modern-day means to conduct one." (Bragg, 1994, Sept. 14, A1)

"Military experts say there is minimum risk to American forces because the 7,000 members of the Haitian military and police forces are poorly trained and ill-equipped. 'They can't even fly a Piper Cub at you.'" (Pentagon official, cited in Gordon, 1994, Sept. 10, I4)

"[The use of force to restore Aristide would result in] . . . casualties and humiliations reminiscent of that in Somalia." (Scowcroft and Melby, 1994, June 1, A21)

"The issue has never been the invasion. . . . The issue is disorder right after the invasion. This could make what happened in Panama look like chicken feed." (Administration official, cited in Schmitt and Gordon, 1994, Sept. 11, I1)

C. Extent of "National Interest Involvement":

i. The international community: 2 *relatively low*

"Unlike the cases of Liberia, Iraq, Bosnia-Herzegovina, Somalia, and Rwanda, thousands of Haitians were not dying daily as a result of a breakdown in civil order or the repression of their government. . . . The overriding concern of the international community, however, seemed to turn more on the fact that a democratically elected leader had been ousted and replaced by a militant group bent on consolidating and maintaining their power." (Murphy, 1996, 265)

ii. United States: 2 to 4 *relatively low* to *relatively high*

U.S. national interest in Haiti was described by von Hippel as multi-dimensional: "1. *Haiti is in the US sphere of influence.* . . . 2. *Democracy was denied to a country in the western hemisphere.* . . . 3. *The refugee problem was threatening to overwhelm the United States.* . . . 4. *The US administration had suffered continual humiliation by the ruling junta since the 1991 coup.* . . . 5. *Human rights abuses were severe.* . . . 6. *Concern for US citizens living in Haiti, albeit a small number.* . . . and 7. 'the total fracturing of the ability of the world community to conduct business in the post-Cold War era.'*" (von Hippel, 2000, 101–03, italics in the original)

"The crisis touched on issues of prestige and control that could be construed as part of the US national interest . . . Three other particular interests also served to transform Haiti's crisis into an issue of national interest: the US history of control over Haitian politics, the refugees coming to the United States, and the protection of democracy in the hemisphere." (Talentino, 2005, 141–42)

"Clinton understood the need to bring the Haiti issue to an early resolution. He was concerned about the possibilities of another surge of refugees and felt pressure both at home and abroad to live up to his pledge to Haiti." (Helis, 2001, 122)

"[The president] believed that the American interests in Haiti set it apart from more distant trouble spots . . . 'It's in our backyard.'" (Bill Clinton, cited in Jehl, 1994, May 20, A1)

"In Haiti, we have a case in which the right is clear, in which the country in question is nearby, in which our own interests are plain, in which the mission is achievable and limited, and in which other nations of the world stand with us." (Bill Clinton, cited in von Hippel, 2000, 103)

"After Somalia and the *Harlan County,* with no end in sight to the Balkan wars, and genocide spreading in Rwanda, the White House needed a foreign policy success." (Helis, 2001, 130–31)

"More parochially, the United States also wanted to avoid a flood of illegal immigrants to its shores provoked by continued repression and poverty in Haiti. There was also considerable domestic pressure . . . to take meaningful action on Haiti as a showing of U.S. moral leadership on racial matters." (Murphy, 1996, 275)

"When brutality occurs so close to your shores, it affects our national interest and we have a responsibility to act." (Clinton, 1994, Sept. 16, A10)

"At root, we have no interest at stake in Haiti so compelling as to warrant unilateral military action." (Thomas Carothers, Senior Associate, Carnegie Endowment for International Peace, 1994, May 12, A25)

"I don't think our vital security issues are at stake [in Haiti]." (Senator John McCain, cited in Greenhouse, 1994, July 10, A9)

"While the situation there continues to be of concern to Washington, Haiti was not of vital interest to the United States." (views of William Perry, U.S. Secretary of Defense, cited in Rohter, 1994, Aug. 18, A9)

"The American people are not convinced that we have vital interests in invading Haiti, despite immigration, which we believe might continue even if Mr. Aristide is returned." (Senator Richard Lugar, cited in Schmitt, 1994, Sept. 1, A10)

"It is the post-invasion circumstances that I fear will bog down U.S. forces in a low-level, open-ended, ill-defined conflict which will require servicemen and women to serve as a virtual palace guard for President Aristide once he is returned to power." (Senator John McCain, cited in Schmitt, 1994, Sept. 1, A10)

"American troops should only be asked to fight for American interests. . . . Risking American lives to restore Aristide to power is not in America's interest." (Senator Robert Dole, cited in Schmitt, 1994, Sept. 2, A9)

"Certainly there was precious little enlightenment in the President's speech . . . on why we should invade Haiti. . . . Mr. Clinton couldn't drum up one compelling reason that a tiny nation whose economy is in shambles and whose military is a shadow of our own posed a risk to our national security. He was reduced to referring to Grenada as though it were Guadalcanal." (Quindlen, 1994, Sept. 17, I23)

D. **Mass Media: March 20 to September 19, 1994**
  i. **"Alerting" function (volume of television and newspaper coverage): N=582; Rank order=1**
    a. **Television coverage: Rank order=1**
       Total (ABC, CBS, NBC): N=272
       In-depth: N=208
    b. ***New York Times* coverage: N=310; Rank order=1**
  ii. **"Evaluative" function (intervention framing in the *New York Times*)**
       Pro-intervention frames: N=27
       Anti-intervention frames: N=51
  iii. **Assessment of media coverage**

Karin von Hipple has argued that "extensive media coverage ensured that the majority of Americans were fully cognizant of the scope of the problem in Haiti as well as the refugee crisis that was plaguing Florida." (2000, 103) Indeed, our data confirm the validity of that assessment as the Haitian crisis ranked first with respect to television news coverage (both total and in-depth), as well as in newspaper coverage, where it garnered over three times the number of stories of any other crisis studied.

Interestingly, however, while the American public was certainly "alerted" to the crisis, media evaluation of the intervention option appeared more negative than positive. In a study of major American network television news coverage leading up to the 1994 intervention, 23 percent of stories were judged to be favorable, 46 percent were judged to be neutral, while 31 percent were seen as unfavorable to President Clinton's intervention policy.[3] (Soderlund 2003, 67) *New York Times* evaluative coverage was even more negative. As judged by Larry Minear and his colleagues, "U.S. policymakers became polarized, reflecting the highly polarized situation in Haiti itself. . . . With policy in flux, . . . the media and public opinion exerted a push-pull influence." (1996, 60–61)

With policy elites divided on the wisdom of an intervention, Lance Bennett's theory of indexing (1990) would lead us to expect significant media attention, and this is exactly what occurred. Indeed, following the *Harlan County* debacle in the fall of 1993, "growing criticism of the United States government's treatment of the Haitian boat people was making it increasingly difficult for Washington to allow the crisis to continue." (See Thompson, 2006, 51–69.)

This judgment appears to accurately describe the political climate that confronted President Clinton toward the end of March 1994, when our study of mass media coverage of the Haitian crisis began, shortly before critical decisions were reportedly made to pursue the route of an armed intervention. As data in Table 6.1 show, media interest in the crisis, although peaking at the time the intervention neared, was quite strong over the entire period of study. Unlike all other crises studied, the overwhelming number of stories originated from the United States (58 percent), mostly from Washington, and filed chiefly by Steven Greenhouse, Douglas Jehl, Michael Gordon, and Elaine Sciolino, with another 32 percent originating from Haiti filed by Howard French, Garry Pierre-Pierre, Rick Bragg, and Larry Rohter. Reporters identified as working for the *New York Times* accounted for 75 percent of material (highest of all ten crises studied), Reuters and the Associated Press contributing a total of 11 percent. As was the case in all crisis coverage, while inside news stories dominated, there were a

Table 6.1 *New York Times* **Coverage of Haiti**

Panel 1 – Date:	N	%	Panel 2 – Dateline:	N	%
First 2 Months	59	19%	United States	180	58%
Second 2 Months	119	38%	Haiti	98	32%
Third 2 Months	132	43%	L.A./Caribbean (other)	16	5%
		100%	Other	0	0%
			Unknown	16	5%
					100%

Panel 3 – Source:	N	%	Panel 4 – Type of Content:	N	%
Local Staff	232	75%	Front-page News	44	14%
AP	16	5%	Inside-page News	201	65%
AFP	0	0%	Editorials	15	5%
Reuters	18	6%	Op-ed Features	32	10%
Other	22	7%	Photos	4	1%
Unknown	22	7%	Letters	5	2%
		100%	Other	9	3%
					100%

Newspaper Coverage, by Date, Dateline, Source and Type (March 20 to September 19, 1994) N=310 large number of front-page stories (44), editorials (15), and op-ed features (32); in all, high-impact items constituted nearly 30 percent of what was massive press coverage.

Coverage of the Haiti crisis in the *New York Times* can be grouped in two time periods—prior to and following the announcement in early May that military intervention was being actively considered. Significantly, in neither period did President Clinton's Haiti policy (which charitably can only be described as befuddled), fare particularly well. In the first period, Clinton was castigated specifically for reneging on his promise not to return intercepted refugees to Haiti and generally for not doing enough to rid the island of the generals. Then, following the announcement that the administration was considering the military intervention option, he was criticized for going too far.

Our study of coverage of Haiti began with a March 23 report by the Congressional Black Caucus, charging that the "Administration has worked in a half-hearted manner to restore . . . [Jean-Bertrand Aristide.]" The Caucus argued that Clinton's "Haiti policy 'must be scrapped' in favor of tougher efforts to restore the nation's exiled President to power." (*NYT*, 1994, Mar. 23, A13) Criticism of President Clinton's policy continued in two op-ed pieces. Bob Herbert noted the "extreme split between . . . [Clinton's] . . . high-toned rhetoric and his administration's shameful behavior regarding Haiti." He singled out the treatment of refugees, the conditions suggested for Aristide's return to Haiti (which he termed "ludicrous"), and the embargo (which was not working). Herbert argued that it was time for the American president to move from words to action. "Meanwhile, the atrocities committed by the police and military continue." (1994, Mar. 23, A21) Amy Wilentz continued the attack: "It seems unlikely that President Clinton wants to go down in history as the man who blocked Haiti's last chance at democracy. Yet, if he continues to ignore gross violations of international sanctions, he is speeding Haiti's tumble into chaos and gangsterism." (1994, Mar. 24, A23)

The issue of whether the United States should mount a military intervention to restore Aristide was first raised on April 10 and received a negative response from the outset:

> I don't think there is any appetite for military action in the Congress or the American people. There is no question we have the military capacity to succeed. The more difficult question is what happens the day after you oust Haiti's military. What do you do? How long do you stay? (Senator Christopher Dodd, cited in Greenhouse, 1994, Apr. 10, A9)

On April 15 sentiments both favoring and opposing a military intervention were reported. Representative David Obey's position was the first reported support for an intervention: "As long as I've been old enough to read and breathe, I've opposed military intervention by the U.S. in the hemisphere. . . . But I feel Haiti is a special circumstance. Haiti is one place where something like this can be done at minimum cost." (cited in Greenhouse, 1994, Apr. 15, A2) However, Steven Greenhouse also reported that at this point, "the administration would not consider military intervention because the idea has little support in Congress or among the public."

Also on April 15, Randall Robinson, chairman of TransAfrica, began a hunger strike that was aimed at changing American policy toward Haiti. Among his demands were an end to the "summary refusal" of entry of Haitian refugees into the United States, the initiation of "comprehensive new trade sanctions," the freezing of "assets of the Haitian coup leaders," and the sealing of "the border with the Dominican Republic . . . with a multinational force." (Robinson, 1994, Apr. 17, IV17) However, a military intervention to restore President Aristide was not one of his stated demands. On April 22, the Haitian president-in-exile himself weighed in, charging that "President Clinton had not shown the 'political will' to make tough decisions to return him to power, adding that if Mr. Clinton had 'done just half of what he promised' the Haitian leader would be back in power." (Jean-Bertrand Aristide, cited in Greenhouse, 1994, Apr. 22, A1) Perhaps mindful that the Haitian Constitution left him vulnerable to impeachment if he were to call for a foreign intervention, Aristide did not press for this option to return him to power.

President Aristide's condemnation of the American president occasioned the first of fifteen editorials that appeared on the Haitian crisis in the New York Times during the study period. Focused on the summary return of refugees to Haiti, the editorial of April 22 put aside the question of intervention, but argued that

> instead of twisting the laws and decency, Washington ought to live up to American principles. Restoring Mr. Aristide to power without recourse to military force may not be possible at this time. Giving a fair hearing and humane sanctuary to those trying to flee a terrorist military regime a few hundred miles off the Florida coast surely is. (NYT, 1994, Apr. 22, A26)

Following the announcement on April 27 of the firing of Lawrence Pezzullo as Special Envoy to Haiti, which was widely seen as a signal by the administration that "its policy has failed," (Weiner, 1994, Apr.

27, A1) Elaine Sciolino, Howard French, and Douglas Jehl combined on a "Special Report" on Haiti, which appeared on the front page of the April 29 edition. It pointed out the failure of the operative policy, the need for a change in that policy, and the reality that there was no agreement between the American and Haitian presidents over strategy, in spite of three meetings between them. While Representative David Obey's call for a military intervention to restore Mr. Aristide to power was noted, the balance of commentary was decidedly unfavorable toward an intervention. For example, Deputy Under Secretary of Defense for Policy, Walter Slocombe, was quoted to the effect that "The Pentagon would not risk American soldiers' lives to put 'that psychopath' back in power."[4] The article concluded that "the Pentagon . . . has made it clear . . . that it has no appetite for putting troops in Haiti, even as military trainers and engineers, until there is a change in the military leadership." (Sciolino, et al., 1994, April 29, A1) Adding to the problem, on May 4 Howard French reported that many analysts had concluded that broader sanctions against the military junta were not likely to be effective. (1994, May 4, A11)

At this point, President Clinton decided that it was "time for . . . [the Haitian generals] . . . to go." He was reportedly "not eager to use force" to dislodge them but indicated that "we can't afford to discount the prospect of a military option." Dismissed Haitian Special Envoy Lawrence Pezzullo argued that the new policy meant "the United States was 'heading irrevocably' toward military intervention." (both cited in Gordon, 1994, May 4, A10) On May 6, it was reported that "units of the 82nd Airborne Division have been placed on alert for possible missions in Haiti." However, aides of President Aristide cautioned that at this time "It would be premature of the United States to use force." (Jehl, 1994, May 6, A10)

On May 7, tougher sanctions on Haiti were reported approved by the UN Security Council, and a second *New York Times* editorial two days later both praised the enactment of these stronger measures and warned against a premature military intervention: "The President's increased resolve is welcome. . . . Real sanctions have never been given a chance. . . . With emotions running high and the White House beset with political problems at home, talk of sending in troops could prove tempting. But the President can best lead now by giving real sanctions a chance to work first." (*NYT,* 1994, May 9, A16)

With the intervention option openly on the table, press commentary increasingly focused on both its need and efficacy. A. M. Rosenthal's op-ed piece supported the president's growing resolve: "It is hard to believe that U.S. armed forces cannot handle the Haitian cops in a few days, if they don't pick up and get out first." (1994, May 10, A23) Most articles, however, took a decidedly cautionary position. In a most prophetic analysis, Thomas Carothers of the Carnegie Endowment for International Peace pointed out that the problems of Haiti involved social polarization and stability would not be achieved by the return of Aristide. Thus, an intervention would create the need for "an extensive and costly long-range assistance program." Moreover, while he judged that "all our options in Haiti are unsatisfactory," he concluded that "armed intervention is among the worst." (1994, May 12, A25) Neither the OAS nor France supported a military intervention until the newly imposed economic sanctions were given a chance to dislodge the generals; in addition, both leading candidates for the presidency of the Dominican Republic were reported as being "opposed to any foreign intervention next door." (French, 1994, May 15, I9)

When the Haitian military junta attempted to legitimize its position by appointing an eighty-one-year-old Supreme Court Justice to the presidency as Aristide's successor, an editorial cautioned the Clinton administration not to overreact, in that the appointment "does not materially change the situation in Haiti." It went on to describe "unilateral action" on the part of the United Sates as "being unwise, given the unhappy history of American meddling in Haiti." In short, the editorial called for a policy that would "allow more stringent measures [sanctions] to have their effect, before resorting to force." (NYT, 1994, May 13, A30)

The president's new "tougher" Haiti policy, which included non-automatic return to Haiti of refugees intercepted at sea, stronger economic sanctions, combined with the possibility of military intervention, continued to come under attack from a variety of critics. Lawrence Pezzullo pointed to the lack of progress stemming from the earlier twenty-year-long American intervention in Haiti: "Every place [in the Caribbean], we've left something behind. In Haiti, we left nothing." The Haitian president-in-exile also became an issue; described as a "wild card," his behavior "makes some officials in Washington wonder whether Father Aristide would turn on his own liberators after riding back to power on their wings." (Sciolino, 1994, May 22, IV5)

Over the summer, supporters of military intervention stressed the issues of Aristide's democratic legitimacy, the repressive nature of the military regime, the suffering of the Haitian people, and the relative ease of a successful military intervention. For example, Senator John Kerry argued that "by tolerating their defiance, we have empowered Haiti's military thugs" and cited the necessity of a policy with "a believable threat of military force." (1994, May 16, A17) In addition, Robert Rotberg, president of the World Peace Foundation and a leading scholar on Haiti, claimed, "There is no hope for Haiti without an immediate military intervention." (cited in Sciolino, 1994, May 18, A1)

For their part, Haiti's generals "appeared to be resolved to ride out the sanctions, convinced that the United States would not mount an armed intervention to unseat them." (French, 1994, May 23, A1) Indeed, it appeared that they had good reason to believe that Clinton would not act: "a non-binding resolution opposing military intervention in Haiti unless there is a 'clear and present danger' to American citizens or interests" was approved by the House of Representatives on May 24 by a vote of 223 to 201. (*NYT*, 1994, May 29, I26)

Toward the end of May, a further argument was advanced against a military intervention—that of the necessity for a long period of what has come to be called "post-conflict peacebuilding." While American intelligence officials were not worried over resistance to an intervention by Haiti's small and poorly trained army, they did raise concerns over what would follow military success. Specifically, it was pointed out that an intervention "would not bring an end to the turmoil and violence that have swept the country, and that an international force to maintain order could be needed there for years." (Gordon and Schmitt, 1994, May 30, I1) On June 1, Brent Scowcroft and Eric Melby claimed further that President Aristide had "shown no flexibility," arguing that "if the Administration orders an invasion to restore . . . [him] . . . it will be making a grave mistake." They concluded with a prophetic commentary: "Those contemplating direct involvement in nation-building ought to hark back to our occupation of Haiti from 1914 to 1933. When we arrived, we encouraged not a vestige of democracy; when we departed, we left none. An invasion today would very likely lead to the same result." (1994, June 1, A21) Howard French also framed the situation in pessimistic terms: "For Haiti . . . a priest-president who before his overthrow . . . seemed to relish the language of class warfare, and an elite that has never been willing to pay taxes or establish even minimal social security for the poor, still seems highly explosive." (1994, June 6, A3) Also during the first week of June, President Aristide proposed his own preferred form of international intervention, which he termed "a surgical action

. . . [as opposed to a military invasion] . . . to remove the thugs within hours. . . . once we do that, we could have the international community in the country within the framework of agreements we have already signed." (cited in French, 1994, June 3, A3) How this "surgery" was to be performed was left unspecified.

A June 11 editorial continued to press for a diplomatic approach:

> After months of ineffectual fumbling and a brief, misguided lurch toward the hasty use of military force, the Clinton administration finally seems headed in the right direction on Haiti. . . . Thanks to a more aggressive diplomatic strategy and a more humane approach to refugees, removing the generals without military intervention has now become a realistic possibility. (*NYT*, 1994, June 11, A20)

In Haiti, however, things looked different. On June 13, sensing that an intervention was imminent, the newly appointed president, Emil Jonassaint, declared a state of emergency: "'Haiti now risks invasion and occupation. A state of emergency is declared taking effect immediately.'" (cited in Reuters, 1994, June 13, A10)

On June 20, it was reported that President Clinton was attempting to "buy off" the Haitian generals by offering them a "comfortable" exile. (Sciolino, 1994, June 20, A1) An editorial on June 23 approved this initiative, but with an important caveat: "Luxury exile for the gang of three [Raoul Cédras, Michel François, and Philippe Biambi] would be a tolerable price to pay for a serious effort to end Haiti's agony. Without that effort, it would be a disgrace." (*NYT*, 1994, June 23, A22) As enhanced sanctions were taking their toll on the Haitian population and its generals were giving mixed signals regarding their willingness to leave (Pierre-Pierre, 1994, June 28), Representative James Oberstar presented a strong case for immediate military intervention in an op-ed piece:

> As we wait for these sanctions to wear down the regime, the Haitian people—starving, the poorest in the hemisphere, suffering the effects of three years of sanctions—will run out of time. Quick military intervention by the United States and others is the only way to restore law, order and constitutional government to the beleaguered nation. (1994, June 25, A23)

If President Clinton's policy was hard to pin down, so too was the exiled Haitian president's. As late as July 1, Aristide indicated he was opposed to a military intervention. He went as far as to indicate that "he would not even agree to return to power under such conditions."[5]

(French, 1994, July 3, IV1) On July 4, it was reported that Clinton's new envoy to Haiti, William H. Gray III, acknowledging "that the fate of Haiti was of 'vital interest' to the United States, . . . [stated that] . . . 'the United States is not contemplating an imminent invasion of Haiti.'" (cited in Sciolino, 1994, July 4, I2)

In early July, on the grounds that the possibility (remote as it was) of gaining asylum in the United States was prompting more Haitians to take to the sea in boats, the Clinton administration again changed its Haitian immigration policy, this time ending the faint hope that Haitians interdicted at sea could gain access to the United States. Reported at this time as well were military exercises widely interpreted as a "rehearsal" for a possible invasion of Haiti. Both of these developments were seen as increasing the chances of an American intervention. On July 7, Elaine Sciolino criticized the president's Haiti policy, describing it "as lurching from one short-term fix to another, often creating new problems that in turn require quick fixes." (1994, July 7, A8) An editorial on the same date specifically criticized the leaking of information on American military exercises and was concerned about where this was heading:

> It is hard to believe that the Pentagon's willingness to discuss . . . "secret" maneuvers is not part of a plan to flush Gen. Cédras and his henchmen out of Haiti. This is a worthy goal, but the timing is amateurish and the underlying message is troubling. . . . Even if U.S. forces . . . were to make quick work of General Cédras and his crew, does Washington really want responsibility for enforcing law and order in a volatile, revenge-minded land? (NYT, 1994, July 7, A18)

Two days later, another editorial called for "a sustainable, consistent policy . . . [combining] . . . "safe havens" for Haitian refugees and "sanctions" for Haiti's business and military leaders. The point was reiterated that the use of force "should be held off the immediate agenda." (NYT, 1994, July 9, I18)

Haiti's military rulers appeared secure in their knowledge that domestic opposition to President Clinton's plans for an invasion made such an option unlikely. (Greenhouse, 1994, July 10) On July 11, in a deliberately provocative move, they ordered foreign human rights observers to leave the country. Both National Security Advisor Anthony Lake and OAS Envoy Dante Caputo characterized the announcement as "outrageous." (cited in Pierre-Pierre, 1994, July 12, A1) The *New York Times* responded to this affront with its third editorial on Haiti in seven days. It acknowledged that the expulsion of the human rights monitors was "a defiant slap at the United Nations and the Organization of American States." Yet, it continued to counsel the Clinton administration "to let recently tightened international sanctions do their work . . . and to find enough safe haven sites, including some in the U.S., to assure that no fleeing Haitian is forced to return home." It also argued that "the Administration should sit tight" on the issue of intervention:

> Force is a blunt instrument. It cannot solve political problems. It kills people, including American troops, who should only be asked to die when vital national interests are involved. It punches holes in the international legal order. It is sometimes necessary but must be used only as a last resort. (NYT, 1994, July 13, A18)

In mid-July, it appeared that President Clinton's position on the use of force had not fundamentally changed from early May: "a step . . . [he wanted to avoid] . . . but will not rule out." (Schmitt, 1994, July 15, A1) However, significantly, the administration began what was described as "an aggressive effort to build public and Congressional support for [the use of force]." The thrust of this media campaign was "a week of television coverage that gave prominence to scenes of brutality." (Jehl, 1994, July 19, A4) Human rights groups in Haiti were not impressed: "We don't want to be used as an excuse for an intervention. . . . They are playing games." (American human rights worker, cited in French, 1994, July 18, A5)

President Clinton's request on July 21 for UN authorization for an invasion of Haiti—the first-ever such request for an intervention in the Western hemisphere—gave new urgency to the issue, with late August cited as the earliest date that an intervention reasonably could be expected. (Jehl, 1994, July 22, A1) It also refocused debate on whether congressional approval of such an invasion would be necessary. A July 24 editorial argued that just such approval (which obviously would not be forthcoming) was necessary for any invasion and that "to invade would be an irresponsible use of the world's most formidable military force." Moreover, it maintained that

> the Clinton Administration has yet to present compelling arguments that invading Haiti is in the best interests of the United States. . . . Horrible things are going on in Haiti. . . . These are good reasons to put the strongest diplomatic pressure and economic pressure on the junta and to

provide sanctuary to fleeing refugees. They are not good reasons to send in the Marines. (*NYT,* 1994, July 24, IV14)

On the same date, in an op-ed article dealing with past American interventions in the Caribbean region, Larry Rohter pointed out that these "have almost uniformly failed to produce the results that policy makers in Washington had hoped for." (1994, July 24, IV1) Representative Ronald Dellums, a member of the Congressional Black Caucus, likewise opposed an invasion of Haiti: "U.S. policy-makers should consider the use of force—anywhere—only as a last resort." (1994, July 24, IV15) At the end of July, Larry Rohter canvassed opinions of Americans living in Haiti and offered the following summary of advice: "Don't invade and, above all, don't get mired in a repeat of the 1915–1934 military occupation." (Rohter, 1994, July 30, I3)

Following the United Nation's authorization of a United States–led invasion force for Haiti, an editorial acknowledged that

> perhaps the threat of force will convince Haiti's top soldiers they should depart. . . . But the threat to use force implies a willingness to use it if the military leaders hold fast, and such an invasion under present circumstances would be a big mistake. . . . The Clinton Administration, under attack from critics on the left and right for alleged timidity in deploying U.S. military power, now reveals a dangerously low threshold for using force in Haiti. (*NYT,* 1994, Aug. 2, A20)

An op-ed article by Joanne Landy, executive director of Campaign for Peace and Democracy, continued the attack against an invasion, claiming that "it is an illusion to believe such an action could restore genuine democracy there." (1994, Aug. 7, IV17) Arguing on the other side, John Judson maintained in a letter to the editor that "if heightened sanctions do not cause the leaders of Haiti to leave soon . . . the military incumbents must be removed by force." (1994, Aug. 11, A22)

In early August, in spite of the green light given to an intervention by the UN, Elaine Sciolino's analysis made clear that there were still basic differences of opinion within the Clinton administration regarding the appropriateness of an invasion. Secretary of Defense William Perry reportedly "opposed a recommendation that would set a deadline for an invasion if the Haitian military leaders did not leave," while Deputy Secretary of State Strobe Talbot was "said to favor an early invasion." These positions were described as reflecting "the extremes of the Administration's thinking on how best to restore . . . Haiti's exiled President." (1994, Aug. 4, A1)

In mid-August another anti-intervention argument appeared—that being the futility of attempting to do anything with Haiti. On this issue, Larry Rohter cited an Army War College study by Donald Schultz and Gabriel Marcella, which concluded that "Haiti's human and material resources are either in such short supply or have been so degraded . . . as to raise serious questions about its continued survival as a society and as an independent nation-state." This assessment led Rohter to suggest "that turning Haiti into a modern state may be impossible." (1994, Aug. 14, IV3)

As August progressed, another crisis in the Caribbean, the Cuban *Balsero* (or Rafter) Crisis, which saw thousands of Cubans take to the waters of the Straits of Florida in makeshift rafts following Fidel Castro's August 12 opening of beaches to would-be émigrés to the United States. (See Soderlund, 2003, 113–38.) This certainly complicated any American military action against the Haitian generals and most likely postponed an invasion until after it had been resolved; as a young Haitian woman concluded, "It is like the U.S. can only solve one problem at a time."[6] (cited in Bragg, 1994, Aug. 26, A10) The crisis also appeared to embolden Haiti's military rulers, who near the end of August reportedly assassinated Father Jean-Marie Vincent, a prominent supporter of President Aristide. However, in perpetrating this act, they may have miscalculated, as Secretary of State Warren Christopher claimed that the killing "underscores the international community's resolve that Haiti's military dictators leave." (cited in Bragg, 1994, Aug. 30, A1)

Among American lawmakers, however, there appeared little such resolve. (See Schmitt, 1994, Sept. 1; Schmitt, 1994, Sept. 2; Schmitt, 1994, Sept. 9; and Gordon, 1994, Sept. 10.) This was not the case among the *New York Times* editorial committee, where there was resolve—that to continue to oppose an invasion of Haiti: "as morally and legally wrong as . . . [the Haitian junta's] . . . actions have been, the United States has no calling to invade countries in the absence of any clear threat to vital American interests or to international peace." Then, citing the lack of public support, the editorial concluded that "unless and until the American people and others throughout the hemisphere are more willing than they are now to bear the risks of an invasion and its likely sequels, including prolonged occupation and deadly clashes with civilians, invading Haiti is a bad idea." (*NYT,* 1994, Sept. 2, A24)

In spite of continued opposition from Congress, the American public, and the *New York Times,* by mid-September it was more or less a foregone conclusion that an invasion was imminent, and commentary began to shift to questions about mission mandates and duration. On these questions, concerned about a repeat of the Somalia experience, Secretary of State Warren Christopher went out of his way to stress the limited nature of any invasion, stating that "it was not the responsibility of the United States to rebuild Haiti's failed institutions or hunt down the three military leaders who currently run the country and oppose Father Aristide's return." (Sciolino, 1994, Sept. 13, A13)

In its editorial commentary, the *New York Times* continued to stress the need for Congressional approval of any invasion:

> To invade Haiti without prior Congressional approval would short-circuit the United States Constitution . . . [as] neither of the situations usually cited as justifying independent action by the Commander in Chief—military crisis or unexpected threat to national security—exists in this case. . . . Mr. Clinton should not abuse his powers and risk damage to his Presidency by plunging ahead. (*NYT,* 1994, Sept. 13, A22)

Further, the editorial argued that President Aristide, if he were to be returned to power by the United States, would likely face difficulties: "A century of Latin American interventions should have taught Washington that it cannot enforce democracy at gunpoint. Haitians elected Father Aristide and still support him, but even his legitimacy may not survive being installed by foreign troops." (*NYT,* 1994, Sept. 13, A22)

On September 14, prior to President Clinton's address to the nation on Haiti, Michael Gordon reported a poll showing that "the American public is strongly opposed to an intervention . . . 66 percent saying they opposed such a move." (1994, Sept. 14, p. A1) Administration officials "acknowledged that the White House had squandered some chances to win public backing for forceful action . . . [saying] . . . they had failed to call sufficient attention to the magnitude of human rights abuses in Haiti," and a communication-counseling group advised the president "'to put a graphic face' on human rights violations there." (Jehl, 1994, Sept. 15, A8) This the president attempted to do, but he failed to change the mind of the *New York Times,* which in an editorial on the day following his speech pointed out that "the fact remains that a Haiti invasion is a mission the country does not believe in, Congress has not approved and Mr. Clinton himself tried to avoid." Mere days before the invasion was to go forward, the editorial reiterated past arguments against an invasion:

No U.S. interests are at stake in Haiti that would justify risking lives, and no urgency exists that could justify short-circuiting Congressional approval and ignoring public opinion. The right policy remains sanctions plus diplomacy and patience. If the President really wanted to demonstrate cool, tough leadership, he would call this invasion back while he still can. (*NYT*, 1994, Sept. 16, A30)

On September 17, it was reported that President Clinton had dispatched former President Carter, along with Senator Sam Nunn and retired General Colin Powell, to Haiti to impress upon the Haitian generals that the "time for them to go" had truly arrived. (Jehl, 1994, Sept. 17, I1) While Clinton had, from the beginning, favored the route of "voluntary exit" for the leaders of Haiti's military government, his aides explained further that "the mission, even if it fails, could provide the President with some badly needed political cover."

Either Cédras gets the message . . . or if Carter and the others get stiffed, it will be very clear to the American people that the Administration has left no stone unturned in seeking a diplomatic solution. If they get stiffed, it will probably help us build public support for what the President is planning. (Unnamed ranking Administration official, cited in Apple, 1994, Sept. 17, I7)

Due to the last minute dispatch of the Carter Mission, the Haitian generals were persuaded to leave the country. Reactions to the success of the Carter Mission varied. Anthony Lewis, in a September 19 op-ed piece, claimed that it "shows what a difference decisive commitment can make in American foreign policy. When at long last President Clinton made clear that he meant business, and former President Carter's mission underlined that determination, the game was over for the Haitian military." (1994, Sept. 19, A19) The *New York Times* editorial board, however, refused to give the American president any credit for the outcome: "the White House should be celebrating its luck, not spinning the public about its diplomatic skill and the virtues of Presidential resolve. President Clinton had reduced himself to the most dismal of foreign policy options: attack or lose face." The editorial ended with the following assessment of the situation:

With U.S. troops and prestige now on the line and Haitian democracy at issue, Americans want this venture to go well. They will try to find reason to cheer Mr. Clinton. In return, they will have every reason to insist that the President will ponder the difference between luck and wisdom. (*NYT*, 1994, Sept. 20, A22)

In spite of voluminous media coverage and an Administration committed to use the media to build public support for an invasion of Haiti, on the eve of the invasion, two-thirds of the American public still opposed the use of force, and it was clear that if the president were to ask Congress for approval, this would be denied. It is also clear that in its editorial voice, the *New York Times* frequently and determinedly opposed an armed intervention throughout the six months prior to the planned launch of an invasion. In total content, as well, there was a decided "anti-invasion tilt" in evaluation, although this did even out considerably as the date for an invasion approached. The previously cited study of television evaluation of the intervention option shows a similar, but less dramatic, media opposition, indicating that volume of media coverage alone will not create a "media push " significant enough to change policy. This conclusion is supported by Andrea Talentino, who argues that

> US public opinion did not support the intervention, due largely to the dubious characterizations of Aristide in the media and the seemingly useless nature of picking a fight against a weakling of a state not critical to national security. In spite of extensive media coverage of the refugees in particular, the so-called CNN effect did not sway the American public in this case. (2005, 143–44)

We may add that, from early May, when the military option was reported as being seriously considered by the White House, the *New York Times* consistently offered arguments opposed to an invasion. What effect these may have had on American policy are speculative, but in the final analysis the president did manage to avoid an invasion by talking the generals out of Haiti, which appears to have been his preferred option all along.

■ Overall Evaluation of the Crisis Response

As Robert Fatton Jr. explains, the US-led intervention in 1994 was not without benefits for Haiti:

> The American occupation of Haiti succeeded in restoring Aristide and preventing, at least temporarily, the country's descent into hell. It opened up the social space necessary to rebuild a popular civil society so brutally squelched under the junta. It offered the people a chance to reestablish the process of democratization while emasculating those institutions that had historically kept the majority destitute. . . . Thus, in spite of their profound ambiguities and contradictions, the intervention and the restoration of Aristide helped rekindle hopes for a better future. (1997, 222)

While most observers would agree that some progress toward democratic governance in Haiti was made in 1994 with the restoration of President Aristide, limitations to that progress are important to note as well. The United States intervention and subsequent UN nation-building efforts at best only restored Haiti to where it had been prior to the September 1991 coup—that is, a country ruled by a civilian president who had been democratically elected. Unfortunately, following Aristide's restoration to power, little further progress was made and, as many predicted, problems in Haiti have persisted.

It has been claimed that the extent to which Aristide was forced to make compromises with what were seen to be his "radical" socio-economic policies to ensure his restoration, weakened him domestically. (Fatton, 1997, 146–48; see also Farmer, 2002, May–June) Additionally, the partisan debates in the United States in both 1993 and 1994 regarding Aristide's character and suitability to rule, certainly appeared to have weakened any firm commitment on the part of the Clinton administration to the elected, and now restored, Haitian president, who was increasingly perceived to be part of the problem. (Pastor, 1997, 131–32; Stotzky, 1997, 48–49) Whatever the case, it is clear that during the six years between the restoration of Aristide and his re-election to the presidency in 2000 (both Aristide's between 1994 and 1996 and René Préval's between 1996 and 2000) little progress was made in solving the country's serious economic, social, and political problems.

Unfortunately for Haiti, the worst was yet to come. At the end of February 2004, following an insurgency that forced the resignation of President Aristide three years into his second presidential term, the United States and the United Nations intervened again in Haiti. This time, however, the international community (largely the United States and France) had refused to intervene to support the democratically elected government of Jean-Bertrand Aristide, waiting instead until the armed opposition to him had gained control of the majority of the country and was poised to attack Port-au-Prince. There seems little doubt that Aristide was put in a "resign or else" position. In this case, the failure of timely support for Aristide's besieged government led to Haiti's collapse into the category of "failed states," necessitating what almost all analysts see as the need for a long-term United Nations peacekeeping force in the country. (See Soderlund, 2006.)

■ **Notes**

1. Thanks go to Ralph Nelson, who, in collaboration with Professor Soderlund, worked on a number of research projects focused on attempts to establish

democracy in Haiti following the ouster of the Duvalier dictatorship. Background material for this chapter relies on material contained in Chapters 3, 4, and 5, written by Soderlund and Nelson for *Mass Media and Foreign Policy: Post-Cold War Crises in the Caribbean,* edited by Soderlund and published by Praeger in 2003.

2. While the 1991 coup has been widely attributed to General Cédras, according to Roland Perusse, it was actually initiated by a group of enlisted men under the leadership of Major [later Lt. Col.] Michel François of the Haitian police, who sent a group of armed men to the home of General Cédras. "Cédras was taken at gunpoint to military command headquarters, where François told Cédras to assume his role as general, or he would be killed or sent away. Cédras complied." (Perusse, 1995, 19)

3. This study of television news covered the six weeks prior to the September 20 intervention. On the basis of a review of the Vanderbilt Television News Archive over the entire six-month period, we find no evidence that would appear to contradict this finding.

4. Reported as "cocktail party conversation," Mr. Slocombe would neither confirm nor deny using the term "psychopath."

5. The Haitian president continued to be vague with respect to support for an invasion. According to Sean Murphy, "In a letter dated July 29, 1994, to Secretary-General Boutros Boutros-Ghali, Aristide called for the international community 'to take swift and determined action' to help Haiti but stopped short of expressly calling for military intervention." (1996, 268)

6. The Balsero crisis also distracted the media from covering events in Haiti. Rick Bragg reported that "foreign journalists, who had chronicled the abuses suffered by Haitians, have left the country by the dozens in the last few weeks, many seeking visas to Cuba." (1994, Aug. 26, A10)

7

Burundi, 1996:
United Nations and
African Intervention Initiatives Falter

Walter C. Soderlund

Background

Burundi is located in the Great Lakes region of Africa. Unusual for contemporary African states, neither it nor its northern neighbor Rwanda is an artificial creation resulting from colonial rule; rather both were traditional African kingdoms that had been colonized by Germany in the late nineteenth century. (Reyntjens 2000, 6) Following the German defeat in World War I, they were turned over to Belgium as a single "mandate" under the League of Nations system of preparing the colonies of the defeated powers for independence. After World War II, they became separate United Nations Trust Territories, again under Belgian control. Burundi and Rwanda share a similar ethnic composition—85 percent Hutu, 14 percent Tutsi, and 1 percent Twa. (Lemarchand, 1970, 1)

In addition to Rwanda, Burundi shares borders with Zaire (later to become the Democratic Republic of the Congo) and Tanzania. Extending over about 28,000 square kilometers, Burundi is one the smallest countries in Africa (roughly the size of Belgium), and in 1993 it had a population of approximately 5.5 to 6 million people, making it the second most densely populated country in Africa. (O'Ballance, 2000, 148) It was also very poor: "With a per capita income of US$140 in 1998, it rank[ed] as the third-poorest country included in World Bank statistics." (Reyntjens, 2000, 5)

Peter Goodspeed notes that "like neighbouring Rwanda, Burundi has a tragic history of ethnic division between the majority Hutus and the ruling Tutsi minority." (2005, Apr. 22, A9) However, according to René Lemarchand, there were important differences between the two:

"Only in Rwanda was Tutsi overrule highly institutionalized. Burundi society was characterized by greater complexity and fluidity, with power gravitating into the hands of a princely oligarchy (the so-called *ganwa*) whose identity was separate from that of either Hutu or Tutsi." (1994, 581, note 2) Lemarchand points to yet another difference:

> Unlike Rwanda . . . Burundi was spared the trauma of ethnic conflict long enough to accede to Independence in 1962 as a constitutional monarchy under a mixed Hutu-Tutsi regime. Not until 1965 did the ripple effects of the Rwanda revolution trigger a sequence of events that led to the overthrow of the monarchy by the army and the capture of the state by Tutsi elements. (1994, 583–84)

■ Roots of the Crisis

Just as the conflicts in Liberia and Sierra Leone are linked, so too are those in Rwanda and Burundi. In fact, Lemarchand maintains that "Rwanda and Burundi cannot be understood independently of each other. Historically, and to this day, ethnic strife in the former has had a profound effect on the destinies of the latter, and vice versa." (1994, 585) The Rwandan Revolution of 1959 not only increased hostilities between Tutsi and Hutu in that country, but set in motion a wave of Tutsi refugees across the border into Burundi, which the refugees then used as a base for regaining power in Rwanda. As one might have predicted, tensions between Tutsis and Hutus within Burundi also increased, leading to large-scale massacres of Hutus by the still-dominant Tutsis—the first such act of violence occurring in 1965, with much larger numbers of Hutus killed in 1972, and again in 1993—the latter resulting in a low-intensity civil war that in 1996 was increasing in intensity and leading to calls for an international intervention.

Although Tutsi-Hutu relations in Burundi were less structured than in Rwanda, Warren Weinstein and Robert Schrire argue that since "there were only two contending ethnic groups at every level of society, and that ethnic bifurcation coincided more generally with other cleavages . . . [this] . . . led elite members of each group to view all or most conflict—independent of its nature—as ethnic." (1976, 10) Moreover, Lemarchand maintains that the spill-over of Hutu-Tutsi conflict from Rwanda to Burundi was more or less inevitable: "Even in the absence of ethnic affinities with their Rwandese kinsmen, it is difficult to see how the Hutu of Burundi could have remained insensitive to the implications of [Hutu] majority rule [in Rwanda]." (1970, 344)

Leonce Ndikumana describes the crucial October 1965 coup d'état led by Hutu army officers that had been preceded in January by the assassination of the Hutu Prime Minister, Pierre Ngendandumwe. That coup failed, and in its aftermath the army was purged of Hutu personnel. As Ndikumana notes: "With the decapitation of the Hutu Leadership, Tutsi gained control of the government and military." (2000, 433)

Much worse violence was yet to come. Peter Goodspeed claims that "in 1972, the Tutsi-dominated army killed up to 200,000 Hutus." (2005, Apr. 22, A9) According to Lemarchand, "The 1972 genocide of Hutu civilians by the all-Tutsi army, following an aborted Hutu-instigated uprising, was the cataclysmic event behind the reconstruction of group identities, i.e., the dehumanisation of Tutsi by Hutu and the denial of Hutu identity by Tutsi." (1994, 590) Filip Reyntjens likewise refers to the 1972 violence as "a major watershed in Burundian contemporary history, and it still provides a crucial point of reference for the two main ethnic groups today." (2000, 7) Warren Weinstein attributes the violence to the "contradictions that reside within Burundi society . . . a small, poor country, highly dependent on foreign aid . . . [which at the same time was] . . . one of the most densely populated states in Africa, leading to fierce competition for few resources." He notes parenthetically that the 1972 killings "generated little interest or comment from governments other that of Belgium." (1972, 27–28)

■ Events Precipitating the Crisis

A democratic election in 1993 was won by an ethnic Hutu candidate, Melchior Ndayaye, and in the view of Edgar O'Ballance, that election "was thought to mark the end of domination by the minority Tutsi tribe." (2000, 148–49) However, on October 21, 1993, the predominantly Tutsi army carried out a coup d'état in which its soldiers murdered Burundi's newly elected president; following the coup "another 300,000 died and 800,000 were forced to flee." (Goodspeed, 2005, Apr. 22, A19)

René Lemarchand maintains that the 1993 assassination of that state's first popularly elected Hutu president contributed directly to the Rwandan genocide in 1994. (1994, 585) It began a smoldering civil war in Burundi that by the summer of 1996 had resulted in the deaths of over 150,000 people. (Reuters, 1996, June 17, A6) It also contributed to the crisis that beset eastern Zaire in the years that followed, since that crisis stemmed in considerable measure from the influx of refugees, mainly Hutu, produced by the 1994 genocide in Rwanda and the civil war in Burundi.

Former Tanzanian President Julius Nyerere identified the two fundamental problems facing Burundi—the "fear of annihilation" on the part of Tutsis and "resentment" over being denied their rights on the part of Hutus. (cited in McKinley, 1996, July 4, A2) In spite of an attempted post-1993 "power sharing" arrangement, whereby the country would have a Hutu president and a Tutsi prime minister, the political situation became increasingly dysfunctional, thanks to a lack of consensus among politicians and the fact that real power remained with the Tutsi-dominated army unable to control a growing Hutu insurgency. Atrocities were committed by both sides, as both sought "to terrorize the population." (McKinley, 1996, July 6, I5) Fears of a repeat of the Rwandan genocide prompted both African and UN efforts at getting an international peacekeeping force into Burundi in the summer of 1996 to attempt to curb the increased violence.

These efforts were frustrated by yet another military coup in Burundi in July 1996, that seemingly had brought an even more hardline Tutsi military government to power. This led to a further deterioration of an already fragile human rights situation in the country. Within a month of the coup, "more that 6,000 people . . . [were] . . . reported to have been killed in various parts of Burundi." (Amnesty International, 1996, Aug. 22) It was the 1996 coup, more specifically how the West should respond to it, that refocused international attention on the problems in Burundi that by this time were not only intertwined with those in Rwanda but were contributing to those in eastern Zaire as well.

Strength of the International Response: Rank order=8
   A. **Did the Humanitarian Crisis Result in an International Intervention? No**

Determinants of the International Response
   A. **Severity of the Crisis: Rank order=4**
      i. **Number of deaths: (short-term) 150,000-plus; (long-term) 250,000 to 350,000**
      "Over the last few years, human rights groups say, up to 150,000 civilians have been killed, often in massacres carried out by Hutu guerrillas or the Tutsi-led army." (Crossette, 1996, July 25, A1)
      "Throughout 1993 there were clear signs of escalating violence emanating from Burundi, where the deaths of up to 250,000

people went largely unnoticed by media and policymakers alike." (Minear, et al., 1996, 63)

". . . in 1993, after Tutsi soldiers murdered Melchior Ndayaye, Burundi's first Hutu president, another 300,000 died and 800,000 were forced to flee." (Goodspeed, 2005, Apr. 22, A9)

"In 1972 . . . tensions burst into massive violence which took the lives of some 100,000–200,000 Burundians." (Weinstein, 1972, 27)

"[In 1972] . . . after an abortive coup by Hutu against their Tutsi rulers, there were massacres of unprecedented magnitude. An estimated 200,000 Hutu were systematically slaughtered." (Melvern, 2004, 10)

ii. **Number of refugees and displaced persons: (short-term) 100,000; (long-term) 500,000 to 1,500,000**

"Population at Risk" (1995) 900,000 (Weiss and Collins, 1996, 5–7, Table I.1)

"The United Nations says more than 100,000 people have been displaced by fighting in Burundi as Hutu-led rebels confront the Tutsi army across wide areas of the country." (Crossette, 1996, May 9, A13)

". . . the UNHCR estimated that more than 500 000 Burundi refugees had fled since the [1993] coup began, 342 000 into Rwanda, 214 000 into Tanzania and 21 000 into Zaire." (O'Ballance, 2000, 149)

"[As of December 1993] . . . the government stated that at least 1.5 million Burundi's had fled their homes." (O'Ballance, 2000, 150)

"Aside from the killings [in the 1993 coup], the violence also caused huge populations movements. About 700,000 people, mainly Hutu, fled to neighbouring countries (400,000 to Rwanda, 250,000 to Tanzania, and 60,000 to Zaïre." (Reyntjens, 1995, 15)

iii. **Likelihood of conflict spreading to other states: 5 *high***

    a. **Number of shared borders: 3**

        Rwanda, Zaire (the Democratic Republic of the Congo), Tanzania

    b. **Involvement of bordering states**

"It is important to stress that Rwanda and Burundi cannot be understood independently of each other. Historically, and to this day, ethnic strife in the former has had a profound impact of the destinies of the latter and vice versa. Just as the Hutu-led revolution in Rwanda has contributed directly to the sharpening of ethnic polarities in Burundi, so the assassination of that state's first popularly elected President . . . at the hands of the all-Tutsi army on 21 October 1993, provides the indispensable backdrop for an understanding of the Rwandan genocide." (Lemarchand, 1994, 585)

"Burundi can only be understood in a broader regional perspective. Particularly since the first Congo War, which in 1996–97 brought Laurent-Désiré Kabila to power in Kinshasa, several conflicts have tended to merge: these include the Great Lakes conflict, which has been the most immediately visible one, and the Sudanese and Angolan civil wars. The geographical proximity of these hotbeds of instability and the play of objective alliances (where all actors reason in terms of 'the enemy of my enemy is my friend') have linked up these conflicts, thus opening the prospect of the emergence of a war zone stretching from Luanda to Asmara." (Reyntjens, 2000, 6)

"If Burundi slips further into chaos, it will spill into Rwanda, its neighbor to the north. . . . The danger is that an ethnic war between Hutu and Tutsi in Burundi and Rwanda could engulf the region, sending hundreds of thousands more refugees into Tanzania and Zaire where 1.7 million Hutu are now living in camps along the border." (McKinley, 1996, July 12, A3)

". . . violence could restart in Burundi . . . [and] . . . spill back over into Rwanda as refugees move from country to country." (Crossette, 1996, July 25, A1)

B. Pre-intervention "Assessment of Risk": 5 *difficult*

"Achieving lasting peace . . . [in the Great Lakes Region] . . . will be as difficult as implementing the Camp David Agreement and as complex as sustaining the Dayton accords." (Madeleine Albright, cited in Lemarchand, 1998a, 41)

"Fearing that Burundi is on the verge of a political collapse, the United Nations is assembling an intervention force that could be used to prevent the country's ethnic Tutsi and Hutu from beginning a genocidal civil war. . . . Before an international force can be sent, however, the United Nations may need as many as 20,000 troops and Security Council approval." (Crossette, 1996, July 25, A1)

"Like the former Yugoslavia, a country as deadly as Burundi may need a Tito more than it needs elections." (McNeil, 1996, July 30, A4)

C. Extent of "National Interest Involvement":

i. The international community: 1 *low*

"We have been in consultation with the [UN] member states. We have received some offers but not enough really to say that if we had to go in today, we will be able to do it. . . . *But what is certain is that . . . [the United States] . . . will not put troops on the ground,* but they will give logistical support and maybe offer airlift capability." When asked if the above response was satisfactory, the Under-Secretary-General for Peacekeeping Operations replied: "It's not an ideal response because in a situation like this you may need to intervene very quickly and . . . you will ideally want to rely on those governments . . . who have extensive logistical support and airlift capabilities to either join the operation or lead it. . . . *at the end of the day if the response is not sufficiently strong, we may not be able to put in a force.*" (Kofi Annan, cited in Hunter-Gault, 1996, Aug. 1, italics added)

"The question is whether enough people in Western Europe or the United States care enough to want their governments to get involved [in Burundi]. . . . The signs are not promising." (Rieff, 1996, June 12, A23)

"For months, Burundi has been under heavy pressure from the United States and the European Union as well as its neighbors to halt the bloodshed. Burundi's foreign aid has been cut off and the economy is in a shambles." (McKinley, 1996, July 4, A2)

"The West has made it known it will not allow Burundi to turn into another Rwanda." (McKinley, 1996, July 12, A3)

". . . Country after country has stalled at committing troops to the [UN] force, and there is a danger of repeating what happened [in Rwanda] in 1994." (Crossette, 1996, July 25, A1)

ii. United States: 1 *low*

"[Burundi is a country] . . . of zero strategic interest to the U.S." (Friedman, 1996, Jan. 24, A19)

"The 1972 genocide in Burundi, resulting in the deaths of one hundred to two hundred thousand Hutu, hardly made a ripple on American consciousness." (Lemarchand, 1998a, 41)

"The Great Lakes region has never been a high priority on . . . [America's] . . . African policy agenda, nor for that matter on the research agenda of political scientists." (Lemarchand, 1998a, 41)

"Burundi, a poor, landlocked, French-speaking country . . . is hardly central to United States policy. There are no historical ties . . . minerals or sea lanes. Until last week [July 25], American interest was mostly humanitarian. . . . But most important, State Department officials want *not* to be the leader in righting the world's Burundi policy." (McNeil, 1996, Aug. 4, IV6, italics in the original)

iii. France: 3 *medium*

"The French, who sent their own force to Rwanda in reaction to the massacre there in 1994, say they do not want to be alone in the field again." (Crossette, 1996, Jan. 30, A2)

iv. Africa: 5 *high*

"You know, the regional heads of states met and took a rather strong stand against the coup d'état and recommended implementation of sanctions. And they are also pressing ahead with the formation of an intervention force." (Kofi Annan, cited in Hunter-Gault, 1996, Aug. 1)

"Africa must end its image 'as a continent synonymous with endless conflict.'" (Benjamin Mkapa, President of Tanzania, cited in AP 1996, June 26, A9)

". . . Only Chad, Malawi and Zambia have committed battalions for possible duty in Burundi . . . [with] . . . Ethiopia, Tanzania and Uganda . . . prepared to join in later. . . . South Africa, with the continent's best equipped army, has not responded to repeated requests to lead or join the force." (Crossette, 1996, July 25, A1)

D. Mass Media: February 10 to August 9, 1996

i. "Alerting" function (volume of television and newspaper coverage): N=45; Rank order=7

   a. Television coverage: Rank order=8

      Total (ABC, CBS, NBC): N=9

      In-depth: N=4

   b. *New York Times* coverage: N=36; Rank order=7

ii. "Evaluative" function (intervention framing in the *New York Times*)

      Pro-intervention frames: N=5

      Anti-intervention frames: N=1

iii. Assessment of media coverage

It should come as no surprise that American mass media did not have a strong history of reporting on events in Burundi. Warren Weinstein notes that this neglect was apparent as early as 1972, with respect to the mass killings that occurred there at that time:

> It is noteworthy that aside from a few newspaper reports that emphasized the sensational aspects of the 1972 revolt and its aftermath, little more was said. While the *New York Times* saw fit to print articles in its Sunday magazine section on Bangladesh and Uganda, it did not print one on Burundi. (1972, 27)

Linda Melvern makes the same point with respect to the 1972 genocide: "After a few days in the headlines, Burundi sank back into obscurity. The killings continued." (2004, 10) Moreover, Lindsey Hilsum notes that in the fall of 1993

> The killing of between 50,000 and 100,000 Burundians and the subsequent exodus of 700,000 people to Rwanda, Tanzania and Zaire was not big news in Britain or the United States. It was slightly bigger in France and much bigger in Belgium. Aid agencies lobbied for coverage and failed. . . . There was a sense of déjá vu and a lack of interest in the complex political causes of the tragedy. (Hilsum, 2007, 170–71)

What is especially noteworthy about media coverage of the 1996 crisis in Burundi is the weakness of the critical dimension of television coverage—a total of nine stories over six months, only four of which qualified as in-depth treatments, can in no way be considered sufficient to have alerted the American people to the existence of a crisis.[1] Coverage in the *New York Times* was somewhat stronger (36 stories), but even that number only places Burundi first among the four least-covered crises.

Our study period begins in February, six months before it became clear in early August that the military coup d'état carried out on July 25 had largely ended active initiatives on the part of both the UN and regional African nations to mount peace enforcement interventions in Burundi.

Coverage of Burundi in the *New York Times* was focused largely on the July coup led by Pierre Buyoya, with close to three-quarters of material dealing with the anticipation of a coup, the coup itself, and its immediate aftermath. Just over half of the material originated from Africa (33 percent from Burundi), while another third came from the United States, most of which originated from the United Nations in New York. Coverage was supplied by local staff and wire services in about equal numbers; James McKinley and Donald McNeil reported for the *New York Times* from Africa, while Barbara Crossette

Table 7.1 *New York Times* **Coverage of Burundi**

Panel 1 – Date:	N	%	Panel 2 – Dateline:	N	%
First 2 Months	5	14%	United States	12	33%
Second 2 Months	5	14%	Burundi	12	33%
Third 2 Months	26	72%	Africa (other)	7	19%
		100%	Other	3	8%
			Unknown	2	6%
					99%

Panel 3 – Source:	N	%	Panel 4 – Type of Content:	N	%
Local Staff	20	55%	Front-page News	1	3%
AP	7	19%	Inside-page News	27	75%
AFP	0	0%	Editorials	2	6%
Reuters	7	19%	Op-ed Features	3	8%
Professional/Academic	2	6%	Photos	1	3%
Other	0	0%	Letters	0	0%
		99%	Other	2	6%
					101%

Newspaper Coverage, by Date, Dateline, Source, and Type (February 10 to August 9, 1996) N=36

covered the United Nations. Inside-page news accounted for 75 percent of content, while high-impact items (one front-page story, two editorials, and three feature/op-ed articles) accounted for 17 percent of total content.

In mid-January, a month prior to our study period, reports of Hutu-Tutsi ethnic violence in Burundi appeared and put the humanitarian intervention issue prominently on the agenda. In a front page story, citing a figure of 100,000 killed to that point, James McKinley and Donald McNeil informed readers that the violence that followed the 1993 coup "is evolving into a civil war that threatens to overwhelm . . . [Burundi's] . . . coalition Government." They also reported the United Nations proposed response—that "troops be sent in to protect relief workers and *for the deployment of a United Nations force to Zaire to intervene should the nation descend into chaos.*" (1996, Jan. 14, I1, italics added)

In an op-ed piece that also appeared in January, Thomas Friedman compared what was happening in Burundi to the murderous events in Rwanda two years earlier: "For the moment, Burundi is Rwanda in slow motion. . . . The best case scenario is for increasing violence; the worst case is for a Rwanda-style cataclysm that will spill hundreds of thousands more refugees across Central Africa." Invoking an argument similar to the one he had advanced four years earlier with respect to Somalia, Friedman pointed out that only the United States "has the power to catalyze the world to get organized to stop mass killing once it starts." He then asked the critical question: "Should the Clinton Administration use that power to try to stop potential genocide in a country of zero strategic interest to the U.S.?" His answer was "yes," because he didn't think "it would take that much, and a little preventive diplomacy here can save a lot of anguish later." Friedman went on to explain that "the Clinton Administration has explored with its allies the idea of putting together a rapid reaction force—with the U.S. contribution confined to logistical support—to curb any mass killing in Burundi if it starts." (1996, Jan. 24, A19) At the end of January 1996, the UN Security Council rejected the idea of a rapid reaction force, passing instead a resolution calling for "restraint" on the part of all parties. It was reported that no further action would be considered until February "at the earliest." (Crosette, 1996, Jan. 30, A2)

At the beginning of our study period in mid-February it was reported that Secretary-General Boutros-Ghali had indeed reopened the rapid reaction force option, requesting a preventive multinational force numbering 25,000 troops to be positioned in Zaire, with "war powers." The United States agreed to the formation of this force but indicated a preference that nations contributing troops keep them at home until needed. (Crossette, 1996, Feb. 22, A6) This initiative, in its American configuration, failed to gain support in the Security Council due to concerns on the part of European nations that "the action could be seen to be authorizing a foreign invasion." (NYT, 1996, March 6, A5) In a March op-ed piece, Cyrus Vance and David Hamburg argued that Burundi was pivotal "to breaking the cycle of mass violence in Central Africa." They did not, however, pursue the idea of an international intervention force being sent there. Instead, they cited the necessity of persuading "extremists in both ethnic groups of the futility and dreadful consequences of violence." (Vance and Hamburg, 1996, Mar. 9, I23)

It was not until early May that increased ethnic violence in Burundi, support for a UN-led intervention on the part of the Clinton administration, and efforts by the UN Secretary-General to find "volunteer" nations to participate in such an effort brought the humanitarian crisis in Burundi to the surface again:

> Concerned that Burundi is again on the verge of widespread violence, the
> Clinton Administration and peacekeeping officials . . . [at the UN] . . . are
> urging an international contingency force to be assembled to restore
> order, if necessary, *without the approval of Burundi's government.* . . . [It
> was reported, however, that] . . . no volunteers have come forward [in re-
> sponse to Boutros-Ghali's request]." (Crossette, 1996, May 9, A13, italics
> added)

Crossette also notes that while the United States was not prepared to
lead or commit troops directly to such a peacekeeping mission, it
would, however, "provide transportation, logistics and communications." She also reports that the administration preferred that the
planning for a possible intervention be done by the UN Department
of Peacekeeping rather than by any single nation. (1996, May 9, A13)

Also contained in the Crossette article is the invocation of the
"state sovereignty" argument by the Burundi government, which ob-
jected to a Chapter VII–based intervention on the grounds "that it is
unacceptable interference that may provoke further bloodshed, not
stop it." A UN spokesperson indicated, however, that with Security
Council approval, the UN did have the power to undertake a military
intervention, in spite of such opposition on the part of Burundi's government. (Crossette, 1996, May 9, A13)

Intermittent reports of ongoing violence continued during May
and June, focused on the killing of three Swiss Red Cross workers in
early June. This was described as "the worst . . . [attack] . . . on foreigners since Burundi's civil war began in 1993." (*NYT,* 1996, June 6,
A3) It was the killing of the Red Cross workers, who were attempting to get safe water to a threatened population, that occasioned an
op-ed piece on Burundi by David Rieff. Rieff explored the perils of
humanitarian action in light of the fact that the groups pursuing the
path of violence do not want humanitarian activities to succeed: "For
those who want the killing to go on, and the hatred and fear to grow,
the presence of humanitarian workers, especially if they are effective,
is dangerous." (1996, June 12, A23) He also counseled Western governments "that underwriting humanitarian organizations is no substitute for political engagement," arguing that

> no humanitarian effort, no matter how brave or inspired, can prevent the
> sack of Monrovia, the siege of Sarajevo, the Rwandan genocide or the
> slow-motion genocide now underway in Burundi. *The hard reality is that
> one stops genocide with diplomatic pressure and, as a last resort, military
> force.* (1996, June 12, A23, italics added)

Rieff's conclusion, however, was that signs for a western military intervention in Burundi did not look promising.

Another initiative for a possible international intervention was reported toward the end of June, when, at a regional conference of African states, Burundi's government, which earlier was reported to have been divided on the issue, made "their first appeal for foreign help to end ethnic killing in the Central African nation." (AP, 1996, June 26, A9) This request led to the formulation of a peacekeeping plan brokered by former Tanzanian President, Julius Nyerere, who called for an African regional intervention force to which Kenya, Uganda, Tanzania, and Ethiopia would contribute troops.

This intervention option raised questions regarding who would control the force, as well as what the nature of its mission would be. Burundi's Tutsi army insisted on command of the force and saw its mission as assisting it in quelling the Hutu rebellion; understandably, the Hutu guerrillas found these conditions unacceptable and rejected them, claiming that Burundi's army was the force that needed to be controlled. (McKinley, 1996, July 4, A2) By mid-July the African initiative appeared hopelessly bogged down over solutions to these important issues, as any agreement had to satisfy the positions of "hardline" Tutsi politicians and the Tutsi army, Hutu and Tutsi moderates, and Hutu guerrilla forces—not an easy task, to say the least. (McKinley, 1996, July 6, I5)

Neither was the UN attempt to organize an international intervention meeting with much success. In spite of Barbara Crossette's warning that "what happened in Rwanda in 1994" was highly possible in its southern neighbor (1996, July 25, A1), responses to requests from Under-Secretary-General Kofi Annan for contributions to an intervention force were disappointing at best, with the United States reported as only willing to contribute to logistics and communications, South Africa not responding at all to requests to lead or join the operation, and only three African states committed to sending troops, with another two willing to send troops later. In that some 20,000 to 25,000 troops were reported needed to arrive at a desired force level, Annan acknowledged, "at the end of the day if the response is not sufficiently strong, we may not be able to put in a force." (cited in Hunter-Gault, 1996, Aug. 1)

On July 25, plans for possible interventions by both the UN and African nations were overtaken by events—specifically, a coup d'état, carried out by Burundi's army and bringing back to power Major

Pierre Buyoya. Buyoya had ruled for a short time following a coup in 1987, and it was he who was responsible for the elections in 1993 that resulted in the election of the Hutu president who was killed shortly thereafter.

Although the coup was a surprise to practically no one (it had been anticipated for several weeks), the *New York Times* did not editorialize on the resulting crisis until it had occurred. The editorial acknowledged that "the festering crisis in Burundi is of a kind that sorely tests the wisdom and capacity of outsiders," and lamented the absence of a UN "standing rapid deployment force" to deal with it, especially in light of the fact that "multinational peacemaking has been discredited in Somalia and Liberia." At this time, however, the *New York Times* was willing to go no further than to endorse condemnation of "any coup led by Tutsi hard-liners." (*NYT*, 1996, July 25, A22)

The initial response to the coup by Secretary-General Boutros-Ghali was that the UN "will not accept a change of government by force or other illegitimate means." (cited in McNeil, 1996, July 26, A3) As for a possible international intervention, the coup seemed to have driven the final nail in its coffin, for while Tutsi hard-liners and Hutu guerrillas could not agree on much, they were of one mind that "they will attack any peacekeeping force that enters [Burundi] without their permission." (McNeil, 1996, July 26, A3)

The coup also prompted the second (and final) *New York Times* editorial on the crisis. This editorial reviewed the reasons for the failure of the peacekeeping initiatives that had taken place to the end of July—namely that "they were quickly repudiated by extremists in both camps. Each side imagined that foreigners would restrain its fighters, leaving its civilians vulnerable to deadly violence." While the editorial promoted diplomacy as a first approach to conflict resolution, it acknowledged that "averting genocide may require a United Nations military presence." Recognizing the risks involved and understanding the reluctance of countries to commit troops to a hostile environment, the editorial nevertheless concluded with a strong call for UN action: "*still, the experience of Rwanda,* where the U.N. failed to halt a bloodbath many believe could have been checked, *must not be repeated in Burundi: There is still time for the U.N. to act.*" (*NYT*, 1996, July 27, I22 italics added)

As it turned out, Major Buyoya appeared, initially at least, not to be the hard-liner that had been anticipated. Instead of further polarizing the situation, he sought to end the ethnic violence by calling for reconciliation between Hutu and Tutsi; his message to the population was "Be Only Burundian." (McNeil, 1996, July 28, I6; see also Mc-Neil, 1996, July 30) By the beginning of August, a rift appeared between African states and Western Europe and the United States. The former took a strong stance against the coup (voting to apply sanctions against Burundi until constitutional rule had been restored, while still discussing "the possibility of putting together an international military force to maintain order in Burundi." (AP, 1996, Aug. 1, A8) The latter appeared to conclude that perhaps Buyoya was the best (if not the only) option available and were "prepared to give . . . [him] . . . a chance."[2] (Crossette, 1996, July 30, A4) In any event, as Donald McNeil reported in a post-coup News Analysis piece,

> American officials, soured by their experience in Somalia, have said they would, at most, transport and feed another country's troops. They have reason to be reluctant. The hilly malarious land would be even harder to invade than Somalia . . . .The Burundian army is well-armed and xenophobic, and the Tutsis have warrior legends to live up to. Meanwhile, the Hutu rebels have said they, too, will shoot at foreign troops. (1996, Aug. 4, IV6)

The conclusion for McNeil was don't expect "an American peace enforcement mission" any time soon—and he was right.

In the months following the July coup d'état, in spite of the conciliatory rhetoric of Major Buyoya, ethnic violence in the country continued, and international concern over the situation remained high. Rwanda's Paul Kagame abandoned Tutsi kinship with Pierre Buyoya and joined with his African neighbors in applying sanctions against Burundi, telling Burundi's new military ruler that he had until "August 15 to restore constitutional rule or all air and road links . . . [between Rwanda and Burundi] . . . would be severed." It was reported on August 9 that Chile, serving at the time on the UN Security Council, proposed a plan calling for sanctions and negotiations, but holding open "the ultimate threat of military intervention." (Crossette, 1996, Aug. 9, A9)

Yet no such intervention occurred. Clearly the July 25 coup had taken the wind out of the sails of any possible international intervention—either UN-led or African-led. Sanctions against Burundi continued, as did the ethnic violence. However, the crisis in Burundi was soon eclipsed in magnitude by the refugee crisis in eastern Zaire (along borders with Rwanda and Burundi), which resulted in the melding of the violence in Burundi with that in Zaire, in what has been called the

"First Congo War." In early October, that crisis brought the issue of an international intervention in the region front and center once again, and prompted a UN authorization of a Canadian-led intervention force—"Operation Assurance"—which was never deployed. (See Chapter 8, this volume.)

▪ Overall Evaluation of the Crisis Response

Unfortunately, the long-standing ethnic conflict between Tutsi and Hutu besetting Burundi did not go away. Finally, on May 21, 2004, the UN Security Council approved the creation of the "United Nations Operation in Burundi" (ONUB). In so doing, it authorized a force of 5,600 military personnel

> in order to support and help to implement the efforts undertaken by Burundians to restore lasting peace and bring about national reconciliation, as provided under the Arusha Agreement. . . . The Council also requested the Secretary-General to conclude agreements with States neighboring Burundi to enable ONUB forces to cross their respective borders in pursuit of armed combatants, as may be necessary while carrying out their mandate. (UN, 2004, May 21)

Some eight years after the failed efforts of 1996, the ongoing ethno-political violence in Burundi finally merited an international intervention.

▪ Notes

1. Six of the nine television stories on Burundi dealt with the July 26 coup and its immediate aftermath, while three reported on violence (including the killing of Red Cross workers) in the period prior to the coup.

2. Following his departure from office in 1993, Major Pierre Buyoya had a positive and ongoing relationship with the United States. This included a grant to his foundation to promote democracy in the region as well as connections with the Carter Foundation. (See McNeil 1996, Aug. 4, IV6.)

8

Zaire (Democratic Republic of the Congo), 1996: "Operation Assurance," The Intervention That Never Was

Walter C. Soderlund and E. Donald Briggs

■ Background

The Democratic Republic of the Congo, in 1996 known as Zaire, is the third-largest country in Africa, about the size of Western Europe or the eastern half of the United States. At the time of the crisis in the mid-1990s, it had a population estimated at between 40 and 45 million people. Zaire was the dominant country in Central Africa, sharing borders with no fewer than nine countries—Sudan, the Central African Republic, the Republic of the Congo, Angola, Zambia, Tanzania, Burundi, Rwanda, and Uganda—and, as such, serves as the crucial link in the cross-Africa "war zone" identified by Filip Reyntjens. (2000, 6)

Ethnic conflicts occurring in its neighbors, especially in Rwanda and Burundi (see Chapters 5 and 7, this volume), exacerbated ethnic tensions in Zaire. As well, over the years Zaire's long-time dictator, Mobuto Sese Seko, had contributed to problems in adjoining states, especially in Angola, through his long-time support of UNITA rebel forces under the command of Jonas Savimbi. (See Chapter 10, this volume.) When Mobutu became seriously ill in 1996, and his regime came under sustained attack, some neighboring states supported him while others contributed military forces to aid in his overthrow.

As with Rwanda and Burundi, the roots of Zaire's problems are to be found in European colonization. Following an initial period during which it was the personal colony of Belgium's King Leopold II, the absolute horrors of which are recounted by Adam Hochschild[1] (1998), the Congo became a formal Belgian colony in 1908, which it remained until achieving its independence in June 1960.

Among the legacies of Belgian colonial rule was an indigenous population that was almost totally unprepared for self-government. As explained by King Gordon:

> The administration of the Belgian Congo, its public and technical services, were run almost exclusively by Europeans. Very few Congolese held positions of executive or operational responsibility. By 1958, no more than 10,000 (out of a population of 13,500,000) were attending secondary or vocational training schools. Until 1956 there was no university in the Congo, and in 1960 there were only seventeen university graduates who had received an education in Europe. The national security force, the *Force publique,* was officered entirely by Belgians and few educational facilities were open to the largely illiterate Congolese troops. (1962, 9–10)

Alan Merriam adds, moreover, that as late as 1955 "the situation in the Congo was one of unsuspecting calm, unbroken by almost any suggestion of independence . . . or even of any concrete thinking of future aims." (1961, 68) Not surprisingly, hasty independence, following years of political neglect, led directly to the collapse of the new Congo government. In the view of Ernest Lefever,

> When externally imposed authority, the only element of order and cohesion in the vast expanse of a territory as large as Western Europe, was abruptly withdrawn, the endemic centrifugal forces of tribalism, regionalism, and conflicting political ambitions asserted themselves. Chaos and violence followed. (1967, 6)

■ Roots of the Crisis

In discussing the Great Lakes region, René Lemarchand refers to a "chain of causality between past and present atrocities." (1998b, 5) In this context, it is important to note that the crisis that beset Zaire in 1996 had obvious roots not only in the "spill-over" of refugees from the Tutsi-Hutu conflicts in Rwanda and Burundi, but also in the events surrounding Congolese independence in 1960 that led to major Belgian and UN interventions into the new country's affairs. These interventions were subsequently followed by the Congo's entanglement in the Cold War machinations of the United States and the Soviet Union.

Troubles for the Congo began immediately upon independence on July 1, 1960, in the form of tribal fighting in Leopoldville. On July 5, the *Force publique* mutinied, refusing to obey the orders of their Belgian officers. The country's Prime Minister, Patrice Lumumba, sided with the mutineers, dismissing the Belgian officers and renaming the force the *Armée Nationale Congolaise* (ANC). Very quickly, the situation spun out of control. Mutinous ANC troops assaulted Europeans, inducing a general state of panic. At this point, Belgium intervened unilaterally. Without permission from the Congolese government, Belgium dispatched paratroopers to restore order and assist in the evacuation of civilians who wanted to leave.

Unfortunately this intervention was not accomplished without Congolese casualties, which incited more unrest. The difficult situation confronting the country was further complicated by a proclamation of independence by the province of Katanga, issued by provincial President Moise Tshombe. Thus, on July 11, less than two weeks following independence, the main components of the "Congo Crisis," as it came to be known in the 1960s, were present—the mutiny of the ANC and the Belgian intervention, followed by the proclaimed secession of Katanga. In the midst of this confusion, the UN was called upon to launch a peacekeeping operation that was to remain in the country for four years. (See Hoskyns, 1965; Lefever, 1967.)

The 1960 United Nations intervention in the Congo (ONUC), which was requested by the Congolese government (thus avoiding the state sovereignty issue), confronted two rival interpretations of the problem to be addressed. The first appeared comparatively simple and focused on the inability of the Congolese government to maintain order, leading to the subsequent Belgian intervention, which at least some saw as aiding Tshombe's bid for Katangan independence. The solution here was to replace the Belgians (including those in Katanga) with UN peacekeepers, and to establish a capacity on the part of the Congolese government to maintain law and order.

The second interpretation of the problem was far more basic and far less simple, calling into question the very viability of a Congolese state. Robert Good framed this version of the problem as follows:

> Was . . . [the Congo] . . . the centralized organism maintained by Belgian imperial power, and bequeathed to the legatees of Belgian rule in the Brussels Round Table Resolutions and the Loi *fundamental*. . . . Or was there a deeper reality based upon the essential disunity and artificiality called the Congo, and evidenced by the inability of a central regime without the aid of imperial power to maintain the cohesion of the whole? (1962, 42)

With the exception of Katanga, which remained a problem for the ONUC until the end of 1962, the replacement of Belgian troops went relatively smoothly and was completed by early September 1960.

(Lefever, 1967) However, also in September, Patrice Lumumba, who has been described as heading "the only political party to have a radical program aiming at transforming the economic structure of Zairian society" that was not based on ethnicity (Naniuzeyi, 1999 678), was dismissed as Prime Minister by the country's president, Joseph Kasavubu, resulting in the further enfeeblement of the Congolese government. For his part, Tshombe remained intractable, refusing to let ONUC troops into Katanga. In February 1961, the UN gave ONUC greater latitude in the use of force, and, over the next two years, with the combined applications of force and diplomatic pressure, the Katangan secession finally ended on January 21, 1963.

While ONUC was eventually successful in ridding the country of Belgian troops and foreign mercenaries and also in preserving the territorial integrity of the country, it was far less successful in establishing the conditions for the maintenance of law and order by training the ANC as a responsible force. According to Lefever,

> The division, disunity, and demoralization within the ANC was both a cause and a symptom of the political and tribal disunity and chaos in the Congo. . . . The indiscipline and irresponsibility of Congolese soldiers was a major, if not *the* major threat to internal law and order throughout the entire period. (1967, 9, italics in the original)

If the Congo did not have enough problems, its politics got caught up in the Cold War, as did those of so many newly independent states in Africa. Patrice Lumumba was assassinated in 1961 by Belgian intelligence operatives supported by the CIA, "because he was reputed to have communist sympathies."[2] (Mgbeoji, 2003, 15) In 1965, President Kasavubu again became involved in a power struggle, this time with Prime Minister Moise Tshombe, and it was the ANC's Commander in Chief, Col. Joseph-Désiré Mobutu (later known as Mobuto Sese Seko), who, "assured of Western backing, intervened once more and seized power on November 24, 1965." (Leslie, 1993, 25) As judged by Ikechi Mgbeoji, "In . . . the conspiracies of the Cold War, Mobutu of Zaire . . . fronted as a bulwark against communism, . . . [and] . . . with support of the United States, ruled and ruined Zaire with an iron fist for thirty-two years." (2003, 37)

Mobutu was also a staunch supporter of the Hutu government of Juvénal Habyarimana in Rwanda. In 1996, it was Mobutu Sese Seko whom Laurent Kabila, leader of the Alliance des Forces Démocratiques pour la Libération du Congo-Zaire (AFDL) and previously a supporter of the assassinated Lumumba, sought to overthrow. Kabila was supported in this effort not only by the MPLA government in power in Angola, but also by Yoweri Musevini in Uganda, and Paul Kagame's Rwandan Tutsi army that had emerged victorious following the 1994 genocide.

During the summer of 1994, a new set of problems emerged for Zaire, as an estimated two million Rwandan Hutu refugees fled into the country and were cared for by the UN and other international relief agencies in a series of camps located near the border. In fact, Lindsey Hilsum maintains that very soon into the media coverage of the Rwandan genocide, the plight of refugees came to overshadow the enormity of the killings that were taking place. (2007, 169) Significantly, no attempt was ever made to separate the Hutu militia and *génocidaires* from the legitimate refugee population. Moreover, the Hutu militia took effective control of the refugee camps, and between 1994 and 1996 it used them as bases for cross-border raids into Rwanda. There were also retaliatory attacks by the Rwandan Tutsi army against the camps. As Bruce Jones has pointed out, the situation had all the components of a catastrophe in the making:

> by the fall of 1994 the international community was facing the growing realization that the regime responsible for the genocide had not been truly defeated, merely chased out of the country—some of them thanks to Operation Turquoise—and were now encamped on Rwanda's immediate border in a country run by a political ally. (2001, 140–41)

▪ Events Precipitating the Crisis

In the fall of 1996, Laurent Kabila's two-decade effort to depose Mobutu Sese Seko was to combine with this more recent set of roots of Zaire's problems, resulting in the "First Congo War." (Reyntjens, 2000, 6) As described by Ian Stewart,

> both Tutsis and Hutus—groups who no longer considered each other human—were living as refugees in Zaire. When rebel leader Laurent Kabila set his sights on ousting Mobutu, he used Mobutu's apparent favoritism toward the Hutus to coax Tutsis into his ranks. Kabila recruited hundred, perhaps thousands, of Tutsis into his ranks. . . . First as Zaire and later as the Democratic Republic of Congo, Central Africa's largest country had become a powder keg waiting for a spark. (2002, 122)

Thus developed the confluence of domestic political conflict, stretching back to the days of Congolese independence, with the post-1994 cross-border aftermath of Hutu-Tutsi violence in Rwanda and Burundi that in 1996 saw perhaps a million refugees caught in the middle of military operations to oust Mobutu.

Beginning in August 1995, Mobutu started a campaign to repatriate Rwandan and Burundi refugees and "some 130,000 were forced out of the camps within a matter of days." (Murphy, 1996, 255–56) As time passed, the situation deteriorated; in addition to being killed by shelling from military operations, the refugees remaining in refugee camps in Zaire faced illness and starvation, to the point where it was estimated that "cholera, dysentery and malnutrition were killing 1,000 people a day." (Massey, 2000, 7)

The crisis, complex as it was, was further complicated by situation of the Bayamulenge—ethnic Tutsis living in Eastern Zaire. The Bayamulenge, then about a million in number, had moved into the region when it was still under Belgian rule, and in 1981, Mobutu Sese Seko saw fit to strip them of Zairean citizenship. If dealing with Mobutu were not difficult enough for the Bayamulenge, in the fall of 1996 they had come under attack from remnants of the Rwandan Hutu Interahamwe, who controlled the refugee camps. In mid-October 1996, Zairean officials further aggravated the situation by giving the Bayamulenge two weeks to leave the country. The plight of the Bayamulenge provided added motivation for Rwanda's Paul Kagame to join Laurent Kabila's campaign to oust Mobutu. Filip Reyntjens noted that the "potential for ongoing conflict involves four government armies; a former army [from Rwanda]; and over 10 rebel movements from five countries." (cited in Massey, 2000, 5) It was to this extraordinarily complex humanitarian crisis in Zaire—the "First Congo War"—which the international community was increasingly called upon to respond in the fall of 1996.

■ The "Almost Intervention"

Following its dismal response to the genocide in Rwanda in 1994, over the spring and summer of 1996 there was considerable pressure on the international community (including the UN and major Western and African nations) to respond to the growing humanitarian catastrophe that was developing in Burundi and spreading across the border into Eastern Zaire. A number of possible options were discussed (see Jones, 2001, 140–48), and, although on November 16, 1996, the international community finally did authorize a humanitarian intervention in Zaire in the form of "Operation Assurance" (a force of fifteen thousand under Chapter VII of the UN Charter), this decision was not arrived at easily. In part, this stemmed from the cruel irony that the majority of refugees in Zaire were Hutus, some former soldiers and some who had committed genocide in Rwanda and had been forced to flee following the defeat of the Rwandan Hutu army and militias by Paul Kagame's RPF. Bruce Jones indicates that "by late fall 1994 and certainly by 1995, the aid agencies were aware that they were feeding *génocidaires* and refueling a genocide movement, but there was little choice but to remain in place." (2001, 146; see also Lautze, et al., 1998, 25; Hilsum, 2007, 173)

On the international side, France in particular pressed for an intervention, although, given the controversy surrounding its "Operation Turquoise" in the Rwandan genocide (which, as pointed out in Chapter 5, was widely seen as attempting to support the Hutu Rwandan government), its motives were highly suspect at best. Some believed that France's real interest was to protect Mobutu Sese Seko, whom it had long supported.[3] France, in turn, was extremely sensitive over the linguistic balance of power in Africa, and suspicious of perceived United States support for the Tutsi side, seeing Washington's reluctance to act over the summer and fall of 1996 as part of an "Anglo-Saxon" plot to withhold an international intervention until Kabila, who was supported by Pual Kagame, had achieved victory. For different reasons, both Great Britain and South Africa were reluctant to become involved in an intervention in Zaire. (Massey, 2000, 11)

For his part, the new Rwandan leader, Paul Kagame, was adamantly opposed to an international intervention, which he feared would protect the surviving remnants of the Hutu Rwandan army and the *Interahamwe* militia, who were using the refugee camps as staging grounds for raids across the border. As was the case with the Rwandan genocide of 1994, Kagame preferred to deal with the problem militarily, this time by supporting Kabila's efforts to oust the Hutu-friendly Zairean dictator. Kagame's strategy was to break the hold of the Hutu militia over the camps and then repatriate the refugees to Rwanda. Thus, "in June 1996 . . . the RPF saw the solution in Eastern Zaire as the relatively simple task of 'taking the war to [the Zairean region of] Goma.'" (Jones, 2001, 147) This strategy was implemented in the form of a major RPF offensive in October and November 1996.

The international response to the crisis, "Operation Assurance," as the planned UN mission was named, was to contain military forces from the United States, Great Britain, Canada, and France (later to be augmented by African forces) under command of a bilingual Canadian, General Maurice Baril. Although sanctioned under Chapter VII, the operation's mandate was in fact quite limited: "to use commensurate force to secure specific humanitarian objectives—the 'effective provision' of aid to refugees and the local population, and the 'voluntary and orderly repatriation' of the refugees." (Massey, 2000, 12) Moreover, the operation's mandate was set to expire at the end of March 1997.

In the end, changing conditions on the ground dictated that the international intervention force that had been approved was never deployed. Precisely at the same time as the UN voted to authorize an intervention in Zaire on November 16, the refugee situation began to clear up on its own. Kabila's AFDL and Kagame's RPF forces attacked and defeated the Rwandan Hutus who were in control of major refugee camps, thus allowing the refugees, on their own, to find their way back across the border into Rwanda in staggering numbers: "By 18 November the [World Food Program] raised their estimate to a total of 500,000 people returning to their Rwandan communities from Mugunga and Kibumba camps with a further exodus of 200,000 refugees from the camps around Katale towards Masisi." (Massey, 2000, 14) Given its limited and refugee-oriented mandate, there appeared to be little that an intervention force could do in addition to what was already in progress. When Canadian Foreign Minister Lloyd Axworthy continued to press for an intervention, the Rwandan government responded, "We don't need them. Unless they are edible, they won't be much good." (cited in Massey, 2000, 14) On November 20, the United States scaled down its contribution to the force, and by mid-December 1996 the refugee situation had improved to the point where the UN decided not to deploy the approved "Operation Assurance" force.

Strength of the International Response: Rank order=7
  A. **Did the Humanitarian Crisis Result in an International Intervention? Almost**
  B. **Type of Response:** Combination
    "Operation Assurance" (approved November 16, 1996):
    UN-sanctioned force, to be led by Canada
  C. **Type of UN Involvement:** Chapter VII
  D. **Size of Proposed Intervening Force:**
    ". . . by 16 November . . . [the international community] . . . furnished both a Security Council mandate and promises for a 15,000-strong force to implement it." (Massey, 2000, 12)

    "On 13 November the U.S. government expressed its commitment in principle to providing up to 5,000 troops to the

MNF. In total, with contributions from France, Spain, and others, the proposed force was to comprise 10,000–15,000 troops." (Jones, 2001, 148)

Determinants of the International Response
A. Severity of the Crisis: Rank order=5
i. Number of deaths (short-term): up to 80,000
"This is the biggest crisis in terms of its humanitarian and potential political dimensions that we have seen in Africa since the 1960s. We seem incapable of picking up the pieces, and they are our pieces." (Leonard Rosenblatt, President, Refugees International, cited in Crossette, 1996, Nov. 9, I1)

"[In November and December 1996] . . . there were initial reports about RPF/AFDL massacres of refugees and other civilians; later international estimates . . . would suggest that the RPF/ADFL had possible killed as many as 80,000 refugees in eastern Zaire." (Jones, 2001, 149)

". . . can one turn a blind eye to the systematic killing of tens of thousands of Hutu refugees in Eastern Congo by the RPA (Rwanda Patriotic Army)?" (Lemarchand, 1998b, 4)

". . . cholera, dysentery and malnutrition were killing 1,000 people a day." (Massey, 2000, 7)

ii. Number of refugees and displaced persons (short-term): 220,000–300,000; (long-term): 700,000 to 2 million
"Population at Risk" (1995): 600,000. (Weiss and Collins, 1996, 5–7, Table I.1)

"[Following the 1994 genocide in Rwanda] . . . between 1m. and 2m. Hutus settled in hellish camps around Goma and Bukavu to join the swelling numbers of Burundian Hutus that had been fleeing to the camps around Uvira in south Kivu since the assassination of President Melchior Ndadaye in October 1993." (Massey, 2000, 3)

"The attacks . . . [on Tutsis in Zaire] . . . have prompted 24,000 people to flee into Rwanda and pushed another 65,000 out of their homes and farms inside Zaire." (McKinley, 1996, June 16, I3)

"[At the end of October 1996] . . . about 700,000 Hutu refugees remained in camps around Goma. . . . Fighting has displaced 220,000 . . . who were in [the camps]." (NYT, 1996, Oct. 31, A10)

"[In late summer 1994] . . . estimates of the number of refugees in eastern Zaire range from 800,000 to 1.2 million. More than half a million Rwandans also fled to Tanzania." (Reed, 1998, 134, footnote 5)

"Two million exiles, mostly Rwandan Hutus who fled when the Tutsis won the war, now lived in crowded camps in Zaire and Tanzania." (Carter, 1995)

iii. Likelihood of conflict spreading to other states: 5 *high*

a. Number of shared borders: 9

Sudan, Central African Republic, Republic of the Congo, Angola, Zambia, Tanzania, Burundi, Rwanda, and Uganda.

b. Involvement of bordering states

"Where ethnic fault lines cut across national boundaries, ethnic conflict inevitably tends to spill from one area to the next. Refugees act as vehicles of ethnic hatred. Over the last forty years in Rwanda, Burundi, and more recently in eastern Congo, refugee-generating violence has led repeatedly to conflict-generating refugee flows." (Lemarchand, 1998a, 42–43)

"The presence of a massive humanitarian aid effort in the absence of a security response would contribute to the process of recycling the Rwandan conflict. Indeed, from the outset the ancien [Rwandan] régime had used aid flows into Goma to its political advantage, and to the detriment of refugees, and begun reestablishing its fight to reclaim power in Rwanda." (Jones, 2001, 144)

"Early in the conflict, the Angolan government contacted the rebel leader, Laurent Kabila, and agreed to a common strategy. The Angolans airlifted a contingent of Kantangese gendarmes, who had been living in Angola after being driven out of Shaba province [Zaire] by Mobutu in the 1960s, to participate in the fighting in the eastern sector. The government provided these troops with military equipment, including heavy weapons, and this force spearheaded the successful offensive against Kisangani, the largest city in the eastern part of the country, which fell to the rebels in the middle of March." (Hare, 1998, 127)

"The Mobutu regime was implicated in the neighbour's wars: it supported the Khartoum government in its war against the southern Sudanese rebellion, which in turn was supported by the USA, Uganda and Eritrea; Zairean territory served as a rear base for attacks by armed movements against Uganda, Rwanda and Burundi; and the support offered by Mobutu to the Angolan rebel movement UNITA . . . did not end with the 1994 Lusaka peace accord." (Reyntjens, 2000, 6)

B. Pre-intervention "Assessment of Risk": 5 *high*

". . . Zaire was perceived as a quagmire into which entry would be difficult and exit both expensive and potentially bloody." (Jones, 2001, 143)

"Undoubtedly, the US regards African intervention as uniquely dangerous and seldom in its national interest." (Massey, 2000, 16)

"As terrible as it may sound, morality has its price, and the world powers have to decide if they are to pay that price, and intervene in a violent, complex, and potentially unresolvable political and ethnic situation." (C. L. Staten, cited in Massey, 2000, 11)

C. Extent of "National Interest Involvement":

i. The international community: 2 *relatively low*

"Other institutions which would normally step in to provide humanitarian relief have failed to do so because world powers have little strategic or economic interest in the region." (Smith, 1996)

"Nobody's interests were at play, with the possible exception of France, which had already been engaged through Operation Turquoise and was not about to enter the region. Finally, there was no major power backing the operation." (Jones, 2001, 143)

"In the 1990's, as Mr. Mobuto's usefulness as a reliable, if corrupt and violent cold-war ally dwindled, he was seen overseas as an embarrassing holdover from another era." (French, 1996, Sept. 13, A3)

"A bankrupt and discredited Government is finding that Zaire has little remaining strategic value and is suddenly alone in the world. . . . The Zairian Government is aware that none of the foreign friends that have intervened to help rescue Mr. Mobutu in the past are likely to assist Zaire militarily to restore control." (French, 1996, Nov. 11, A6)

ii. United States, Canada, and Great Britain: 2 *relatively low*

". . . There is strong evidence that Africa sits very low on America's list of priorities." (Massey, 2000, 10)

"Given the entrenched position of the FGOR [Former Government of Rwanda], it was asserted that moving the camps and separating the two groups [Hutu militia and genuine refugees] would have required a heavily armed and sizable military expedition which was authorized to use force. While the US actively supported the attainment of these goals, the crisis in eastern Zaire came after those in Somalia, Yugoslavia and Rwanda, and the Clinton administration simply was not willing to invest the necessary diplomatic, military and financial resources to undertake the project, nor was it willing to take such a risk just prior to an election." (Reed, 1998, 145)

"Frozen by the [1996 presidential] election . . . [the Clinton administration] . . . is unlikely to want to make a public issue of another African crisis. . . . Administration officials repeat that no Americans will be sent to the region." (Crossette, 1996, Nov. 2, I6)

"The key event was the decision by the White House, presumably provoked by mounting international pressure, to sanction the deployment of between 3,000 and 4,000 troops and logisticians in the region, of which 1,000 would be on the ground around Goma." (Massey, 2000, 12)

"In the operation . . . [that Canada] . . . initiated in Zaire in 1996, we . . . decided to do something and lacked the capacity to do it on our own or in concert with others. When we had accumulated those resources, we failed to follow through." (Adelman, n.d., 18)

"In contrast to France's highly interventionist policy, British armed intervention following the east-of-Suez withdrawal has been highly infrequent and limited." (Massey, 2000, 11)

iii. France: 4 *relatively high*

"France was by far the most vociferous state calling for military intervention." (Massey, 2000, 8)

"France's interest in Zaire was motivated by commercial considerations and Zaire's tremendous reservoir of minerals, but also by the shared language." (Rouvez, 1994, 170)

"If the post-colonial interventionist reflex, à la Jacques Foccart, had waned, it certainly had not perished entirely. The continuing presence of Foccart . . . within the *cellule africaine* in Chirac's Elysée Palace, ensured a strong interventionist lobby committed to rescue the Mobutu regime in time-honoured fashion." (Massey, 2000, 9)

"Regardless of the truth behind French claims that the UN was dragging its feet in an effort to win the AFDL time to take the Mugunga camp, it was clear that Paris desperately needed an intervention, yet for almost the first time, felt incapable of acting unilaterally." (Massey, 2000, 16)

iv. Rwanda and Uganda: 5 *high*

"Whilst the *de facto* military intervention by Rwanda and Uganda in support of the AFDL did not definitively end the refugee crisis, it did effectively extinguish the possibility of a large-scale peace enforcement mission." (Massey, 2000, 14)

"The best solution for Rwanda and Uganda was for the AFDL [Kabila's force] to supply a swift military solution prior to (or without the need for) any peacekeeping intervention." (Massey, 2000, 6)

v. South Africa: 2 *relatively low*

"The only genuine regional power, South Africa had indicated that domestic constraints precluded anything other than a marginal role in any intervention." (Massey, 2000, 16)

"The *apartheid* regime [in South Africa] had been an historic supplier of mercenaries to bolster the Mobutu dictatorship, and had made covert arms sales to the Habyaramana regime [in Rwanda]." (Massey, 2000, 11)

D. Mass Media: May 21 to November 20, 1996
  i. "Alerting" function (volume of television and newspaper coverage): N=120; Rank order=6
    a. Televison coverage: Rank order=4
       Total (ABC, CBS, NBC): N=44
       In-depth: N=29
    b. *New York Times* coverage: N=76; Rank order=6
  ii. "Evaluative" function (intervention framing in the *New York Times*)
     Pro-intervention frames: N=13
     Anti-interventionframes: N=7
  iii. Assessment of media coverage

Although the potential of a refugee crisis in Zaire had been on the media radar screens since the summer of 1994, Simon Massey reports that in the fall of 1996, "with few journalists and aid workers in Kivu [Zaire], the status and magnitude of the refugee population in the theatre of war was indeterminate." (2000, 6) Despite the difficulties in getting information from the region, the Zairean crisis ranked number six in combined television and newspaper coverage and received over one hundred reports in American mass media outlets over a six-month period of study. More significantly, Zaire ranked fourth in television coverage, placing it ahead of conflicts in Liberia and East Timor on that all-important "alerting" medium of crisis reporting.

In short, given the lack of resolve in the United States regarding the wisdom underlying humanitarian intervention following the Somalia disaster—the "Somalia Syndrome"—it is reasonable to see this case as one where media coverage might have been a crucial component in creating the necessary pressure to finally bring a reluctant Clinton administration "on-side" for an intervention in eastern Zaire in the fall of 1996.

New York Times coverage of the Zairean crisis was virtually non-existent over the late spring and summer of 1996, with only three stories appearing prior to the serious escalation of the crisis in October. Just over half of total reporting originated from Africa, with a third coming from the United States. Reporters on *New York Times* assignment provided almost three-quarters of content, chiefly James McKinley and Howard French from Africa, and Barbara Crossette reporting from the UN in New York, with the balance of material contributed by Reuters and the Associated Press. As with all crises studied, inside-page

Table 8.1 *New York Times* **Coverage of Zaire**

Panel 1 – Date:	N	%	Panel 2 – Dateline:	N	%
First 2 Months	1	1%	United States	26	34%
Second 2 Months	2	3%	Zaire	23	30%
Third 2 Months	73	96%	Africa (other)	19	25%
		100%	Other	7	9%
			Unknown	1	1%
					99%

Panel 3 – Source:	N	%	Panel 4 – Type of Content:	N	%
Local Staff	55	72%	Front-page News	13	17%
AP	5	7%	Inside-page News	50	66%
AFP	0	0%	Editorials	5	7%
Reuters	9	12%	Op-ed Features	4	5%
Other	7	9%	Photos	0	0%
		100%	Letters	1	1%
			Other	3	4%
					100%

Newspaper Coverage, by Date, Dateline, Source and Type (May 21 to November 20, 1996) N=76 news dominated coverage, accounting for nearly two-thirds of content; high-impact items accounted for a very respectable 29 percent of content: front-page news coverage (17 percent), editorials (7 percent), and op-ed pieces. (5 percent)

On June 16, James McKinley began the process of alerting the American public to the impending crisis in Zaire by outlining the problem: Hutu refugees who had fled Rwanda in 1994 were encouraging Zairean Hutus to attack their Tutsi neighbors. It was also noted that Zairean troops had failed to control the violence, leading Rwanda's Paul Kagame to use the term "ethnic cleansing" to describe what was happening. (McKinley, 1996, June 16, I3) Over the summer, however, there were no follow-up stories, and Zaire's problems were not covered again until September 13, when Howard French reported that President Mobutu was seriously ill and assessed the significance of this for the country. While neither the problem of refugees nor that of ethnic violence were specifically mentioned, the future for Zaire was portrayed as grim: "I don't want to say this, but if things fall apart here suddenly, what we could face is another Yugoslavia." (Bernardin Mungul Diaka, Former Governor of Kinshaha, cited in French, 1996, Sept. 13, A3)

Toward the end of September, clashes between Rwandan and Zairean military units along the border were reported, and on October 11 the plight of the Banyamulenge was first noted: "A United Nations spokeswoman . . . [reported] . . . that the situation had grown explosive since [Zairean] Government troops had ordered about 400,000 Banyamulenge to leave within a week." (AP, 1996, Oct. 11, A4) The Banyamulenge (with considerable help from Rwanda's Tutsi army) responded by attacking UN-run refugee camps, thereby unleashing yet another flood of refugees, numbering in the hundreds of thousands, further into Zaire. It was at this point that the issue of humanitarian intervention came to dominate the international agenda in a major way.

In late October, the UN became engaged in efforts to control the situation as, in addition to the need to deal with the extensive human suffering taking place among the refugees, it feared "the possibility that the conflict will draw in Rwanda and Burundi." (Reuters, 1996, Oct. 25, A8) On October 26, a Tutsi businessman claimed that "if the international community doesn't get involved and stop this now, it will be worse than Rwanda." (cited in McKinley, 1996, Oct. 26, I7)

As the magnitude of the chaos in eastern Zaire increased, two rival options for dealing with the crisis emerged in reporting. One of these was proposed in a late October op-ed piece by Philip Goure-vitch, contributing editor to *The Forward*. Gourevitch argued that the refugee camps had "become bases for a vicious war against Rwanda and local populations in Zaire . . . [as well as] . . . the greatest threat to the perilous regional balance." Thus, rather than continuing to subsidize the camps at the cost of a million dollars a day, he suggested that they should be shut down and their inhabitants repatriated to Rwanda. (Oct. 28, A19) This was the solution also favored by Paul Kagame, and ultimately it was the one that carried the day.

The second option, that of an international intervention to aid the refugees, was complicated not only by the state sovereignty issue (Rwanda, where at least some troops would have to be deployed, was opposed to an intervention), but by the perception that "Zaireans have a very strong feeling of resentment about a foreign intervention taking place on their territory." (Panos Mountzis, UN High Commissioner for Refugees in Goma, cited in McKinley, 1996, Oct. 28, A8) As well, the truly confusing nature of the military conflict on the ground and the uncertain condition and location of the refugee population on whose behalf an intervention would be mounted contributed to indecision. In spite of these complications, over the first three weeks of November, in a period of intense media coverage of the crisis (three-quarters of total coverage appeared from November 1 to November 20), the intervention option appeared to have won out, in spite of continuing United States reluctance to allow the Security Council to approve an intervention force.

At the beginning of November, a *New York Times* editorial supported President Clinton's proposal for an "African Crisis Response Force" operating under UN authority, to respond to the Zairean crisis. It argued that if adequately funded and not designed to avoid Western political engagement, it would be "a constructive instrument of international cooperation rather than a cynical hiring of African soldiers to carry out dangerous chores for the West." (*NYT*, 1996, Nov. 1, A34) On November 2, it was announced that Boutros Boutros-Ghali had appointed Raymond Chrétien, Canadian Ambassador to the United States, "as an envoy to the region . . . to mediate a regional agreement to end the fighting and recommend how to establish a larger United Nations presence." This marked the beginning of an active Canadian role in the crisis. At the same time, Kofi Annan issued a call for volunteer nations to either lead or contribute troops to an intervention force "before everything blows up in our faces" (cited in Crossette, 1996, Nov. 2, I6)

On the following day, Howard French cautioned that the collapse of Zaire could set a dangerous precedent "for secession and adventurism in a host of other fragile postcolonial constructions from Nigeria to Angola, . . . [concluding that] . . . the international community cannot ignore this terrible business for long." (French, 1996, Nov. 3, IV3) Indeed, UN officials claimed that there were "no obvious solutions to the crisis short of a military intervention." France called for immediate action, which at this point focused on providing "a safe passageway" for refugees to return to Rwanda, a plan that would require Rwandan cooperation. (McKinley, 1996, Nov. 4, A3)

A second editorial appeared on November 5, urging immediate action on the part of the Clinton administration. It argued that "solving the refugee emergency cannot wait. . . . The outside world, led by the United States, must act quickly to save . . . [the refugees] . . . from starvation and a possible cholera epidemic. . . . A sensible solution is to create internationally protected corridors so that Hutu refugees can return home to Rwanda." (NYT, 1996, Nov. 5, A22) Jacques De-Millano, vice president of Doctors Without Borders, maintained that "'it's too late for a soft diplomatic approach' . . . [calling instead for an international force] . . . to invade Zaire immediately and set up zones in which aid agencies can operate." (cited in McKinley, 1996, Nov. 5, A8) McKinley reported further that "prompted by France, American officials are now considering whether to send some American troops to Central Africa for logistical support for an intervention force to protect and feed up to 1.4 million refugees." However, neither the United States nor Great Britain were yet ready to endorse a UN mission into eastern Zaire; as Madeleine Albright noted, there were "a lot of questions and a lot of problems, and not enough answers." (cited in Erlanger, 1996, Nov. 6, A8) On November 9, the UN Secretary General referred to the situation in Zaire as "a new genocide. . . . I will call it genocide by starvation." (Boutros Boutros-Ghali, cited in Crossette, 1996, Nov. 9, I1) France continued to press for Security Council approval of an intervention force, but the United States voted against a French resolution authorizing such a force, reiterating the need for "a clear mission." (Myers, 1996, Nov. 10, A18)

A break in the stalemate appeared on November 13, when Canada came forward with an offer to lead an intervention force, to be composed of between ten thousand and fifteen thousand troops, and to be furnished by a dozen nations, significantly including the United States, which had seemingly agreed to provide armed protection for aid convoys. (Crossette, 1996, Nov. 13, A8) However, the United States continued to stand in the way of Security Council approval of the mission: "Administration officials said they feared a foreign venture into a chaotic landscape of rival militias and endangered refugees could end in disaster." This led French Defense Minister, Charles Million to complain that "the United States must not drag its feet any longer." (cited in Crossette, 1996, Nov. 13, A8)

Yet, continue to drag its feet it did. On November 13, the *New York Times* ran an editorial that focused on the contentious need to separate "the 100,000 or so Hutu fanatics responsible for the massacres [of 1994] from the much larger numbers who were not" and called upon the UN to respond "promptly but prudently." (*NYT*, 1996, Nov. 13, A22) How this extremely difficult task was to be accomplished was left unexplained. For its part, the Clinton administration acknowledged that "U.S. participation in this important humanitarian mission is vital." (White House Press Secretary Michael McCurry, cited in Mitchell, 1996, Nov. 14, A1) However, in spite of this verbal recognition of the need for international intervention, the United States continued to haggle over terms of the force's mandate, insisting that it "would not disarm militias and would not force its way into the refugee camps or police them." A spokesman for Senator Jesse Helms was not impressed with the nuance, indicating, "This smells like Somalia all over again." (Marc Theisman, cited in Mitchell, 1996, Nov. 14, A14)

David Rieff, in an op-ed article appearing on November 14, called for a cautious approach to a possible intervention. He criticized international aid agencies for being "the last interventionists in the post-cold war world," claiming that "the oratory of post-cold war humanitarians is eerily reminiscent of that of cold warriors who believed that there was no part of the world in which Communism did not have to be confronted." He cautioned as well that ill-thought-out interventions could worsen situations in the long run: "Americans should not let the moral fervor of interventionism blind them to the implications of military action. If the United States goes in, it should be with the understanding that such humanitarian moves are rarely, if ever, quick, clean or easy." (1996, Nov. 14, A23)

In spite of continuing reservations, the United States ultimately agreed to commit its troops to significant ground operations, namely "to capture and hold the airport at Goma and open a corridor from there to the Rwandan border," but it continued to block Security Council approval of the mission until its concerns regarding mission mandate and duration were met. (Crossette, 1996, Nov. 15, A7) A

November 15 editorial praised President Clinton for having "responded humanely and judiciously to the challenge of saving a million desperate refugees trapped by a war in eastern Zaire." At the same time, the editorial supported the American position of needing to clarify the terms and conditions of the mission and cited as well the need to get Congress on-side for the commitment of American troops to the intervention force. (*NYT*, 1996, Nov. 15, A23)

On the same day (November 16) that the Security Council voted to authorize the intervention under Chapter VII, it was reported that refugees had begun their trek back to Rwanda in huge numbers. In spite of UN, Canadian, and French arguments that an intervention force was still needed, the Clinton administration immediately began to "reassess" the need for the mission it had just voted to approve, and on November 20 it announced that American troops would not be going into Zaire after all. In the view of Bruce Jones, the American pull-out signaled "the death knell for the mission." (2001, 149)

The proposed intervention and the American role in decision making leading up to it occasioned multiple evaluations. According to Iain Guest, a senior fellow at the United States Institute of Peace, the voluntary repatriation of refugees was a blessing in disguise: "It seems to have spared us the ultimate nightmare: to go into the Mgunga camp to try to feed refugees and separate them from the militia, and have neither the force nor the mandate with which to do it." (cited in Erlanger, 1996, Nov. 16, I6) An unnamed State Department official complained, "Zaire was just embarrassing. . . . We were bounced by the French and the United Nations into acting on a clear humanitarian issue, rather than taking any kind of lead." Morton Abramowitz, president of the Carnegie Endowment for International Peace, likewise offered the opinion that the United States had acted "because I suspect we were feeling increasingly isolated." (both cited in Erlanger, 1996, Nov. 18, A6) The final *New York Times* editorial on the crisis recognized that the need for an intervention still might exist, and called for a "careful" reassessment. It also pointed out that "the international community will have to provide some kind of impartial monitoring of the security problem to keep the deadly cycle of killing, reprisals and mass flight from resuming." (*NYT*, 1996, Nov. 19, A24)

There was a relatively strong pro-intervention tilt in intervention framing (13 pro- vs. 7 anti-), and President Clinton moved from an initial position of opposing the use of American troops to one of committing troops to possible combat operations in eastern Zaire to secure and guard the Goma airport and ensure the protection of refugees on their way back to Rwanda. In this, he was cautiously supported by the editorial positions expressed by the *New York Times*. It is not unreasonable to suggest that, in addition to pressure from the UN, France, and Canada, as well as from respected international aid agencies, mass media contributed to this change of policy just prior to the November presidential election.[4] Thus, we consider Zaire to have met the test of a possible "media push"—adequate alerting, combined with framing that tended to be supportive of an intervention. We must, however, add the caveat that in spite of this combined pressure, the Clinton administration was certainly not going to be rushed into an intervention that it had not carefully thought out with respect to a limited mission mandate as well as a precise deadline for an exit. It is also clear that the United States abandoned its commitment to participate in the intervention just as soon as conditions appeared to permit such action. In spite of the president's statement on November 16 that "the world's most powerful nation must not turn its back on so many desperate people and so many innocent children who are now at risk," (Clinton, 1996, Nov. 16, I7) two days later Secretary of Defense William Perry commented with respect to the fate of the mission, "We are not the Salvation Army." (cited in Reuters, 1996, Nov. 18, A6)

▪ Overall Evaluation of the Crisis Response

In December 1996, with the refugee crisis that had occasioned the need for an intervention seemingly on the way to resolution, the UN decided not to send an intervention force to Zaire. The result, according to Bruce Jones, was that "by January 1997, what once seemed like a war for control of the Rwanda-Zaire border area had become a war for the Kivu region and then a war for the whole of Zaire." (2001, 148) On May 18, 1997 Laurent Kabila entered Kinshasa, finally taking control of the country that Mobutu Sese Seko had just abandoned after three decades of misrule. The victorious Kabila immediately renamed the country the Democratic Republic of the Congo.

With the end of the Mobutu dictatorship, there was initial optimism that the two "roots" of the Democratic Republic of the Congo's crisis had been dealt with. Unfortunately, this optimism proved to be misplaced. While Laurent Kabila's victory "was expected to lead to the end the internecine conflicts in Zaire . . . , events have proven expectations wrong." (Mgbeoji, 2003, 169, footnote 5) In fact, according to Ian Stewart, "The change from Mobutu to Kabila sent an already unsettled and volatile region into a chaotic tailspin in 1997 and 1998. Mobutu's had been a remorseless reign of corruption, oppression, and despotism, but it had been stable—a source of certainty in an otherwise shaky part of Africa." (2002, 116)

Nor, unfortunately, were the problems associated with the deep-seated conflict between Hutu and Tutsi put to rest. Filip Reyntjens refers to the post-Mobutu period as the "Second Congo War," during which "Rwandan and Hutu forces, which were opposed to Kabila in 1996–97, now side[d] with him in the context of an 'anti-Tutsi' alliance." (2000, 6) Specifically, the "Second Congo War" began when ethnic Tutsi Bayamulenge in eastern Zaire

> rebelled against the rule of Kabila alleging that he was no better than the late Mobutu and accusing him of corruption, tribalism, and dishonesty of intention in claiming to return the country to democratic rule. . . . It has been alleged that the rebels who now occupy a significant portion of Congo are backed by the governments of neighbouring Rwanda and Uganda, and because of this the Congolese government refuses to negotiate with the rebels, described as "pawns of Rwanda and Uganda." (Mgbeoji, 2003, 169, footnote 5)

In light of the very limited mandate and short time in the field of the proposed "Operation Assurance" intervention force, it is unclear how it would have responded to the new round of violence that followed Laurent Kabila's victory over Mobutu. What is clear, however, is that an enormous amount of "mission creep" would have been needed in order for it to have done so effectively. Be that as it may, according to Winston Jalloh, in the years following 1998, the continuing conflict in the Democratic Republic of the Congo claimed over three million lives. (2004, 33)

While the immediate mission to protect refugees that was assigned to "Operation Assurance" may have seemingly "solved itself," the more fundamental problem of bringing peace and stability to the people of the Democratic Republic of the Congo and its neighbors certainly had not. In fact, Bruce Jones claims "that the political and security responses to the postgenocide crisis in Rwanda were wholly insufficient in the face of events on the ground." He goes on to specify the linkages:

> The human consequences of the postgenocide crisis did not rise to the level of suffering experienced during the genocide yet are extraordinary by any

other standard. As many as 80,000 civilians were killed; hundreds of thousands of refugees were forced back into a country where their security was far from guaranteed. . . . [Zaire] . . . was embroiled in war; and eastern Zaire became a battleground of regional competition. A small civil war became a genocide, and a genocide in a small country became a war in a huge region. The failures of peacemaking in Rwanda and the subregion could not have been more complete. (2001, 150–51)

■ Notes

1. In a book that should be mandatory reading for students of international relations, Adam Hochschild describes in horrific detail the conditions in King Leopold's Congo colony, where during his rule, the population of the Congo was reduced by half. The implication of this statistic is that as a result of outright murder, starvation, exhaustion, exposure, and disease, an estimated ten million Congolese had been killed. (1998, 233)

2. According to Hochschild, "CIA chief Allen Dulles authorized . . . [Lumumba's] . . . assassination." He quotes Richard Bissell as indicating that President Eisenhower "would have preferred to have him taken care of some other way than by assassination, but he regarded Lumumba . . . as a mad dog . . . and he wanted the problem dealt with." (Richard Bissell, cited in Hochschild, 1998, 302) Further, John Stockwell relates a story told by a CIA officer about "driving about . . . [Lubumbashi] . . . after curfew with Patrice Lumumba's body in the trunk of his car, trying to decide what to do with it." Stockwell initially believed that the officer "had been trying to help. It was not until 1975 that . . . [he] . . . learned the CIA had plotted Lumumba's death." (1978, 105)

3. It was reported that France supported Mobutu Sese Seko against a major insurgency in 1977 by selling the dictator "35 *Puma* and *Alouette* helicopters, 17 *Mirgage 5s,* and 290 light armored vehicles." (Rouvez, 1994, 170)

4. An examination of Vanderbilt Television News Archive likewise indicates a reasonably strong effort at alerting the American population to the crisis in eastern Zaire. All three major networks had correspondents in Africa covering the crisis, with the first report filed by ABC's Sheila MacVicar on November 1. In total, reports from correspondents on the scene appeared in twenty-five of the forty-four stories aired. As near as can be determined, twenty-five stories as well showed video of refugees in flight and/or conditions in the camps that housed them, with the refugee issue discussed in at least an additional five brief anchor-read reports. International intervention, involving the UN, France, the United States, or Canada, was discussed in twenty-two stories. These two issues dominated coverage, and it is reasonable to assume that the American viewing audience was able to make the connection between them.

9

Sierra Leone, 1997:
ECOMOG II, UNOMSIL, UNAMSIL

Walter C. Soderlund

■ Background

Located on the West Coast of Africa, Sierra Leone is a country roughly the size of New Brunswick with a population in the 1990s of about 4.2 million people (Pratt, 1999, 7). It shares borders with Liberia and Guinea.

The history of Sierra Leone had been intertwined with that of neighboring Liberia long before the disastrous events of the 1990s. According to Christopher Clapham,

> they share the peculiar legacy of Creoledom, and the late nineteenth-century expansion from the coastal settlements into a hinterland itself divided between numerous ethnic groups; they have analogous administrative hierarchies, and distributions of educational and professional skills; and they have similar economies, based principally on the export of primary materials—especially minerals—by foreign-managed corporations, and only relying to a secondary extent on indigenously-produced cash crops. The sharp break comes in the political legacy of colonialism in Sierra Leone and of long independence in Liberia. (1976, 1–2)

Britain was the colonial master of Sierra Leone and its interests in the area date back to 1618 and 1633, when trade charters were granted to the Company of Adventurers of London Trading to Africa and the Company of Royal Adventurers into Africa. A. B. Cotay claims that "these companies were the forerunners of British colonial expansion in the so-called 'dark continent' of Africa . . . [as] . . . in 1807 and 1808 the British Crown took over the administration of Sierra Leone from the chartered companies" creating a formal Colony

(Cotay, 1959, 210). Andrea Talentino points out that Sierra Leone also "served as a base for a British antislavery squadron through the early and mid-1800s." (2005, 204) An additional British "Protectorate" of Sierra Leone was created in 1896 out of territory in the interior claimed by Liberia (Mgbeoji, 2003, 7).

Just as Liberia had been settled by freed slaves from the United States, Sierra Leone had served a similar purpose for the British somewhat earlier: "In 1787 three ships landed in Freetown harbour . . . with 500 of these unfortunate men to start the first settlement in Sierra Leone." (Cotay, 1959, 211) Over the years, freed slaves who had been settled in Nova Scotia following the American Revolution, some from Jamaica, as well as those liberated by the British Navy from slave ships on route to the Western Hemisphere, were added to the earlier arrivals. (Fyfe, 1979, 22–30)

Much as was the case in Liberia, Sierra Leone was divided between the "Colony"—Freetown and surroundings, dominated by the "Creoles" (descendants of the resettled ex-slaves)—and the "Protectorate" (home to the country's indigenous population, "variously referred to as 'up-country people,' 'countrymen,' or 'provincials.'") (Cartwright, 1970, 5, footnote 4) In the Protectorate, two tribal groups out of about eighteen dominated—the Mende and the Temne—each accounting for about 30 percent of the population (see Cartwright, 1970, 14, Table 1.1). However, as Martin Kilson points out,

> In general . . . [the administrative and judicial systems] . . . meant that British rather than traditional or indigenous authority must govern the behavior of persons not bound by customary rules. Such persons were, of course, foreigners (European and Lebanese), though the Creoles were partially included. More specifically, this conception of the colonial situation meant that matters affecting the economic activity of foreigners such as land rights, mineral or agricultural concessions, commercial contracts, and debts were invariably subject to British colonial authority. (1969, 16)

According to Clapham, in Sierra Leone "the Creoles never acquired full control over their own government, and were much less well placed than their Liberian equivalents to manage and profit from the expansion into the hinterland that took place in both territories at the end of the nineteenth century." (1976, 7) In 1951, again unlike the situation in Liberia, the Creoles lost power to the Provincials "when most Creole political leaders went into an embittered political isolation rather than countenance sharing power with the Protectorate people." (Cartwright, 1970, 5) Creole elite power was eroded in other areas as well: "Creole dominance in the bureaucracy ha[d] been chal-lenged and diminished in the 1970s by a wider recruitment of provin-cials . . . and by the manipulation of the size of the state apparatus as well as entry and promotion procedures." (Riley, 1982, 107–108) It was, then, the cleavage between the Northern Mende-speaking and the Southern Mel-speaking populations that was paramount in Sierra Leonean politics, not the creole-indigenous split that characterized Liberia (Pratt, 1999, 9).

Independence for Sierra Leone followed a series of steps that were typical of British decolonization at the end of World War II: a "repre-sentative government" was elected in 1951, followed by "home rule" in 1957, whereby Britain retained power over "external affairs and in-ternal security." (Cotay, 1959, 212) Full independence was achieved in 1961.

During the 1950s and 1960s politics in Sierra Leone, while peace-ful, was described by Stephen Riley as "unusually competitive." (1982, 106) However, in 1968 the degree of competition began to narrow. The Sierra Leone Peoples Party (SLPP) that had led the country to indepen-dence lost an election to the All Peoples Congress (APC), a party that, over the next ten years, successfully established a one-party state. Ac-cording to Riley,

> President Siaka Stevens and his changing coterie of political supporters have acted with consummate political skill to extend political control and prevent effective opposition, both by promises of preferment, political ma-noeuvers and generated fear, as well as by the use of political violence, particularly during the elections of 1973, and 1977 and the 1978 one-party referendum campaign. (1982, 107)

President Stevens held on to power until 1985, when "foreign debt, rampant inflation, currency devaluation, budget deficits, corruption and declining exports led to chronic fuel, power and food short-ages," (Pratt, 1999, 9) and "a peaceful and carefully-managed trans-fer of power occurred." (Fashole Luke and Riley, 1989, 133) Major-General Joseph Momoh now assumed the presidency, an office he was to hold until he was deposed by a military coup d'état in 1992, staged by soldiers who had served in the ECOMOG intervention force in Liberia and had become dissatisfied and politicized (Howe, 1996/97, 157). "By the end of the 1980s the economic growth rate was consis-tently negative" (Talentino, 2005, 205), and, according to Amos Saw-yer, "Momoh's ineptitude took Sierra Leone further along the path to violent collapse." (2004, 443)

■ Roots of the Crisis

In the mid-1980s Sierra Leone was listed as "one of the poorest countries in the world, with a G.N.P. *per capita* of U.S. $310 . . . , an average life expectancy of only 41 years, and as many as 154 of every 1,000 infants . . . dying every year before they reach their first birthday. Data on the distribution of incomes and life-chances further suggest the existence of an extremely unequal society." (Fashole Luke and Riley, 1989, 137) These conditions were to have an impact on what was to come for Sierra Leone, because economic circumstances such as these led predictably to social and political instability.

According to a report filed with the Canadian Centre for Foreign Policy Development written by Member of Parliament David Pratt, a Special Envoy to Sierra Leone,

> during the Momoh years there were two trends, largely unnoticed at the time, that would have important ramifications later. One was the continued and dramatic growth in the number of unemployed and disaffected youth. They drifted from the countryside in one of two directions: either to Freetown and other urban centres, or to the diamond fields of Kono. In either case they became socialized in a climate of violence, drugs and criminality. The other trend was a growth in student militants. During the second half of the 1980s, many university students had been radicalized in part by the violence of the government suppression of their demonstrations, and in part by their exposure to new ideas, including the thoughts of Col. Qaddafi, as expressed in *The Green Book*. (1999, 10)

Ibrahim Abdullah and Patrick Muana specifically link the problem of disaffected youth noted above to the societal violence that consumed the country in the 1990s:

> The roots of the RUF lie in Freetown, where a rebellious youth culture began to evolve in the 1940s, based on the lumpen "rarray boys." These first-generation lumpens were predominantly foot soldiers for the politicians of the time. . . . [Later] . . . politicians continued to try to control the wilder elements, seeking a ready supply of thugs to do their dirty work. . . . Students immersed in the rebellious youth culture became the articulate mouthpiece of a disaffected youth cohort attacking APC rule and calling for fundamental change. (1998, 173–174)

It was this group of "disaffected and unemployed youths on the fringes of both urban and rural society" from which Charles Taylor's ally Foday Sankoh recruited the Revolutionary United Front (RUF). (McGregor, 1999, 483)

Diamonds, which were discovered in the 1930s, have also contributed to instability in Sierra Leone. A. B. Cotay, Commissioner for Sierra Leone and Gambia in the late 1950s, relates that following the diamond boom of 1955–57, the prime minister "thinks that the discovery of pebbles—as he calls diamonds—is not a blessing to the country, because law and order are breaking down, and immorality, drunkenness are taking grip of the country." (Cotay, 1959, 213) Andrea Talentino documents the extent of corruption in the diamond industry:

> When Stevens took power in 1968, Sierra Leone was the fourth-largest diamond producer in the world, earning approximately $200 million per year from the gems. But corruption and smuggling led to a dramatic decrease in exports and a corresponding pinch on government revenues. When Stevens left office in 1985, the government made only $100,000 per year on diamonds. (2005, 205)

In addition to the societal instability caused by the lure of riches, there is consensus that control of the diamond fields by rebel groups during the civil war, and the resulting illicit trade in the gems, provided a major source of funds for the RUF throughout the decade of the 1990s.

■ Events Precipitating the Crisis

Just as the conflict in Rwanda spilled over into Burundi and Zaire, so too did the Liberian conflict spill over into Sierra Leone. Without the upheaval in neighboring Liberia, it is at least questionable whether the problems in Sierra Leone (although these certainly should not be underestimated) would have resulted in the horrific events visited upon that nation in the 1990s. For example, Talentino argues that "in spite of Sierra Leone's problems, insurgency did not spring from within. Instead it was developed without as a part of [Charles] Taylor's attempt to enhance his own position by encouraging criminal behavior and violence." (2005, 207; see also Chapter 2, this volume)

The conflict that began in Liberia at the end of 1989 quickly spread to Sierra Leone, when in 1991 the country became a "second front" for Charles Taylor's NPFL. Libyan-trained Foday Sankoh, a nearly illiterate former enlisted soldier who had been imprisoned over his involvement in an attempted coup against President Stevens and who had studied "revolution" in Libya, was recruited to attack Sierra Leone in order to register Taylor's disapproval of Sierra Leone's support for the ECOWAS intervention in Liberia. The insurgent group, which Andrew McGregor claims lacked both an ideology and "a coherent political agenda," (1999, 484) took the name Revolutionary United Front. Yeketeil Gershoni explains, "The war in Sierra Leone appeared to follow the Liberian experience: with many casualties, displacement of population, destruction of economic and administrative structures and anarchy replacing the rule of law and order." (1997, 55) In April 1991, the government of Sierra Leone immediately attempted to get help from the United Nations, but none was forthcoming (Mgbeoji, 2003, 24). In the fall of 1992, Sierra Leone again asked for military assistance, but this was no more successful than earlier requests for help (Talentino, 2005, 208).

Herbert Howe recounts that as the decade passed the wars in Liberia and Sierra Leone continued to feed off one another:

> The Liberian conflict exacted wider political casualties. Sierra Leonean soldiers, mostly ECOMOG veterans, fought RUF in early 1992. This was destroying the country's economy, and the ECOMOG soldiers suffered from missing paychecks, irregular supplies, and minimal logistics support. In April 1992, these soldiers overthrew Joseph Momoh, Sierra Leone's president. (1996/97, 157)

A symbiotic relationship between Taylor and Sankoh continued into the late 1990s and beyond: "Taylor lent out his country for use as a conduit through which to smuggle guns and money into Sierra Leone. Selling Sierra Leone's diamonds on the international market, Taylor laundered the gem revenues for Sankoh in return for a hefty percentage of the profits." (Stewart, 2002, 49)

Following the 1992 coup, General Momoh was replaced by a National Provisional Ruling Council (NPRC), which in 1995 decided to employ mercenaries under contract to Executive Outcomes to combat the RUF rebels.[1] The NPRC held power until an election in 1996, which saw Ahmad Tejan Kabbah emerge victorious as Sierra Leone's president. It was in this election that the RUF's practice of amputating hands, arms, legs, ears, and lips, the signature atrocity of the conflict, began to pick up in momentum. According to Ian Stewart, Kabbah's slogan was "'The future is in your hands,' . . . [and Sankoh], . . . [e]mploying the kind of twisted logic reserved for madmen and zealots . . . reasoned he could stop the voting by cutting off every potential ballot-casting hand in the country. . . . Some of the more brutal rebels put a macabre spin on the president's words, often telling their victims, 'Go ask Kabbah for your hands back.'"[2] (2002, 58) The scale of amputations as well as the widespread use of children as fighters marks the conflict in Sierra Leone as one of the world's most mindless and heartless (Jalloh, 2004).

In May 1997, about six months following a peace accord signed with rebel forces, the Kabbah government was overthrown in a military coup resulting in a period of joint rule by the Armed Forces Revolutionary Council (AFRC) and Foday Sankoh's RUF. According to Pratt,

> the period of joint AFRC-RUF rule was characterized by a complete break-down of law and order, and by a collapse of the formal economy. Schools, banks, commercial services and government offices ceased to function, while rape and looting became the order of the day. As Amnesty International put it, *[t]he rule of law completely collapsed and violence engulfed the country*. (1999, 14, italics in the original)

It was "the overthrow of the democratic government of President Anmed Tejan Kabbah [that] triggered intervention in 1997." (Talentino, 2005, 200)

▪ The Intervention

In May 1997 the Organization of African Unity asked ECOWAS, which had troops stationed in the country to support the Liberian intervention, to extend the mandate of ECOMOG to include Sierra Leone. While the crisis in Sierra Leone had been ongoing since 1991 and was to continue until 2002, it is mass media coverage over the six months leading up to this crucial juncture in the conflict that we have chosen to examine for this study. Following the May coup, both the United States and Great Britain sent military forces to evacuate their own as well as citizens of other western countries from Freetown, which had become the site of increasingly intense fighting. However, by June 9, when these evacuation operations had been completed, it was clear that no Western nation (Britain and the United States being the most likely candidates) would intervene to end the ongoing civil war. Again, as was the case in Liberia, it fell to a Nigerian-led ECOWAS intervention force to attempt to reestablish order and return a democratically elected government to Sierra Leone in what were extremely difficult circumstances. And, much like its predecessor force in Liberia, ECOMOG II "effectively became the government's security force, making it a party in the conflict." (Talentino, 2005, 216)

In July 1998 the UN created an Observer Mission in Sierra Leone (UNOMSIL), but its complement was less than 700 personnel. A much

larger UN mission (UNAMSIL) was created in October 1999 to oversee the peace process envisaged in the Lome Peace Accord that had
been signed by the warring parties in July of that year.

Hostilities continued, however, and in May 2000, when it again
appeared that RUF forces would overrun Freetown, the British landed
military forces "to evacuate British citizens and to help secure the airport for UN peacekeepers." Subsequently, "in a dramatic shift of
strategy and mission, the British took control of UN forces and organized government forces for an offensive against RUF rebels while
the UN protected key points." Foday Sankoh was captured (later to
die in prison) and with his removal, the British intervention effectively ended the conflict. In January 2002, President Kabbah "declared the civil war officially over." (Mills, 2005)

Strength of the International Response
　A. **Did the Humanitarian Crisis Result in an International Inter-
　　vention? Yes**
　B. **Type of response: Combination**
　　• **ECOMOG II 1997:** led by Regional Power—Nigeria
　　"On 26 May 1997, the Organization of African Unity (OAU)
　　also condemned the coup, and called for an immediate restora-
　　tion of the constitutional order, urging the leaders of ECOWAS
　　to take immediate action against the coup makers. The opera-
　　tional mandate of ECOWAS's military arm, the West African
　　Monitoring Group (ECOMOG) was consequently extended
　　from Liberia to Sierra Leone in order to prevent the total
　　breakdown of law and order." ("Overview of Pre-UNAMSIL
　　Interventions." n.d.)
　　• **UNOMSIL 1998:** led by the UN
　　• **UNAMSIL 1999:** led by the UN, later by Great Britain
　C. **Type of UN Involvement:**
　　• **ECOMOG II:** Chapter VIII
　　• **UNOMSIL:** Chapter VI
　　• **UNAMSIL:** Chapter VII
　D. **Size of Intervening Forces: Rank order=4**
　　• **ECOMOG II: 4,000–10,000**
　　"[Following the 1997 coup] . . . the Nigerians are . . . esti-
　　mated to have about 4,000 troops in Sierra Leone." (Concilia-
　　tion Resources, 1997 September/October)
　　"[In 1997] . . . ECOMOG's mandate was upgraded from
　　sanction enforcement to actual military intervention to oust the

AFRC/RUF. The ECOMOG contingent in Sierra Leone is led by Nigerian Commander Brigadier General Maxwell Khobe and composed of approximately 9,000 troops, predominantly Nigerian with several Guinean support battalions." (Africa Action, 1998, Dec. 18).

"By the end of August [1997] ECOMOG had 10,000 troops in the country." (Talentino, 2005, 213)

• UNOMSIL: 61

"[In July 1998 the] . . . UN Security Council voted to create UN Observer Mission in Sierra Leone (UNOMSIL)." (Mills, 2005)

"At its peak [UNOMSIL] consisted on 61 uniformed personnel, including five civilian police monitors." (Pratt, 1999, 24)

• UNAMSIL: 6,000 to 17,500

"On October 22, [1999] the UN Security Council approved the U.N. Mission in Sierra Leone (UNAMSIL). The operation, given an initial six month mandate, authorized the deployment of a 6,000-member U.N. peacekeeping force. UNAMSIL's mandate, under the U.N. Charter's Chapter VII, included assisting the disarmament and demobilization process, ensuring the security of U.N. civilian personnel, assisting the delivery of humanitarian aid, and providing support for the new elections." (Human Rights Watch, 1999)

Determinants of the International Response
A. Severity of the Crisis: Rank order=7
i. Number of deaths (short-term): 10,000 to 50,000-plus

"The recent military overthrow of Sierra Leone's elected government . . . threatened to reignite a civil war in which at least 10,000 people died." (*NYT,* 1997, June 6, A30)

"By . . . [the end of May 1997] . . . estimates of dead in the rebel war ranged upwards from 50,000." (Pratt, 1999, 14)

"The conflict . . . killed 50,000 people, forced millions to flee their homes, destroyed the country's economy and shocked the world with its images of amputated limbs and drug-addled boy soldiers." (Polgren, 2007, Mar. 25, I1)

"Sierra Leone is an example, unfortunately not unique, of a nation in which the collapse of political and social structures made external intervention appear the only humanitarian solution." (McGregor, 1999, 483)

ii. Number of refugees and internally displaced persons: (short-term) 160,000; (long-term) 2.5 to 3 million

"Population at Risk" (1995) 1.5 million. (Weiss and Collins, 1996, 5–7, Table I.1)

"[Following the 1997 coup] . . . one hundred thousand people were officially registered as displaced, and sixty thousand were registered as refugees." (Talentino, 2005, 212)

"At different times in the previous six years [since 1991], estimates of the number of displaced people were as high as 2.5 million—more than half of the entire population." (Pratt, 1999, 14)

iii. **Likelihood of conflict spreading to other states: 4** *relatively high*

    a. **Number of shared borders: 2**

      Guinea and Sierra Leone

    b. **Involvement of bordering states**

"Without external support, be it diplomatic, military or humanitarian, the conflict in Sierra Leone, which is actually a regional conflict, has the potential to destabilize the whole of Western Africa." (Pratt, 1999, 39)

"The current troubles in Sierra Leone can be traced back to the 1990 ECOMOG intervention in Liberia. As Sankoh began organizing his movement, Charles Taylor, the Liberian guerrilla leaders, began to arm the RUF in retaliation for the two battalions of the SLA which Sierra Leone provided to help the Nigerian-led ECOMOG forces in Liberia." (McGregor, 1999, 484–485)

"Foday Sankoh, leader of RUF, was a senior mobilizer and occasional envoy of Charles Taylor, and the core of the invading force was drawn from Taylor's 'special forces.'" (Sawyer, 2004, 446)

". . . ongoing conflict in Sierra Leone has engendered refugee movements into neighboring Guinea and Liberia." (CIA, 2002)

B. **Pre-intervention "Assessment of Risk": 4** *relatively high*

"Both factions in ECOWAS regarded the war in Sierra Leone as an extension of the war in Liberia, and assumed that it would end when Liberia's war ended. Moreover, seeing that their intervention in Liberia led to chaos, the two factions in ECOWAS were duly wary of repeating their mistake." (Gershoni, 1997, 67)

"Nigeria may have felt that Sierra Leone offered greater rewards than risks." (Talentino, 2005, 221)

C. Extent of "National Interest Involvement":

i. The international community: 1 *low*

"The United Nations response to the Sierra Leone crisis may be described as ambiguous and reactive at best." (McGregor, 1999, 492)

"It was only in 2001 that the UN formally acknowledged the links between the conflicts in Sierra Leone and Liberia, and the entrepreneurial role of Taylor in this conflict system." (Sawyer, 2004, 447)

"Although the Commonwealth secretary general, Emaka Anyaoku, claimed that military intervention was 'totally justified,' the Commonwealth nations are divided over their treatment of Nigeria's role in Sierra Leone." (McGregor, 1999, 494)

"What is more disturbing about the global response or lack thereof to the Sierra Leone conflict is that such a tragedy, which United Nations Human Rights Commissioner Mary Robinson acknowledged was twenty-five times more horrendous than the Kosovo tragedy, elicited little or no early response for the great powers." (Mgbeoji, 2003, 44)

"The recent surge in atrocities against civilians in Sierra Leone has raised a limited level of awareness from the international community regarding the human rights implications of the crisis." (Human Rights Watch, cited in Africa Action, 1998, Dec. 18)

". . . thousands of Sierra Leoneans were killed and mutilated mainly because there was no large scale, international intervention in the early stages of the war." (Brown, 2005, Dec. 13)

ii. United States: 1 *low*

"At the time of the peace accord . . . [November 1996] . . . Secretary-General Annan asked the Security Council to approve a modest peacekeeping force, but member states, notably the United States, declined to consider the prospect." (Talentino, 2005, 211)

iii. Africa: 5 *high*

"As for the OAU, the Nigerian intervention was welcomed by its chairman, Robert Mugabe, and its secretary-general, Salim Ahmed Salim, at the Zimbabwe summit in June 1997." (McGregor, 1999, 494)

"Any actions taken with respect to the conflict in Sierra Leone will inevitably have a significant impact on the security situation in and policies of Guinea, Liberia, Côte d'Ivoire, Burkina Faso, Ghana and Nigeria." (Pratt, 1999, 16)

"Nigeria has long sought to establish itself as a regional hegemon and has pursued policies specifically designed to solidify that role. Sierra Leone offered an important opportunity to demonstrate its leadership in the region and its dominance in ECOWAS. If the UN endorsed ECOMOG as a regional model, Nigeria's status at home and abroad would benefit." (Talentino, 2005, 221)

"Nigerian views on the military intervention in [Sierra Leone] remain divided, as was the case when former Nigerian dictator General Ibrahim Babangida engineered the establishment of ECOMOG to intervene in the Liberian civil war. At the time, Babangida's interest in Liberia was largely seen to be an attempt to save his friend President Samuel Doe . . . from warlord Charles Taylor and his forces. Now Abacha has staked out Nigeria's position as defending a democratically-elected president, Kabbah, against a military faction backed by RUF forces loyal to Foday Sankoh, a former protege of Taylor, recently sworn in as Liberia's own democratically-elected president." (Conciliation Resources, 1997, September/October)

"The motives of Nigerian intervention were two-fold: there was a natural desire for regional security; but General Sani Abacha also wanted international legitimacy for this discredited military regime." (McGregor, 1999, 482)

"In particular, Nigeria must have hoped intervention would help reduce its status as an international pariah for the egregious human rights record of its repressive dictatorship." (Talentino, 2005, 222)

"It is well known that public opinion in Nigeria was against continued . . . [deployment] . . . of Nigerian troops as a part of ECOMOG in Sierra Leone, however, the Nigerian Army was interested in staying in Sierra Leone due to the massive benefits they were getting from illegal diamond mining." (Jetley, 2000, May)

"Restoring an elected government in Sierra Leone might ease the international isolation faced by Nigeria; quashing a revolt by army officers in another country might send a message to disgruntled Nigerian officers." (French, 1997, May 30, A13)

"Nigeria's dictator, Gen. Sani Abacha, did not order his troops into action out of any commitment to democracy. . . . the Nigerian leader seems mainly interested in establishing his own country as West Africa's dominant military power and regional policeman." (*NYT,* 1997, June 6, A30)

"For . . . Nigeria's primary opponents in ECOWAS, intervention was appealing for contradictory reasons. Liberia [under Charles Taylor], Burkina Faso, and Côte d'Ivoire were closely allied with each other and opposed to any further boosts to Nigerian power. Intervention through the rubric of ECOWAS gave them significant advantages. Like Nigeria they could appear to support widely embraced principles . . . and still be able to provide covert assistance to RUF. In addition, they could hope to drain Nigerian resources by perpetuation of the conflict in this fashion and therefore hope to restrict rather than expand its power." (Talentino, 2005, 223)

"Ghana is seen as a moderating influence on Nigerian ambitions, and its continued involvement in the Sierra Leone peacekeeping force is strongly encouraged by Britain and the United States." (McGregor, 1999, 492)

". . . Guinean military involvement in ECOMOG can also be expected, especially as Guinea has security concerns about a rebel movement operating from the Sierra Leone side of their common border. Aside from Guinea, however, most francophone members of ECOWAS (Benin, Burkina Faso, Côte d'Ivoire, Mali, Mauritania, Niger, Senegal, and Togo) are reluctant to become involved." (McGregor, 1999, 492)

D. Mass Media: December 10, 1996 to June 9, 1997
  i. "Alerting" function (volume of television and newspaper coverage): N=25; Rank order=8
    a. Television coverage: Rank order=7
      Total (ABC, CBS, NBC) N=8
      In-depth N=2
    b. *New York Times* coverage: N=17; Rank order=8
  ii. "Evaluative" function (intervention framing in the *New York Times*)
    Pro-intervention frames: N=2
    Anti-intervention frames: N=2
  iii. Assessment of media coverage

In January 1998, reporting on yet another RUF offensive against Freetown, Associated Press (AP) West Africa Bureau Chief Ian Stewart, who was to be seriously wounded a few days later, recounted the following conversation with AP Headquarters in New York over a story on Sierra Leone that he had submitted: "I filed my story by eight in the evening. . . . I waited an hour before calling New York to check whether there were any editing questions. 'It hasn't been edited yet,' I was told. 'Isn't it on the budget?' I asked. The 'budget' was the AP's daily list of top stories on the wire. 'Nope,' I was told. 'The General Desk feels it's just another story about a little war in Africa.'"(2002, 185)

Human Rights Watch concluded that Stewart's experience was far from unique, and pointed to crisis over-kill as one of the reasons why there was so little media interest: "Overshadowed by conflict in Liberia and events elsewhere on the continent, Sierra Leone has largely escaped the attention of the international community. . . . The recent surge in atrocities against civilians . . . has had to compete with other refugee-related emergencies for the attention of international players." (cited in Africa Action, 1998, Dec. 18) Veteran British Broadcasting Corporation (BBC) correspondent Mark Doyle, who provided a crucial link in getting information out on the Rwandan genocide, suspects that racism may have played a role as well, claiming that "it is not an exaggeration to suggest, just tentatively, that the international reaction to Sierra Leone might have been very different if all those people with their limbs chopped off had been white." (cited in Mgbeoji, 2003, 44)

Table 9.1 *New York Times* Coverage of Sierra Leone

Panel 1 – Date:	N	%	Panel 2 – Dateline:	N	%
First 2 Months	0	0%	United States	1	6%
Second 2 Months	1	6%	Sierra Leone	11	65%
Third 2 Months	16	94%	Africa (other)	5	29%
		100%			100%
Panel 3 – Source:	N	%	Panel 4 – Type of Content:	N	%
Local Staff	6	35%	Front-page News	0	0%
AP	5	29%	Inside-page News	15	88%
AFP	1	6%	Editorials	1	6%
Reuters	5	29%	Op-ed Features	0	0%
		99%	Photos	1	6%
					100%

Newspaper Coverage, by Date, Dateline, Source and Type (December 10, 1996 to June 9, 1997) N=17

For whatever reason, as the numbers indicate, during the six month period of our study, United States mass media simply did not become engaged with the civil war in Sierra Leone. This was in spite of its renewed intensity and the unique cruelty associated with amputations and the use of child soldiers—factors that normally would tend to increase media interest (see Galtung and Holmboe-Ruge, 1965; Gans, 1979). Perhaps contributing to the lack of media interest was the American government's position to reject any form of intervention other than sending marines to evacuate American and other Western nationals, indicating to assignment editors that the story "didn't have legs" and thus did not merit the investment of resources.

In the months prior to the May 27 coup that toppled President Kabbah's government, the *New York Times* had run only one story on Sierra Leone. As was the case in Burundi, clearly it was the coup that deposed the elected president, along with Western and African responses to it (accounting for fully 94 percent of stories), that provided the focus for journalistic interest in Sierra Leone. That only 6 percent of stories originated in the United States is another indication of how little the humanitarian crisis engaged the interest of American decision-makers.

Almost all of the crisis coverage originated from Africa (94 percent)—65 percent from Sierra Leone (furnished by the three major wire services) and another 30 percent from Côte d'Ivoire, reported by *New York Times* reporter Howard French. With the exception of one editorial and one stand-alone photo on the front page, all material dealing with Sierra Leone appeared on inside news pages and tended to focus on day-to-day happenings on the ground. A very modest six percent of content was considered to be "high impact."

In terms of an international intervention in Sierra Leone, two dimensions stand out. First, with the exception of a rather weak comment from UN Secretary-General Kofi Annan that "if the use of international force becomes a last resort and inevitable, then it may have to come to that," (cited in AP, 1997, June 5, A12) there was literally no discussion of the need for or the appropriateness of a Western intervention. While there was one reference to the State Department's "concern for the future of Sierra Leone's democracy," (Reuters, 1997, May 27, A10) there was no discussion regarding whether Washington was either prepared to, or indeed should, do anything about restoring it.

The most interesting aspect of intervention coverage deals with the amount of attention focused on, and the mixed evaluations given to, the Nigerian-led ECOWAS intervention, particularly Nigeria's underlying motives. While wire service reports originating from Sierra Leone were generally supportive of Nigerian/ECOWAS efforts on behalf of the deposed elected government, it was in *New York Times* reporting (both in reports from Howard French and in the one editorial that appeared on the crisis) that Nigeria was taken to task. The editorial charged that "the Nigerian leader [Sani Abacha] seems mainly interested in establishing his own country as West Africa's dominant military power and regional policeman," (*NYT*, 1997, June 6, A30) while Howard French reported that "Washington expressed disapproval of Nigeria's intervention, saying it preferred peaceful settlement." (French, 1997, June 9, A6) In total, two stories supported the Nigerian intervention, while the same number opposed it.

While French was generally supportive of what he saw as a trend toward Africans taking increased responsibility for dealing with African problems, by this point in the evolution of the Sierra Leone conflict two things should have been fairly obvious: (1) that efforts at "peaceful settlement" had not worked, and (2) that in neighboring Liberia, ECOMOG I had not been up to the task of peace enforcement. These considerations, however, did not appear to enter into the discussion of intervention in *New York Times* reporting. Also, with one exception, where the use of the all-encompassing term "atrocities" was used by Howard French to describe the tactics employed by rebel forces (1997, June 3, A10), there was no in-depth discussion of the truly bizarre and evil aspects of the civil war in Sierra Leone, which should have become evident long before the May 1997 coup.

In addition to the possibility of a Nigerian intervention, news stories dealt with the violence associated with and following the coup and the American and British evacuations of Westerners from the country.[3] Somewhat remarkably in our judgment, the possibility of a Western military intervention six years into the civil war never became a part of media discussion of the crisis.

■ Overall Evaluation of the Crisis Response

S. Byron Tarr stresses the linkages between Sierra Leone and Liberia: "[they] were created under similar circumstances. In both, concentrated political power enforced ethnic and class cleavages. Poor governance increased inequality in income distribution and persistent decline in output, leading to political discontent." (Tarr, 1993, 80)

And, eventually, in 1991, a civil war in Liberia spread into Sierra Leone, with horrendous consequences. The war did eventually end. As Andrea Talentino notes, "By the end of 2001 disarmament had been completed throughout the country except in two eastern districts. The RUF leadership had fragmented and its strength as a fighting organization was much diminished." As a result, she concluded that "Sierra Leone has become a cautious example of success in intervention." (2005, 215) While this may be the case, the costs of the decade-long conflict were extraordinary. In the judgment of Ikechi Mgbeoji,

> the Sierra Leone conflict is probably unmatched in its savagery and wickedness. Children as young as two months were regularly hacked to death and often had their limbs cut off by the "Cut Hands Commando" units of the rebels. By the end of the Sierra Leone conflict in May 2002, the RUF rebellion had killed 50,000 Sierra Leoneans, mutilated over 100,000, pushed over 1 million into neighbouring states as refugees, and internally displaced over 2 million (half the population). (2003, 43)

Our analysis shows that American mass media neither alerted the population to this crisis, other than in a most cursory manner (overall Rank Order 8), nor did the *New York Times* ever seriously discuss the pros and cons of a possible Western intervention in Sierra Leone, focusing its limited editorial attention instead on dissecting and criticizing the motivations underlying the Nigerian intervention. Talentino confirms that "pressure on the UN to respond [in Sierra Leone] came from international actors, *not the media.*" (2005, 218, italics added) For American media, it appears that Sierra Leone truly was, as Ian Stewart's editors described it, "just another . . . little war in Africa."

■ **Notes**

1. The name "Executive Outcomes" cleverly disguises the true nature of the organization which during the 1990s was a mercenary group composed of former members of the South African Defense Force who hired themselves out to various African governments and companies in need of military security. Headed by Eeben Barlow, the group (which was reported to have been dissolved in 1998) claimed to have "500 military advisers and 3,000 highly trained multi-national special forces soldiers" under its command. In addition to its well-documented participation in the civil wars in Sierra Leone and Angola, the organization is reputed to have been active in a number of African countries including Uganda, Zambia, and Ethiopia (see Lobaido, 1998, Aug. 11). Andrew McGregor notes as well the involvement of Sandline International, a British mercenary group, operating on behalf of the Sierra Leone government (1999, 488).

2. The cutting off of hands is yet another cruel practice brought to Africa by Europeans. In his book, *King Leopold's Ghost,* Adam Hochschild relates that in order to be paid their bounty for Congolese natives killed, Belgian soldiers would often simply cut off their hands to claim their reward (1998, 164–166; see photos following 116).

3. A perusal of the Vanderbilt TV News Archive indicates that American network television news reports focused almost exclusively on the "evacuation of foreigners" dimension of the crisis.

10

Angola, 1999:
1,000 UN Military Observers Removed, 30 UN Civilian Observers Returned

E. Donald Briggs and Walter C. Soderlund

■ Background

Angola is one of two crises studied that occurred in ex-Portuguese colonies, the other being East Timor. In neither of these did the independence process proceed smoothly, but the crises that beset both in the late 1990s were the result of quite unique sets of circumstances. (For East Timor, see Chapter 11, this volume.)

For Angola, 1999 marks not so much the development of a new crisis as it does the third or fourth surge in the intensity of the civil war that had gone on in that country since its independence from Portugal in 1975, a conflict that even then was essentially an extension of the independence struggle begun in the early 1960s. (See James, 1991.) Nor does 1999 mark the first instance in which the international community attempted to facilitate the end of hostilities—in fact, efforts in this direction were far more robust at earlier stages of the drawn-out crisis. While in this sense Angola exhibits characteristics different from most other peacekeeping/peace enforcement situations, the 1999 crisis stemming from yet another renewal of the civil war did present the international community with a clear case of humanitarian emergency, and for that reason it is included in this study.

Located in South West Africa, bordered by the Atlantic Ocean on the west, Republic of Congo and Zaire on the north, Zambia on the east, and Namibia on the south, Angola is a relatively large country (three times the size of California), with a relatively sparse population (estimated at 10 million), "divided into eight major ethnic groupings . . . and fractured politically along ethnic lines." (Page Fortuna, 1993a, 376) Unlike the great majority of African countries, Angola is also rich in resources (notably diamonds and oil, among other minerals), has abundant fertile agricultural land (it was once the world's third-largest coffee producer), and is blessed with a number of good seaports. It would thus appear to have all the necessary material bases for becoming one of Africa's principal success stories.

Angola was, of course, a colonial domain or "overseas province" of Portugal for nearly five hundred years; Portugal, as James Ciment tells us, was "always an imperial anomaly, . . . the first European nation to colonize Africa and virtually the last to leave." (1997, 35) Portuguese explorers first made contact with the Angolan area of West Africa in the late fifteenth century (see Wheeler, 1971, Chapter 2), and shortly thereafter it became one of the most important centers of the Atlantic slave trade. Paul Hare has suggested that something like 40 percent of all the slaves taken from Africa came from Angolan ports. (1998, 4)

The slave trade in fact defined Portugal's relations with its Angolan "province" for most of the colonial period. That meant that it was in an almost continuous state of military pacification, and that in the four centuries after 1575 "rarely did a year pass" without a military campaign somewhere in the territory. (Wheeler, 1969, 428) This was somewhat less true in the "era of comparative quiescence" following 1925, but military operations of one kind or another were never far away at any time. (Wheeler, 1969, 426)

It is probably true, however, that there were no serious challenges to Portuguese rule until segments of Angolan society caught the decolonization fever of the post–World War II era. Two nationalist movements, the Popular Movement for the Liberation of Angola (MPLA), which drew its support from the Mbundu people, and the National Front for the Liberation of Angola (FNLA), which drew its support from the Bakongo people, were founded in the 1950s. Lisbon was aware of the grievances that had grown up, and it implemented reforms that, by 1958, it was convinced had ensured racial harmony in Angola for the foreseeable future. Trouble, however, began with the non-political Baixa "Cotton Revolt" of 1960, which resulted in the massacre of a disputed number of ill-armed peasants and continued in February 1961 with attacks on a police patrol, a prison, a police barracks, and the radio station in Luanda, the capital. Repression, arrests, and executions followed, and by March a full-scale insurrection was underway. (See Pélissier, 1971, Chapter 8.) Douglas Wheeler describes the situation Portuguese military leaders confronted in 1961:

Over 100 administrative posts and towns had been wiped out, taken, or paralyzed by African nationalist groups; over 1,000 Europeans were dead and an unknown number of Africans; the economy of North Angola was crippled; communications were largely out or damaged; and thousands of Portuguese refugees were camped in Luanda, or on their way back to Portugal.

The insurrection failed, but warfare aimed at ending Portuguese colonial rule continued, and by 1967–68,

the strength of the [Portuguese] army in Angola had reached approximately 50,000, or some 15–16 times the number of European troops which had been in the country in early 1961. . . . The war against the African nationalists by then was costing Portugal about $300,000 a day, and perhaps $20 million a year. (both quotes from Wheeler, 1969, 431)

It was at this time that Angola became "a fixture on the agendas of the [UN] Security Council and General Assembly, in the context of the organization's focus on the struggle for self-determination in Africa." (Lodico, 1996, 104)

Significantly for events that were to afflict Angola for decades to come, a third nationalist group came into existence in 1966. The National Union for the Total Independence of Angola (UNITA), supported by the Ovimbundo people, was founded by Jonas Savimbi, following his desertion from the FNLA after five years of membership. UNITA began attacks against Portuguese positions in Angola almost immediately. By the time of independence nine years later, it had become a significant threat and the chief rival of the MPLA for control of the state-to-be.

Events in Portugal itself, rather than in Angola, brought about independence. On the night of April 24–25, 1974, a group of leftist officers within the Portuguese military ranks, calling itself the Armed Forces Movement, and acting largely out of dissatisfaction over colonial policy, overthrew the government of Marcelo Caetano that had assumed power following the longstanding dictatorship of Antonio de Salazar. The new government was keen on disengaging from its colonies as quickly as possible. A conference of the leaders of the three Angolan nationalist groups was arranged in January 1975. The result was the Alvor Agreement, in which it was agreed that all three independence groups were "the sole and legitimate representatives of the Angolan people . . . [and that] . . . full independence and sovereignty of Angola shall be solemnly proclaimed on November 11 [1975]."

(Ciment, 1997, 47) One representative from each organization was to join in a triumvirate transitional government until elections could be held for a constituent assembly. As might have been expected, the three groups turned on each other within weeks of signing the Alvor Agreement, each "trying to establish itself as the legitimate government of the oil-diamond-coffee-cotton-rich country." (Ciment, 1997, 2)

International factors as well intruded into Angolan politics. Yvonne Lodico has observed that "it would be hard to find a time . . . in Angola's history in which there were not several external influences feeding its internal strife," (1996, 104) and in the mid-1970s it was the Cold War that provided the pretext for major international involvement, as overseas supporters of each group now intensified their efforts to boost their clients into the seat of power. The Soviet Union had long provided limited arms and moral support to the fraternal socialists of the MPLA, and sharply increased its assistance now that independence was in sight. Cuba, which had been supplying advisors and military trainers to the MPLA since 1965, likewise upped the ante and eventually provided in the neighborhood of 17,000 troops to fight in the MPLA cause. The latter undoubtedly saved the MPLA from defeat at the hands of UNITA. In Washington's view, and in that of some commentators, the Cuban forces were in Angola as proxies for the Soviets.[1] But while Moscow may have approved of their participation, and provided transport for the bulk of their troops, others have argued convincingly that the decision to intervene was Cuba's alone, in pursuit of its "strong commitment to further the cause of socialism" and determination to enhance its own "leadership role in the Third World." (Klinghoffer, 1980, 115) Gillian Gunn maintains that the Cubans decided to intervene without even consulting Moscow and that by so doing they gave the Soviets the option of refusing to support the move and thus appearing weak, or allowing themselves to be dragged in deeper than they had intended to go. She concluded that "left to their own initiative, the Soviets would probably have been far more circumspect in Angola." (1992, 48–49) Not even superpowers are always able to call the tune.

For its part, the FNLA received support from China, which appears simply to have wanted to thwart Soviet objectives as much as possible, and from Mobutu Sese Seko's government in Zaire. The FNLA leader, Holden Roberto, lived in Zaire most of the time, and he was also Mobutu's brother-in-law. In addition, there were ethnic ties between the FNLA's principal followers in Angola and people living in adjoining areas of Zaire. What is more surprising, and not often mentioned in discussions of Angolan history, the FNLA also received American support in the form of both money and arms through the CIA. Roberto himself received an annual retainer of $10,000 from the CIA in the early 1960s, despite the fact that Portugal was an American Cold War ally. In 1974 Roberto was handed $300,000 of CIA money to allow him to buy a television station and a daily newspaper in Luanda. (Meredith, 2005, 136, 315)

By 1975, the United States had decided, apparently at the urging of Zambia's President Kenneth Kaunda, to provide major support for UNITA as well. Secretary of State Henry Kissinger became convinced that concerted action was necessary to prevent the Soviets from carving out a new sphere of influence in Africa. As he put it, "Our concern in Angola is not the economic wealth or the naval base. I don't care about the oil or the base, but I do care about the African reaction when they see the Soviets pull it off and we don't do anything." (cited in Meredith, 2005, 316) Planeloads of Soviet arms began arriving in July 1975.

South Africa also weighed in, principally in support of UNITA, but with their own forces in addition to whatever economic and material aid could be supplied. Ian Spears has argued that in doing so, it acted as a proxy of the United States, just as Cuba was doing on behalf of the Soviet Union. (1999, 563) Since South Africa's military forces carried out operations in Angola that favored UNITA on several occasions during the conflict, the conclusion is both neat and plausible. It should not be forgotten, however, that South Africa had ample reasons of its own to be concerned about developments in Angola. Ideologically the conservative South African regime was perhaps even less enthusiastic about socialist next-door neighbors than the United States, but more importantly, it wished to avoid a government in Luanda that would support and assist the Southwest Africa Peoples' Organization (SWAPO), the "rebel" group in Namibia with which it was battling. But the involvement may have been greater than anyone in Pretoria had intended. Gunn quotes a South African military official involved in the decision to assist UNITA:

> We had a request from . . . [MPLA rivals] . . . for aid, and we decided to expend a relatively small sum initially. . . . Our intuitive feeling was that we should have the most friendly power possible on that border. . . . We [subsequently] found that our new allies were totally disorganized. They could not utilize cash, so we provided arms. They could not use the arms

so we sent in officers to train them to use the arms. The training process was too slow, so we handled the weapons ourselves. We got pulled in gradually, needing to commit ourselves more if the past commitment was not to be wasted." (cited in Gunn, 1992, 49–50)

All the Angolan nationalist groups assumed that the one that controlled Luanda on November 11, 1975, would receive the reins of power from the departing Portuguese. Fierce clashes between FNLA and MPLA partisans in Northern Angola resulted, thanks to the well-trained Cuban troops, in FNLA defeat. In Southern Angola, the South African Defense Force (SADF) prevented MPLA inroads against UNITA, itself still militarily weak and unable to mount a serious challenge to MPLA strength. Hence, it was the MPLA that was in a position to assume power when, as scheduled on November 11, the Portuguese, as one commentator put it, "brought five centuries of colonial rule to a pathetic, whimpering end." (Fred Bridgland, cited by Ciment, 1997, 51; see also Stockwell, 1978, 213–16)

The cost of the conflict had been high. By January 1976, 100,000 Angolans, perhaps 1,200 Cubans, and 100 South Africans had died, and more than 50,000 people had fled to Zaire and Zambia. In military terms, it was estimated that the war had cost $6.7 billion in arms and property losses. "The Angolan war of independence was easily the costliest and most destructive conflict in modern sub-Saharan history, though it would pale next to the horrors to come." (Ciment, 1997, 53–4)

▪ Roots of the Crisis

Jonas Savimbi devoted the immediate post-independence years to building UNITA into a force capable of challenging the MPLA, and to establishing the international support that would make that possible. United States aid, for instance, had ceased in December 1975 with the passage of legislation (the Clark Amendment), which prohibited aid to the Angolan groups, and it was vital that it be regained. Savimbi was successful, thanks in part to a visit to the United States in 1976, and he was also able to come to some sort of understanding with the South Africans. By 1980 "the pieces were . . . beginning to come together for the escalation of Savimbi's war against the MPLA." (Ciment, 1997, 64) Following Ronald Reagan's election, American aid was more readily forthcoming. The Clark Amendment was repealed in 1985, and more or less permanent war came to Southern Angola. Much of this was again conducted by the SADF, though Savimbi always ridiculed the very idea of cooperation with a regime based on racial discrimination. (See Ciment, 1997, 71.) Ciment maintains, however, that at the very least UNITA received diesel fuel and other non-military supplies courtesy of Pretoria (1997, 2), quite apart from the benefits derived from South African operations themselves. A major UNITA offensive against the MPLA in 1983 was stopped 125 miles south of Luanda. In United States–mediated talks the following winter, the Lusaka Accords were signed. These provided for a military disengagement, the withdrawal of the SADF from Angola, and an international monitoring commission to see that no party took advantage of the situation. (Ciment, 1997, 73) It would appear, however, that none of the parties kept the agreement for longer than it took to return to their respective bases, and by 1985, full-scale hostilities had been resumed, though without notable success on any side.

In December 1988, the United States, Cuba, South Africa, and Angola concluded the Tripartite Accords, which, in effect, traded South Africa's withdrawal from Angola for Cuba's similar action and provided for the creation of the United Nations Angola Verification Mission (UNAVEM I) to verify Cuba's pullout. (Lodico, 1996, 107) It also agreed that Namibia should begin the transition to independence (see Page Fortuna, 1993a), thus removing the most important reason for South Africa to be concerned with the outcome of the Angolan civil war.

This neither ended Angola's civil war nor the efforts to bring about that end. There were new talks in Bicesse, Portugal, in 1990, assisted this time not only by Portugal itself, but by the United States and the Soviet Union as well. The Bicesse Accords were signed in May 1991, just a week after the last Cuban troops left Angola. (Ciment, 1997, 196) The Accords provided for a ceasefire within two weeks, the integration of MPLA and UNITA forces into a single national army, and internationally monitored elections in the fall of 1992. The Security Council also established UNAVEM II to oversee the process. (Page Fortuna, 1993b)

When elections were held the following September, the MPLA emerged victorious by a substantial margin. Savimbi, however, immediately declared the elections fraudulent, despite the testimony from monitors to the contrary, and resumed hostilities. Further negotiations produced the Lusaka Protocols (as distinct from the earlier Lusaka Accords), the chief focus of Paul Hare's book *Angola's Last Best Chance for Peace* (1998). The Protocols were signed in Zambia on November 20, 1994, though Savimbi declined to attend and sign personally, citing inadequate security.

By this time the Cold War was over, the Clinton administration was in office in Washington, and attitudes toward the Angolan situation had changed dramatically. The new administration not only recognized the MPLA government in Luanda, it also lifted sanctions against selling it military equipment and advocated a UN embargo against UNITA. (Ciment, 1997, 198) The Protocols, produced after eight months of negotiation, gave UNITA a share of power, including three of the country's nineteen governorships, and four cabinet posts, though none of the "key" ones that Savimbi had demanded. (Ciment, 1997, 199) In February 1995, the Security Council authorised a 7,500-man UN peacekeeping force, UNAVEM III, though it did not even begin to deploy until April 1995. (Hare, 1998, 87) Yvonne Lodico describes the difficult conditions facing UNAVEM III:

> The new operation deployed into a country in which the basic infrastructure was almost totally devastated and 35 percent of the population . . . has been displaced from their homes. Intensifying the humanitarian situation, land mines could be found throughout the country . . . , [making Angola] . . . the most mine-polluted country in the world. (1996, 124)

■ Events Precipitating the Crisis

A number of factors might be pointed to as precipitating the 1999 Angolan crisis: the failure of the Lusaka Protocols—or the failure of the international community to persuade the parties to abide by them; the basic distrust between Angolan leaders; or perhaps the unrealities of the concept of "power sharing," however "fair" it may have seemed to those who proposed it.

In the months following the Lusaka Protocols, both sides accused the other of violations of the ceasefire, and Savimbi declined to commit himself to any personal role in the new government. But at least some demobilization of UNITA forces seems to have taken place, some UNITA members took the legislative seats allotted to them, and outside observers seemed to feel that affairs were moving generally in the right direction. Madeleine Albright, United States Ambassador to the United Nations, for instance, said on visiting Angola in January 1996, that the two parties needed "just a final push" to make the peace stick. (cited in Ciment, 1997, 218) The UN appears to have considered that push to have been delivered, as in July 1997 it decided that UNAVEM III could be replaced by a small, thousand-man team of military observers, police, and human rights workers (MONUA). (Hare, 1998, 128–29)

But serious difficulties quickly developed over the transfer of UNITA-controlled areas to state administration. Two of these, Negage, the site of the main airport in Northern Angola, and Cuango, the center of the richest diamond-mining area in the Northeast, were particularly important to both parties. Savimbi charged that the government used "undue military pressure in taking over Negage, making further cohabitation impossible." (Hare, 1998, 141–42) Savimbi distrusted Jose Eduardo dos Santos, the MPLA leader, and that distrust was reciprocated. During the final months of 1997 and early 1998, the situation deteriorated quickly. Attacks against "government institutions and personnel, especially the national police . . . had, according to MONUA, the characteristics of an organized military operation identified with UNITA. In many cases, MONUA personnel also came under attack." (Hare, 1998, 144) In June 1998, the Secretary-General expressed alarm at developments in Angola and stated that the situation was "attributable, for the most part, to the failure of UNITA to fulfill its obligations under the Lusaka Protocols." (Kofi Annan, cited in Hare, 1998, 145) In December 1998, the Angolan government requested that the UN remove MONUA, and began an intensified attack against UNITA forces. (Spears, 1999, 568–69) It was not until October 1999 that the departed MONUA was replaced by a thirty-man civilian observer team.

In the full-scale renewal of the civil war that followed, the government did not initially fare very well. By the latter part of July 1999, UNITA controlled approximately 70 percent of the country, and in the process drove "more than a million Angolans off the land and into the cities." (Daley, 1999, July 26, A1) Well over ten years after the departure of Cuban troops, Angola was again engulfed in unrelenting conflict. Savimbi has largely taken the blame for this, and it is true that without him UNITA probably would have given up the struggle earlier than it did. But it should not be forgotten that MPLA officials were scarcely less recalcitrant and manipulative.

Strength of the International Response: Rank order=9
   A. **Did the Humanitarian Crisis Result in an International Intervention? Yes**
      A thirty-person civilian observer team
   B. **Type of Response:** UN-led civilian observer team
      "[In October 1999] . . . the United Nations Security Council voted . . . to send a team of 30 civilians to maintain a United Nation presence in Angola, described as Africa's most dangerous country." (AFP, 1999, Oct. 17, I5)

C. **Type of UN Involvement:** Chapter VI
D. **Size of Intervening Force:** Thirty civilian observers

Determinants of the International Response
  A. **Severity of the Crisis: Rank order=8**
    i. **Number of deaths: (short-term) indeterminate; (long-term) 500,000 to 1,000,000**
    "About 350,000 [Angolans] died in 16 years of bloody civil war." (Lewis, 1992, Nov. 16, A17)
    ". . . the war . . . left the country devastated and killed half a million people." (Talbot, 2002, Apr. 13)
    "A million Angolans face starvation as the food supplies dwindle." (Reuters, 1999, June 23, A6)
    "One million people died, four million others got displaced and the same number of families are separated throughout the country as a result of 27 years of armed conflict in Angola." (Doctors without Borders, cited in *People's Daily*, 2002, Oct. 11)
    ii. **Number of refugees and displaced persons: (short-term) 1 million to 1.2 million; (long-term) 2 to 3.5 million**
    "Population at Risk" (1995) 3.7 million. (Weiss and Collins, 1996, 5–7, Table I-1)
    "Population in Need" (1999) "more than 3 million." (Weiss and Collins, 2000, 5, Table I.1)
    "By January 1999, after just one month of fighting, an estimated 250,000 Angolans had been forced from their homes. The number rose to 800,000 by May and to an estimated 1 million by June—almost one-tenth of Angola's population." (Spears, 1999, 563)
    "More than 1.2 million Angolans have fled their homes since December, when Government forces and UNITA rebels resumed fighting." (Reuters, 1999, June 23, A6)
    "At least 200 people are dying every day in Angola of illness related to malnutrition, and 1.7 million people are homeless." (Crossette, 1999, Aug. 24, A9)
    ". . . 3.5 million people, a third of the population, have fled their homes." (Talbot, 2002, April 13)
    iii. **Likelihood of conflict spreading to other states: 5 *high***
      a. **Number of shared borders: 4**
        Democratic Republic of the Congo, Republic of Congo, Namibia, Zambia

b. Involvement of bordering states

". . . the war in Angola is only one dimension of a much larger regional conflict. An 'arc of conflict' extends from Angola through the two Congos, Rwanda, Burundi, Uganda, the Sudan, Ethiopia, Eritrea, and Somalia." (Spears, 1999, 563)

". . . the conflicts in Congo and Angola have fed off each other and continue to do so." (Crocker, 1999, Aug. 6, A19)

"African leaders, like Felix Houphouet-Boigny of Ivory Coast and Mobutu Sese Seko of Zaire were open supporters [of Jonas Savimbi], other presidents cultivated strong diplomatic and commercial ties right until the end." (Simpson, 2002, Feb. 25)

"Internationally, Angola provided military support to Laurent Kabila's . . . struggle to overthrow Mobuto Seso Seko in neighbouring Zaire. . . . [Mobutu's] . . . overthrow in May 1997 meant an end to Zaire's military support both to UNITA and to separatist rebels in the oil-rich Cabinda region. . . . [Angola] . . . kept a force of some 7,000 troops in the DRC to sustain the regime and protect their common border." (Spears, 1999, 567)

"For months Angola has accused Zambia of allowing the Angolan rebel group UNITA to resupply via Zambia. But Zambia denies such cooperation, saying the accusations emanate from its refusal to allow Angolan troops to use Zambian territory to attack the rebels." (Daley, 1999, May 11, A8)

B. Pre-intervention "Assessment of Risk": 5 *high*

"No African nation is as sadly recidivist as Angola. Agreements to end the power struggle between the rebels led by Jonas Savimbi and the Government have been within reach in 1975, 1991, and 1994, but never successfully grasped." (Crocker, 1999, Aug. 6, A19)

"Opportunists with a Leninist sense of power are in charge on both sides in Angola. Neither places a high priority on peace or people. Barring victory, both prefer war over peace." (Crocker, 1999, Aug. 6, A19)

C. Extent of "National Interest Involvement":
i. The international community: 3 *medium*

"Angola's economic significance can hardly be overstated. . . . [Its] wealth can be found in, among other things, its enormous supply of oil and diamonds." (Spears, 1999, 564)

"As for the United Nations, having just been asked to leave, it is unlikely to mount any sort of major peace mission to Angola beyond making itself available to facilitate negotiations should the two parties decide to bargain." (Spears, 1999, 578)

ii. United States: 3 *medium*

"The irony of some as-yet defined intervention is that, as unlikely as it is, the West (most likely the United States) would be stepping in to protect a government it had long opposed during the cold war years from a rebel movement it had long supported. One expatriate businessman . . . noted that 'the US would step in, but only if there was a serious threat to the oil business.'" (Spears, 1999, 578)

"As Africa's second largest producer of oil, Angola provides the United States with 7 percent of its oil imports." (Spears, 1999, 564)

"Kissinger saw the Angolan conflict solely in terms of global politics and was determined the Soviets should not be permitted to make a move in any remote part of the world without being confronted by the United States." (Stockwell, 1978, 43)

"When Nixon resigned in August 1974, Kissinger became even more concerned that the Soviets might take advantage of US domestic problems to expand their international influence. The fall of Saigon in April 1975 heightened Washington's suspicion that Moscow would see it as weak and vacillating. Kissinger concluded, therefore, that the United States had to 'resist marginal accretions of Soviet power even when the issues seem ambiguous.' Angola just happened to be the next perceived 'marginal accretion.'" (Gunn, 1992, 51)

"In fact, Angola had little plausible importance to American national security and little economic importance beyond *robusta* coffee it sold to American markets and the relatively small amounts of petroleum Gulf Oil pumped from the Cabindan fields." (Stockwell, 1978, 43)

iii. Africa: 5 *high*

"When the Portuguese announced their decolonization timetable for Angola following the April 1974 coup d'état in Lisbon, there was little doubt that Zaire would continue to be intimately involved in the politics of independent Angola." (Crocker, 1976, 5)

"There is also a significant geopolitical factor. Oil-rich Cabinda would be a tempting prize in the struggle over succession to Portuguese rule: Zaire's sponsorship of a Cabinda separatist movement reflects the desire at least to explore an expansionist option." (Crocker, 1976, 6)

"President Mobutu was motivated to intrude in Angola both by family concerns—the FNLA leader was his brother-in-law—and by strategic considerations. With only a sliver of territory linking it to the sea, Zaire traditionally sent its mineral wealth to foreign markets through Angola's Benguela rail line. In addition, the mineral-rich Zairean province of Shaba bordered Angola, and Mobutu constantly feared Angolan actors would assist secessionist Shaba rebels. Helping a friendly leader take power in Luanda was therefore clearly advantageous to Mobutu." (Gunn, 1992, 49)

"On September 11 [1975], Mobutu committed his elite Seventh and Fourth Commando Battalions . . . and the tide swung back in favor of the FNLA north of Luanda." (Stockwell, 1978, 163)

"Since the closure of the Zambian-Rhodesian border to rail traffic in 1973, some 40 percent of Zambia's copper exports have been carried on the Benguela railroad through the middle of Angola. That rail link is now severely damaged and could require a year to repair, under favorable circumstances. Thus Lusaka has a substantial economic interest in seeing peace restored to Angola." (Crocker, 1976, 7)

"Like Angola's black-governed neighbors, South Africa perceives important national interests to be at stake in Angola; unlike them, however, it has the capacity for direct, physical intervention on a substantial scale." (Crocker, 1976, 8)

"Support by South Africa for UNITA/FNLA was a means of assuring that 'the most friendly power possible' would be installed in Angola. South Africa feared that a hostile government would aid both the ANC's anti-apartheid efforts and the struggle of Namibian guerrillas to force South African troops out of their homeland." (Gunn, 1992, 49)

D. Mass Media: April 18 to October 17, 1999
   i. "Alerting" function (volume of television and newspaper coverage): N=15; Rank order=9
      a. Television coverage: Rank order=10
         Total (ABC, CBS, NBC): N=0
         In-depth: N=0
      b. *New York Times* coverage: N=15; Rank order=9

ii. "Evaluative" function (intervention framing in the *New York Times*)
Pro-intervention frames: N=0
Anti-intervention frames: N=2
iii. Assessment of media coverage

In his appraisal of the seemingly endless Angolan civil war, Ian Spears noted that "the apparent invisibility of the crisis is hardly surprising, given the usual media coverage of wars in Africa." (1999, 563) Our study of media coverage of Angola begins on April 18, 1999, six months prior to the decision by the UN to renew its presence in Angola by the modest deployment of 30 civilian observers. If we use a comparative perspective to evaluate United States mass media coverage of the Angolan crisis, we may rephrase Spear's assessment as follows: *Even, in light of the usual media coverage of wars in Africa, the apparent invisibility of this crisis is surprising.* No coverage of the crisis at all on network television news, combined with a mere fifteen stories in the *New York Times,* places Angolan just ahead of last place Sudan in terms of media visibility. Moreover, it should be noted that ten of the twelve *New York Times* inside page news stories dealing with the crisis were of the one-paragraph "World Briefing" variety. This accounts for the large number of "Unknown"

Table 10.1 *New York Times* **Coverage of Angola**

Panel 1 – Date:	N	%	Panel 2 – Dateline:	N	%
First 2 Months	3	20%	United States	3	20%
Second 2 Months	8	53%	Angola	1	7%
Third 2 Months	4	27%	Africa (other)	0	0%
		100%	Other	0	0%
			Unknown	11	73%
					100%

Panel 3 – Source:	N	%	Panel 4 – Type of Content:	N	%
Local Staff	4	27%	Front-page News	1	7%
AP	1	7%	Inside-page News	12	80%
AFP	4	27%	Editorials	0	0%
Reuters	4	27%	Op-ed Features	1	7%
Freelance/Academic	1	7%	Photos	0	0%
Other	1	7%	Letters	1	7%
		102%			101%

Newspaper Coverage, by Date, Dateline, Source and Type (April 18 to October 17, 1999) N=15 datelines and provides further evidence of the lack of interest in the Angolan crisis.

There is little doubt regarding the invisibility of the war in Angola—fifteen items overall, of which only two were considered to be high-impact items. The dearth of coverage was at least partly a consequence of the fact that military operations were not going well for the Angolan government and that it had employed censorship to hide reverses on the ground. On July 26, in the only front-page story appearing on Angola, Suzanne Daley documented the difficulties involved in getting information on the military situation:

> Information about how the war is going is spotty. Most of the country is not accessible, and the Government has done its best to keep news to a minimum, including ordering a blackout on war news in January. Since then a half-dozen journalists have been beaten up or threatened for reporting on it anyhow, including reporters for the Voice of America and the BBC. (1999, July 26, A7)

On August 11, the Associated Press further reported that following the broadcast of an interview with Jonas Savimbi, two journalists and the Director of a Catholic radio station had been arrested. The story noted that "Rádio Ecclésia is one of the few independent sources of information in Angola, where the Government has imposed a blackout on news about fighting with the rebels since the beginning of the year." (AP, 1999, Aug. 11, A6)

In that there was not much news about the fighting, as was the case in Sudan, the censorship strategy can be seen to have been at least partially successful. However, the reality that over the summer of 1999 UNITA was on the offensive, and that the Angolan government was in retreat, came through very clearly in the limited *New York Times* reporting that appeared, with government reversals covered in five stories. A successful government offensive against UNITA in September was also noted, although only in two brief stories.

Beyond the issues of government defeats and censorship, reporting focused primarily on two issues: the human suffering experienced by the Angolan people and UNITA's financing its war through illegal trade in diamonds. Suzanne Daley's front-page story detailed the horrors encountered by those uprooted by the seemingly endless war: "Aid workers say they are beginning to see a new phenomenon among this population—an indifference to life. Many of the refugees, they say, do not seem to be even trying to survive anymore." (1999, July 26, A7) On August 24, Barbara Crossette, in a short piece in the

World Briefing section, reported the view of a World Food Organization spokesperson that "Angola, a potentially rich country torn for three decades by civil war, was living at a level of despair that exists virtually nowhere else in the world today." (Catherine Bertini, cited in Crossette, 1999, Aug. 24, A9)

Both Raymond Bonner and Chester Crocker highlighted the importance of the illicit trade in diamonds to the continuation of UNITA's capacity to prolong the conflict. According to Bonner, "The flow of uncut diamonds from rebel-held mines to market centers around the world—valued at hundreds of millions of dollars a year— is keeping rebel armies in Angola, Congo and Sierra Leone supplied with tanks and assault rifles and even uniforms and beer." (Bonner, 1999, Aug. 8, I3) Although lacking in specifics as to how this might be accomplished, both reports referred to the need to curtail the illicit diamond trade in order to bring peace to Angola.

While the suffering of the Angolan people was made quite clear in a number of stories, a specific connection to a possible American-led intervention was made in only one—that in an op-ed piece by Chester Crocker. While he claimed that "for the people of Angola the permanent war is intolerable," his assessment of how the United States should respond to this situation was quite guarded. Crocker certainly questioned the wisdom of the United States leading an intervention in support of the Angolan Government:

> Perhaps, instead of debating which political bed to jump into tomorrow, the United States would be better advised to engage not only with the Government of Angola but also with Angola's fragile civil society institutions, the churches, the humanitarian agencies and those "autonomous" leaders who are now speaking out against the unconscionable behavior of incumbent political elites. . . . Kofi Annan is right to call for the real friends of Angola to engage in the search for peace. . . . *But one wonders if this is best done by having American military and diplomatic resources placed at the disposal of the recognized but unaccountable Government of Angola.* (1999, Aug. 6, A19, italics added)

■ Overall Evaluation of the Crisis Response

For the record, the war in Angola continued unabated until Jonas Savimbi was killed in action in February 2002. Then, a scant two weeks later, a ceasefire was arrived at. Now, more than five years later, it appears that Angola is at last set upon a firm path to peace and prosperity. This fact raises two questions: First, was Jonas Savimbi some sort of evil incarnate, solely responsible for three decades of destruction within his own country? Second, if the first question is even largely true, how can so many, and perhaps especially so many in the media, have been deceived by him for so long?

Savimbi had no shortage of detractors after his death or, for that matter, in the closing years of his life. As early as 1992, for example, Anthony Lewis referred to him as "another creature of the Cold War," grouped with such notorious figures as Mobutu Sese Seko and Said Barre. (1992, Nov.16, A17) Christopher Clapham derided Savimbi's "appeal to local ethnic sentiments and traditions, including the burning of witches," and denounced his hypocrisy in representing himself as a democrat to the United States and an ally of apartheid to South Africa. (1998, 17) To Chris Simpson, he was a "pariah" at the time of his death, and most of his obituaries were "predictably damning." (2002, February 25) Megesha Ngwiri exemplified Simpson's observations: "Jonas Malhiro Savimbi . . . should have been taken out and shot 27 years ago, thus saving at least a million lives. He is Angola's greatest tragedy." (cited in de Rezende, 2002, May)

While the suggestion that Savimbi even pretended to be a supporter of apartheid is scarcely credible, the charge is a good indication of the "anything goes" criticism of him following the breakdown of the Lusaka Protocols. There was, of course, more than a little truth in their criticisms, but as usual with wholesale condemnations, the other side of Savimbi tended to be overlooked at this stage. Paul Hare, as United States special representative for the peace process in Angola from 1993 to 1998, was scarcely a Savimbi booster, but he points out that the MPLA government provided some justification for UNITA intransigence by its maneuvers at home and abroad during 1998 (1998, 142–43), just as it had not been blameless at earlier stages of the civil war. Savimbi almost certainly must bear the major share of the blame for the extended hostilities, but he probably should not be made the sole culprit, except in the sense that it was undoubtedly his charismatic leadership that kept UNITA in the fray for so long. In the final analysis, therefore, one is forced to agree with Ngwiri that without him a good many lives would have been saved. One wonders, however, whether the same might not be said of dos Santos.

Why, then, did it take twenty-five years to reach such a conclusion about Savimbi, and how were successive American governments "fooled" by him? In Elaine Windrich's assessment, "The image of Jonas Savimbi as a 'freedom fighter' deserving of U.S. support was largely a product of the publicity efforts of the Pretoria regime and American right-wing pressure groups that had a unique access to the Reagan/Bush White House." (1992, 1) Savimbi appears, in fact, to have realized early on that any possibility of his success depended as much on good publicity as on good weaponry. The United States was, of course, particularly important in this regard, and it was, down at least to the Clinton administration, predisposed in favor of any proposition that could be cast in an anti-communist mold. When he visited Washington in 1986, Savimbi was welcomed to the White House itself, and President Reagan spoke at that time of UNITA's winning "a victory that electrifies the world and brings great sympathy and assistance from other nations to those struggling for freedom." (Simpson, 2002, Feb. 25) In light of such statements, it would have been surprising to find much severe criticism of Savimbi in the mainstream media prior to 1993, and such criticism would have been neither appropriate nor helpful once the United States turned seriously to trying to cajole UNITA and MPLA to join forces. Nonetheless, one is left to ponder the extent to which Savimbi's original media image in the United States as a "freedom fighter," elaborately constructed by public relations professionals and promoted by paid lobbyists, had managed to override a two-decade-long record of at best questionable behavior.[2]

Nor is it easy to see how the UN could have done more to prevent the tragedy of Angola. As Ian Spears asked in his concluding remarks on the conflict:

> How does one negotiate an end to a war that has persisted with only two interruptions for 25 years (longer if one considers the pre-independence struggle), where substantial resources have been committed by the international community, where most of the obvious methods of conflict resolution have been tried and failed, where there is little incentive to negotiate yet again with an aggressive adversary, and finally, where a seemingly endless supply of diamonds and oil fuels the respective parties' capacity to make war? (1999, 581)

How indeed? It may be an unpalatable truth, but we are forced to recognize that some conflicts cannot be solved by outside intervention, at least not at a cost that is acceptable. Unfortunately, it appears that a good many conflicts, perhaps especially those occurring in Africa, are no less intractable than the Angolan one, although not always in the same way.

■ Notes

1. James Stockwell, the man in charge of the CIA operation in Angola ("IAFEATURE"), places blame for the escalation of Cold War intrusion into

Angola on the United States. "Uncomfortable with recent events, and frustrated by our humiliation in Vietnam, Kissinger was seeking opportunities to challenge the Soviets. Conspicuously, he had overruled his advisors and refused to seek diplomatic solutions in Angola." (1978, 43) Stockwell points out further that "although allied with the MPLA throughout the early seventies, the Soviets had shut off their support in 1973. Only in March 1975 did the Soviet Union begin significant arms shipments to the MPLA. Then, in response to the Chinese and American programs, it launched a massive airlift." (1978, 68)

2. The professional promotion of Savimbi peaked in 1986 with his visit to the United States, where in Washington he met "with President Reagan at the White House, George Shultz at the State Department, Caspar Weinberger at the Pentagon and various senators and congressmen. . . ." The visit also included appearances by Savimbi on television programs such as *Sixty Minutes, Nightline, MacNeil-Lehrer News Hour,* and *Good Morning America.* (Windrich, 1992, 50)

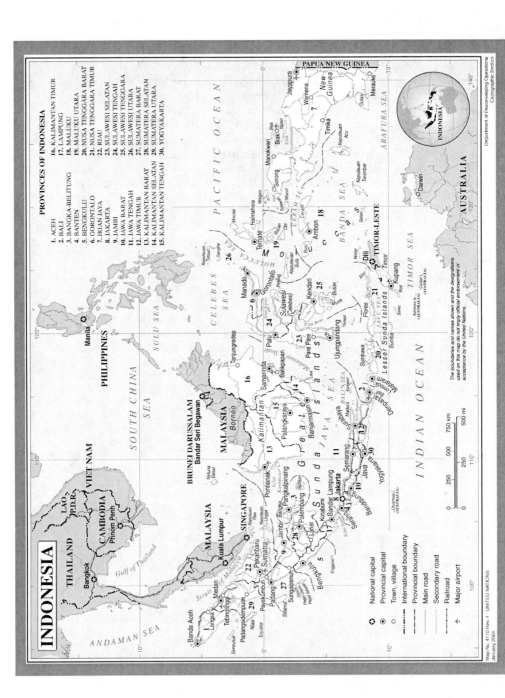

INDONESIA

PROVINCES OF INDONESIA

1. ACEH
2. BALI
3. BANGKA-BELITUNG
4. BANTEN
5. BENGKULU
6. GORONTALO
7. IRIAN JAYA
8. JAKARTA
9. JAMBI
10. JAWA BARAT
11. JAWA TENGAH
12. JAWA TIMUR
13. KALIMANTAN BARAT
14. KALIMANTAN SELATAN
15. KALIMANTAN TENGAH
16. KALIMANTAN TIMUR
17. LAMPUNG
18. MALUKU
19. MALUKU UTARA
20. NUSA TENGGARA BARAT
21. NUSA TENGGARA TIMUR
22. RIAU
23. SULAWESI SELATAN
24. SULAWESI TENGAH
25. SULAWESI TENGGARA
26. SULAWESI UTARA
27. SUMATERA BARAT
28. SUMATERA SELATAN
29. SUMATERA UTARA
30. YOGYAKARTA

⊕ National capital
◉ Provincial capital
○ Town, village
-·-·- International boundary
—— Provincial boundary
—— Main road
—— Secondary road
—+— Railroad
✈ Major airport

The boundaries and names shown and the designations
used on this map do not imply official endorsement or
acceptance by the United Nations.

0 250 500 750 km
0 250 500 mi

Map No. 4110 Rev. 4 UNITED NATIONS
January 2004

Department of Peacekeeping Operations
Cartographic Section

11

East Timor (Timor-Leste), 1999: INTERFET, "Operation Warden"

Walter C. Soderlund and E. Donald Briggs

■ Background

East Timor is a very small country, about the size of Maryland, sharing an island in the southern reaches of the Indian Ocean with West Timor, a province of Indonesia. It lies about 430 kilometers north of Australia and in 1999 it had an estimated population of between 800,000 and 870,000 people. Although small in terms of population, East Timor is composed of a number of different ethnic groups, as evidenced by the active use of sixteen indigenous languages.

Initially, the Portuguese arrived on the island of Timor as traders early in the 16th century, with the entire island becoming the colony of Portuguese Timor in 1702. Dutch incursions over the years eventually led to the loss of the western half of Timor in 1859, with the formal boundary between East (Portugal) and West Timor (the Netherlands) established in 1916. At the time of its independence in 1950, Indonesia, as the successor state to the Netherlands, took control of West Timor, making it a province of the Indonesia federation.

According to Matthew Jardine, over "the first 300 years of colonial rule, Portugal showed less interest in East Timor than in any of its other colonies, . . . [but] . . . by the end of the 19th century, this situation had begun to change rapidly." (1995, 19) At this point, in an effort to reap some financial benefits from the colony, modest economic and social development was attempted. Further, in 1930, under Antonio Salazar, a new Colonial Act "centralized control over the colonies, bringing them under direct rule of Lisbon." Under this legislation, the population of East Timor was divided into two categories: "*indigenes* ('unassimilated' natives) and *nao indigenes* including mestos (whites) and 'assimilated' natives." (Taylor, 1999, 12–13) The Portuguese language, culture, and Catholicism were promoted in the colony, mainly through the development of Church-run schools. This resulted in East Timor, along with the Philippines, approaching independence with a majority Catholic population; it also differentiated East Timor from the Western half of the island, which was Muslim. However, at the time its political future was being determined in the mid-1970s, it was claimed that in spite of Portuguese efforts to promote economic and social development, East Timor "remained one of the most economically backward colonies in all Southeast Asia."[1] (Jardine, 1995, 20)

During the Second World War, East Timor was attacked and eventually occupied by Japan. However, in 1942, in what became known as the "Battle of Timor," Australian and Timorese volunteers fought the Japanese invaders, leading to the death of some 60,000 Timorese, which, as John Taylor points out, accounted for 13 percent of East Timor's population. Following a brutal Japanese occupation, Portugal reasserted its control over the colony at the war's end. A 1947 Australian War Graves Commission Report conveys a sense of post–World War II conditions in East Timor: "Forced labour under the whip goes on from dawn to dusk, and the Portuguese colonists . . . live with the same mixture of civility and brutality as they had 350 years ago." (cited in Taylor, 1999, 14) While there was some nationalist sentiment and unrest following the Second World War, sufficient to prompt Portugal to take repressive measurers, unlike the situation in Angola, where there was widespread armed resistance, "until 1974, Portugal enjoyed unchallenged colonial authority over East Timor, which remained one of the world's most deprived backwaters." (Head and Tenenbaum, 2002, May 18)

■ Roots of the Crisis

The Portuguese coup d'état of April 1974 (discussed in Chapter 10, this volume) provided the catalyst for subsequent developments in East Timor as it "encouraged nationalist movements . . . calling for gradual independence from Lisbon—a position initially favored by the new Portuguese government." (Burr and Evans, 2001) As was the case in Angola, three major political parties figured in the events determining the future of East Timor: the Timorese Democratic Union (UTD), a conservative, elite-centered group, oriented toward and supported by Portugal; the Revolutionary Front for an Independent East

Timor (FRETILIN), a more popular, left-leaning group, committed to "the universal doctrines of socialism and democracy," (Jardine, 1995, 26) and the Timorese Popular Democratic Association (APODETI), a group that "called for an 'autonomous integration into the Republic of Indonesia in accordance with international law' on the grounds of ethnic and historical links."[2] (Lawless, 1976, 949)

According to William Burr and Michael Evans,

> Early signals from the Indonesian government indicated that it was prepared to support East Timorese independence, but Jakarta soon became interested in turning the region into the country's twenty-seventh province. Fears that an independent East Timor could be used as a base by unfriendly governments or spur other secessionist movements in Indonesia had convinced hard-liners in the military to press for annexation of the territory. (2001)

In July 1975, the Lisbon government put forth "a timetable for home-rule, including the election of a popular assembly that would determine East Timor's future, with Portuguese sovereignty ending no later than October 1978." (Burr and Evans, 2001) It is significant that all of this was happening in 1975—the year that the United States finally had to acknowledge defeat in Vietnam—for this meant, just as it had in Angola, that with Henry Kissinger serving as Secretary of State, the Cold War would intrude in a major way on East Timor's political future.

Initially the UTD and FRETILIN cooperated in the pursuit of independence, and Robert Lawless describes this period as providing "the best opportunity for the establishment of an independent East Timor." However, at the end of May 1975, the two movements split, leading Lawless to argue that "the breakup of this coalition sealed the fate of East Timor and ensured the subsequent invasion and attempted takeover by Indonesia." (1976, 948) The breakup also resulted in fairly widespread socio-political violence. This culminated in an attempted UTD coup against FRETILIN in August, during which the "UTD seized key installations in Dili, including the radio station, airport, and some administrative buildings, and demanded immediate independence for East Timor and imprisonment of FRETILIN members." (Lawless, 1976, 952)

The UTD coup not only failed, but also prompted FRETILIN to mount a counter-coup that was so successful that by the end of August, FRETILIN had gained control of nearly the entire colony. The Portuguese garrison "withdrew to the island of Ataúro, and for all practical purposes Portuguese control of Timor had ended after some 450 years." (Lawless, 1976, 953) Shortly thereafter, "on November 28, Fretilin declared East Timor's independence—apparently in the belief that a sovereign state would have greater success appealing to the UN [for assistance]." (Burr and Evans, 2001) FRETILIN renamed the colony the Republica Democratica de Timor Leste, and among a small number of nations recognizing FRETILIN "as the representative party of the East Timorese people," were Albania, China, Vietnam, and Angola. (Lawless, 1976, 953)

The proclamation of independence did not sit well with Indonesia, which almost immediately "declared East Timor a part of Indonesia." (Lawless, 1976, 953) While Indonesia had made plans for a military invasion of East Timor ("Operation Komodo"), there was some fear of negative reactions to an invasion on the part of Indonesia's major international trade and investment partners.

Such misgivings were laid to rest by a visit to Jakarta by United States President Gerald Ford and Secretary of State Henry Kissinger in early December 1975. William Burr and Michael Evans reconstruct the discussion over East Timor from a record of a December 6 meeting among Ford, Kissinger, and Indonesian President Suharto, released by the Ford Library to the National Security Archive in 2001. In this meeting, it was Suharto who brought up the issue of East Timor: "We want your understanding . . . if we deem it necessary to take rapid or drastic action." Burr and Evans report that "Ford was unambiguous. 'We will understand and will not press you on the issue.'" Kissinger seemed concerned primarily with the timing of the Indonesian invasion: "'it is important that whatever you do succeeds quickly' but that 'it would be better if it were done after we returned to the United States.'" (cited in Burr and Evans, 2001) Thus reassured, the Indonesian Army invaded East Timor on December 7, 1975, only one day after the American president and secretary of state had left the country.

The invasion was not the quick success for which both Suharto and Kissinger had hoped. It was reported "that more than 450 Indonesian troops were killed in the first four weeks of the Indonesian invasion, and the 15,000 to 20,000 Indonesian force failed to subdue large areas of East Timor or to find and destroy the 3,000 or so Fretilin troops." (Lawless, 1976, 956) East Timor remained a "closed province" from 1975 until 1989, and as such, it was off limits to journalists and foreign observers. (Sherlock, 1996) For Mike Head and Linda Tenenbaum, the "international community" bears a heavy responsibility not only for the attempted conquest, but for the ongoing guerrilla war (waged by FRETILIN's "army" known by the acronym FALINTIL), and the large-scale Indonesian repression that followed:

> After suffering a devastating defeat in 1975 in Vietnam, the US and Australian governments feared that the fledgling independence movement in East Timor, led by FRETILIN, could trigger instability across the Indonesian archipelago. The Suharto junta was actively encouraged to invade the half-island in December 1975. *For the next two decades, successive Australian and US governments solidly backed Indonesia's bloody suppression of Timorese resistance, at the cost of 200,000 lives.* (Head and Tenenbaum, 2002, May 18, italics added)

■ Events Precipitating the Crisis

Immediately following the 1975 invasion, the UN passed a resolution calling on Indonesia to leave East Timor, but this had no effect. (Nevins, 2002, 627–28) In spite of continued guerrilla resistance, Indonesia appeared determined to prevail in its annexation of the territory, although its control never seemed to extend much beyond the major towns and strategic locations. (Jardine, 1995, 50–57)

During the 1990s, however, a number of developments led to a change of policy on the part of Indonesia. The first was the end of the Cold War, which, as we have seen elsewhere, had the effect of neutralizing western fears of possible communist gains in the Third World. Second, there was a growing international awareness of the extent of the Indonesian repression in East Timor, created in part at least by Internet sites such as that maintained by East Timor Action Network and the writings of political activists such as Noam Chomsky. Indonesian repression was given major visibility by the Santa Cruz Cemetery massacre in November 1991[3] (Jardine, 1995, 16–17), and by the awarding of the Nobel Peace Prize in 1966 to Carlos Belo, the Roman Catholic Bishop of Dili, and independence leader José Ramos-Horta. Contributing more directly to the chain of causality was the end of the Suharto dictatorship in 1998, combined with a financial collapse in Indonesia, resulting in what was described as "a deep crisis. A country that achieved decades of rapid growth, stability and poverty reduction is now near economic collapse. . . . *no country in recent history, let alone one the size of Indonesia, has ever suffered such a dramatic reversal of fortune.*" (World Bank Report, cited in Cobb, 1999, Sept, 21, italics in the original)

In the winter and the spring of 1999, Indonesia's new President, B. J. Habibe, finally responded to international pressure to deal with the status of East Timor, twenty-four years after it had become an issue. Although East Timor had been under de facto Indonesian control since 1975, significantly the United Nations had never recognized Indonesian sovereignty over the territory. (UN, 2006) As Joseph Nevins tells us, "Portugal was still the territory's 'administering power' under international law as the U.N. did not judge East Timor as having undergone a proper process of decolonization." (2002, 626) On May 5, 1999, Indonesia agreed to enter into discussions with the United Nations regarding a vote on "autonomy within Indonesia," in what was referred to as a "process of consultation." (UN, 1999)

A UN Assistance Mission in East Timor (UNAMET) was created in June to negotiate with Indonesia. It had a mandate "to advise the Indonesian Police . . . [and] . . . to maintain contact with the Indonesian Armed Forces." (UN, 1999) UNAMET was composed of 280 civilian police officers and 50 military liaison officers. In addition, a "core group" of states (Australia, Japan, the United Kingdom, and the United States) "acted as an informal advisory body to the U.N. secretary-general during the consultation process." (Nevins, 2002, 628)

Indonesia agreed to a "free and fair" ballot and to provide security for the registration process and the vote. The consultation process proceeded over the summer with an uncomfortable level of intimidation and violence perpetrated by anti-independence militias, widely believed to be under the control of the Indonesian army. While the UN pressed Indonesia to allow an international force to go to East Timor to supervise the autonomy ballot scheduled (after one postponement) for the end of August, Indonesia refused to agree to this.

This refusal presented the UN and the Core Group with a dilemma. Although intelligence reports indicated that Indonesia planned a violent response if the autonomy within Indonesia option were to be rejected, under the agreement negotiated with the Indonesian government the responsibility to provide security rested with its army, which had promised to carry out its duties faithfully. Moreover, if the international community were to press Indonesia to accept an international force, it was feared that this might result in the derailing of the entire consultation process. In stark terms, Australian Foreign Minister Alexander Downer outlines the problem facing the UN and the international community:

It was clear that Indonesia . . . would not agree to the establishment of an international security/peacekeeping force in East Timor before the ballot. President Habibe categorically rejected Australian calls for him to invite a peacekeeping force into East Timor in the lead-up to the vote. . . . to have pushed the idea with Jakarta would have resulted in the cancellation of the 30 August vote." (cited in Nevins, 2002, 634)

In addition, Secretary-General Kofi Annan pointed out that "no country, I mean no country, would accept to deploy its forces without Indonesia's agreement." (cited in Nevins, 2002, 635)

The autonomy proposal was turned down by a margin of 78.5 percent to 21.5 percent, with 95 percent of those registered casting ballots. (UN, 1999; see also Wheeler and Dunne, 2001) In the final analysis, given the sensitivity on the part of both Indonesia and the international community to the "sovereignty issue," it is hard to see how very much more could have been done to get an international security presence in East Timor prior to the major violence that broke out in early September, upon the announcement of rejection of the autonomy option.[4]

■ The Intervention

The period of post-referendum violence in East Timor, carried out by Indonesian army units and militias, lasted for a period of about three weeks. On September 9, about a week into the intensified violence, President Clinton called for an international force to intervene in East Timor, *if Indonesia could not control the violence.* Shortly thereafter, violence forced UNAMET to leave the territory, and on September 15 the UN Security Council authorized a multinational force (INTERFET) under Chapter VII to "take *'all necessary measures'* to restore security to the crisis-ravaged territory." (Cobb, 1999, Sept. 21, italics in the original)

INTERFET was led by Australia, which supplied the majority of troops, and was empowered "1. To restore peace and security in East Timor . . . ; 2. To protect and support UNAMET in carrying out its tasks . . . ; [and] . . . 3. To facilitate humanitarian assistance operations." (Cobb, 1999, Sept. 21) Importantly, President Habibe agreed to both the intervention and INTERFET's mandate, and the force landed without Indonesian resistance on September 20. While the intervention did end the violence, the interval between the announcement of the referendum vote and the arrival of the peacekeeping force proved to be devastating for East Timor. According to Joseph Nevins, during the approximately three weeks that followed [the announcement of the vote,] the TNI [Indonesian Army] and its militia destroyed an estimated 70% of the territory's buildings and infrastructure, forcibly deported about 250,000 people to Indonesia, raped untold numbers of women, and killed upward of 2,000 people—to create what many have called "ground zero." Arguably, Indonesia's scorched-earth campaign was unprecedented in terms of its degree of destruction in the context of departing colonial powers in the 20th century. (2002, 623–24)

Strength of the International Response: Rank order=5

A. Did the Humanitarian Crisis Result in a International Intervention? Yes

B. Type of Response: Chapter VII

C. Type of UN Involvement:
An Australian-led, UN-authorized force, with 25 countries contributing troops

D. Size of the Intervening Force: 8,000
"Australia contributed about 4,500 of a force of 8,000." (Jackson, 2000, 24–25)

Determinants of the International Response

A. Severity of the Crisis: Rank order=9

i. Number of deaths: (short-term) 1,400 to 7,000; (long-term) over 200,000

"The price of voting had been high—between 5,000 and 6,000 people had been killed by paramilitaries since Habibe's [January] announcement, thousands more had fled their homes, and many were still being held by the paramilitaries in camps." (Taylor, 1999, xxix)

"[As of mid-June,] . . . since January, political violence, carried out mainly by militias and gangs that want to remain part of Indonesia, has claimed more than 100 lives, mostly those of independence supporters." (NYT, 1999, June 15, A19)

"[Following the August 30 vote] . . . the TNI and its militia . . . killed upward of 2,000 people." (Nevins, 2002, 623)

"[The UN Food and Agriculture Organization] . . . puts the figure [of] those killed at 7,000." (Crossette, 1999, Sept. 15, A11)

"What happened in September 1999 was only the final act of more than 20 years of atrocities and destruction perpetrated by the Indonesian military in East Timor. Well over 200,000 East Timorese—about one-third of the pre-invasion population—lost their lives as a result of Indonesia's December 7, 1975, invasion and subsequent occupation, an outcome that many scholars have characterized as genocidal in nature." (Nevins, 2002, 626)

ii. Number of refugees and displaced persons: (short-term) 40,000 to 300,000

"[On September 19] . . . the UN's humanitarian co-ordinator for East Timor, states that 300,000 refugees are hiding in remote areas of East Timor, and 150,00 are living in camps in West Timor." (Taylor, 1999, 229)

"On the eve of the referendum, it is reported that 60,000 people have fled their homes in the last two months." (Taylor, 1999, 227)

"As many as 200,000 people, nearly a quarter of East Timor's population, have been driven from their home within the last four days by militias opposed to independence." (Crossette, 1999, Sept. 8, A1)

"The Indonesian Government estimates that 93,000 people have fled East Timor since the violence erupted last week . . . [with] . . . another 23,000 . . . trapped on the East Timor side of the border." (Lander, 1999, Sept. 13, A1)

"The 50,000 displaced East Timorese around the town of Dare, whose numbers are equivalent to half the population of the Capital six miles to the north, have no milk for their children or medicines to combat diarrheal diseases and malaria." (Crossette, 1999, Sept. 16, A10)

"About 250,000 East Timorese left the country, and in some cases they were forced out of the country." (Paul and Spirit, 2002)

iii. Likelihood of conflict spreading to other states: 1 *low*

    a. Number of shared borders: 1

      Indonesia (West Timor)

    b. Involvement of bordering states

      Indonesian support for (or inability to control) paramilitary militias was the major cause of the violence.

B. Pre-intervention "Assessment of Risk": 2 to 3 *relatively low to medium*

"There is a wide spectrum of possibilities regarding the security situation in the territory. To a very great degree the security of the operation will depend on the size, composition, location, and most importantly the intent of the TNI and to a lesser degree the militia. It is estimated the TNI has approximately 15,000 troops in East Timor—including 2000 Kopassus . . .

[Indonesian Special Forces] . . . in addition to 8,000 police. Estimates of the militia force vary widely. Due to the history of the province, public support and sympathy do not lie with the militia in any large numbers. This augurs against a protracted guerrilla war in the absence of TNI support." (Cobb, 1999, Sept. 21)

"At the low-risk end of the spectrum, the operation will be essentially straightforward and well within the capabilities of the INTERFET." (Cobb, 1999, Sept. 21)

"The relative ease with which the . . . INTERFET force finally entered East Timor on September 20, 1999, the lack of Indonesian military resistance, as well as—most importantly—the nature of the TNI-militia scorched-earth campaign together made it clear that Indonesia had no intention of staying in East Timor. It is thus unlikely that any sort of international military intervention without Jakarta's permission would have resulted in significant TNI resistance." (Nevins, 2002, 641)

"There are very considerable concerns for the INTERFET at the high-risk end of the security spectrum. The TNI/militia backed anti-UN resistance could be used in an attempt to back earlier TNI claims that it was unable to maintain security in the territory." (Cobb, 1999, Sept. 21)

"ADF casualties are to be expected in what has already become the greatest single challenge to Australian foreign policy and defence policies in a generation." (Cobb, 1999, Sept. 21)

C. Extent of "National Interest Involvement":
i. The international community: 2 *relatively low*

". . . the destruction of East Timor was definitively shaped by the broader international context. The New Order's major foreign sponsors and allies—Australia, Britain, Japan, and the U.S.—turned a blind eye to mounting evidence that pointed clearly toward the impending disaster that eventually occurred." (Zinoman and Peluso, 2002, 548)

"Many of the world's wealthiest and most powerful countries played a key, if not decisive, role in facilitating Indonesia's illegal war of conquest and occupation. That the U.N. took no effective action to enforce its resolutions—especially those passed by the Security Council . . . is a manifestation of that complicity." (Nevins, 2002, 628)

ii. United States: 2 *relatively low*

"Frankly, with respect to East Timor (which most Americans would hardly be able to locate on a map) making a case that it was of either strategic or economic interest to the US would be a hard task. Basically, the US national interest, exactly like Australia's, was to stay on good terms with Jakarta." (Bell, 2000, 173)

"Certainly if you look at East Timor by itself, I cannot see any national interest there that would be overwhelming . . . [and] . . . would call for us to deploy or place U.S. forces on the ground in that area." (General Henry Shelton, Chairman of the Joint Chiefs of Staff, cited in Shenon, 1999, Sept. 10, A12)

". . . Indonesia is a strategically important country for the United States in Asia, one that serves as a counter balance to China as well as Japan." (Perlez, 1999, Sept. 12, IV1)

"[In 1975] U.S. strategists . . . were concerned that Fretilin might usher in a pro-socialist country: a 'Cuba in the Indian Ocean.'" (Catalinotto, 2006, June 8)

"For senior [U.S.] officials, the fate of a post-colonial East Timor paled in comparison to the strategic relationship with the anti-communist Suharto regime." (Burr and Evans, 2001)

"The U.S. authorized Indonesia's invasion and, by doing so, is arguably guilty of aiding and abetting the international crime of aggression. . . . [President] Ford later admitted that, given a choice between East Timor and Indonesia, the U.S. 'had to be on the side of Indonesia.'" (Nevins, 2002, 630)

iii. Indonesia: 5 *high*

"East Timor is still a nuisance internationally, leading to many misunderstandings, even among our allies, and creating difficulties in our diplomatic work." (Ali Alatas, Indonesian Representative to the UN, cited in Taylor, 1999, 179)

"Indonesia is also in the middle of a political transition and is concerned about the demonstration effect ceding territory will have on other long-standing separatist movements in Aceh and Inan Jaya." (Cobb, 1999, Sept. 21)

". . . [President] Habibe was fed up with continued international condemnation. 'Why do we have to hang on to East Timor if it is hurting us so much and the East Timorese feel so unhappy about it?'" (Dewi Fortuna Anwar, Presidential Policy Advisor, cited in Taylor, 1999, xvii)

". . . Habibe argued that, whatever the composition of the next government, it would have to honour the referendum result: 'The next president has to do it. . . . We don't want to be burdened by the problem of East Timor after January 2000.'" (cited in Taylor, 1999, xviii)

iv. Australia: 4 to 5 *relatively high* to *high* (but complex)

"The Aussies are ready to put troops into Timor because they know that if Indonesia implodes, the boat people are headed for Australia." (Friedman, 1999, Sept. 8, A23)

"To put the [intervention] outcome in the bluntest *real-politik* terms, those decisions of September 1999 meant that Canberra exchanged an easy quasi-alliance with an emerging power of 211 million people for a fragile and probably conflictual relationship with a very vulnerable small nation of 800,000." (Bell, 2000, 175)

"Having abandoned the East Timorese people to invasion and genocide for a quarter of a century, a bewildered Australian Government was forced into a military intervention in late 1999." (Anderson, 2003, 113)

"Australia, which had sacrificed the rights of the people of East Timor on the altar of good relations with Indonesia, found itself leading an intervention force that challenged the old certainties of its 'Jakarta first' policy." (Wheeler and Dunne, 2001)

"While Australian popular sentiment demanded an intervention in solidarity with the East Timorese people (who in 1999 were experiencing massacre and dislocation), the intervention also represented a considered step of 'forward defence' right up to Australia's most sensitive border, that with Indonesia. Although there was no direct military confrontation (as the Indonesian withdrawal had been negotiated), Australian troops entered a power vacuum, with the aim of stabilizing and asserting control over the entire political transition." (Anderson, 2003, 117)

". . . the aim of the . . . [Australian] . . . military intervention is to establish a UN protectorate in East Timor through which Australian and other imperialist powers will seek to reinforce and prosecute their business and strategic interests across the resource-rich Indonesian archipelago." (Beams, 1999, Sept. 8)

"By the time Australian troops landed in Dili in mid-September 1999, with the ostensible brief of 'protecting' the East Timorese people, the carnage was already complete. But by leading the UN's

INTERFET force, the Howard government had placed itself in the box seat to demand a substantial say in whatever administration the UN set up." (Head and Tenenbaum, 2002, May 18)

"According to the current border—fixed by the 1989 Timor Gap Treaty between Australia and Indonesia—Australia controls the overwhelming portion of the oil and gas reserves. Under that treaty the Suharto regime handed Canberra a generous slice of the offshore exploration fields in return for Australia's support for, and formal recognition of, the 1975–76 Indonesian annexation of East Timor." (Head, 2000, October 25)

"The relationship [between Australia and Indonesia] was important because Indonesia was the most populous Muslim country in the world. It was a developing country offering numerous complementary interests. A successful relationship was a precondition of a successful engagement with Asia." (Don Watson, former speech writer for Prime Minister Paul Keating, cited in Crowell, 2006, Aug. 2)

"Since the earliest days of the revolutions against the Dutch . . . Australian policy-makers . . . have acted on the assumption that securing good relations with Jakarta is and always will be among Australia's highest diplomatic priorities." (Bell, 2000, 172)

"Of all Western countries, Australia was perhaps the one whose support for Indonesia's occupation was most steadfast. Given its geographic proximity, wealth of resources, and sheer size, Indonesia has long been important to Australia." (Nevins, 2002, p. 628)

"Canberra shamefully 'broke ranks' with the other Western powers . . . [over Indonesian annexation of East Timor] . . . according recognition to East Timor as a province of Indonesia, whereas the UN continued to regard it as a Portuguese colonial territory under Indonesian occupation, pending a UN supervised vote on self-determination." (Bell, 2000, p. 172)

"The East Timor Crisis has shaken an already unstable Indonesian political elite and deeply soured relations with Australia. Notwithstanding some Indonesian voices in support of the UN intervention . . . Indonesian-Australian relations have reached an all time low." (Cobb, 1999, Sept. 21)

v. Great Britain: 1 *low*

"In July 1975, Sir John Archibald Ford, British Ambassador to Jakarta, wrote to the Foreign Office that 'the people of

Portuguese Timor are in no condition to exercise their right to self-determination.' It was in British interest, he opined, 'that Indonesia should absorb the territory as soon and as unobtrusively as possible; and that if it comes to the crunch and there is a row in the U.N. we should keep our heads down and avoid siding with the Indonesian government.'" (cited in Nevins, 2002, 632)

    vi. Japan: 3 *medium*

"As international scrutiny and criticism of Jakarta's occupation mounted beginning in the 1990s, Japan remained arguably Indonesia's most unwavering supporter among the wealthy capitalist countries." (Nevins, 2002, 633)

    vii. New Zealand: 3 *medium*

"New Zealand . . . played a key role in the Australian-led military occupation of East Timor in late 1999 and has significant financial interests [in East Timor.]" (Head and Tenenbaum, 2002, May 18)

D. Mass Media: March 21 to September 20, 1999
    i. "Alerting" function (volume of television and newspaper coverage): N=165; Rank order=4
      a. Televison coverage: Rank order=6
        Total (ABC, CBS, NBC): N= 33
        In-depth: N=22
      b. *New York Times* coverage: N=132; Rank order=4
    ii. "Evaluative" function (intervention framing in the *New York Times*)
      Pro-intervention frames: N=30
      (most premised on Indonesian consent)
      Anti-intervention frames: N=9
    iii. Assessment of media coverage

Nick Beams argues that the September 1999 Australian-led intervention into East Timor can be attributed to an Australian version of the "CNN effect"—specifically, that the Australian action had been "prepared by a sustained media campaign aimed at stampeding the genuine and legitimate public outrage at the actions of the militias into political support for the largest Australian military intervention since the Vietnam War." Ironically, Beams notes, the same media, "for most of the past two decades . . . supported the military occupation of East Timor, as well as backing the Suharto dictatorship in Indonesia." (1999, Sept. 8)

In our opinion, the following excerpt from the editorial "What must be done in East Timor," published in the *Sydney Morning Herald* on September 8, 1999 (at the very time the Australian government was making decisions regarding a possible intervention), is about as strong an endorsement of the need for a humanitarian intervention as we encountered since *New York Times* editorials pressing for greater American involvement in Somalia in the fall of 1992:

> Australia, however reluctantly and without waiting for others, must lead the way—in force. Mr. Howard talks of up to 2,000 Australian troops, but still the talk is conditional on receiving international support and Indonesian agreement. The time for such talks has passed. On Indonesia's past performance, its declaration of martial law yesterday must be suspected as intended more to gain time than resolve the crisis. Australia should end this dangerous period of uncertainty. It should declare its intention to move troops into East Timor if Indonesia doesn't restore order immediately and if, in that event, the UN Security Council fails to call together urgently a peacekeeping force. (cited in Beams, 1999, Sept. 8)

In the six months prior to the landing of INTERFET on September 20, 1999, in spite of limited involvement of what might be termed conventional United States national interests, the *New York Times* published 132 stories on East Timor. An additional 33 television stories (22 of which were considered in-depth treatments) brings the total media coverage to 165 stories, placing East Timor fourth overall among the crises studied. Thus, it appears that the function of altering the American population with respect to East Timor had been performed adequately.

Our study of media coverage of East Timor crisis begins on March 21, six months prior to the landing of INTERFET on September 20, 1999. Reports of violence perpetrated by pro-Indonesian militias dominated media coverage in the spring and summer, with much of what appeared prior to August 27 found in the one-paragraph World Briefing section (23 items). Overall, the percentage of high-impact items (front-page stories, editorials, and op-ed pieces) stood at 20 percent, most of this beginning on August 27 in response to a serious outbreak of militia-instigated violence just prior to the referendum vote and some three weeks before the landing of INTERFET.

Actual and potential misdeeds of the paramilitary militias and the Indonesian military dominated coverage throughout the study period. Fully one-third of content originated in the United States, with Barbara Crossette reporting from the UN the primary contributor, followed

Table 11.1 *New York Times* **Coverage of East Timor**

Panel 1 – Date:	N	%	Panel 2 – Dateline:	N	%
First 2 Months	24	18%	United States	45	34%
Second 2 Months	16	12%	East Timor	28	21%
Third 2 Months	92	70%	Indonesia	20	15%
		100%	Australia	9	7%
			Asia (other)	5	4%
			Unknown	25	19%
					100%

Panel 3 – Source:	N	%	Panel 4 – Type of Content:	N	%
Local Staff	86	65%	Front-page News	12	9%
AP	13	10%	Inside-page News	85	64%
AFP	5	4%	Editorials	4	3%
Reuters	5	4%	Op-ed Features	11	8%
Other	20	15%	Stand Alone Photos	5	4%
Unknown	3	2%	Letters	11	8%
		100%	Other	4	3%
					99%

Newspaper Coverage, by Date, Dateline, Source and Type (March 21 to September 20, 1999) N=132

by Philip Shenon in Washington. East Timor and Indonesia were the next most important countries of origin of material (21 percent and 15 percent, respectively), with *New York Times* correspondent Seth Mydans the main provider of that content. What was unusual in the case of East Timor was the presence of a large number of letters to the editor (11), originating from writers located in the United States, Australia, and Indonesia; interestingly, these were the main source of arguments pressing the case for an intervention going forward without Indonesian consent.

Coverage in the *New York Times* of what was to become the East Timor crisis began on March 19 (two days prior to the beginning of our study period) with a report in the "World Briefs" section in which José Ramos-Horta, co-winner of the Nobel Peace Prize in 1996 and champion of independence for East Timor, argued that the Indonesian military intended "'to disrupt the vote and intimidate the people,' . . . [maintaining that] . . . the ballot [on autonomy] should not be held until Indonesian troops are withdrawn." (cited in Lander 1999, Mar. 19, A4) Following that warning, our story count begins with the report of the killing of seventeen East Timorese by pro-Indonesian militia groups, an act that prompted José Alexandre

(Xannana) Guzmao, a major independence leader under house arrest in Jakarta, to order "his supporters to resume their war against Indonesian troops." It was noted that this marked a reversal of "a policy of restraint" that had been in place over the previous months. Guzmao reportedly felt "lied to" by Indonesia about the upcoming consultation process, "and he accused the international community of 'passivity' in trusting the Indonesian military more than the people of East Timor." (AFP, 1999, Apr. 6, A14) Two days later, Bishop Carlos Belo, in response to another act of militia violence (the killing of the largest number of East Timorese since the Santa Cruz Cemetery massacre in 1991), reiterated Guzmao's warning, demanding "that the international community help prevent more violence in the territory." (AP, 1999, Apr. 8, A6) Thus began the process of "alerting" the American public to the crisis, and of course these early warnings turned out to be prophetic.

Over the next few weeks, reports of violence linked to pro-Indonesian militia groups continued. Eurico Gutterres, head of one such paramilitary group, reportedly ordered his troops "to conduct a cleansing of all those who have betrayed integration. . . . Capture or kill them if you need." (cited in *NYT*, 1999, Apr. 18, I4) In spite of this, Guzmao rescinded his call to supporters for renewed warfare and a peace accord was signed by all parties on April 22. The accord committed "the separatists and the militias supporting the Indonesian government to 'stop killing, intimidation and terror.'" (*NYT*, 1999, Apr. 22, A6)

The first *New York Times* editorial on East Timor appeared on April 23, and it placed the blame squarely at the feet of Indonesia for the violence that was occurring: "Deadly violence returned to East Timor last week and militias backed by Indonesia's army are clearly to blame." The editorial also correctly identified the strategy behind the violence perpetrated by the militias: "Their goal is to thwart a plan . . . to let Timor's people choose between autonomy and independence." It also identified a role for the United States and the international community in the consultation process. "A tentative cease-fire . . . is not enough. The United States and other countries must insist that Mr. Habibe disarm and disband the militias." An international intervention was not called for; rather the editorial urged Washington to use its economic leverage to "warn Indonesia that international loans could be suspended unless it acts. . . . These are critical days for East Timor. *A strong international message to Jakarta can make a difference.*" (*NYT*, 1999, Apr. 23, A24, italics added)

At the same time, observers on the ground in Dili were pessimistic about East Timor's future. In an inside-page news article on April 26 filed from Dili, Seth Mydans wrote, "It is unclear whether this sad and battered territory can survive a potential end to its long separatist war. Many analysts fear that the prospect of settlement will only ignite an uglier, more intractable conflict." Mydans argued,

> neither side is prepared to accept a result that goes against them, . . . [and] . . . the Indonesian military has already begun a process of Timorization of the war. The truckloads of men who terrorized Dili last week were some of the thousands of recruits who have joined rag-tag military-backed "militias" since the start of the year. These groups, which support continued integration with Indonesia, are carrying out a war of intimidation from which the military has officially withdrawn. (Mydans, 1999, Apr. 26, A3)

On May 5, the day that the August 8 vote on autonomy was announced, the first op-ed piece appeared, written by Anciceto Guterres Lopes, Director of Yayasan HAK (Legal Aid, Human Rights and Justice Foundation) in Dili. Guterres Lopes claimed that "the recent wave of violence . . . reveals that the Habibe Government is reneging on a promise of a peaceful solution to East Timor's disputed political status." Citing the words of a militia spokesperson, "We will kill as many people as we want," he argued that "the militias have no other aim than to sow chaos and terror." However, just as with the *New York Times* editorial, Guterres Lopes did not call for an international intervention, asking instead that the United States consider "cutting off all military aid and training until a valid vote on independence is held in East Timor."[5] (1999, May 5, A25)

Thus, when the date for the vote on autonomy was first set in early May, the *New York Times* had begun to alert the American people (with chilling accuracy, it turned out) to what in varying degrees of intensity lay ahead for East Timor. However, neither the volume nor prominence of this coverage was very high, as many inside-page news items were of the one-paragraph "World Briefing" variety.

On May 25, with the autonomy vote still scheduled for August 8, the UN announced that it was "sending up to 280 . . . civilian police advisors" to East Timor. (Reuters, 1999, May 25, A10) Yet barely a month later, amid "growing concerns about security and logistics," the Secretary-General postponed the referendum date without announcing a new one. The same news report cited an Amnesty International report that accused "Indonesia of using militia groups to intimidate those favoring independence over autonomy under Indonesia." (Miller, 1999, June 23, A6)

Around mid-July, two reports further detailed Indonesia's role in the upcoming referendum. The first reported a visit of thirteen Indonesian cabinet ministers to East Timor, who "vowed to do their best to insure that an independence vote proceeds peacefully." It was noted that UN officials pressed them to get "the police to crack down on anti-independence militiamen who have killed dozens of civilians and attacked and threatened United Nations personnel." (AP, 1999, July 13, A4) On July 20, a reputed internal Indonesian Government report presented quite a different view of Indonesia's position, praising the activities of pro-Indonesian militias and accusing the UN of "bias towards independence." The report forecast "violence if independence forces won and anticipated non-Timorese who control many businesses would leave." Further, it predicted that "'at best . . . aspects of society will be controlled by the church,' while the United Nations and Australia will control the rest." (cited in *NYT,* 1999, July 20, A6)

Sporadic and relatively low-profile warnings about both occurring and anticipated violence continued to appear over the summer, and as late as August 24, an op-ed article by Bishop Carlos Belo still focused on "diplomatic interventions" as the "only hope there is to avoid a new blood bath." The Bishop did, however, end the article by calling upon the Indonesian government to "permit the entry of international peacekeepers." (1999, Aug. 24, A15)

Importantly in terms of our research focus, international intervention in the form of a peacekeeping mission of armed troops had never been discussed as a serious option in *New York Times* reporting prior to the outbreak of post-referendum violence. What had been suggested was that violence was likely, and that the international community had a responsibility to pressure Indonesia to get its army and militia groups under control and do what was promised in terms of providing security. This, it was argued, could be done through threats of withholding loans and withdrawing military support and training.

It was the reality of the widely predicted violence actually coming to pass that prompted sustained and serious coverage of the crisis by the *New York Times.* Beginning on August 27, three days prior to the vote on autonomy, anti-independence mobs roamed Dili, torching two buildings and killing four people (Mydans, Aug. 27, A12) and, on the next day, President Clinton "warned the President of Indonesia that relations with the United States will be severely damaged if there is mass violence during next week's referendum." (Shenon, 1999, Aug. 28, A4) Over the next three weeks, 88 items of newspaper content (accounting for two-thirds of total coverage) appeared until September 20, the day INTERFET landed on the island.[6]

A September 2 editorial agreed that President Clinton had been right in warning Indonesia that "failure to control the militias would damage relations with Washington." It went on to place the responsibility for maintaining security on Indonesia, arguing that "President Habibe must send disciplined and reliable police and military forces into East Timor with orders to disarm the militias and see that the referendum results are carried out." (NYT, 1999, Sept. 2, A26) On September 3, amid reports that "some nations [are] threatening to send in their own troops to maintain order," Stanley Roth, Assistant Secretary of State, pointed out what appeared to be fairly obvious: "[Indonesia] . . . can't say they don't want the international community to come in with peacekeepers if they're not going to provide security themselves." (cited in Mydans, 1999, Sept. 3, A9)

In early September, a new reality confronted UN and international decision makers. As Dili burned and its inhabitants fled, it was now clear that their strategies of pressuring Indonesia to provide security had proven notably unsuccessful. While a stand-alone photo of East Timorese lined up to cast their vote on a largely violence-free voting day appeared on the front page on August 31, it was not until violence erupted in full fury following announcement of the results of the vote on September 4 that the East Timor crisis garnered its first front-page news story. The article reported, "Violence has swept through the territory . . . since the vote. Its continuation could turn a new East Timor state into the scene of a civil war . . . [and noted that] . . . shooting, burning, killing and terror of the ragtag militia gangs may be beyond the control even of the Indonesian military that created them." (Mydans, 1999, Sept. 4, A1) On the very next day, "foreseeing 'chaos' and a 'new genocide,'" José Alexandre Gusmao appealed to the UN for "armed help" (cited in Mydans, 1999, Sept. 5, I6) Amid reports of a large number of killings and with UN workers trapped in their compound, José Ramos-Horta claimed, "We are facing an imminent extraordinary humanitarian catastrophe right under the eyes of the Security Council, and they are not acting."

In spite of this, between September 4 and September 15, little was done to end the violence, and Australian Prime Minister John Howard provided the reason for the inactivity: "You can't go into the territory of another country without that country's approval." (both cited in

Mydans, 1999, Sept. 6, A1) Robin Cook, British Foreign Secretary, agreed with Howard: "Nobody is going to fight their way ashore. . . . [But] if the Government of Indonesia cannot get its own security forces to restore order, it should allow the international community to assist in an orderly transition. . . . As yet we have not seen the right action."[7] (cited in Crossette, 1999, Sept. 6, A8) While Barbara Crossette reported on September 7 that "key nations are moving toward sending a force to restore order if the Indonesian military refuses to do so," (Crossette, 1999, Sept. 7, A1) it took an additional eight days of arm-twisting (and perhaps growing media pressure on Western decision makers) before Indonesia agreed to the deployment of an international force of peacekeepers.

In a September 7 op-ed piece, Anthony Lewis claimed that the current situation in East Timor is the "price paid for Kissingerian realism," noting further that "the international community has been silent about all that has happened over the past 24 years, and so feeble, that it has a responsibility to act firmly now." Lewis concedes, however, that the use of American troops abroad "is always, rightly, a delicate decision." (1999, Sept. 7, A19)

On September 8, Seth Mydans cited a Dutch journalist's report that "the whole city [of Dili] is being destroyed and houses are being looted. The situation is getting worse and worse." (Tjiske Lingsma cited in Mydans, 1999, Sept. 8, A12) Also on September 8, an editorial called for an international intervention as "a last resort" but still hedged on intervening without Indonesian permission: "The United Nations Security Council should immediately endorse Australia's attempt to assemble a quick-reaction international peacekeeping force, and countries with economic influence should use it *to press Indonesia to end the violence now or let the peacekeepers in.*" (*NYT,* 1999, Sept. 8, A22, italics added) At that point, the United Sates was still reluctant to move, as Secretary of Defense William Cohen indicated that there were no plans to insert "any peacekeeping troops." (cited in Becker and Shenon, 1999, Sept. 9, A1) However, Barbara Crossette reported movement in the Security Council, "with China and Russia joining in condemning the violence." But she noted as well that "all governments continue to insist that Indonesia be given every possible chance to reassert control." (1999, Sept. 9, A8)

On September 10, President Clinton began to ratchet up the arm-twisting, insisting that "if Indonesia does not end the violence, it must invite the international community to assist in restoring security." (cited in Shenon, 1999, Sept. 10, A1) Clinton's position was reaffirmed in a September 10 editorial that pointed out that "time is running out for Indonesia to disarm and disband the army-backed militias . . . unless Jakarta can bring these militias to heel . . . an international peacekeeping force will be needed." At the same time, the editorial continued to press Indonesia to accept an international force: *"East Timor's safety and freedom require that Jakarta agree to international peacekeepers."* (1999, Sept. 10, A24, italics added) This was not enough for Suzan Mackey, a former UN Observer to the Consultation Process. Writing to the paper from Australia, she argued, "It is time for a peacekeeping force in East Timor; the United States has a moral obligation to be involved after its complicity in the history that has brought East Timor to this point." (1999, Sept. 10, A24)

September 11 saw President Clinton moving a step closer to intervention, as he announced that "'It is now clear that the Indonesian military is aiding and abetting the military violence . . . ' [and] . . . that an international peacekeeping force was crucial." (cited in Mydans, 1999, Sept. 11, A1) He also announced that American arms sales to Indonesia had been suspended. At the same time, Kofi Annan raised the stakes for Indonesian leaders, telling them that if they "did not accept immediate international military assistance to restore order in East Timor, . . . [they] . . . might be guilty of crimes against humanity." (Crossette, 1999, Sept. 11, A6) Another letter to the editor raised the "moral responsibility" argument: "If we accept the mantle of leader of the free world, we should accept the moral responsibility it imposes." (Hamilton, 1999, Sept. 11, A10)

In a September 11 op-ed piece, Harvard professor Stanley Hoffman took the Clinton administration to task for its lack of a firm response to the violence in East Timor: "The Clinton Administration, which once defined its mission in foreign affairs as the spread of democracy, has responded . . . [in East Timor] . . . in a weak, dilatory manner." Hoffman made a strong case as well that "the sovereignty issue shouldn't hold us back . . . [because] . . . *Indonesia is an illegal occupier in East Timor, not a legal sovereign."* He concluded that the time has come for the United States to move, *"with or without Indonesia's consent."* (1999, Sept. 11, A11, italics added) This was the strongest piece promoting a case for international intervention that was not premised on the need for prior Indonesian approval.

In the days that followed, Bishop Carlos Belo was forced to flee East Timor after his house was burned. At long last, on September 12 Indonesia conceded that it had "lost control" over its forces in East

Timor, yet paradoxically it claimed that "the time is not right for inviting international troops." (Mydans, 1999, Sept. 12, I1) Finally, a day later, Indonesia announced that it had agreed to "invite" an international force into East Timor—a force to which the United States contribution was described by President Clinton as "limited but important." (cited in Mydans, 1999, Sept. 13, A1) The final editorial on the East Timor crisis appeared on September 14, in which President Habibe was praised for accepting an international force. At the same time, the editorial held the Indonesian President's feet to the fire: "Most crucial, Mr. Habibe cannot be permitted to stall. There will soon be nothing left of East Timor to save." (*NYT*, 1999, Sept. 14, A22)

Once the Indonesian government had issued an "invitation" to intervene, things went relatively smoothly for the authorization and organization of INTERFET, and upon its arrival in East Timor on September 20, the Australian commander of the UN force "praised the cooperation of the Indonesian forces." (Mydans, 1999, Sept. 20, A1)

In an op-ed piece appearing on September 15, just after Indonesia's acceptance of a UN force, Thomas Friedman attempted to place United States foreign policy decision-making with respect to the East Timor intervention in perspective. In so doing, he asked four questions:

"*1. Is there some strategic rationale for U.S. involvement?*" Friedman's answer was yes, if others did the heavy lifting:

> Roughly 40 percent of the world's trade passes through the sea lanes around Indonesia, the world's fourth largest nation. If contributing a few logistic personnel—to a U.N. force made up of Australians and Asians—helps resolve Indonesia's ugliest internal strife, it has some strategic benefit.

"*2. Can we make a reasonable difference at a reasonable cost?*" Friedman's answer was again yes, assuming that the main burden of the intervention fell to others:

> In East Timor, assuming that Asians and Aussies staff the U.N. force, we should be able to make a reasonable difference—instituting a free and fair U.N.-sponsored vote for independence by the people of East Timor—at a reasonable cost. For a relatively small price we will be upholding the rule of international law and the U.N.'s credibility, and showing how U.S. power can be leveraged.

"*3. Can we make a sustainable difference at a reasonable cost?*" Friedman's answer was probably yes:

East Timor is more like Kuwait than Kosovo. It's a territory occupied by bad guys. If the U.N. comes in and the bad guys gradually leave or are isolated, East Timor should be self-governing at a sustainable cost.

"4. Can we walk and chew gum at the same time?" Friedman's answer was hopefully yes: He argued that interventions in distant places could be done,

as long as we don't lose focus on what are still the killer strategic issues for America . . . [such as arms control]. . . . If the administration can do the big stuff and the small stuff, it will set an important precedent—and it is not too late. . . . History is not kind to leaders who just do the capillaries, not arteries. (all quotations from Friedman, 1999, Sept. 15, A29, italics in the original)

It hardly needs pointing out that "moral responsibility" and "responsibility to protect" arguments were virtually absent from Friedman's critique. Nor was the question addressed as to whether an intervention, which in John Taylor's estimation was "too little, too late," (1999, xxxi) should have been attempted some two weeks earlier, without Indonesian permission.

■ Overall Evaluation of the Crisis Response

In the final analysis, Indonesia, with its well over 200 million people, proved to be infinitely more important to the world's major powers than was East Timor, with its 800,000. The nearly twenty-four years of de facto control over East Timor by Indonesia had been legitimized by Australian recognition of Indonesian sovereignty, and by the fact that the latter's military occupation of East Timor was never challenged in any significant way by other major international powers. In addition, when reports of intimidation and more serious instances of violence were reported on a more or less continuous basis over the summer of 1999, the international community repeatedly choose not to confront Indonesia over its behavior (Nevins, 2002, 637–39).[8]

When the widely predicted violence finally occurred, did media coverage of the crisis (now quite intense) serve as a key ingredient in changes to the well-established Australian and American policies of currying favor with Indonesia? In our opinion, the answer is a chary yes. Media coverage, if doing nothing else, kept the crisis on the minds of the American mass public, and in its framing, pressed for Indonesian consent to an international intervention. It must be stressed, however, that calls for an international intervention were cautious, in that for the most part, they hinged on getting Indonesia to accept a peacekeeping force voluntarily. Unfortunately, in the final analysis, the resulting intervention came too late to be of great help to East Timor. While the international response to the violence following the referendum vote was probably as quick as one could reasonably have hoped for (about a week to the actual landing of troops, as opposed to the six months needed to get UNAMIR II into Rwanda some five years earlier), nevertheless, as Nevins has claimed, the results of three weeks of uncontrolled violence were devastating for East Timor.

One is left to wonder what would have happened in East Timor if Indonesia had not finally agreed to allow an international intervention force into the territory. This is a critical point, and it might have been the "fifth question" asked by Thomas Friedman. Norms regarding the relative weight of the principles of state sovereignty and protection of human rights may have changed following the end of the Cold War, but East Timor does not present a strong case for suggesting that the first has been reduced to insignificance. Rather it suggests that state sovereignty continues to be a powerful influence on elites, both media and governmental, when discussions regarding international intervention are considered, at least when there are grounds to fear offending an important state.

Following the traumatic events of 1999, for a time East Timor slipped out of the headlines, and it appeared that with its independence in 2002, following a transitional period of UN administration and the final withdrawal of Australian peacekeepers in 2005, East Timor (now Timor-Leste) might emerge as a success story for international intervention.

Unfortunately, such hopes were dashed in the summer of 2006, when civil strife in the new country reached a magnitude that prompted a second Australian-led intervention. Trouble began with unrest in the newly created Timor-Leste army between former FALINTIL guerrilla fighters (concentrated in the western region of the country) and those less involved in the resistance to Indonesian occupation, who tended to come from the eastern region. Easterners felt discriminated against in terms of promotions, and in February 2006 they began a strike that resulted in the dismissal of nearly 600 soldiers, nearly half of the 1,400-strong army. In early May, clashes between the dismissed soldiers and police resulted in "tens of thousands" fleeing violence in Dili. (BBC News, 2006, May 5)

Toward the end of May, continued clashes between soldiers and police, combined with increased gang-related violence, led to a political crisis and to Foreign Minister Ramos-Horta's call for international assistance in restoring order. Australia, New Zealand, Portugal, and Malaysia responded with an intervention force "Operation Astute" numbering over 1,300 troops. (ABC News Online, 2006, June 10) In August 2006, the United Nations responded to the renewed violence and instability with its own new mission to Timor-Leste, the United Nations Integrated Mission in Timor-Leste (UNMIT)—this mission focused on "stability, national reconciliation, and democratic governance for Timor-Leste." (UN, 2007)

■ Notes

1. The Portuguese record in preparing East Timor for independence is less than exemplary. According to statistics cited by Denis Freney, "By the end of 1975 there were three Timorese engineers, two medical doctors, one dentist, two psychologists, two Political Science graduates and three agricultural scientists." (1975, 17) Nor did Indonesia appear to do much better; as of 1999, Seth Mydans reported an illiteracy rate in East Timor of 80 percent. (1999, Aug. 29, A3) At the time of its independence in 2002, Timor-Leste was reported to be "the world's poorest country." (ABC News Online, 2006, July 10)

2. Matthew Jardine claims that APODETI "appears to have been largely a project of the Indonesian military's intelligence service. The last thing Indonesia wanted was another independent country on its border, and it was dedicated to making sure this never happened." (1995, 26)

3. Matthew Jardine describes the Indonesian army's 1991 response to a memorial mass for a slain guerrilla fighter, by quoting American reporter Allan Nairn, who witnessed the event:

Without warning, and without provocation, "soldiers raised their rifles, and took aim. Then, acting in unison, they opened fire. . . . Men and women fell, shivering in the street, rolling from the impact of the bullets. . . . The soldiers jumped over the fallen bodies and fired at the people still upright. They chased down young boys and girls and shot them in the back." When it was over, more than 250 people had been killed and hundreds more wounded.

Jardine notes that Nairn and fellow American journalist Amy Goodman were badly beaten by Indonesian soldiers and that the massacre had been videotaped by British journalist Max Stahl. The video was widely distributed in the West, leading to numerous editorials in Western newspapers supporting East Timorese self-determination. (1995, 16–17)

4. For some, there still remains a question of whether the violence following the vote was the result of out of control "rogue elements" within the Indonesian military or was "state orchestrated." On the basis of a careful examination, Joseph Nevins concludes that the "second explanation is far more persuasive than the first." (2002, 624–25) Coral Bell concurs with this assessment. (2000, 171)

5. On the day after his article appeared in the *New York Times,* Guterres Lopes's life was threatened. This prompted United States Senator Russell Feingold to comment that "if Mr. Lopes and other human rights advocates were harmed, it would have 'a devastating impact' on relations with the United States.'" (cited in Shenon, 1999, May 6, A4)

6. United States network television news coverage of the crisis in East Timor did not begin until August 29, with a thirty-second preview of the upcoming referendum on CBS. What were described as "graphic scenes . . . of violence," were first shown in a twenty-second anchor-read story on September 1. Over the next few days, there were a large number of other references in the reporting to "scenes of violence."

7. Perceptions among key UN decision makers that Indonesian agreement was necessary prior to the deployment of any international force were widespread. "I can assure you that the Security Council will not give the green light if there is no permission on the part of the Indonesian government." (Peter van Walsum, Netherlands Representative and President of the Security Council for September, cited in Crossette, 1999, Sept. 8, A1) "There is no taste in Council or the world for going to war with Indonesia." (Robert Fowler, Canadian Representative on the Security Council, cited in Crossette, 1999, Sept. 8, A1)

By September 5, in reports originating mainly from London the length of stories began to increase, with the focus clearly on the post-referendum violence. On September 7, the first report from Jakarta was aired on NBC, which was joined there by ABC on September 8, and by CBS on September 10. International intervention was an issue that was discussed, and there appear to have been arguments presented both supporting and opposing the deployment of an international force. For example, on September 6, Australian journalist John Pilger claimed the "ethnic cleansing" was occurring (NBC), while on September 8, United States National Security Advisor Sandy Berger was reported as offering the opinion that American troops are not world police. (CBS) Unfortunately, the limited amount of information provided in the abstracts does not permit us to comment on whether TV news coverage dealt with the issue of an intervention proceeding without Indonesian consent. Once the UN had approved INTERFET, the origin of reporting shifted to Darwin, Australia, while the focus of stories appeared to shift to the plight of refugees who were arriving there from East Timor. On September 20, Mike Lee covered the arrival of INTERFET in Dili for ABC, the only report actually filed from East Timor.

8. For example, in addition to the steady stream of reports of violence contained in *New York Times* reporting, representatives of the Carter Center working in East Timor concluded in early August that "top representatives of the government of Indonesia have failed to fulfill their main obligation under the May 5 Agreements and in many cases have actively sought to undermine the popular consultation process." (Preston and Flies, 1999, Aug. 8) Just prior to the vote, former President Carter reiterated the charge. (Mydans, 1999, Aug. 29, A3)

12

Conclusion: Assessing the Comparative Impact of Mass Media on Intervention Decision-making

Walter C. Soderlund and E. Donald Briggs

■ Introduction

Our case studies call for a number of preliminary observations before we turn to our conclusions derived from the structured-focused comparison. A matter of terminology might be mentioned first. The situations we have analyzed, some of which occasioned international intervention, were customarily referred to as "crises," and we have generally followed suit. It needs to be noted, however, that few of them precisely fit the classic definition of a crisis. Charles Hermann penned the definition most often cited: "a situation that (1) threatens the high-priority goals of the decision-making unit, (2) restricts the time available before the situation is transformed, and (3) surprises the members of the decision-making unit." (1969, 29) Given that most of the post–Cold War crises explored here tended to be peaks in conflicts ongoing for a decade or longer, they could scarcely have come as a surprise to anyone. Moreover, with the partial exceptions of Haiti and East Timor, they rarely constituted a threat to the well-being of any major international players. Rather, they were situations that, due to their longevity, intensity, apparent insolubility, or particular relevance to human rights, became of reluctant international concern only after prolonged gestation periods. A new term should probably be coined to describe them. Perhaps "continuing crisis syndrome" conveys the essence of what is involved somewhat better than the term "crisis" alone. For the sake of simplicity, however, we will continue to use the term "crisis" to refer to the situations under study.

Secondly, consideration needs to be given to the characteristics that our case studies share, and the extent to which these, singly or together, may explain the tragic events that occurred. The logical place to start is that, with the somewhat technical exception of Liberia, all of our crisis situations occurred in former European colonies. Having been on the receiving end of the plunder-and-run policies practiced by colonial powers, it might be suggested that the crises these societies experienced were the outgrowth, direct or indirect, of the colonial experience, and there is much truth to this. At the same time, care needs to be taken with the pervasive, but oversimplified, notion that everything undesirable that happens, especially in Africa, can be explained, and/or excused, by the depredations of the former colonial masters. At the very least, this common factor has to be weighed in the light of several other common characteristics shared by our violence-plagued states.

For instance, it hardly needs to be pointed out that we are dealing exclusively with a group of very poor to extremely poor countries. They are located at the very bottom of UN indices of poverty,[1] although Angola and, to some extent, Zaire and Sudan are blessed with substantial resources and good economic prospects. But where poverty is the norm, control and appropriation of government revenue is one of the few reliable avenues to wealth. As Filip Reyntjens has observed with respect to Burundi,

> Burundi has faced conflict during most of its history since independence in 1962. While strife has generally been interpreted as "ethnic," it is in fact political, aimed at maintaining or capturing power. Controlling the state is of major importance in a poor country like Burundi, as it is the main avenue for accumulation and reproduction of a dominant class. (2000, 5; see also Meredith, 2005; Fatton, 2006)

Moreover, the link between poverty and political violence is important because the majority of crises studied resulted from civil wars, possible separation, or independence, where control of the entire state was the ultimate prize. The one exception to this generalization was Haiti, where the population, although unhappy with their military government, was not engaged in organized violence aimed at overthrowing it. (See Talentino, 2005; Shamsie and Thompson, 2006.)

The truth is that even the governments of poor countries have money; it is the people who do not. If money does not come from mineral resources like diamonds, copper, or oil, it comes from those abroad trying to buy influence, or to prevent others from acquiring it (as in the days of Soviet-American Cold War rivalry), or as the result of other foreign paranoias, such as that of France with respect to suspected Anglo conspiracies against francophones in Rwanda and Zaire. Money comes as well in the form of less self-serving "aid packages" from well-intentioned sources, genuinely seeking to improve the well-being of those less fortunate than themselves. Whatever its source, personal greed and corruption often appear to siphon a great deal of the aid into private bank accounts. Martin Meredith, for example, has exhaustively documented the unbelievable extent to which government resources in almost every African country have been treated as the personal property of political leaders, often to the tune of multiple billions of dollars. (2005) It does not seem too extreme to refer to this as a pervasive political culture, or to suggest that in such situations violent conflict over access to the only available source of riches is almost to be expected.

Without question, post-independence governments in Africa in particular have been almost universally bad, and the same holds true for Haiti. One observer of the African political scene has in fact categorized post-independence governments as "so bad as to lead to a resistance born of desperation, and to consequences of prolonged immiseration, exploitation and state decay." (Clapham, 1998, 3) Apart from the glimpses of this provided by our case studies, one might mention the situation in Nigeria, where vast oil revenues appear to have benefited few but the power elite, and Zimbabwe, where Robert Mugabe has managed to reduce the second most thriving economy in southern Africa to the brink of bankruptcy, with 80 percent unemployment and an inflation rate that was predicted to reach an astounding 3,700 percent by the end of 2007. (Perry, 2007, Apr. 23) But while the vast majority of challengers to those in power have cited corruption and misuse of office as the justification for beginning conflicts causing millions of deaths, it is almost impossible to find an instance where these challengers proved to be an improvement over their predecessors when they finally gained control of the state. One cannot help but wonder, therefore, how much the exploitation or misery of the people at large was ever a serious motivation for the actions of self-styled reformers.

In addition to being both poor and misgoverned, almost all of our crisis states were also "ethnically challenged" to one degree or another. It would be simplistic to describe all of the crises as entirely or even essentially ethnic in nature, but Rwanda and Burundi certainly were very largely so, and ethnic (tribal/clan) allegiances played a significant role in several others (Liberia, Sierra Leone, Somalia, Sudan, Zaire, and Angola). It has not been unusual for African political leaders, either in power or aspiring to it, to adopt the view that only their own clansmen are to be trusted (Rwanda and Somalia providing particularly clear examples), and to assume that members of other groups would naturally act more or less exclusively in their own group's interest if given access to power. Conflict in such circumstances, of course, becomes a zero-sum game in which there is no room for compromise.

Ethnic considerations in the form of tribal allegiances were also responsible for the spill-over of crises across borders, which was a prominent feature of all our African crisis situations. Conflicts spread across national borders either as a result of neighboring governments opting to aid ethnic kin through the supply of arms, financial support, or the provision of safe havens for military training or the like, or as a result of refugees seeking shelter among their fellow tribesmen "next door" and more or less forcing the intervention of their host governments out of self-protection. While spill-overs are not confined to situations in which there is kinship-across-the-border, they probably occur more readily and involve greater numbers where people can assume that they will at least not be received with hostility on the other side of the border. Large numbers of refugees are inevitably a problem for a host state, as we saw even for the United States with respect to Haiti and as was feared in Australia with respect to East Timor.

In addition, of course, as has been documented in the case studies, the Cold War in its active phase played some role in the events leading up to every crisis examined, and it appears to have been a primary causal factor for those in Somalia, Angola, and East Timor. We will discuss the impact of the end of the Cold War below in our discussion of national interest.

It cannot be concluded, however, that any single one of the factors discussed above, or even a combination of them, inevitably leads to humanitarian crises of the magnitude that result in calls for international intervention. There are other poor, ethnically or religiously diverse ex-colonies that were a part of the strategic considerations of either the United States or the Soviet Union that have not succumbed to societal breakdowns similar to the majority of our case studies. India and Pakistan are perhaps examples, although neither has suffered from governments as unrelentingly vicious as those in our African sample. It seems reasonable to suggest, however, that the more of these factors that are in play, the greater the likelihood of serious disorder in which there will be pressure for internationally imposed solutions.

The circumstances under which the international community will succumb to pressure to "do something" about situations of human tragedy, and especially how important the mass media are in producing such a response, has been the primary focus of our study. We therefore turn now to an examination of our structured-focused comparison of the ten humanitarian crises for what it reveals about when international rescue missions are likely to be undertaken and when they are not.

■ Strength of International Responses

Beginning with Table 12.1, the extent of the "international response to crises" (our dependent variable) was considerable, with Somalia (where the response was substantial) and Sudan (which was limited to relief operations) serving as the book-end cases.

Table 12.1 Rank Order of Crises, Based on Strength of International Response

Rank	Crisis	Size of Intervention Force
1	Somalia	29,000–45,000
2	Haiti	20,000–29,000
3	Liberia	12,500–16,000
4	Sierra Leone	4,000–10,000
5	East Timor	8,000
6	Rwanda	3,000–3,600
7	Zaire (Democratic Republic of the Congo)*	
8	Burundi**	
9	Angola***	
10	Sudan****	

Notes: *A UN intervention "Operation Assurance" was to be composed of 10,000–15,000 troops. To be led by Canada, it was authorized and organized in the fall of 1996, but never deployed.

**Interventions to be undertaken by African states as well as by the UN were discussed in the summer of 1996, but never organized; a UN mission was finally deployed, but not until 2004.

***Thirty civilian observers were sent by the UN in November 1999.

****Beyond ongoing relief operations, no intervention took place in 1992.

■ Crisis Severity

The "severity of crisis" rank order shown in Table 12.2 is based on a combination of the number of deaths (short-term and long-term), the number of refugees and internally displaced persons (short-term and long-term), and the actuality or likelihood of cross-border spill-over, as perceived by intervention decision makers at the time. First, it must be pointed out that the "statistics" dealing with these particular "deadly

Table 12.2 Rank Order of Crises, Based on Overall Severity

Rank	Crisis	Rank on International Response
1	Rwanda	6
2	Somalia	1
3	Sudan	10
4	Burundi	8
5	Zaire	7
6	Liberia	3
7	Sierra Leone	4
8	Angola	9
9	East Timor	5
10	Haiti	2

quarrels," to use the language of Lewis F. Richardson and Quincy Wright (1960), appear to be far less than exact.[2] That said, the overall range with respect to the above-mentioned factors, with Rwanda and Haiti occupying the extremes, is certainly great enough to enable us to make reasonable estimates as to relative crisis severity.

The Spearman Rank Order Correlation between "crisis severity" and "strength of the international response" is –0.18, indicating at best a weak negative relationship between the two variables.[3] This result is skewed, however, by Haiti and East Timor. In these cases, relatively few people were killed, and there were relatively few refugees in the period leading up to the international response; the prospects for spill-over were limited as well. If we remove these two cases from the calculation, leaving an all-African sample of eight crises, the rank order correlation increases to +0.14, indicating an equally weak positive relationship between the severity of a crisis occurring on the African continent and the strength of an international response to it. Our conclusion is that, by itself, crisis severity does not appear to be a particularly good predictor of international crisis intervention.

■ Perceived Risk

Table 12.3 categorizes the ten crises in terms of the pre-intervention assessment or perceived risk involved in an intervention. With respect to the humanitarian crises of the 1990s, it took some time for those making intervention decisions to understand the perils inherent in what have been described as "wars of a third kind." At the beginning of the decade, the ECOWAS intervention into the Liberian conflict was seen by Nigerian decision makers as a relatively easy operation. This, of course, turned out to be anything but the case. Some two

Table 12.3 Category of Crisis, Based on Perceived Intervention Risks*

Category	Crisis
low	Liberia
	Somalia
	Haiti
medium	East Timor
	Rwanda
high	Burundi
	Zaire
	Sierra Leone
	Angola
unclear	Sudan

Note: *Crises are listed chronologically, within category.

years later, those in the United States planning the intervention in Somalia seem to have learned little from the problems encountered by ECOMOG in Liberia, and they likewise seriously underestimated the risks involved. The resulting disaster was followed by the opposite mind-set—the so-called "Somalia Syndrome"—as operationalized in the spring of 1994 in Presidential Decision Directive 25 (PDD-25) that severely restricted the conditions under which the United States would become involved in future humanitarian operations.[4]

In hindsight, it was unfortunate for the concept of humanitarian intervention that the Somalia intervention occurred so early in the post–Cold War period and turned out so badly. With the exception of Liberia and Sudan, all cases involving humanitarian intervention in the 1990s were viewed by the media (and seemingly by decision makers as well) through the lens of the Somalia operation, which, despite the considerable resources applied to it, was almost universally considered a total failure. How appropriate, we may therefore ask, were the lessons learned from the Somalia experience?

Somalia involved the extreme application of a particular set of circumstances that came to be identified with the terms "collapsed states" or "failed states." (See Zartman, 1995; Mazrui, 1995; Gros, 1996; Rotberg, 2002.) As we now know, state collapse is a fairly rare phenomenon, involving a long process of debilitating violent events, each eroding the capacity of the state to govern, and culminating in the more or less total disappearance of a government capable of exercising control. Thus, state failure leaves in its wake chaos and anarchy, with such order as may exist supplied by local warlords.

To one degree or another, over half of the 1990 post-colonial crises studied involved states that had either collapsed or were on the path to collapse—in addition to Somalia, these are Liberia, Sierra Leone, Zaire, Burundi, and Angola. In the view of some commentators, the collapse of these states cannot be attributed to chance. Ikechi Mgbeoji, for instance, maintains that "the mutilation of precolonial African nations into ahistorical units run by self-indulgent elites . . . [is] . . . a time bomb waiting to explode." Moreover, he goes on to warn that "the collapsing artifices known as African states create an inherent demand for foreign intervention." (2003, 26)

In our view, Mgbeoji overstates the case somewhat. The notion that prior to colonization Africa was neatly divided into a series of "natural" states, with borders corresponding to areas of ethnic habitation, will not bear historical scrutiny. With few exceptions, tribal groups were intermixed throughout the continent, and such boundaries as there were prior to European colonization were the result of the ebb and flow of conflict and conquest, just as they were in earlier times in other parts of the world. Though the fact is seldom recognized, all state boundaries are largely artificial creations that have scant logic other than they reflect what could be agreed upon at a particular point in time—the border between Canada and the United States being one excellent example of this. Still, in the case of Africa, it is undoubtedly true that colonial map-making did nothing to improve inter-tribal relations, and in a number of cases created rivalries that had not previously existed.

There were a number of glib assumptions on the part of decision makers regarding the ease with which an organized Western military force could whip a bunch of half-civilized warlords into line. Moreover, media assessments of the risks involved in intervention do not appear to have taken particular notice of differences in the state of governance in crisis areas. On this point, it must be remembered that four of the ten crises studied involved relatively strong state governments that were, to use a euphemism, "behaving badly." Indeed, in the case of Rwanda, the state was sufficiently strong to have orchestrated a genocide that exceeded Nazi Germany's record of killing a large number of people in a brief period of time (Hatzfeld, 2005).[5] In different ways, Sudan, Haiti, and Indonesia (through its actions in East Timor) present similar examples of state power run amok. Strategies that failed in dealing with the chaos of failed states like Somalia may have been successful in curbing the excesses of states that were still able to control the groups perpetrating violence.

What more often concerned opponents of intervention was the expected duration of any operation undertaken—getting in and stabilizing a situation was typically seen as relatively simple compared with establishing a longer-term solution and getting out again. Proponents of intervention, on the other hand, tended to think largely in the shorter term and were able on that basis to downplay considerably the risks involved. It is clear, however, that following the debacle in Somalia, understandable sympathy for people in dire situations was tempered by considerations of cost in terms of casualties, length of commitment, and the troubling recognition that success was both difficult to define and far from certain.

▪ National Interest

Even in the clearest of circumstances, what is truly in the "national interest" of a nation-state is never a foregone conclusion. Rather, the nature of the national interest is usually open to a number of interpretations and in the final analysis is constructed out of vigorous debate among powerful domestic interest groups. The degree of controversy in defining the national interest was most clearly evident with respect to Haiti, which was portrayed by supporters of an intervention as vital to American interests, while opponents argued that it was marginal to those interests. Every crisis studied affected the national interests of some other country, particularly any country that shared a boundary with the crisis-afflicted state, or that was close enough to be affected by an outflow of refugees. Table 12.4 attempts to categorize the level of post–Cold War conventional national interests of possible intervening powers in humanitarian crisis-affected states.

With the end of the Cold War, Third World countries that had been important in the strategic calculations of Great Power in the

Table 12.4 Category of Crisis, Based on Perceived "National Interest"*

Category	Crisis	Country with "Interests"
high	Liberia	Nigeria
	Haiti	U.S.
	East Timor	Australia
	Sierra Leone	Nigeria
medium	Rwanda	France
	Burundi	France
	Zaire	France
	Angola	U.S.
low	Somalia	U.S.
unclear	Sudan	

Note: *Crises are listed chronologically, within category

1960s, 1970s, and 1980s, and thus had attracted the attention and support of the United States and the Soviet Union (Somalia, Sudan, the Congo (Zaire), Liberia, Angola, and East Timor prominently among them), had for the most part lost their political/military significance. This altered political reality was first suggested by the withdrawal of Cuban troops from Angola in 1988 and became widely apparent by the early 1990s, literally at the time that conflicts in Liberia, Somalia, and Sudan were building in intensity.

As we have seen in our analysis of media crisis coverage in the *New York Times,* the question of whether the concept of a universal humanitarian interest would, to some extent, replace the more parochial concept of security and economics-based national interests was never really debated in the case of the Liberian civil war, while very little if anything was debated with respect to the Sudanese civil war. It was not until the summer of 1992 that the horrible consequences of state failure in Somalia (chaos, famine, and death) put that issue on the agenda in a major way. It seems doubly unfortunate, therefore, that the failure of "Operation Restore Hope" should call into question the practicality of embracing the moral responsibility to protect populations at risk as an operative principle just as it seemed to be gaining ascendancy.[6]

Perceptions of the national interest and of the basis on which states should intervene in the affairs of another changed also. Andrea Talentino states the case convincingly:

> The practice of intervention changed . . . and became part of conflict resolution approaches that, in extreme cases, required military force to end violence and provide support for reconstruction programs. . . . Taken all together, these changes reflected a normative revolution that seemed to raise principle above power and redefine legitimacy in the context of responsibility. . . . [Intervention moved] . . . away from its traditional uses; rather than primarily benefiting the intervener, operations were intended to benefit the target. (2005, 276–77)

The revolution in thinking was genuine enough, and might be said to still be going on. (See ICISS, 2001.) But during the 1990s, Somalia put a severe crimp in its application. Apart from Somalia itself, only Zaire among our cases provides clear examples of "humanitarian responsibility" being accepted as the primary influence on intervention decision-making. In others, the rhetoric of moral and humanitarian concerns was frequently present, but closer examination reveals that unless traditional strategic or economic interests were there as well, humanitarian rescue missions were a decidedly unattractive option for states capable of mounting such operations.

It will be recalled, for example, that France's intervention in Rwanda was justified on the basis of the highest-sounding humanitarian principles, but few would argue with the suggestion that it was occasioned primarily by the perception that French language, culture, and national honor were in need of protection. Similarly, Haiti has been described as a case of humanitarian intervention, and President Clinton's emphasis on "restoring democracy" there is consistent with that characterization. Nevertheless, given its location in the Caribbean, Haiti was of special interest to the United States, and the problem of instability there, leading to an influx of Haitian boat people into Florida, was clearly a pressing domestic concern. Finally, while motivations for the Australian-led intervention in East Timor were complex, there is little doubt that there were important security and economic issues at stake, including Australian interests in off-shore oil reserves in the Timor Gap, and again, the fear of refugees streaming from the conflict. At the same time, as was true with the UN and other nations, there was a very real and profound concern that Indonesia was not living up to its commitments to provide security for the referendum process it had agreed to undertake. However, evidence of intimidation and violence by militias, combined with Indonesia's inability or unwillingness to deal with this, continued to be reported throughout the summer, and the truth is that nothing was done, despite considerable pressure from humanitarian groups. Even at the peak of post-referendum violence in September 1999, Australia and the United States made Indonesian acceptance of an intervention force an absolute prerequisite for taking any direct action, despite extraordinarily questionable Indonesian claims to sovereignty over East Timor. It thus seems clear that traditional concepts of the national interests have not yet become entirely irrelevant, despite continuing humanitarian rhetoric. Professor Ronald Steel makes a forceful case to this effect, characterizing "humanitarian intervention . . . as the exception rather than the rule." He argues that "intervention will occur where it can be done relatively cheaply, against a weak nation, in an area both accessible and strategic, where the public's emotions are aroused, and *where it will not get in the way of other political, economic or military needs.*" (1999, Sept. 12, IV19, italics added)

It should be noted, however, that even when humanitarian rhetoric must be regarded with some skepticism, it may serve a purpose. It is a reminder, in the first instance, that such a principle is a "proper" basis for international action, and that more selfish interests cannot be pursued too blatantly without incurring international censure. In more practical terms, it provides a basis for recruiting the assistance of other nations in the cause. As Thomas Friedman observed in his analysis of the United States decision to intervene in Somalia, "where there are principles and no strategic interests at stake—or real opposition forces on the ground—[it is] relatively easier for Washington to organize an international coalition to respond." (1992, Dec. 5, I1) By framing the need for a Haitian intervention in humanitarian terms, the United States not only managed to get UN legitimization for the intervention, but had over twenty nations following it into Haiti in the fall of 1994.[7] The truth is that in the post–Cold War world the US sheriff clearly did not like to ride alone; it was much more comfortable leading a posse. (See Haass, 1999, 144.) Nor is there any reason to think that this is a unique position.

The irony of this, particularly as far as African states are concerned, is that while humanitarian considerations were rarely sufficient to compel crisis intervention, in the 1990s neither did most of the major world powers have significant conventional interests there to prompt an intervention. Virtually all scholars conclude that once the Cold War had ended, the African continent was not a high priority on the American foreign policy agenda. This reality was confirmed by its refusal to become involved in the Liberian civil war—this in spite of long-standing historical ties to Liberia, the presence of extensive communications facilities, a request from the Liberian government for American armed support, an intervention capability at hand, and widely held expectations that an American intervention would be forthcoming. Thus, to the extent the United States would become involved in African crisis intervention, some justification other than traditionally defined national interest would have to be invoked.

As we saw in the case of Somalia, this turned out to be the "moral responsibility of a world leader" argument presented so forcefully by the *New York Times* over the summer and fall of 1992. However, the intervention in Somalia that these editorials and op-ed pieces may have helped to produce, in turn provided a grim reality check on the notion of an abstract "responsibility to protect" as a motivation for intervention. Not until the refugee crisis in eastern Zaire in 1996 and the post-referendum violence in East Timor in 1999 do we again see arguments advanced in the media for Western intervention based on purely humanitarian grounds; in both cases, a far more cautious involvement was called for than was advanced for Somalia.

Both Alan Rouvez (1994) and Simon Massey (2000) reviewed the continuing interests of former European colonial powers in Africa and arrived at similar conclusions: Britain was largely out of the picture, Belgium was still involved, but only to a limited degree, leaving only France among the Great Powers still interested in post-colonial Africa. It appeared that French interests centered on the conventional areas of trade, investment, and military aid, though, as we have observed previously, the more abstract notions of preserving French language and culture and a romantic sense of honor in doing right by its former colonies were also evident. Consequently, many questioned the supposed humanitarian motivation of the "Operation Turquoise" intervention in Rwanda, despite its being sanctioned by the United Nations. France likewise was the chief advocate for multi-national interventions in Burundi and Zaire in 1996, the latter at a time when the government of Mobuto Sese Seko, a prominent French client, was under serious attack from his foes, both domestic and foreign.[8]

Not surprisingly, African states had the greatest interest in controlling political and social violence on their continent. At least those neighboring or otherwise close to a conflict area had to contend with the inevitable flood of refugees (sometimes numbering in the millions), resulting from porous borders and divided ethnic groups. Refugees present a double problem. On the one hand, they have to be cared for in at least some minimal fashion (though international aid agencies assist in that), but they may also be disruptive by engaging in political or criminal activity that creates difficulties for the host state. Moreover, it should not be forgotten that conflict next door creates opportunities as well as challenges, especially when there are outstanding irredentist claims or territorial disputes. At the extreme, the national interest of neighbors may be in prolonging or extending conflict rather than containing it.

Of course, it should be remembered as well that African states that do wish to control violence in their neighbors rarely have the resources to do so effectively and, when they try, are perhaps even more likely to become just another conflicting faction than are the more powerful and remote Western powers. Moreover, as we saw with the ECOWAS interventions in Liberia and Sierra Leone, components of the intervening force had conflicting national interests, which made them more opponents than collaborators in a single cause.

Unfortunately, the reality is that decisions regarding intervention will continue to depend on whether coming to the rescue of "other people" far from home is important in some sense other than conscience alone. In short, the issue of humanitarian versus national interest motivations for international rescue missions is far from simple, but it seems clear from our findings that there is little ground for thinking that traditional conceptions of national interest have yet been superceded in any fundamental way.[9]

■ Mass Media—the "Alerting" Function

With respect to the media alerting variable as shown in Table 12.5, data upon which the rank ordering is based are quite precise, and the extent of differences in media coverage is considerable. In that Haiti is located in the Western Hemisphere, and over twenty thousand American troops were scheduled to spearhead a long-discussed and controversial invasion, it is not surprising that Haiti stands by itself in terms of media interest. In addition to Haiti, we find that crises in Somalia and Rwanda both exceeded two hundred items of content over a six-month period, while those in East Timor, Liberia, and Zaire all exceeded well over one hundred items. We have concluded that for these six crises, the volume of media attention was sufficient to have alerted the American population to an ongoing serious situation. Contrariwise, we believe that crises in Sudan, Burundi, Sierra Leone, and Angola all failed to capture media attention to the extent that we can even begin to consider media coverage to have been a factor, either positive or negative, in intervention decision-making.

Table 12.5 Rank Order of Crises, Based on Combined Volume of Television and Newspaper Coverage *

Rank	Crisis	Number of Stories	Rank on International Response	Rank on Crisis Severity
1	Haiti	582	2	10
2	Somalia	270	1	2
3	Rwanda	242	6	1
4	East Timor	165	5	9
5	Liberia	132	3	6
6	Zaire	120	7	5
7	Burundi	45	8	4
8	Sierra Leone	25	4	7
9	Angola	15	9	8
10	Sudan	13	10	3

Note: *Assuming 30 day months, 180 stories indicate on average one story per day dealing with the crisis appeared in at least one of four mainstream U.S. media outlets over a six-month period.

If we look at the Spearman Rank Order Correlation between "volume of media coverage" on the one hand, and "strength of the international response" on the other, we find a correlation coefficient of +.79 that would appear to suggest a consistent, relatively strong relationship between the two variables; for the all-African sample, this correlation remains basically unchanged at +0.81. Significantly, crisis severity failed to predict volume of media coverage much better than it did the international response (−.04 vs. −0.18).

However, in spite of the rather impressive correlations related to media coverage and international response, one must remember that while correlation is necessary to establish causality, it is not sufficient to do so. An additional factor that complicates a causal linkage is that in two crises (Liberia and Sierra Leone), by and large the West passed on intervention, and the relatively strong responses to these crises were undertaken by the West African regional organization, ECOWAS, led by Nigeria. In our estimation, based on the necessity of an adequate media alert, overall there are at best six cases where media coverage was sufficient even to suggest that a media push might be an important factor in intervention decision-making: In chronological order, these are Liberia, Somalia, Rwanda, Haiti, Zaire, and East Timor. In order to probe further whether media coverage was, in fact, pushing decision makers toward intervention against their better judgment, as argued by proponents of the CNN effect, a case-by-case review of the coverage of these crises in the *New York Times* may be useful to assess how possible international intervention responses were, in fact, evaluated and presented to readers.

▪ Mass Media—the "Evaluation" Function

Liberia

In spite of close historical ties, described by Kenneth Noble as "the closest the United States ever had to a colony in Africa," (1990, May 25, A3) and what might be seen as at least adequate alerting on the part of mass media to the horrors that were occurring in Liberia, a United States–led humanitarian intervention into the crisis was never an issue that was discussed in media coverage of the crisis. American policy was firmly committed to non-intervention, and the *New York Times* offered no criticism of this policy, which remained unchanged for the duration of that nation's long and costly civil war.

Somalia

On the eve of the landing of United States intervention forces in Somalia, perhaps forgetting his earlier chastisement of television news networks for their late arrival on the scene (see Chapter 3, footnote 4), Walter Goodman presented a textbook case for the CNN effect:

> it was television's wrenching pictures from Somalia that goaded a reluctant Administration to act. . . . once the pictures appeared of fly-tormented faces and bloated bellies of dying babies, the effect was stunning. The natural reaction of Americans against the gun-happy druggies who were stealing their food, became too much for Washington to resist. (1992, Dec. 8, C20)

Certainly, the volume of media coverage of the Somalia crisis, second only to that generated by Haiti, was more than sufficient to have alerted the American population to the seriousness of the situation there. Likewise, our analysis of evaluative coverage in the *New York Times* is certainly consistent with a media push toward intervention— first in getting the American aircraft to fly in food supplies, and later in committing troops to protect that food from predatory warlords and roving gangs. Note as well that prior to the sustained media attention given to Somalia over the summer and fall of 1992, United States policy was one of non-intervention. That this policy then changed in the direction suggested by *New York Times* editorials supports the conclusion of a relatively strong media impact on two separate decisions to intervene.

Rwanda

The Rwandan genocide in the spring and summer of 1994 was the first major crisis following the disastrous 1993 intervention experience in Somalia to command the attention of the international community in terms of "needing to do something quickly." Mass media in the United States clearly alerted the population to the crisis, although in fairness it is doubtful whether anyone in North America could grasp the full extent of the horror that was occurring.

However, in terms of evaluating an appropriate international response to the genocide, the *New York Times* seemed as much in the grip of the "Somalia Syndrome" as was the Clinton administration. The government did not want an intervention, and the influential newspaper did little in the way of creating a media push to change that policy—indeed, it may be said to have reinforced government "coolness" toward that option. However, since there was no change to government policy, it is difficult to assess whether the media evaluations affected governmental decisions not to take any action, in spite of the truly horrific level of organized killing.

Haiti

Haiti presents the only case where the United States government actively considered a policy of military intervention relatively early on in the crisis study period, albeit as a last resort. Partly due to fears of "another Somalia," and perhaps just as importantly due to dislike of exiled Haitian President Jean-Bertrand Aristide, important political elites (some Democrats as well as Republicans) opposed an American intervention to restore him. As a result, over the summer of 1994, the Clinton administration consciously used mass media as an instrument to bring the American people on-side for an intervention as well as to neutralize opposition in Congress. (Minear et al., 1996, 60–61)

The American media had certainly adequately covered the September 1991 coup d'état that had overthrown Haiti's elected president, the repression carried out by the subsequent military government, and the resulting out-flow of refugees. Beyond that, events in Haiti had been covered extensively in the intervening years, especially the ignominious retreat of the *USS Harlan County* from Port-au-Prince in the fall of 1993 that effectively ended hopes of implementing the Governors Island Agreement.

However, in the case of Haiti we see evidence of the *failure* of a media push to influence policy. In spite of providing massive coverage of the crisis, the *New York Times* clearly had not bought into the wisdom of committing American troops to the restoration of President Aristide and made this position clear in editorial after editorial. Over the summer of 1994, neither elite nor popular opposition to an intervention (nor media opposition) had any apparent impact on administration policy, except perhaps to reinforce Clinton's often-stated preference for a negotiated departure of the generals over their forceful removal—a policy that, after three years of trying, finally proved successful at the very last minute in September 1994.

Zaire

The refugee crisis in eastern Zaire was the direct result of the Rwandan genocide in 1994, where the lack of more forceful action on the part of the international community was a cause of both deep reflection and increasing shame. The same Hutu-Tutsi antagonisms that had fed the 1994 genocide in Rwanda were again present in Zaire, so the crisis had to be treated as significant. However, the option of an international intervention was only very cautiously considered.

It seems relatively clear that the Clinton administration initially did not favor United States participation in an intervention, and its support for a UN-led intervention appeared half-hearted as well. However, when the crisis exploded in October 1996 with the expulsion of the Bayamulenge and increasing Rwandan military involvement, the administration did change its policy to the point of agreeing to commit troops to limited, but potentially significant, ground combat roles.

We must bear in mind, however, that both the mandate and the mission duration of the proposed "Operation Assurance" were quite limited; in particular, the former was restricted to providing "safe corridors" for the movement of refugees and significantly did not include separating Hutu militia and former Rwandan army troops from the general refugee population. While the *New York Times* was a somewhat reluctant supporter of a minimal role for the United States in eastern Zaire, the change in the administration's position with respect to an intervention appears to have been prompted more by international pressure—mainly from France and Canada—than from media-generated public pressure. (Erlanger, 1996, Nov. 18) Indeed, as soon as circumstances permitted (i.e., "voluntary" return of huge numbers of refugees to Rwanda), the United States quickly backed away from an intervention that ultimately never took place.

East Timor

Following Somalia and Zaire, East Timor appears to offer the only other case for significant media impact on the decision to mount an international intervention—in this case, however, the chief focus is on Australian decision-making. Coral Bell outlines the case underlying the importance of mass media in modern-day diplomacy:

As a point of diplomatic history, the management of the East Timor crisis is likely to be seen as the first ever success for a technique or strategy suggested long ago, in the early days of the League of Nations. It was then called the "hue-and-cry" option, the notion being that if enough diplomatic pressure was generated, the government targeted would lose its nerve and re-think its policy. In effect, international public opinion, carefully orchestrated, would act as a substitute for armed force.

She goes on to point out that earlier failures of this strategy occurred in

a world in which . . . the communications media had hardly begun climbing to their present overwhelming universality and capacity for pressure. The well-known "CNN effect," which is now almost decisive, was hardly imaginable in the pre–World War II society of states. (2000, 172)

For Bell, the previously discussed "norm change" that had undermined the sanctity of state sovereignty, combined with intense media pressure on decision makers, is fundamental to understanding the change in Australian policy, which up to September 1999 had been focused on maintaining good relations with Indonesia. (See also the arguments in Beams 1999 and Anderson 2003.) However, as has been noted, there were also important Australian economic and security interests at stake in East Timor, and, in the final analysis, it is important to understand that no action was taken by the UN, Australia, or any other country until the Indonesian government had agreed to the deployment of an intervention force, albeit with much arm-twisting, to which mass media no doubt contributed.

The United States approached the crisis in East Timor most cautiously, relying on the promises by the Indonesian government and military to maintain order long after it was clear that not only was security not being provided, but that the Indonesian security forces were either condoning, or actually participating in, the violence. While the Clinton administration did continue to press Indonesia to allow a force of international peacekeepers into East Timor, at the same time it appeared extremely reluctant to support any deployment of international troops without the prior approval of Indonesia, which, after literally weeks of uncontrolled violence carried out by pro-Indonesian militias, was finally achieved prior to the deployment of INTERFET on September 20. It appears that extensive media coverage in East Timor held the feet of all governments involved to the fire, a process that finally led to a negotiated solution apparently acceptable to all.

Table 12.6 presents, in summary form, our assessments of media impact (both alerting and evaluation) on United States crisis decision-making.

Table 12.6 Summary Estimate of "Alerting" and "Evaluative" Functions

Crisis	Adequacy of Alert	Initial U.S. Policy	Media Evaluation	Media Impact
Liberia 1990	Adequate N=132	Opposed	No support for U.S. intervention/ no criticism of failure to intervene	None
Somalia 1992	High N=270	Opposed	Strong support for U.S. intervention/ significant criticism of failure to intervene	Significant
Sudan 1992	Totally Inadequate N=13	Indeterminate	No support for U.S. intervention/ no criticism of failure to intervene	None
Rwanda 1994	High N=242	Favored an "African Crisis Response Force"	Recognized that "something" needed to be done, but that the situation was beyond help	Minimal
Haiti 1994	Extremely High N=582	Considered intervention as a last resort	Strong criticism of intervention/little support for one	Minimal
Burundi 1996	Inadequate N=45	Moderately supportive of an African or UN-led intervention	Mixed	None
Zaire 1996	Adequate N=120	Opposed to a UN intervention/ later agreed to commit troops	Cautiously supportive of intervention	Moderate
Sierra Leone 1997	Inadequate N=25	Opposed	No support for U.S. intervention/weak criticism of ECOWAS intervention	None
Angola 1999	Totally Inadequate N=15	Indeterminate	No support for U.S. intervention/weak support for failure to intervene	None
East Timor 1999	High N=165	Focused on diplomatic efforts to get Indonesia to accept UN peacekeeping force	Supported diplomatic and economic pressure/moved to support intervention as a "last resort"	Moderate

■ Final Thoughts

The above findings confirm that the relationship among mass media, public opinion, and government action is both interactive and complicated, and unfortunately they do not provide a basis for a simple choice between the diametrically opposed claims of the CNN effect advocates and Edward Herman and Noam Chomsky's "propaganda model" (1988) that posits that media serve as little more than "handmaidens to governments." As many news persons are prepared to admit, their organizations do serve, to a large extent, as conduits of information from government to the public—they are, after all, *news* organizations, and what governments propose to do, are considering doing, or simply think about with respect to situations affecting the state and the world in general, is certainly news. Media outlets would scarcely be doing their duty, or anyone a favor, if they failed to convey fully such matters to the publics they serve.

But news people are not robots that neutrally communicate government statements via some telephone-like connection. They are people with opinions of their own—indeed, given the business they are in, they could hardly avoid having them—and they frequently express those opinions through editorials, special features, columns, or simply by the slant or emphasis they choose to give to stories they air or write. Newspapers in particular also allow op-ed space for the expression of informed opinion by persons outside the industry itself, and they print letters-to-the-editor, which often adopt positions concerning issues of the day. Through such mechanisms, there is at least the potential for influencing any who are open to arguments, sometimes based on reason, sometimes based on emotion.

With respect to decision-making in international crises, it is important to reiterate that our findings indicate little correlation overall between crisis severity and either the level of international response (–0.18) or the level of media interest (–0.04); however, for the all-African sample, both correlations improved to +0.14 and +0.52 respectively. What did predict the strength of the international response, *regardless of crisis severity,* was the volume of media coverage—the "alerting function" associated with the CNN effect: The rank-order correlation for the entire sample was +0.79, while for the all-African sample it was +0.81.

This suggests that the alerting function clearly is of some importance. And, while this by no means constitutes a wholesale endorsement of the CNN effect, it does appear to indicate that in the overall mix of factors leading to an international intervention, *the international community is more likely to respond to a serious crisis in a country of marginal strategic or economic importance if the mainstream media are effective in alerting populations to the crisis.*

A second factor that must be considered, however, is whether an adequate "media alert" is accompanied by a convincing case for intervention on moral or humanitarian grounds, or the opposite, or something in between. Robert Entman has observed that "the public's actual opinions arise from *framed information,* from selected highlights of events, issues, and problems, rather than from direct contact with the realities of foreign affairs." (2004, 123, italics added) In other words, alerting may not be enough. There is, of course, the "pictures speak louder than words" argument, which holds that images of atrocities on the TV screen, for instance, do more to sway public opinion than thousands of pages of print, especially since many people rely for their news more on the electronic than the print media. But it is difficult to imagine that even graphic pictures by themselves would create consistent positions concerning the response of a government to an international crisis. (See Almond, 1950; Devine, 1970.) If the elite press mounts sustained opposition to becoming involved in distant peoples' troubles, or even studied indecision about it, public opinion is unlikely to coalesce in favor of humanitarian rescue to the extent that decision makers would feel compelled in this direction. In partial denial of what is probably the most quoted axiom in media studies (media don't tell the public *what to think,* but what to *think about*), we would nonetheless suggest that *a public alerted to a humanitarian crisis is more likely to direct significant pressure on its government to act in one direction or another if media have tended to lean in a similar direction.*

The circumstances under which such pressure might be effective in forcing a reluctant government to take action against its better judgment are another matter. In principle, democratic governments are (and should be) responsive to public and media pressures because, if for no other reason, they need to get re-elected. In the American system, continuing public pressure for action on humanitarian grounds is likely to influence members of Congress before members of the administration, because at any time the majority of them will be facing the electorate in not more than two years, while the president may have up to twice as long, and may largely disregard electoral pressure during the second term. Congress, however, has weight even with lame-duck presidents, so determined media/public campaigns may be indirectly effective on White House decision-making.

Against obstinate resistance, however, such a process may take a very long time. As the Iraqi insurgency has demonstrated only too plainly, presidents are not without means of fending off public and/or congressional pressures when they are firmly committed to a particular course of action. We therefore conclude that *media/public opinion pressure will be more effective in influencing government action when it accords with existing inclinations or can tip the balance in situations of indecision. Only rarely, however, and only over a significant period of time, can such pressure change an entrenched policy direction.*

To state the case bluntly, the CNN effect appears to be more hyperbole than fact. Among our ten case studies there is little evidence of significant media influence, except in Somalia, with some in Zaire and East Timor. Nonetheless, it is difficult to imagine any government undertaking extensive international intervention solely in pursuit of humanitarian causes, unless the media are largely on-side, or at least not substantially opposed. And for groups interested in promoting an international response to a humanitarian crisis, media campaigns appear to be about the only tactics available to them.

For some time, there have been modest urgings in the direction of intervention in the ongoing conflict in Darfur, which some have termed a genocide. In spite of clear parallels to the Rwandan tragedy and norm changes with respect to state sovereignty reflected in the "responsibility to protect" doctrine, western governments have shown little inclination to acquiesce to such demands. At this point in time (June 2008), following the approval in mid-April 2007 by the Sudanese government of a limited UN force joining the African peacekeeping force on the ground in Darfur, the UN took over control of the operation in January 2008 and UN troops have been deployed. However, as was the case in East Timor, while the Darfur intervention is moving slowly, continued media/public pressure directed at all parties directly involved in the conflict may induce the Sudanese government to control activities of the Janjaweed militia and rebel groups in Darfur to agree to a negotiated political solution.

Undoubtedly, one of the principal reasons why humanitarian interventions such as proposed for Darfur are resisted is the less-than-reassuring historical experience with cases such as we have examined. The unfortunate truth is that while the international community has been fairly successful in conducting *peacekeeping* operations, it has encountered severe problems organizing and carrying out those that have entailed *peace enforcement*. It is never easy, in the first place, to persuade states to participate in the latter type of operations, which, together with typical bureaucratic fumbling in the United Nations

Secretariat, means that getting them off the ground is often delayed beyond the point where they might be most effective. Critics have habitually complained that in confronting humanitarian crises the international community does not do enough, or do it quickly enough. While this is true, it does not take into account the fact that the United Nations is in no sense a united body, but rather a forum for diplomatic discussion and negotiation among states, each of which has its own views and frequently its own axe to grind.

However, the problems associated with launching an intervention pale in contrast to those encountered once a force is in the field. Manpower contributions agreed to by participating countries may very well not arrive in a timely fashion, and those from less-developed states may arrive with little or no appropriate equipment. But perhaps the greatest problem of all is in the area of "command and control." This has several components. First, some states, perhaps understandably, are reluctant to place their troops under UN command, and some restrict the geographic areas or types of activities in which their troops may be involved.[10] Needless to say, this creates a co-ordination nightmare for any UN commander. Secondly, and most important of all, the real commanders of such operations are not the generals who nominally head them, but the bureaucrats in the UN Peacekeeping Division who frequently have more of an ear for political niceties than for military necessities. Anyone who doubts how utterly maddening this can be, and how destructive of any efficiency in carrying out the ostensible task at hand, should read Lieutenant General Romeo Dallaire's *Shake Hands With the Devil* (2003), about his experiences in Rwanda, and Major General Lewis MacKenzie's *Peacekeeper: The Road to Sarajevo* (1993), about his earlier efforts in Bosnia. As both MacKenzie and Dallaire have testified, it is bad enough having your request for essential equipment or urgent clarifications/modifications of rules of engagement denied, but it is worse having them fall into a void from which they emerge, if at all, only weeks later in a garbled form. From the cases we have studied, as well as others we are familiar with, it is not difficult to conclude that the United Nations is organizationally incapable of managing large-scale military field operations with any degree of efficiency.

There is yet another problem. Critics have charged that despite the best intentions, interventions to protect and rescue the oppressed may, in fact, make the situation worse. As argued by Katherine Newland, "Not only have humanitarian interventions failed to protect people adequately from terrible suffering and death, but they have in many cases seemed to exacerbate or prolong that suffering." (cited in MacFarlane, 1999, 539) This was most evident in the ECOWAS interventions in Liberia and Sierra Leone, where the ECOMOG intervening forces became long-term parties to the conflict. However, if intervening troops attempt to disarm or contain one faction, as American forces did in Somalia, they are engaging on the side of opposing factions. Even if they merely attempt to prevent one group from committing atrocities on another (as General Dallaire wanted to do in Rwanda), such action would not be seen as neutral by those whose objectives are thwarted. In peace enforcement, the reality is that there is no such thing as neutrality.

For all of these reasons, it is difficult to be optimistic about the future of humanitarian interventions. As Michael Davis has stated:

> Humanitarian crises of vast proportions, often brought on by communal or ethnic conflicts, have been among the defining events of the post-Cold War World order. The cries of human anguish caused by these events have captured our global media and our political debate. We have, however, inherited an international regime that, in its current state of practice, often appears inadequate to the task of coping with these events. International responses to humanitarian crises are often too late, and when they do occur, they are often inadequate. (2003, 3–4)

It might be added that, at least for the most complex situations, like the Somalia quagmire, which is as deep and unrelenting today as it was in 1994, or entrenched ethnic hatreds such as those in Rwanda, there may be little that can be done, short of long-term occupation of the territory and the establishment of a rigorous system of control, authoritarian enough to prevent the kind of insurgency that has bedeviled American objectives in Iraq, and is coming to do the same with the NATO operation in Afghanistan. It is not a popular thing to say, and certainly not a comfortable one to accept, but the stark truth is that there may be some problems that outside intervention cannot solve, and where attempting to do so may even be counterproductive. The trick, of course, is to distinguish these situations from those where a timely helping hand from outside may prevent much bloodshed and suffering.

One would have to be a supreme optimist to expect that in the foreseeable future conflict will disappear, or that we, as human beings, will cease to feel the need to intervene to alleviate the human suffering caused by it. Nor will the United Nations cease to try to organize humanitarian interventions when there seems to be some possibility of doing so, and where, rightly or wrongly, the venture is thought to have some possibility of success. And that is probably as it should be. Regardless of its deficiencies, the United Nations is the "only game in town" when it comes to dealing with international humanitarian disasters, and sometimes it is better to take even inadequate action than to live with the consequences of not having tried.

▪ Notes

1. Only seven of the ten countries studied are ranked on the UN Human Development Index, and all are located in the bottom quartile. Sudan ranks highest (138 out of 175), while Sierra Leone occupies the 175th and last position. Presumably, conditions in Liberia, Somalia, and East Timor were such that needed data were not available to allow rankings to be made. (UN, 2003b)

2. In some cases, estimates on the number of deaths, refugees, and displaced persons caused by these crises differed by many hundreds of thousands. (See Gilkes, 1993, 23; Kuperman, 2001, 21; Johnson, 2003, 143, footnote 1.) Given the length of time over which some of these crises persisted, the disorganized nature of most, combined with widespread societal poverty, famine, targeting of civilians, questionable census figures, and government censorship, this is understandable. In the absence of accurate hard numbers, the confusion is added to by the tendency for humanitarian groups to promote an international intervention by overstating to some extent the degree of suffering on the ground. This is also seen as aiding in raising funds for their relief efforts. On this topic, see the excellent discussion by Lindsey Hilsum on the role of NGOs in the area of "fact inflation." (2007, 183–84)

To some extent, this has complicated the construction of our rank order of crisis severity, but in that we are dealing with ordinal rather than interval data, we believe we have created a sufficiently accurate ordering based on how each crisis was likely to have been perceived at the time intervention decisions were being made. When in doubt, we gave preference to those crises that appeared most acute in nature, thus likely to create a large-scale loss of life in a relatively short period of time. Admittedly, this process is somewhat subjective, and while we do not wish to imply that any crisis was not serious, we believe the process we followed yielded a reasonable picture of crisis severity as perceived by decision makers at the time that a possible intervention was being discussed.

3. The Spearman Rank Order Correlation coefficient is a statistical measure appropriate to ordinal data and shows the degree to which two sets of ordinal rankings are similar. The measure varies from +1.0, when the two rank orders are in perfect agreement, to -1.0, when they are in perfect disagreement. Scores around zero indicate that there is no relationship between the two rank orders. (See Blalock, 1972, 416–17.)

The formula for computing the Spearman Rank Order Correlation is

$$r_s = 1 - \frac{6\sum Di^2}{N(N^2-1)}$$

4. Howard Adelman points out that PDD-25, which "ruled out rapid international response to crises like the Rwandan genocide . . . [was] . . . signed into effect one month after the Rwandan genocide began . . . [but that] . . . the conditions of that directive governed policy at that time." (n.d., 15; see also Daalder, 1996)

5. Admittedly, Rwanda was a difficult case, for in addition to the genocide (in which civilians were targeted), there was the more conventional civil war between the Rwandan army and RPF forces, making a terrible situation even more difficult to understand. (See Chaon, 2007.)

6. It may be that, just as the Korean War ended hopes for "collective security" as a viable response to inter-state conflict, the Somalia intervention appears to have played a similar role for humanitarian intervention as a response to intra-state conflict.

7. For a more charitable assessment of motivations underlying President Clinton's policies, see Mandelbaum, 1996.

8. It was reported that, following its intervention in Rwanda in 1994, France felt that it could not intervene unilaterally in the region again. Interestingly, it was the United Sates that provided the major opposition in Security Council decision-making to French initiatives for UN sponsorship of multinational operations in both Burundi and Zaire in 1996.

9. It may well be the case that in the post-September 11 world, the nature of what is considered "in the national interest" has changed again—this time giving new significance to the phenomenon of "state failure." In light of Afghanistan's role in sheltering Osama bin Laden's al Qaeda prior to September 11, 2001, we have seen new attention paid to the consequences of the rule of warlords that tends to follow in the wake of state collapse. Thus, it is possible that international intervention in humanitarian crises will, in fact, increase in the post–September 11 environment, with the renewed chaos in Somalia a case to watch. If international intervention does increase, in light of the problems encountered in Afghanistan and Iraq, in whatever form it may be justified rhetorically, we judge that it will not be due to the altruistic motive of coming to the rescue of at-risk populations, but rather in response to a new-found national interest—fear of the consequences that allowing chaos to take hold may bring.

10. Critical to the undermining of a UN-commanded force is the understandable reluctance of any popularly elected government to give up command of its armed forces in situations where casualties are likely. The more difficult the mission, the less likely it is that command of troops will be relinquished—and this reality is not likely to change.

Contributors

E. Donald Briggs (Ph.D., University of London, 1961) is Professor Emeritus of Political Science at the University of Windsor, where he taught international relations and African politics from 1963 until his retirement in 1999. His interest in mass media dates back to his Ph.D. dissertation, *The Anglo-French Incursion into Suez, 1956,* which analyzed press opinion regarding the legality of the 1956 Suez invasion. Among his publications are *Media and Elections in Canada* (1984) and "The Zapatista Rebellion in Chiapas, 1994" (2003). For many years he was the coordinator of the World University Service Canada (WUSC) program at the University of Windsor, in which capacity he was responsible for sponsoring fifteen refugee students to Canada from conflict-ridden countries in Africa, many from those studied in this book.

Kai Hildebrandt (Ph.D., University of Michigan, 1990) is Associate Professor of Communication Studies at the University of Windsor. He co-authored *Germany in Transition* (1981) and co-edited *Television Advertising in Canadian Elections* (1999). An expert in the use of quantitative and qualitative research methods, he recently completed a comparative study of legal education focused on issues of access to, and success of, legal education. He is the co-editor of *Canadian Newspaper Ownership in the Era of Convergence* (2005) and is currently working on a project assessing the impact of media ownership convergence in reducing the diversity of content available to Canadian audiences.

Abdel Salam Sidahmed (Ph.D., Charles University, Prague, Czech Republic, 1991) is Associate Professor of Political Science at the University of Windsor. From 1995 to 2005 he held a number of positions at the International Secretariat, Amnesty International, London, including the post of Director of the Middle East Program. His authored and co-authored publications include: *Sudan* (2005 in the Routledge Curzon Contemporary Middle East Series); *Politics and Islam in Contemporary Sudan* (1997); and *Islamic Fundamentalism* (1996—nominated for the 1998 Grawemeyer Award for Ideas Improving World Order). He was an Honorary Research Fellow, Institute of Middle Eastern and Islamic Studies, University of Durham, and lectured at Centre of Middle Eastern and Islamic Law in the School of Oriental and African Studies, University of London.

Walter C. Soderlund (Ph.D., University of Michigan, 1970) is Professor Emeritus in the Department of Political Science at the University of Windsor. He is the author of *Media Definitions of Cold War Reality* (2001) and *Mass Media and Foreign Policy* (2003) as well as the co-editor of *Television Advertising in Canadian Elections* (1999), *Profiles of Canada* (2003), and *Canadian Newspaper Ownership in the Era of Convergence* (2005). He has a long-standing interest in intervention, beginning in the late 1960s with research for his Ph.D. dissertation, *The Functional Roles of Intervention in International Politics.* He has also worked extensively in the area of international communication, where his focus has been on the Caribbean, especially the way in which events in Cuba and Haiti have been portrayed in North American media and the possible impact of this coverage on U.S. foreign policy. Following his retirement in 2002, he served for a year as the founding director of the University of Windsor's Centre for Studies in Social Justice and in 2004 organized Assumption University's Centre for Religion and Culture.

References

Abbott, E. (1988). *Haiti: An Insider's History of the Rise and Fall of the Duvaliers.* New York: Simon and Schuster.

ABC News Online. (2006, July 10). "Timeline: Unrest in East Timor." Retrieved Jan. 6, 2007, from http://abc.net.au/news/indept/featuretimes/s1646987.htm.

Abdullah, I. and P. Muana (1998). "The Revolutionary Front of Sierra Leone." In C. Clapham (Ed.). *African Guerrillas.* London: James Currey, 172–93.

Abiew, F. (1999). *The Evolution of the Doctrine and Practice of Humanitarian Intervention.* The Hague: Kluwer Law International.

Adam, H. (1999). "Somali Civil Wars." In T. Ali and R. Matthews (Eds.). *Civil Wars in Africa: Roots and Resolution.* Montreal, QC and Kingston, ON: McGill-Queen's Press, 169–92.

Adeleke, A. (1995). "The Politics and Diplomacy of Peacekeeping in West Africa: The ECOWAS Operation in Liberia." *The Journal of Modern African Studies, 33,* 569–93.

Adelman, H. (n.d.). "The Role of Non-African States in the Rwandan Genocide." Retrieved September 22, 2006, from http://www.yorku.ca/crs/publications/OCEP%20PDFs/H%20A%The%20Role%20of%20Non-African%20States%20in%20Rwandan%20Genocide.PDF.

(AFP) Agence France Presse. (1999, Apr. 6). "Timor Separatist Urges Violence Against Army." The *New York Times,* A14.

(AFP) Agence France Presse. (1999, Oct. 17). "U.N. Presence for Angola." The *New York Times,* I5.

Africa Action. (1998, Dec. 18). "Security Council Meets in Open Session to Consider Situation in Sierra Leone." *Africa Policy E-Journal.* Retrieved March 23, 2006, from http://www.africaaction.org/does98/s19812.htm.

Alao, A., J. Mackinlay and F. Olonisakin (1999). *Peacekeepers, Politicians, and Warlords: The Liberian Peace Process.* New York: United Nations University Press.

Ali, T. and R. Matthews (1999). "Civil War and Failed Peace Efforts in Sudan." In T. Ali and R. Matthews (Eds.). *Civil Wars in Africa: Roots and Resolution.* Montreal, QC and Kingston, ON: McGill-Queen's Press, 193–220.

Alier, A. (1992). *Southern Sudan: Too Many Agreements Dishonored.* Reading, UK: Ithaca Press.

Allen, C. (1999). "Editorial: Ending Endemic Violence: Limits to Conflict Resolution in Africa." *Review of African Political Economy, 26,* 317–22.

Allison, G. and P. Zelikow (1999). *The Essence of Decision. Explaining the Cuban Missile Crisis.* 2nd ed. New York: Addison Wesley Longman.

Almond, G. (1950). *The American People and Foreign Policy.* New York: Harcourt Brace.

Amnesty International. (1996, August 22). "Burundi: More than 6,000 People Have Been Killed Since the Coup D'État." Retrieved July 17, 2006 from http://151.1.143/news/1996/1160202796.htm.

Anderson, J. (1992). "New World Order and State Sovereignty: Implications for UN-Sponsored Intervention." *Fletcher Forum, 16,* 127–37.

Anderson, T. (2003). "Aid, Trade, and Oil: Australia's Second Betrayal of East Timor." *Australian Journal of Political Economy,* 113–27. Retrieved September 22, 2006, from http://www.jape.org.Jape52_110_Anderson.pdf.

Anglin, D. (2002). *Confronting Rwandan Genocide: The Military Options. What Could and Should the International Community Have Done?* The Pearson Papers, Paper Number 6. Cornwallis Park, NS: The Canadian Peacekeeping Press.

Aning, E. (1999). "Eliciting Compliance from Warlords: The ECOWAS Experience in Liberia, 1990–1997." *Review of African Political Economy, 26,* 335–48.

(AP) Associated Press. (1990, July 28). "Rebels Attack Center of Liberia Capital." The *New York Times,* I3.

(AP) Associated Press. (1990, Aug. 5). "Liberian Rebel Says He'll Arrest Foreigners to Stir World Attention." The *New York Times,* I19.

(AP) Associated Press. (1992, Sept. 16). "2,400 U.S. Marines on the Way to Somalia." The *New York Times,* A10.

(AP) Associated Press. (1992, Sept. 20). "Somali Fighter Wants U.S. Marines to Leave." The *New York Times,* I10.

(AP) Associated Press. (1994, Apr. 19). "Massacres Spreading in Rwanda." The *New York Times,* A3.

(AP) Associated Press. (1994, May 11). "U.S. Discusses Peace Effort." The *New York Times,* A9.

(AP) Associated Press. (1996, June 26). "Burundi Issues Appeal for Help to End Killings." The *New York Times,* A9.

(AP) Associated Press. (1996, Aug. 1). "Africans Vote for Sanctions Against Coup." The *New York Times,* A8.

(AP) Associated Press. (1996, Oct. 11). "Zaire Fights Displaced Tutsi Suspected of Attacks." The *New York Times,* A4.

(AP) Associated Press. (1997, June 5). "Rebels Told to Give Up in West Africa." The *New York Times,* A12.

(AP) Associated Press. (1999, Apr. 8). "Militiamen Backed by Indonesia Kill 25 in East Timor, Cleric Says." The *New York Times,* A6.

(AP) Associated Press. (1999, July 13). "East Timor: High-Level Visit." The *New York Times,* A4.

(AP) Associated Press. (1999, Aug. 11). "Angola's Government Crackdown on Radio." The *New York Times,* A6.

Apple, R.W. Jr. (1994, Sept. 17). "Changing Tack on Haiti." The *New York Times,* I1.

Barkin, S. (1997). "Legitimate Sovereignty and Risky States." In G. Schneider and P. Weitsman (Eds.). *Enforcing Cooperation: Risky States and Inter-governmental Management of Conflict.* New York: St. Martin's Press, 16–36.

BBC Online. (1998, Dec. 11). "Millions Dead in Sudan Civil War." *World: Africa.* Retrieved Sept. 9, 2006, from http://newsbbc.co.uk/1/hi/world/africa/232803.stm.

BBC News. (2006, May 5). "Residents Flee East Timor Capital." Retrieved January 6, 2007, from http://news.bbc.co.uk.2/hi/asia-pacific.4975722.stm.

Beams, N. (1999, Sept. 8). "Australia Prepares Military Intervention in East Timor: What Are the Real Motives?" *World Socialist Web Site.* Retrieved August 14, 2006, from http://www.wsws.org/articles/1999/sep1999/tim-s 08.shtml.

Becker, E. and P. Shenon (1999, Sept. 9). "With Other Goals in Indonesia, U.S. Moves Gently on East Timor." The *New York Times,* A1.

Bell, C. (2000). "East Timor, Canberra and Washington: A Case Study in Crisis Management." *Australian Journal of International Affairs,* 54, 171–76.

Bellegarde-Smith, P. (2004). *Haiti: The Breached Citadel.* Toronto: Canadian Scholars' Press.

Bello, C. (1999, Aug. 24). "A Day of Reckoning in East Timor." The *New York Times,* A15.

Bennett, W. L. (1988). *News: The Politics of Illusion.* 2nd Ed. New York: Longman.

Bennett, W. L. (1990). "Toward a Theory of Press-State Relations in the United States." *Journal of Communication,* 43, 103–25.

Berman, L. and E. Goldman (1996). "Clinton's Foreign Policy at Midterm." In C. Campbell and B. Rockman (Eds.). *The Clinton Presidency: First Appraisals.* Chatham, NJ: Chatham House Books, 290–324.

Berry, N. (1990). *Foreign Policy and the Press: An Analysis of The New York Times Coverage of U.S. Foreign Policy.* New York: Greenwood Press.

Beshir, M. O. (1968). *The Southern Sudan: Background to the Conflict.* London: C. Hurst and Company.

Beshir, M. O. (1992). *Southern Sudan: Too Many Agreements Dishonoured.* Reading, UK: Ithaca Press.

Blalock, H. (1972). *Social Statistics*. (2nd ed.). New York: McGraw-Hill.

Blechman, B. (1995). "The Intervention Dilemma." *The Washington Quarterly*, 18, 63–73.

Blight, J. and T. Weiss (1992). "Must the Grass Suffer? Some Thoughts on Third World Conflicts After the Cold War." *The Third World Quarterly*, 13, 229–53.

Bogdanish, W. and J. Nordberg. (2006, Jan. 29). "Mixed U.S. Signals Helped Haiti Towards Chaos." The *New York Times*, I1.

Bonner, R. (1992, Dec. 2). "Buy Up the Somali's Guns." The *New York Times*, A23.

Bonner, R. (1999, Aug. 8). "U.S. May Try to Curb Diamond Trade that Fuels Africa's Wars." The *New York Times*, I3.

Boutros-Ghali, B. (1993). "UN Peacekeeping in a New Era: A New Chance for Peace." *The World Today*, 49, 66–69.

Bragg, R. (1994, Aug. 26). "U.S.-Cuba Strain Cools Haiti's Invasion Fever." The *New York Times*, A10.

Bragg, R. (1994, Aug. 30). "Priest Who Aided President is Killed by Gunmen in Haiti." The *New York Times*, A1.

Bragg. R. (1994, Sept. 14). "Haiti's Forces: Poorly Armed and Seasoned Only in Terror." The *New York Times*, A1.

Brown, M. (1993). *Ethnic Conflict and International Security*. Princeton: Princeton University Press.

Brown, P. (2005, December 13). "Blood Diamonds." *Worldpress.org*. Retrieved March 14, 2006, from http://www.worldpress.org/Africa/2193.cfm.

Brune, L. (1998). *The United States and Post-Cold War Interventions: Bush and Clinton in Somalia, Haiti and Bosnia, 1992–1998*. Claremont, CA: Regina Books.

Burr, M. (1993). *Quantifying Genocide in the Southern Sudan, 1983–93*. Washington, DC: US Committee for Refugees.

Burr, W. and M. Evans (2001). "East Timor Revisited: Ford, Kissinger and the Indonesian Invasion, 1975–76." *National Security Archive Electronic Briefing Book No. 62*. Retrieved August 14, 2006, from http://www.gwu.edu/~nsarchiv/NSAEBB/NSAEBB62/.

Carlson, I., H. Sung-Joo and R. Kupolati (1999). *Report of the Independent Inquiry into the Actions of the United Nations During the Genocide in Rwanda*. New York: The United Nations. Retrieved April 7, 2002, from http.www.un.org/News.ossag/rwanda report.htm.

Carothers, T. (1994, May 12). "The Making of a Fiasco." The *New York Times*, A25.

Carter, J. (1995, Sept. 17). "The Crisis in Rwanda and Burundi." The Carter Center. Retrieved April 7, 2006, from http://www.cartercenter.org/doc 56.htm.

Cartwright, J. (1970). *Politics in Sierra Leone, 1947–1967*. Toronto: University of Toronto Press.

Catalinotto, J. (2006, June 8). "Behind Australia's intervention in East Timor." *Workers World.* Retrieved August 14, 2006, from http://www.workers .org./2006/world/east-timor-0615/.

Chaon, A. (2007). "Who Failed in Rwanda, Journalists or the Media?" In A. Thompson (Ed.). *The Media and the Rwanda Genocide.* Ottawa: International Development Research Centre, 160–66.

Chopra, J. (1998). "Introducing Peace-Maintenance." *Global Governance,* 4, 1–18.

Chopra, J. and T. Weiss (1992). "Sovereignty Is No Longer Sacrosanct: Codifying Humanitarian Intervention." *Ethics and International Affairs,* 6, 95–117.

(CIA) U.S. Central Intelligence Agency. (2002). *The World Factbook 2002– Sierra Leone.* Retrieved April 4, 2003, from http://www.cia.gov/cia/ publications/factbook/geos/sl.html.

Ciment, J. (1997). *Angola and Mozambique: Postcolonial Wars in Southern Africa.* New York: Facts On File, Inc.

Clapham, C. (1976). *Liberia and Sierra Leone: An Essay in Comparative Politics.* Cambridge: Cambridge University Press.

Clapham, C. (1998). "Introduction: Assessing African Insurgencies." In C. Clapham (Ed.). *African Guerrillas.* London: James Currey, 1–18.

Clark, J. (1993a). "Debacle in Somalia." *Foreign Affairs,* 72, 109–23.

Clark, J. (1993b). "Debacle in Somalia: Failure of the Collective Response." In L. F. Damroach (Ed.). *Enforcing Restraint: Collective Intervention in Internal Conflicts.* New York: Council on Foreign Relations Press, 205–39.

Clinton, W. (1994, Sept. 16). "In the Words of the President: The Reasons why the U.S. May Invade Haiti." The *New York Times,* A10.

Clinton, W. (1996, Nov. 16). "Remarks by President Clinton on Bosnia and Central Africa." The *New York Times,* I7.

Cobb, A. (1999, Sept. 21). "East Timor and Australia's Security Role: Issues and Scenarios." Parliament of Australia, Parliamentary Library. Retrieved August 14, 2006, from http://www.aph.gov.au/Library/Pubs/CIB .1999-2000/2000cib03.htm.

Cohen, B. (1963). *Press and Foreign Policy.* Princeton, NJ: Princeton University Press.

Cohen, B. (1994). "Introduction to Media and Foreign Policy: A View from the Academy." In W. L. Bennett and D. Paletz (Eds.). *Taken By Storm: The Media, Public Opinion, and U.S. Foreign Policy in the Gulf War.* Chicago: University of Chicago Press, 8–11.

Conciliation Resources. (1997, Sept.–Oct.). "Nigerian Intervention in Sierra Leone." Retrieved March 23, 2006, from http;//www.c-rorg/pubs/occ_ papers/briefing2shtml.

Cotay, A. (1959, July). "Sierra Leone in the Post-War World." *African Affairs,* 53, 210–20.

Crocker, C. (1976). *Report on Angola.* Washington, DC: Center for Strategic and International Studies, Georgetown University.

Crocker, C. (1996). "The Varieties of Intervention: Conditions for Success." In C. Crocker and F. Osler Hampson (Eds.). *Managing Global Chaos: Sources of and Responses to International Conflict.* Washington, DC: USIP Press, 183–96.

Crocker, C. (1999, Aug. 6). "Death is the Winner in Africa's Wars." The *New York Times,* A19.

Crossette, B. (1996, Jan. 30). "U.N. Pressing for Restraint, Delays Its Action on Burundi." The *New York Times,* A2.

Crossette, B. (1996, Feb. 22). "In About Face U.S. Proposes Standby Force for Burundi." The *New York Times,* A6.

Crossette, B. (1996, May 9). "To Quell Violence in Burundi, an International Force is Urged." The *New York Times,* A13.

Crossette, B. (1996, July 25). "U.N. Asks Intervention Force As Burundi Nears Collapse," The *New York Times,* A1.

Crossette, B. (1996, July 30). "Fearing Strife, U.N. Withholds Report on Death of Burundian." The *New York Times,* A4.

Crossette, B. (1996, Aug. 9). "Rwanda Joins Effort to Isolate Burundi." The *New York Times,* A9.

Crossett, B. (1996, Nov. 2). "In Face of African Crisis, No Plans for World Action." The *New York Times,* I6.

Crossette, B. (1996, Nov. 9). "U.N. Says Military Must Act to Save Refugees in Zaire." The *New York Times,* I1.

Crossette, B. (1996, Nov. 13). "Canada Proposes Zaire Aid Force." The *New York Times,* A1.

Crossette, B. (1996, Nov. 15). "U.S. Sets Conditions for Using Troops to Aid Refugees in Zaire." The *New York Times,* A7.

Crossette, B. (1999, Aug. 24). "Angola: Malnutrition's Deadly Toll." The *New York Times,* A9.

Crossette, B. (1999, Sept. 6). "Security Council Presses Indonesia to Restore Order." The *New York Times,* A8.

Crossette, B. (1999, Sept. 7). "A Push to Intervene is Gathering Backers at the UN." The *New York Times,* A1.

Crossette, B. (1999, Sept. 8). "U.N. Says a Quarter of East Timorese Have Fled." The *New York Times,* A1.

Crossette, B. (1999, Sept. 9). "As Support for Intervention Grows, Indonesia Persuades U.N. to Delay Evacuation of Mission." The *New York Times,* A8.

Crossette, B. (1999, Sept. 11). "Annan Warns Indonesia That Inaction May Lead to Criminal Charges." The *New York Times,* A6.

Crossette, B. (1999, Sept. 15). "U.N. Presses to Organize International Force for East Timor." The *New York Times,* A11.

Crossette, B. (1999, Sept. 16). "U.N. Prepares Peacekeepers as Timorese Fight to Survive." The *New York Times,* A10.

Crowell, T. (2006, Aug. 2). "East Timor's Blighted Independence." *Asia Times Online.* Retrieved August 14, 2006, from http://www.atimes.com/atimes/Southeast_Asia/HH02Ae01.html.

Daadler, I. (1996). "Knowing When to Say No: The Development of US Policy for Peacekeeping." In W. Durch (Ed.). *UN Peacekeeping, American Politics, and the Uncivil Wars of the 1990s.* New York: St. Martin's Press, 35–67.

Daley, S. (1999, May 11). "Angola, Zambia: Meetings Planned." The *New York Times,* A8.

Daley, S. (1999, July 26). "Hunger Ravages Angolans in Renewed Civil War." The *New York Times,* A1.

Dallaire, R. (2003). *Shake Hands with the Devil: The Failure of Humanity in Rwanda.* Toronto: Random House Canada.

Davis, M. (2003). "The Emerging World Order: State Sovereignty and Humanitarian Intervention." In M. Davis, W. Dietrich, B. Scholdan, and D. Sepp (Eds.). *International Intervention in the Post-Cold War World: Moral Responsibility and Power Politics.* Armonk, NY: M. E. Sharpe, 3–39.

Dellums, R. (1994, July 24). "Squeeze the Dominican Republic." The *New York Times,* IV15.

Deng, F. (1973). *Dynamics of Identification: A Basis for National Integration in the Sudan.* Khartoum: Khartoum University Press.

Deng, F. (2001). "Sudan—Civil War and Genocide: Disappearing Christians in the Middle East." *The Middle East Quarterly,* 8. Retrieved September 8, 2006, from http://www.meforum.org/article/72.

de Rezende, I. (2002, May). "An Unmourned Death." *World Press Review,* 49. Retrieved February 5, 2006, from http://www.worldpress.org/Africa/507.cfm.

Des Forges, A. (1994, May 11). "Genocide: It's a Fact in Rwanda." The *New York Times,* A25.

Destexhe, A. (1995). *Rwanda and Genocide in the Twentieth Century.* New York: New York University Press.

Devine, D. (1970). *The Attentive Public. Polyarchical Democracy.* Chicago IL: Rand McNally.

Donnelly, J. (1998). "Human Rights: A New Standard of Civilization?" *International Affairs,* 74, 1–13.

Dunn, D. E. (1999). "The Civil War in Liberia." In T. Ali and R. Matthews (Eds.). *Civil Wars in Africa: Roots and Resolution.* Montreal, QC and Kingston, ON: McGill-Queen's Press, 89–121.

Dupuy, A. (2004). "Class, Race and Nation: Unresolved Contradictions of the Saint-Domingue Revolution." *Journal of Haitian Studies,* 10, 6–21.

Eckstein, H. (1975). "Case Study and Theory in Political Science." In F. Greenstein and N. Polsby (Eds.). *Handbook of Political Science.* Vol. VII. Reading, MA: Addison-Wesley, 79–138.

Edwards, S. (2004, Mar. 11). "Kagame Implicated in Genocide." *National Post,* A13.

Edwards, S. (2004, Apr. 7). "Genocide's 'Bad Guy' Is in Doubt." *National Post,* A10.

Edwards, S. (2006, Nov. 27). "Rwanda's Leader's Murder Still Awaits UN Probe." *National Post,* A12.

Ellis, S. (1995). "Liberia 1989–1994: A Study of Ethnic and Spiritual Violence." *African Affairs*, 94, 165–97.

Ellis, S. (1998). "Liberia's Warlord Insurgency." In C. Clapham (Ed.). *African Guerrillas*. Oxford: James Currey, 155–71.

Entman, R. (1993). "Framing: Towards a Clarification of a Fractured Paradigm." *Journal of Communication*, 43, 51–58.

Entman, R. (2004). *Projections of Power: Framing News, Public Opinion, and U.S. Foreign Policy*. Chicago, IL: University of Chicago Press.

Erlanger, S. (1996, Nov. 6). "U.S. May Send Troops to Zaire to Aid Those Fleeing Fighting." The *New York Times*, A8.

Erlanger, S. (1996, Nov. 16). "As Thousands of Refugees Leave Camps in Zaire, U.S. Reassesses the Need for Military Force." The *New York Times*, I6.

Erlanger, S. (1996, Nov. 18). "Waiting for Clinton: Allies Still Hope for U.S. Leadership in Crises." The *New York Times*, A6.

Faison, S. (1992, July 25). "U.N. Head Proposes Expanded Efforts for Somali Relief." The *New York Times*, I1.

Farmer, P. (1994). *The Uses of Haiti*. Monroe, ME: Common Courage Press.

Farmer, P. (2002, May/June). "Haiti's Wretched of the Earth." *Tikkun*. Retrieved Jan. 3, 2005, from http://www.tikun.org/magazine/index/cfm/action.tikkun/issue.tik0405/article.040521.html.

Fashole Luke, D. and S. Riley (1989). "The Politics of Economic Decline in Sierra Leone." *The Journal of Modern African Studies*, 27, 133–41.

Fatton, R. (1997). "The Rise, Fall, and Resurrection of President Aristide." In R. Rotberg (Ed.). *Haiti Renewed: Political and Economic Prospects*. Washington, DC: The Brookings Institution Press, 136–53.

Fatton, R. (2006). "The Fall of Aristide and Haiti's Current Predicament." In Y. Shamsie and A. Thompson (Eds.). *Haiti: Hope for a Fragile State*. Waterloo, ON: Wilfrid Laurier University Press, 15–24.

Fauriol, G. (1988). "The Duvaliers and Haiti." *Orbis*, 32, 587–607.

Findlay, T. (1999). *The Blue Helmets' First War: Use of Force by the UN in the Congo, 1960–64*. Clementsport, NS: Canadian Peacekeeping Press.

Finnemore, M. (1998). "Military Intervention and the Organization of International Politics." In J. Lepgold and T. Weiss (Eds.). *Collective Conflict Management and Changing World Politics*. Albany, NY: State University of New York Press, 181–204.

Fixdal, M. (1998). "Humanitarian Intervention and Just War." *Mershon International Studies Review*, 42, 283–312.

French, H. (1994, Apr. 2). "Months of Terror Bring Rising Toll of Deaths in Haiti." The *New York Times*, I1.

French, H. (1994, May 4). "Embargo Seen as Insufficient for the Return of Aristide." The *New York Times*, A11.

French, H. (1994, May 15). "Hands Off Haiti, Say Dominicans." The *New York Times*, I9.

French, H. (1994, May 18). "Americans Approve Forceful Steps to Restore Ousted Haitian President." The *New York Times*, A1.

French, H. (1994, May 23). "Haiti's Generals Remain Defiant as a Strict Embargo Takes Effect." The *New York Times,* A1.

French, H. (1994, June 3). "Doubting Sanctions, Aristide Urges U.S. Action." The *New York Times,* A3.

French, H. (1994, June 6). "Resolving a Crisis: Can Haiti Emulate South Africa?" The *New York Times,* A3.

French, H. (1994, July 3). "Haiti Longs for Help from the Land It Fears." The *New York Times,* IV1.

French, H. (1994, July 18). "Aristide's Stand on Invasion Is Seen as Reflecting Distrust of U.S." The *New York Times,* A5.

French, H. (1996, Sept. 13). "In Zaire, They Finally Ask, Who Follows Mobutu?" The *New York Times,* A3.

French, H. (1996, Sept. 30). "Booming City, Flush with Rats and Dying Children." The *New York Times,* A4.

French, H. (1996, Nov. 3). "Yes, Things Can Get Worse in Africa." The *New York Times,* IV3.

French, H. (1997, May 30). "Nigerian Military Action in Sierra Leone Backs a Larger Purpose." The *New York Times,* A13.

French, H. (1997, June 3). "Nigeria Set Back by Sierra Leone Rebels, Flies in More Troops." The *New York Times,* A10.

French, H. (1997, June 9). "Once Again, Africa Deals with Crisis on Its Own." The *New York Times,* A6.

Freney, D. (1975). *Timor: Freedom Caught between the Powers.* Nottingham, UK: Spokesman Books for the Bertrand Russell Peace Foundation.

Friedman, T. (1991, Oct. 3). "The OAS Agrees to Isolate Chiefs of Haitian Junta." The *New York Times,* A1.

Friedman, T. (1992, Dec. 5). "Crossing a Line, and Redrawing It." The *New York Times,* I1.

Friedman, T. (1996, Jan. 24). "The Next Rwanda." The *New York Times,* A19.

Friedman, T. (1999, Sept. 8). "The Mean Season." The *New York Times,* A23.

Friedman, T. (1999, Sept. 15). "The Four Questions." The *New York Times,* A29.

Fromuth, P. (1993). "The Making of a Security Community: The United Nations After the Cold War." *Journal of International Affairs,* A6, 341–366.

Fyfe, C. (1979). *A Short History of Sierra Leone.* (New Edition). London: Longman.

Galtung, J. and M. Holmboe-Ruge (1965). "The Structure of Foreign News: The Presentation of the Congo, Cuba, and Cyprus Crises in Four Norwegian Newspapers." *Journal of Peace Research,* 2, 65–91.

Gamson, W. (1989). "News as Framing." *American Behavioral Scientist,* 33, 157–61.

Gans, H. (1979). *Deciding What's News: A Study of CBS Evening News, NBC Nightly News, Newsweek and Time.* New York: Pantheon.

Gelb, L. (1992, Nov. 19). "Shoot to Feed Somalia." The *New York Times,* A27.

Gelb, L. (1992, Dec. 6). "Not Set in Stone." The *New York Times,* IV19.

George, A. (1979). "Case Studies and Theory Development: The Method of Structured, Focused Comparison. In P. Lauren (Ed.). *Diplomacy: New Approaches in History, Theory, and Policy.* New York: The Free Press, 43–68.

Gershoni, Y. (1985). *Black Colonialism: The Americo-Liberian Scramble for the Hinterland.* Boulder, CO: Westview Press.

Gershoni, Y. (1997). "War Without End and an End to a War: The Prolonged Wars in Liberia and Sierra Leone." *African Studies Review,* 49, 55–76.

Giardet, E. (1996). "Reporting Humanitarianism: Are the New Electronic Media Making a Difference?" In R. Rotberg and T. Weiss (Eds.). *From Massacres to Genocide: The Media, Public Policy, and Humanitarian Crises.* Washington, DC: The Brookings Institution, 43–68.

Gilboa, E. (2005). "The CNN Effect: The Search for a Communication Theory of International Relations." *Political Communication,* 22, 27–44.

Gilkes, P. (1993, November-December). "From Peacekeeping to Peace Enforcement: The Somalia Precedent." *Middle East Report,* 185, 21–24.

Good, R. (1962). "The Congo Crisis: A Study of Post-colonial Politics." In L. Martin (Ed.). *Neutralism and Nonalignment: The New States in the World.* New York: Praeger, 34–63.

Goodman, W. (1992, Sept. 2). "Why It Took TV So Long to Focus on the Somalis." The *New York Times,* C18.

Goodman, W. (1992, Dec. 8). "Re Somalia: How Much Did TV Shape Policy?" The *New York Times,* C20.

Goodspeed, P. (2005, Apr. 22). "Burundi Vote Misses Deadline Amid Violence." *National Post,* A19.

Gordon, J. K. (1962). *The United Nations in the Congo: A Quest for Peace.* New York: Carnegie Endowment for International Peace.

Gordon, M. (1992, Aug. 15). "With U.N.'s Help, U.S. Will Airlift Food to Somalia." The *New York Times,* I1.

Gordon, M. (1992, Dec. 4). "U.N. Backs a Somali Force as Bush Vows a Swift Exit; Pentagon Sees Longer Stay." *New York Times,* A1.

Gordon, M. (1992, Dec. 6). "Envoy Asserts Intervention in Somalia is Risky and Not in Interests of U.S." The *New York Times,* I14.

Gordon, M. (1992, Dec. 8). "Big Test for Small Force: Logistics of Somali Aid." The *New York Times,* A18.

Gordon, M. (1994, May 4). "Clinton Says Haiti Military Must Go Now." The *New York Times,* A10.

Gordon, M. (1994, June 16). "U.S. To Supply 60 Vehicles for U.N. Troops in Rwanda." The *New York Times,* A12.

Gordon, M. (1994, Sept. 10). "U.S. Hopes Talk of War Forces Out Haiti Army." The *New York Times,* I4.

Gordon, M. (1994, Sept. 14). "Top U.S. Officials Outline Strategy for Haiti Invasion." The *New York Times,* A1.

Gordon, M. and E. Schmitt (1994, May 30). "Weighing Options, U.S. Aides Assess Invasion of Haiti." The *New York Times,* I1.

Gordon, M. and M. Mazzetti (2007, Apr. 8). "North Koreans Arm Ethiopians as U.S. Assents." The *New York Times,* A1.

Goulding, M. (1993). "The Evolution of United Nations Peacekeeping." *International Affairs,* 69, 451–64.

Gourevitch, P. (1996, Oct. 28). "Zaire's Killer Camps." The *New York Times,* A19.

Gray, R. (1961). *A History of the Southern Sudan, 1839–1899.* Oxford, Oxford University Press.

Greenhouse, S. (1994, Apr. 10). "Haiti Policy in Stalemate." The *New York Times,* A9.

Greenhouse, S. (1994, Apr. 15). "Clinton Policy Towards Haiti Comes Under Growing Fire." The *New York Times,* A2.

Greenhouse, S. (1994, Apr. 22). "Aristide Condemns Clinton's Haiti Policy as Racist." The *New York Times,* A1.

Greenhouse, S. (1994, July 10). "Lawmakers Oppose an Invasion of Haiti Now." The *New York Times,* A3.

Greenwood, C. (1993). "Is There a Right of Humanitarian Intervention?" *The World Today,* 49, 34–40.

Gros, J.-G. (1996). "Towards a Taxonomy of Failed States in the New World Order: Decaying Somalia, Liberia, Rwanda and Haiti." *Third World Quarterly,* 17, 455–71.

Gunn, G. (1992). "The Legacy of Angola." In T. Weiss and J. Blight (Eds.). *The Suffering Grass: Superpowers and Regional Conflict in Southern Africa and the Caribbean.* Boulder, CO: Lynne Rienner, 39–54.

Guterres Lopes, A. (1999, May 5). "East Timor's Bloodiest Tradition." The *New York Times,* A25.

Haass, R. (1999). *Intervention: The Use of American Military Power in the Post-Cold War World* (Rev. Ed.). Washington, DC: Brookings Institution Press.

Hall Jamieson, K. and P. Waldman (2003). *The Press Effect: Politicians, Journalists, and the Stories that Shape the Political World.* New York: Oxford University Press.

Hallward, P. (2004, May-June). "Option Zero in Haiti." *New Left Review,* 27. Retrieved January 10, 2006, from http://www/newleftreview.net .NLR26102.shtml.

Hamilton, J. (1999, Sept. 11). "How East Timor is Like Kosovo." The *New York Times,* A10. (letter)

Harding, A. (2001, April 21). "Oil and Sudan's Civil War." *BBC News.* Retrieved Sept. 9, 2006, from http://news.bbc.co.uk/1/hi/programmes/from_our_own_correspondent/1287188.stm.

Hare, P. (1998). *Angola's Last Best Chance for Peace: An Insider's Account of the Peace Process.* Washington, DC: United States Institute of Peace.

Hatzfeld, J. (2005). *Machete Season: The Killers in Rwanda Speak.* (Trans. Linda Coverdale). New York: Farrar, Straus and Giroux.

Head, M. (2000, October 25). "Timor Gap Dispute Highlights Motives Behind Australian Intervention." *World Socialist Web Site.* Retrieved August 14, 2006, from http://wsws.org/articles.2000/oct2000/tim-o25.shtml.

Head, M. and L. Tennenbaum (2002, May 18). "East Timor's 'Independence': Illusion and Reality." *World Socialist Web Site.* Retrieved August 14, 2006, from http:www.wsws.org/articles/2002/may2002/timo-m18.shtml.

Hector, C. (1988). "Haiti: A Nation in Crisis." *Peace and Security,* 3, 6–7.

Helis, J. (2001). "Haiti: A Study in Canadian-American Security Cooperation in the Western Hemisphere." In D. Haglund (Ed.). *Over Here and Over There: Canada-US Defence Cooperation in an Era of Interoperability.* Kingston, ON: A special issue of the *Queen's Quarterly,* published in cooperation with the Conference of Defence Associations Institute, 113–44.

Henderson, E. and J. D. Singer (2000). "Civil War in the Post-Colonial World, 1946–1992." *Journal of Peace Research,* 37, 275–99.

Herbert, B. (1994, Mar. 23). "Pretty Words on Haiti." The *New York Times,* A21.

Herman, E. and N. Chomsky (1988). *Manufacturing Consent: The Political Economy of the Mass Media.* New York: Pantheon Books.

Hermann, C. (1969). *Crises in Foreign Policy Decision-making.* Indianapolis, IN: Bobbs-Merrill.

Hilsum, L. (2007). "Reporting Rwanda: The Media and the Aid Agencies." In A. Thompson (Ed.). *The Media and the Rwanda Genocide.* Ottawa: International Development Research Centre, 167–87.

Hochschild, A. (1998). *King Leopold's Ghost: A Story of Greed, Terror, and Heroism in Colonial Africa.* New York: Houghton Mifflin.

Hoffman, P. and T. Weiss (2006). *Sword & Salve: Confronting New Wars and Humanitarian Crises.* Lanham, MD: Rowman and Littlefield.

Hoffmann, S. (1999, Sept. 11). "Principles in the Balkans, but Not in East Timor." The *New York Times,* A11.

Hoge, W. (2006, Dec. 2). "U.S. Proposing Regional Force to Monitor Somalia Violence." The *New York Times,* A7.

Holsti, O. (1969). *Content Analysis for the Social Sciences and Humanities.* Reading, MA: Addison-Wesley.

Holzgrefe, J. (2003). "The Humanitarian Intervention Debate." In J. Holzgrefe and R. Keohane (Eds.). *Humanitarian Intervention: Ethical, Legal, and Political Dilemmas.* Cambridge: Cambridge University Press, 15–52.

Homer-Dixon, T. (1994). "Environmental Scarcities and Violent Conflict: Evidence from Cases." *International Security,* 19, 76–116.

Hoskyns, C. (1965). *The Congo Since Independence, January 1960–December 1961.* London: Oxford University Press.

Howe, H. (1996/97). "Lessons of Liberia: ECOMOG and Regional Peacekeeping." *International Security,* 21, 145–76.

Human Rights Watch. (1999). "Sierra Leone: Human Rights Developments." Retrieved March 23, 2006, from http://www.hrw.org/wr2k/Africa-09.htm.

Hunter-Gault, C. (1966, Aug. 1). "Burundi in Crisis." *Online NewsHour.* Retrieved April 7, 2004, from http://www.pbs.org.newshour/bb/africa/august96/burundi_8-1.html.

(ICISS) International Commission on Intervention and State Sovereignty. (2001). *The Responsibility to Protect: Report of the International Commission on Intervention and State Sovereignty.* Ottawa: International Development Research Centre. Retrieved January 18, 2006, from http://www.iciss.ca.pdf/Commission-Report.pdf.

Innes, A. (2004). "Political Communication in Wartime Liberia: Themes and Concepts." *Centre D'Études des Politiques Étrangères et de Sécurité, 26,* 1–34. Retrieved November 20, 2006, from http://www.er.uquam.ca/nobel/cepes/pdf/no26.pdf.

Iorio, S. and S. Huxman (1996). "Media Coverage of Political Issues and the Framing of Personal Concerns." *Journal of Communication, 46,* 97–115.

Ives, K. (1995a). "The Lavalas Alliance Propels Aristide to Power." In D. McFadyen and P. La Ramée (Eds.). *Haiti: Dangerous Crossroads.* Boston: South End Press, 41–45.

Ives, K. (1995b). "The Unmaking of a President." In D. McFadyen and P. La Ramée (Eds.). *Haiti: Dangerous Crossroads.* Boston: South End Press, 65–87.

Ives, K. (1995c). "Haiti's Second U.S. Occupation." In D. McFadyen and P. La Ramée (Eds.). *Haiti: Dangerous Crossroads.* Boston: South End Press, 107–18.

Iyengar, S. and D. Kinder (1987). *News That Matters: Agenda-setting and Priming in a Television Age.* Chicago: University of Chicago Press.

Iyengar, S. (1991). *Who Is Responsible: How Television Frames Political Issues.* Chicago: University of Chicago Press.

Jackson, M. (2000). "Something Must Be Done? Genocidal Chaos and World Responses to Mass Murder in East Timor in 1995–1978 and 1999, and in Burundi in 1992 and 1994." Paper presented at the Meeting of the Northeastern Political Science Association, Albany, N.Y.

Jakobsen, P. (1996). "National Interest, Humanitarianism or CNN: What Triggers UN Peace Enforcement After the Cold War?" *Journal of Peace Research, 33,* 205–15.

Jalloh, W. (2004). *War Is No Child's Play. A Look at the Use of Child Soldiers in Sub-Saharan Africa with a Case Study of Sierra Leone.* M.A. Major Paper. Department of Political Science, University of Windsor.

James, A. (1995). "Peacekeeping in the Post-Cold War Era." *International Journal, 50,* 241–65.

James, C. L. R. (1963). *The Black Jacobins: Toussaint L'Ouverture and the San Domingo Revolution.* 2nd ed. New York: Vintage.

James III, W. M. (1991). *A Political History of the Civil War in Angola 1974–1990.* New Brunswick, NJ: Transaction Publishers.

Jardine, M. (1995). *East Timor: Genocide in Paradise.* Tucson, AZ: Odonian Press.

Jefferies, J. (2001). "The United States and Haiti: An Exercise in Intervention." *Caribbean Quarterly*, 47, 71–94.

Jehl, D. (1994, May 6). "Clinton's Options on Haiti: Even Harsher Choices Ahead." The *New York Times*, A10.

Jehl, D. (1994, May 18). "U.S. is Showing a New Caution on U.N. Peacekeeping Missions." The *New York Times*, A1.

Jehl, D. (1994, May 20). "Clinton Spells Out Reason He Might Use Force in Haiti." The *New York Times*, A1.

Jehl, D. (1994, June 10). "Officials Told to Avoid Calling Rwanda Killings 'Genocide'." The *New York Times*, A8

Jehl, D. (1994, July 19). "Clinton and Haiti: Domestic Issues Complicate Choice." The *New York Times*, A4.

Jehl, D. (1994, July 22). "Clinton Seeks U.N. Approval of Any Plan to Invade Haiti." The *New York Times*, A1.

Jehl, D. (1994, Sept. 15). "Clinton Plans Speech to Head Off Clash with Congress." The *New York Times*, A8.

Jehl, D. (1994, Sept. 17). "Holding Off, Clinton Sends Carter, Nunn and Powell to Talk to Haitian Junta." The *New York Times*, I1.

Jetley, V. (2000, May). "Report on the Crisis in Sierra Leone." Retrieved March 23, 2006, from http://www.sierra-leone.org/jetley0500.html.

Johnson, D. (1989). *John Garang: The Call for Democracy in Sudan*. London: Kegan Paul International.

Johnson, D. (2003). *The Root Causes of Sudan's Civil Wars*. Oxford, UK: James Currey.

Johnson-Sirleaf, E. (2007, Mar. 21). "Stand with Us, Canada; What Gives Liberia Hope." *The Globe and Mail*, A19.

Jonas, G. (2004, Feb. 13). "Aristide's Haiti." *The Windsor Star*, A6.

Jones, B. (1999). "Civil War, the Peace Process, and Genocide in Rwanda." In T. Ali and R. Matthews (Eds.). *Civil Wars in Africa: Roots and Resolution*. Montreal, QC and Kingston, ON: McGill-Queen's Press, 53–86.

Jones, B. (2001). *Peacemaking in Rwanda: The Dynamics of Failure*. Boulder, CO: Lynne Rienner.

Judson, J. (1994, Aug. 11). "Haiti's Thugs May Listen to Nothing but Force." The *New York Times*, A22. (letter)

Kennan, G. (1993, Sept. 30). "Through a Glass Darkly." The *New York Times*, A25.

Kerry, J. (1994, May 16). "Make Haiti's Thugs Tremble." The *New York Times*, A17.

Khalid, M. (1985). *Nimeiri and the Revolution of Dis-May*. London: Routledge and Kegan Paul.

Kilson, M. (1969). *Political Change in a West African State: A Study of the Modernization Process in Sierra Leone*. New York: Atheneum Press.

Kinzer, S. (1994, May 25). "European Leaders Reluctant to Send Troops to Rwanda." The *New York Times*, A1.

Klarevas, L. (2000). "The United States Peace Operation in Somalia." *Public Opinion Quarterly,* 64, 523–40.

Klinghoffer, A. (1980). *Angolan War: A Study of Soviet Policy in the Third World.* Boulder, CO: Westview Press.

Krause, C. (1990, June 13). "Strategic Interests Tie U.S. to Liberia." The *New York Times,* A3.

Krause, C. (1992, Nov. 27). "Washington Seeks Conditions on Plan for Somali Force." The *New York Times,* A1.

Kuperman, A. (2001). *The Limits of Human Intervention: Genocide in Rwanda.* Washington, DC: The Brookings Institution.

Laber, J. (1994, Apr. 20). "Don't Write off Rwandan Violence as Ethnic." The *New York Times,* A18. (letter)

Lander, M. (1999, Mar. 19). "Indonesia: Timor Pullout Urged." The *New York Times,* A4.

Lander, M. (1999, Sept. 13). "East Timorese Flee Homes, and Encounter More Danger." The *New York Times,* A1.

Landy, J. (1994, Aug. 7). "Suppose We Invade Haiti: Then What?" The *New York Times,* IV17. (letter)

Larson, W. (1990). "Television and U.S. Foreign Policy: The Case of the Iran Hostage Crisis." In D. Graber (Ed.). *Media Power in Politics.* 2nd ed. Washington, DC: CQ Press, 301–12.

Lautze, S., B. Jones, and M. Duffield. (1998). *Strategic Humanitarian Coordination in the Great Lakes, 1996–1997: An Independent Assessment.* New York: United Nations, Office of Humanitarian Affairs, Policy, Information and Advocacy Division. Retrieved December 5, 2006, from http://129194.252.80/catfiles.11145.pdf.

Lawless, R. (1976). "The Indonesian Takeover of East Timor." *Asian Survey,* 16, 948–64.

Lefever, E. (1967). *Uncertain Mandate: Politics of the U.N. Congo Operation.* Baltimore, MD: The Johns Hopkins Press.

Lemarchand, R. (1970). *Rwanda and Burundi.* New York: Praeger.

Lemarchand, R. (1994). "Managing Transition Anarchies: Rwanda, Burundi, and South Africa in Comparative Perspective." *The Journal of Modern African Studies,* 32, 581–604.

Lemarchand, R. (1998a). "U.S. Policy in the Great Lakes: A Critical Perspective." *Issue: A Journal of Opinion,* 26, 41–46.

Lemarchand, R. (1998b). "Genocide in the Great Lakes: Which Genocide? Whose Genocide?" *African Studies Review,* 41, 3–16.

Lewis, A. (1992, Nov. 16). "Cold War Wreckage." The *New York Times,* A17.

Lewis, A. (1992, Nov. 20). "Action or Death." The *New York Times,* A31.

Lewis, A. (1994, Sept. 19). "Resolution Matters." The *New York Times,* A19.

Lewis, A. (1999, Sept. 7). "The Fruits of Realism." The *New York Times,* A19.

Lewis, I. M. and J. Mayall (1996). "Somalia." In J. Mayall (Ed.). *The New Interventionism, 1991–1994: United Nations Experience in Cambodia,*

Former Yugoslavia and Somalia. New York: Cambridge: Cambridge University Press, 94–124.

Lewis, P. (1992, Nov. 27). "U.N. Chief to Ask Use of Force to Back Somali Aid." The *New York Times*, A14.

Lewis, P. (1992, Dec. 1). "U.N.'s Chief Requests New Force to Ease the Somalis' Misery Now." The *New York Times*, A1.

Lewis, P. (1992, Dec. 6). "U.N. Says Somalis Must Disarm Before Peace." The *New York Times*, I15.

Lewis, P. (1994, Apr. 22). "Security Council Votes to Cut Rwandan Peacekeeping Force." The *New York Times*, A1.

Lewis, P. (1994, Apr. 29). "U.S. Expects U.N. to Toughen Haiti Embargo." The *New York Times*, A13.

Lewis, P. (1994, Apr. 30). "U.N. Council Urged to Weigh Action on Saving Rwanda." The *New York Times*, A1.

Lewis, P. (1994, May 1). "U.S. Examines Way to Assist Rwanda." The *New York Times*, A1.

Lewis, P. (1994, May 3). "U.N. Chief Seeks An African Peace Force for Rwanda." The *New York Times*, A3.

Lewis, P. (1994, May 12). "U.S. Opposes Plan for UN Force in Rwanda." The *New York Times*, A9.

Lewis, P. (1994, May 14). "Security Council Agrees on Plan to Send Peace Force to Rwanda." The *New York Times*, A1.

Lewis, P. (1994, May 17). "U.N. Backs Troops for Rwanda, But Terms Bar Any Action Soon." The *New York Times*, A1.

Lewis, P. (1994, May 26). "Boutros-Ghali Angrily Condemns All Sides for Not Saving Rwanda." The *New York Times*, A1.

Libenow, J. G. (1987). *Liberia: The Quest for Democracy.* Bloomington, IN: Indiana University Press.

Lippmann, W. (1922). *Public Opinion.* New York: Harcourt Brace.

Livingston, S. and T. Eachus (1995). "Humanitarian Crises and U.S. Foreign Policy: Somalia and the CNN Effect Reconsidered." *Political Communication,* 12, 413–29.

Livingston, S. (1996). "Suffering in Silence: Media Coverage of War and Famine in the Sudan." In R. Rotberg and T. Weiss (Eds.). *From Massacres to Genocide: The Media, Public Policy and Humanitarian Crises.* Washington, DC: The Brookings Institution, 68–89.

Livingston, S. (2007). "Limited Vision: How Both the American Media and Government Failed Rwanda." In A. Thompson (Ed.). *The Media and the Rwanda Genocide.* Ottawa: International Development Research Centre, 188–97.

Lobaido, A. (1998, Aug. 11). "Executive Outcomes: A New Kind of Army for privatized global warfare." Retrieved August 27, 2006, from http://.www.worldnetdaily.com/news/article?ARTICLE_ID=16671.

Lodico, Y. (1996). "A Peace that Fell Apart: The United Nations and the War in Angola." In W. Durch (Ed.). *UN Peacekeeping, American Politics, and the Uncivil Wars of the 1990s.* New York: St. Martin's Press, 103–33.

Lorch, D. (1994, Apr. 21). "The Massacres in Rwanda: Hope is Also a Victim." The *New York Times*, A3.

Lorch, D. (1994, May 21). "Thousands of Rwandan Dead Wash Down to Lake Victoria." The *New York Times*, A1.

Lowenkopf, M. (1976). *Politics in Liberia. The Conservative Road to Development.* Stanford, CA: Hoover Institution Press.

Lyons, G. and M. Mastanduno (1995). *Beyond Westphalia? State Sovereignty and International Intervention.* Baltimore, MD: The John Hopkins University Press.

Lyons, T. (1994). "Crises on Multiple Levels: Somalia and the Horn of Africa." In A. Samatar (Ed.). *The Somali Challenge: From Catastrophe to Renewal?* Boulder, CO: Lynne Rienner, 189–207.

Lyons, T. and A. Samatar (1995). *Somalia: State Collapse, Multilateral Intervention and Strategies for Political Reconstruction.* Washington, DC: The Brookings Institution.

MacFarlane, S. N. (1999). "Humanitarian Action and Conflict." *International Journal*, 54, 537–61.

MacKenzie, L. (1993). *Peacekeeper: The Road to Sarajevo.* Vancouver, BC: Douglas and McIntyre.

Mackey, S. (1999, Sept. 10). "Fleeing the Killing in East Timor." The *New York Times*, A24. (letter)

Mackinlay J. and J. Chopra (1992). "Second Generation Multilateral Operations." *The Washington Quarterly*, 15, 113–31.

Maingot, A. (1986–87). "Haiti: Problems of a Transition to Democracy in an Authoritarian Soft State." *Journal of Interamerican Studies and World Affairs*, 28, 75–102.

Makinda, S. (1993). "Somalia: From Humanitarian Intervention to Military Offensive?" *The World Today*, 49, 184–86.

Malinkina, O. and D. McLeod (2000). "From Afghanistan to Chechnya: News Coverage by Izvestia and The *New York Times*." *Journalism and Mass Communication Quarterly*, 77, 37–49.

Mandelbaum, M. (1996). "Foreign Policy as Social Work." *Foreign Affairs*, 75, 16–32.

Massey, S. (2000). "Operation Assurance: The Greatest Intervention That Never Happened." *The Journal of Humanitarian Assistance.* Retrieved April 7, 2006, from http://www.jha.ac/articles/a036.htm.

Mazrui, A. (1995). "The African State as a Political Refugee." In D. Smock and C. Crocker (Eds.). *African Conflict Resolution: The U.S. Role in Peacemaking.* Washington: United States Institute of Peace Press, 9–25.

Mazrui, A. (1997). "Crisis in Somalia: From Tyranny to Anarchy." In H. Adam and R. Ford (Eds.). *Mending Rips in the Sky: Options for Somali Communities in the 21st Century.* Lawrenceville, NJ: Red Sea Press Inc., 5–11.

McCombs, M. and D. Shaw (1972). "The Agenda-Setting Function of Mass Media." *Public Opinion Quarterly*, 36, 176–87.

McCombs, M. and D. Shaw (1993). "The Evolution of Agenda-Setting Research: Twenty-Five Years in the Marketplace of Ideas." *Journal of Communication,* 43, 58–67.

McGregor, A. (1999). "Quagmire in West Africa: Nigerian Peacekeeping in Sierra Leone (1997–98)." *International Journal,* 54, 482–501.

McKinley, J. and D. McNeil (1996, Jan. 14). "In the Grisly Shadow of Rwanda, Ethnic Violence Stalks Burundi." The *New York Times,* I1.

McKinley, J. (1996, June 16). "Stoked by Rwandans, Tribal Violence Spreads in Zaire." The *New York Times,* I3.

McKinley, J. (1996, July 4). "African Peacekeeping Plan for Burundi Gains Ground." The *New York Times,* A2.

McKinley, J. (1996, July 6). "The Toll of Ethnic Revenge: Dead Women and Children." The *New York Times,* I5.

McKinley, J. (1996, July 12). "Chaos in Burundi Could Sow Misery Next Door." The *New York Times,* A3.

McKinley, J. (1996, Oct. 26). "Zaire War Breeds a Human Catastrophe." The *New York Times,* I7.

McKinley, J. (1996, Oct. 28). "From African Tangle, Explosion." The *New York Times,* A8.

McKinley, J. (1996, Nov. 4). "War in Eastern Zaire Leaves Relief Agencies Scrambling." The *New York Times,* A3.

McKinley, J. (1996, Nov. 5). "Zaire Rebel Calls a Truce, but Refugees Remain in Danger." The *New York Times,* A8.

McNeil, D. (1996, July 26). "Burundi Army Stages Coup, and New Fighting is Feared." The *New York Times,* A3.

McNeil, D. (1996, July 28). "Be Only Burundian, Coup Leader Urges Ethnic Rivals." The *New York Times,* I6.

McNeil, D. (1996, July 30). "New Leader of Burundi: Authoritarian Democrat." The *New York Times,* A4.

McNeil, D. (1996, Aug. 4). "Burundi in Crisis: America Sits and Watches." *New York Times,* IV6.

Melvern, L. (2000). *A People Betrayed: The Role of the West in Rwanda's Genocide.* Claremont, South Africa: New Africa Education Publishing.

Melvern, L. (2004). *Conspiracy to Murder: The Rwandan Genocide* (Rev. Ed.). London: Verso.

Melvern, L. (2007). "Missing the Story: the Media and the Rwanda Genocide." In A. Thompson (Ed.). *The Media and the Rwanda Genocide.* Ottawa: International Development Research Centre, 198–210.

Meredith, M. (2005). *The Fate of Africa.* New York: Public Affairs Press.

Mermin, J. (1997). "Television News and American Intervention in Somalia: The Myth of a Media-Driven Foreign Policy." *Political Science Quarterly,* 112, 385–403.

Merriam, A. (1961). *Congo: Background of Conflict.* Evanston, IL: Northwestern University Press.

Merrill, J. (1968). *The Elite Press: Great Newspapers of the World*. New York: Pitman Publishing Corporation.

Mgbeoji, I. (2003). *Collective Insecurity: The Liberian Crisis, Unilateralism, and Global Order*. Vancouver, BC: UBC Press.

Miller, J. (1999, June 23). "East Timor: U.N. Delays Key Vote." The *New York Times*, A6.

Mills, T. (2005, April). "Sierra Leone Civil War, 1991–2002." *Land Forces of Britain, the Empire and Commonwealth*. Retrieved March 23, 2006, from http://www.regiments.org/wars/20thcent/91sierra.htm.

Millspaugh, A. (1931). *Haiti Under American Control, 1915–1930*. Boston, MA: World Peace Foundation.

Minear, L., C. Scott, and T. Weiss (1996). *The News Media, Civil War, and Humanitarian Action*. Boulder, CO: Lynne Rienner.

Mitchell, A. (1996, Nov. 14). "Clinton Offers U.S. Troops to Help Refugees in Zaire." The *New York Times*, A1.

Mitchell, R. and T. Bernaur (1998). "Empirical Research on International Environmental Policy: Designing Qualitative Case Studies." *Journal of Environment and Development*, 7, 4–31.

Moeller, S. (1999). *Compassion Fatigue: How the Media Sell Disease, Famine, War and Death*. New York: Routledge.

Morales, W. (1994). "US Intervention and the New World Order: Lessons from Cold War and Post-Cold War Cases." *Third World Quarterly*, 15, 77–101.

Morley, M. and C. McGillion (1997). "'Disobedient' Generals and the Politics of Redemocratization: The Clinton Administration and Haiti." *Political Science Quarterly*, 112, 363–84.

Muldoon, J. (1995). "What Happened to Humanitarian Intervention?" *The Bulletin of the Atomic Scientists*, 51, 60–61.

Murphy, S. (1996). *Humanitarian Intervention: The United Nations in an Evolving World Order*. Vol. 21, Procedural Aspects of International Law Series. Philadelphia, PA: University of Pennsylvania Press.

Mydans, S. (1999, Apr. 26). "With Peace Accords at Hand, East Timor's War Deepens." The *New York Times*, A3.

Mydans, S. (1999, Aug. 27). "Anti-Independence Frenzy Leaves 4 Reported Dead in East Timor as Referendum Approaches." The *New York Times*, A12.

Mydans, S. (1999, Sept. 4). "In East Timor, Decisive Vote for a Break from Indonesia." The *New York Times*, A1.

Mydans, S. (1999, Sept. 5). "Danger Rises as East Timor Faces Freedom." The *New York Times*, I6.

Mydans, S. (1999, Sept. 6). "East Timor Falls Into Gangs' Hands; Killings Reported." The *New York Times*, A1.

Mydans, S. (1999, Sept. 8). "The Timor Enigma." The *New York Times*, A12.

Mydans, S. (1999, Sept. 11). "Militias in Timor Menace Refugees at U.N. Compound." The *New York Times*, A1.

Mydans, S. (1999, Sept. 12). "Jakarta Concedes a Loss of Control of East Timor Forces." The *New York Times,* I1.

Mydans, S. (1999, Sept. 13). "Indonesia Invites a U.N. Force to Timor." The *New York Times,* A1.

Mydans, S. (1999, Sept. 20). "Australian Forces Reach East Timor to Aid in Recovery." The *New York Times,* A1.

Myers, S. (1996, Nov. 10). "U.N. Fails to Authorize Peace Force for Zaire." The *New York Times,* A18.

Nairn, A. (1994, Oct. 24). "Our Man in FRAPH: Behind Haiti's Paramilitaries." *The Nation,* 458–61.

Naniuzeyi, M. (1999). "The State of the State in Congo-Zaire: A Survey of the Mobutu Regime." *Journal of Black Studies,* 29 (Special Issue: "Political Strategies of Democracy and Health Issues and Concerns in Global Africa"), 669–83.

Nardin, T. (2006). "Introduction." In T. Nardin and M. Williams, *Humanitarian Intervention.* New York: New York University Press, 1–28.

Natsois, A. (1996). "Illusions of Influence: The CNN Effect in Complex Emergencies." In R. Rotberg and T. Weiss (Eds.). *From Massacres to Genocide: The Media, Public Policy and Humanitarian Crises.* Washington, DC: Brookings Institution, 149–68.

Ndikumana, L. (2000). "Towards a Solution to Violence in Burundi: A Case for Political and Economic Liberalisation." *The Journal of Modern African Studies,* 28, 431–59.

Neack, L. (1995). "UN Peacekeeping: In the Interest of Community or Self?" *Journal of Peace Research,* 32, 181–96.

Nelson, R. and W. Soderlund (1992). "Press Definitions of Reality during Elections in Haiti." *Media Development,* 39, 46–49.

Nevins, J. (2002). "The Making of 'Ground Zero' in East Timor in 1999: An Analysis of International Complicity in Indonesia's Crimes." *Asian Survey,* 42, 623–41.

Newbury, C. (1998). "Ethnicity and the Politics of History in Rwanda." *Africa Today,* 45, 7–24.

Newbury, D. (1997). "Irredentist Rwanda: Ethnic Conflict and Territorial Frontiers in Central Africa." *Africa Today,* 44, 211–22.

Niblack, P. (1995). *The United Nations Mission in Haiti: Trip Report.* Santa Monica, CA: Rand Corporation.

Nicholls, D. (1996). *From Dessalines to Duvalier: Race, Color and National Independence in Haiti.* New Brunswick, NJ: Rutgers University Press.

Noble, K. (1990, May 25). "Liberia Capital Fearful as War Nears." The *New York Times,* A3.

Noble, K. (1990, June 5). "Liberian Warfare Has Roots in 1985." The *New York Times,* A7.

Noble, K. (1990, June 16). "Liberian President Criticizes U.S." The *New York Times,* I3.

Noble, K. (1990, July 15). "In Besieged Liberian Capital, Hunger and Sleepless Nights." The *New York Times,* I1.

Noble, K. (1990, Aug. 21). "Liberian Leader, Rejecting Truce Offer Won't Quit." The *New York Times,* A11.

Noble, K. (1990, Aug. 22). "West African Force Sent to Liberia." The *New York Times,* A3.

Norris, P. (1995). "The Restless Searchlight: Network News Framing of the Post-Cold War World." *Political Communication,* 12, 357–70.

(*NYT*) The *New York Times.* (1990, July 26). "Sanctuary for Liberian Victims." The *New York Times,* A18. (editorial)

(*NYT*) The *New York Times.* (1990, Aug. 6). "The Uses of Force." The *New York Times,* A12. (editorial)

(*NYT*) The *New York Times.* (1990, Aug. 21). "Some Liberians Accuse the U.S. of Betrayal." The *New York Times,* A10.

(*NYT*) The *New York Times.* (1992, July 23). "The Hell Called Somalia." The *New York Times,* A22. (editorial)

(*NYT*) The *New York Times.* (1992, Aug. 2). "The Scourging of Africa." The *New York Times,* IV16. (editorial)

(*NYT*) The *New York Times.* (1992, Aug. 18). "Finally, Help for Somalia." The *New York Times,* A18. (editorial)

(*NYT*) The *New York Times.* (1992, Sept. 1). "A Foreign Legion for the World." The *New York Times,* A16. (editorial)

(*NYT*) The *New York Times.* (1992, Nov. 4). "Don't Forsake Somalia." The *New York Times,* A30. (editorial)

(*NYT*) The *New York Times.* (1992, Dec. 1). "Do It Right in Somalia." The *New York Times,* A24. (editorial)

(*NYT*) The *New York Times.* (1992, Dec. 4a). "Intervention in Somalia: White House and U.N. Muddy the Issue." The *New York Times,* A30. (editorial)

(*NYT*) The *New York Times.* (1992, Dec. 4b). "Intervention in Somalia: Congress Just Can't Let George Do It." The *New York Times,* A30. (editorial)

(*NYT*) The *New York Times.* (1992, Dec. 5). "What's the Goal in Somalia." The *New York Times,* I18. (editorial)

(*NYT*) The *New York Times.* (1992, Dec. 8). "The World's Only Other Cop." The *New York Times,* A24. (editorial)

(*NYT*) The *New York Times.* (1994, Apr. 10). "Double Tragedy in Africa." The *New York Times,* IV18. (editorial)

(*NYT*) The *New York Times.* (1994, Apr. 23) "Cold Choices in Rwanda." The *New York Times,* A24. (editorial)

(*NYT*) The *New York Times.* (1994, Mar. 23). "Black Caucus Urges Tougher Haiti Policy." The *New York Times,* A13.

(*NYT*) The *New York Times.* (1994, Apr. 22). "Treat Haitians Fairly." The *New York Times,* A26. (editorial)

(*NYT*) The *New York Times.* (1994, May 3). "Horror in Rwanda, Shame in the U.N." The *New York Times,* A23. (editorial)

(*NYT*) The *New York Times*. (1994, May 9). "Haiti: Sanctions at Last." The *New York Times*, A16. (editorial)

(*NYT*) The *New York Times*. (1994, May 13). "Stay Calm on Haiti." The *New York Times*, A30. (editorial)

(*NYT*) The *New York Times*. (1994, May 18). "Look Before Plunging into Rwanda." The *New York Times*, A22. (editorial)

(*NYT*) The *New York Times*. (1994, May 29). "Votes in Congress." The *New York Times*, I26.

(*NYT*) The *New York Times*. (1994, June 11). "The Makings of a Haiti Policy." The *New York Times*, A20. (editorial)

(*NYT*) The *New York Times*. (1994, June 15). "Shameful Dawdling in Rwanda." The *New York Times*, A24). (editorial)

(*NYT*). The *New York Times*. (1994, June 23). "Retiring Haiti's Junta." The *New York Times*, A22. (editorial)

(*NYT*) The *New York Times*. (1994, June 24a). "Few Allies Help France." The *New York Times*, A8.

(*NYT*) The *New York Times*. (1994, June 24b). "France's Risky Rwanda Plan." The *New York Times*, A26. (editorial)

(*NYT*) The *New York Times*. (1994, July 7). "Which Haiti Policy?" The *New York Times*, A18. (editorial)

(*NYT*) The *New York Times*. (1994, July 9). "Needed: Steady Hands on Haiti." The *New York Times*, I18. (editorial)

(*NYT*) The *New York Times*. (1994, July 13). "No Good Reason to Invade Haiti." The *New York Times*, A18. (editorial)

(*NYT*) The *New York Times*. (1994, July 24). "War Fever Over Haiti." The *New York Times*, IV14. (editorial)

(*NYT*) The *New York Times*. (1994, Aug. 2). "A U.N. License to Invade Haiti." The *New York Times*, A20. (editorial)

(*NYT*) The *New York Times*. (1994, Sept. 2). "Still a U.S. Invasion, Still Wrong." The *New York Times*, A24. (editorial)

(*NYT*) The *New York Times*. (1994, Sept. 13). "Congress Must Vote on Haiti." The *New York Times*, A22. (editorial)

(*NYT*) The *New York Times*. (1994, Sept. 16). "To the Shores of Port-au-Prince." The *New York Times*, A30. (editorial)

(*NYT*) The *New York Times*. (1994, Sept. 20). "Haiti: Relief, Not Victory." The *New York Times*, A22. (editorial)

(*NYT*) The *New York Times*. (1994, Mar. 6). "Security Council Urges Diplomacy in Burundi." The *New York Times*, A5.

(*NYT*) The *New York Times*. (1996, July 25). "Burundi at the Edge." The *New York Times*, A22. (editorial)

(*NYT*) The *New York Times*. (1996, July 27). "The Risk of Carnage in Burundi." The *New York Times*, I22. (editorial)

(*NYT*) The *New York Times*. (1996, Oct. 31). "In the Heart of Africa, a Slide Toward War." The *New York Times*, A10.

(*NYT*) The *New York Times*. (1996, Nov. 1). "An African Peace Force." The *New York Times*, A34. (editorial)

(*NYT*) The *New York Times*. (1996, Nov. 5). "Help the Hutu Refugees." The *New York Times*, A22. (editorial)

(*NYT*) The *New York Times*. (1996, Nov. 13). "Coping With an African Emergency." The *New York Times*, A22. (editorial)

(*NYT*) The *New York Times*. (1996, Nov. 15). "Rescue Mission to Africa." The *New York Times*, A23. (editorial)

(*NYT*) The *New York Times*. (1996, Nov. 19). "Help Still Needed in Central Africa." The *New York Times*, A24. (editorial)

(*NYT*) The *New York Times*. (1997, June 6). "Nigeria's Game in Sierra Leone." The *New York Times*, A30. (editorial)

(*NYT*) The *New York Times*. (1999, Apr. 18). "In Timor, Separatists Attacked by Militias." The *New York Times*, I4.

(*NYT*) The *New York Times*. (1999, Apr. 22). "All Factions in the Violence in East Timor Sign a Peace Accord." The *New York Times*, A6.

(*NYT*) The *New York Times*. (1999, Apr. 23). "Indonesia's Responsibility in East Timor." The *New York Times*, A24. (editorial)

(*NYT*) The *New York Times*. (1999, June 15). "East Timor: Calmer for Autonomy Vote." The *New York Times*, A19.

(*NYT*) The *New York Times*. (1999, July 20). "Jakarta Reportedly Predicts East Timor Will Vote to Split Off." The *New York Times*, A6.

(*NYT*) The *New York Times*. (1999, Sept. 2). "Respecting the Vote in East Timor." The *New York Times*, A26. (editorial)

(*NYT*) The *New York Times*. (1999, Sept. 8). "East Timor Under Siege." The *New York Times*, A22. (editorial)

(*NYT*) The *New York Times*. (1999, Sept. 10). "Helping East Timor, and Indonesia." The *New York Times*, A24. (editorial)

(*NYT*) The *New York Times*. (1999, Sept. 14). "An Effective Force for East Timor." The *New York Times*, A22. (editorial)

O'Ballance, E. (2000). *The Congo-Zaire Experience, 1960–98*. London: MacMillan Press Ltd.

Oberstar, J. (1994, June 25). "Liberate Haiti." The *New York Times*, A23.

O'Brien, C. (1962). *To Katanga and Back: A UN Case History*. New York: Simon and Schuster.

Olson, J. (1995). "Behind the Recent Tragedy in Rwanda." *GeoJournal, 35*, 217–22.

"Overview of Pre-UNAMSIL Interventions." (n.d.) Published in Monograph No. 68 *Peacekeeping in Sierra Leone, UNAMSIL Hits the Home Straight*. Retrieved March 23, 2006, from http://www.iss.co.za/Pubs/Monograph/No68/Chap2.html.

Page, B. and R. Shapiro (1983). "Effects of Public Opinion on Policy." *American Political Science Review, 77*, 175–90.

Page Fortuna, V. (1993a). "United Nations Angola Verification Mission I." In W. Durch (Ed.). *The Evolution of UN Peacekeeping: Case Studies and Comparative Analysis*. New York: St. Martin's Press, 1993, 376–87.

Page Fortuna, V. (1993b). "United Nations Angola Verification Mission II." In W. Durch (Ed.). *The Evolution of UN Peacekeeping: Case Studies and Comparative Analysis*. New York: St. Martin's Press, 1993, 388–405.

Pastor, R. (1997). "A Popular Democratic Revolution in a Predemocratic Society: The Case of Haiti." In R. Rotberg (Ed.). *Haiti Renewed: Political and Economic Prospects*. Washington, DC: The Brookings Institution Press, 118–35.

Paul, J. and M. Spirit (2000). "Riots Rebellions Gun Boats and Peacekeepers." Retrieved August 24, 2006, from http://britains-smallwars.com/RRGP/EastTimor.html.

Pease, K. and D. Forsythe (1993). "Human Rights, Humanitarian Intervention, and World Politics." *Human Rights Quarterly*, 15, 290–14.

Pélissier, R. (1971). "The Armed Revolt of 1961." In D. Wheeler and R. Pélissier, *Angola*. New York: Praeger, 173–92.

People's Daily. (2002, Oct. 11). "One Million People Died During Civil War in Angola: Report." Retrieved January 5, 2006, from http://english.people.com.cn/200210/11/eng20021011_104868.shtml.

Perlez, J. (1992, July 12). "U.N. Observers Delay Visit to Somalia." The *New York Times*, I12.

Perlez, J. (1992, July 19). "Deaths in Somalia Outpace Delivery of Food." The *New York Times*, I1.

Perlez, J. (1992, July 31). "U.S. Says Airlifts Fail Somali Needy." The *New York Times*, A9.

Perlez, J. (1992, Aug. 2). "The Disaster Begins to Sink In." The *New York Times*, IV6.

Perlez, J. (1992, Aug. 19). "1,000 Boys Return to Camp in Sudan." The *New York Times*, A5.

Perlez, J. (1992, Sept. 16). "A Hidden Disaster Grown in Sudan, Aid Officials Say." The *New York Times*, A1.

Perlez, J. (1992, Sept. 20). "Profile: Mohammed Sahnoun. A Diplomat Matches Wits With Chaos in Somalia." The *New York Times*, IV4.

Perlez, J. (1992, Nov. 27). "Somalia Aid Workers Split on Troops." The *New York Times*, A14.

Perlez, J. (1992, Dec. 4). "Expectations in Somalia." The *New York Times*, A1.

Perlez, J. (1992, Dec. 5). "Anxiety and Fear in Somalia in the Waiting for U.S. Forces." The *New York Times*, I1.

Perlez, J. (1999, Sept. 12). "Command Performance: America Talks and (Some) Others Listen." The *New York Times*, IV1.

Perry, A. (2007, Apr. 23). "Land of Chains and Hunger." *Time*, 21.

Perusse, R. (1995). *Haitian Democracy Restored, 1991–1995*. Lanham, MD: University Press of America.

Pierre-Pierre, G. (1994, June 28). "Haiti's Strongman Reported Ready to Retire." The *New York Times*, A6.

Pierre-Pierre, G. (1994, July 12). "Haiti Orders Out Foreign Monitors of Human Rights." The *New York Times*, A1.

Plummer, B. (1988). *Haiti and the Great Powers: 1902–1915*. Baton Rouge, LA: Louisiana State University Press.

Polgreen, L. (2007, Mar. 25). "Diamonds Move From Blood to Sweat and Tears." The *New York Times*, I1.

Power, S. (2003). *"A Problem from Hell." America and the Age of Genocide*. New York: Perennial.

Pratt, D. (1999, April 23). *Sierra Leone: The Forgotten Crisis*. Ottawa, ON: Canadian Centre for Foreign Policy Development.

Preston, B. and G. Flies (1999, Aug. 8). "Pre-Election Statement on East Timor Elections, Aug. 8, 1999." *The Carter Center*. Retrieved August 24, 2006, from http://www.cartercenter.org/doc267.htm.

Prunier, G. (1997). *The Rwanda Crisis: History of a Genocide*. New York: Columbia University Press.

Prunier, G. (1998). "The Rwandan Patriotic Front." In C. Clapham (Ed.). *African Guerrillas*. London: James Currey, 119–33.

Quindlen, A. (1992, Aug. 12). "Somalia's Plagues." The *New York Times*, A19.

Quindlen, A. (1994, Sept. 17). "The Face-Saving Intervention." The *New York Times*, I23.

Rawson, D. (1994). "Dealing with Disintegration: U.S. Assistance and the Somali State." In A. Samatar (Ed.). *The Somali Challenge: From Catastrophe to Renewal?* Boulder, CO: Lynne Rienner, 147–87.

Reed, W. C. (1998). "Guerrillas in the Midst: The Former Government of Rwanda (FGOR) & the Alliance of Democratic Forces for the Liberation of Congo-Zaire (ADFL) in Eastern Zaire." In C. Clapham (Ed.). *African Guerrillas*. London: James Currey, 134–71.

Reuters. (1990, July 21). "Liberian Guerrillas Capture Monrovia's Northern Sector." The *New York Times*, I3.

Reuters. (1990, July 31). "Liberia Troops Accused of Massacre in Church." The *New York Times*, A1.

Reuters. (1994, May 24). "Vatican is Critical." The *New York Times*, A3.

Reuters. (1994, May 28). "U.N. Chief Seeks Rwandan Aid." The *New York Times*, A5.

Reuters. (1994, June 13). "Haiti Declares an Emergency." The *New York Times*, A10.

Reuters. (1994, June 16). "France May Move In to End Rwanda Killing." The *New York Times*, A12.

Reuters. (1996, June 6). "Red Cross Suspends Operation in Burundi." The *New York Times*, A3.

Reuters. (1996, June 17). "Aid Workers Say Army Kills Civilians in Burundi." The *New York Times*, A6.

Reuters. (1996, Oct. 25). "Zaire Fighting Endangers Refugees, U.N. Says." A8.

Reuters. (1996, Nov. 18). "U.S. Weighing G.I. Relief Mission." The *New York Times,* A6.

Reuters. (1997, May 27). "Sierra Leone Military Arrests 5 Cabinet Officials After Coup." The *New York Times,* A10.

Reuters. (1999, June 23). "Angola Famine Alert." The *New York Times,* A6.

Reuters. (1999, May 25). "East Timor: U.N. Sending Police Aides." The *New York Times,* A10.

Reyntjens, F. (1995). *Burundi: Breaking the Cycle of Violence.* London: Minority Rights Group International.

Reyntjens, F. (2000). *Burundi: Prospects for Peace.* London: Minority Rights Group International.

Richardson, L. (1960). In Q. Wright (Ed.). *Statistics of Deadly Quarrels.* Pittsburgh, PA: Boxwood Press.

Rieff, D. (1996, June 12). "Death in Burundi." The *New York Times,* A23.

Rieff, D. (1996, Nov. 14). "Intervention Has a Price." The *New York Times,* A23.

Rieff, D. (2002). *A Bed for the Night: Humanitarianism in Crisis.* New York: Simon and Schuster.

Riley, S. (1982). "Sierra Leone Politics: Some Recent Assessments." *Africa: Journal of the International African Institute,* 52, 106–09.

Riley, S. (1993). "Intervention in Liberia: Too Little, Too Partisan." *The World Today,* 49, 42–43.

Rioux, J.-S. (2003). "Third Party Interventions in International Conflicts: Theory and Evidence." Paper presented at the Meeting of the Canadian Political Science Association, Halifax, NS.

Robinson, P. (2000). "The Policy-Media Interaction Model: Measuring Media Power During Humanitarian Crisis." *Journal of Peace Research,* 37, 613–33.

Robinson, P. (2001). "Operation Restore Hope and the Illusion of a News Driven Intervention." *Political Studies,* 49, 941–56.

Robinson, P. (2002). *The CNN Effect: The Myth of News, Foreign Policy and Intervention.* New York: Routledge.

Robinson, R. (1994, Apr. 17). "Haiti's Agony, Clinton's Shame." The *New York Times,* IV17.

Rogers, E. and J. Dearing (1988). "Agenda-Setting Research: Where Has it Been, Where Is It Going?" In J. Anderson (Ed.). *Communication Yearbook, Vol. 11.* Beverley Hills, CA: Sage Publications, 555–94.

Rosenblatt, R. (1994, June 5). "A Killer in the Eye." The *New York Times,* VI38.

Rosenthal, A. (1994, May 10). "The Haitian Mirror." The *New York Times,* A23.

Rotberg, R. (2002). "The New Nature of Nation-State Failure." *The Washington Quarterly,* 25, 85–96. Retrieved Oct. 3, 2006, from http//:64.233.167.104/search?q=cache:ajA-cZxcFQJ.www.twq.com/02summer/rotberg.pdf+rotberg+washington+quarterly+hl=en&gl=ca&ct=dnk+cd=1.

Rotberg, R. and T. Weiss (1996). *From Massacres to Genocide: The Media, Public Policy and Humanitarian Intervention*. Washington, DC: The Brookings Institution.

Rohter, L. (1994, July 24). "Close to Home: Remembering the Past; Repeating It Anyway." The *New York Times*, IV1.

Rohter, L. (1994, July 30). "Americans in Haiti Fear an Invasion." The *New York Times*, I3.

Rohter, L. (1994, Aug. 14). "Haiti is a Land Without a Country." The *New York Times*, IV3.

Rohter, L. (1994, Aug. 18). "Haitian Chief Buffs Image on the Streets." The *New York Times*, A9.

Rouvez, A. (1994). *Disconsolate Empires: French, British and Belgian Military Involvement in Post-Colonial Sub-Saharan Africa*. Lanham, MD: University Press of America.

Ruay, D. (1994). *The Politics of Two Sudans: The South and the North, 1821–1969*. Uppsala, Sweden, Institute of African Studies.

Sahnoun, M. (1994). *Somalia: The Missed Opportunities*. Washington, DC: United States Institute of Peace Press.

Salih, M. A. and L. Wohlgemuth (1994). "Introduction: Reality and Myth about the Somalia Crisis and the UN Intervention." In M. A. Salih and L. Wohlgemuth (Eds.). *Crisis Management and the Politics of Reconciliation in Somalia*. Uppsala, Sweden: Nordiska Africainstitutet, 5–9.

Salwen, M. (1988). "Effect of Accumulation of Coverage on Issue Salience in Agenda-Setting." *Journalism Quarterly*, 65, 100–06.

Samatar, A. (1994). "Introduction and Overview." In A. Samatar (Ed.). *The Somali Challenge: From Catastrophe to Renewal?* Boulder, CO: Lynne Rienner, 3–19.

Samatar, S. (1991). *Somalia: A Nation in Turmoil*. Minority Rights Group International.

Sawyer, A. (2004). "Violent Conflicts and Governance Challenges in West Africa: The Case of the Mano River Basin Area." *Journal of Modern African Studies*, 42, 437–63.

Schmidt, H. (1971). *The United States Occupation of Haiti, 1915–1934*. New Brunswick, NJ: Rutgers University Press.

Schmidt, W. (1992, Nov. 28). "Europeans Cautious." The *New York Times*, I6.

Schmidt, W. (1994, Apr. 8). "Troops Rampage in Rwanda; Dead Said to Include Premier." The *New York Times*, A1.

Schmidt, W. (1994, Apr. 18). "Rwandan Puzzle: Is Uganda Taking Sides?" The *New York Times*, A6.

Schmitt, E. (1990, Aug. 8). "Marines Evacuate 21 More in Liberia." The *New York Times*, A3.

Schmitt, E. (1992, Dec. 1). "U.S. Assesses Risks of Sending Troops to Somalia." The *New York Times*, A10.

Schmitt, E. (1994, July 15). "Making Moves For Haiti Action." The *New York Times*, A1.

Schmitt, E. (1994, Sept. 1). "Legislators in U.S. Differ Over Haiti." The *New York Times*, A10.

Schmitt, E. (1994, Sept. 2). "Pentagon Estimates It Will Cost $427 Million to Invade Haiti." The *New York Times*, A9.

Schmitt, E. (1994, Sept. 9). "Some Lawmakers Say Clinton Can Order Haiti Invasion." The *New York Times*, A8.

Schmitt, E. and M. Gordon (1994, Sept. 11). "Looking Beyond Invasion: U.S. Plans Haiti Police Force." The *New York Times*, I1.

Sciolino, E. (1992, Dec. 2). "Doubts at the CIA." The *New York Times*, A18.

Sciolino, E. (1992, Dec. 6). "Reluctant Heroes: Getting In Is the Easy Part of the Mission." The *New York Times*, IV4.

Sciolino, E. (1994, Apr. 15). "For the West, Rwanda is Not Worth the Political Candle." The *New York Times*, A3.

Sciolino, E. (1994, May 18). "Clinton's New Policy on Haiti Yields Little Progress So Far." The *New York Times*, A1.

Sciolino, E. (1994, May 22). "Haiti? Oh, We've Been There." The *New York Times*, IV5.

Sciolino, E. (1994, June 20). "Exile in Style Being Offered to Haiti Chiefs." The *New York Times*, A1.

Sciolino, E. (1994, July 4). "Haiti Invasion Not Imminent, Envoy Says." The *New York Times*, I2.

Sciolino, E. (1994, July 7). "Clinton's Problem: What Price Democracy?" The *New York Times*, A8.

Sciolino, E. (1994, Aug. 4). "Top U.S. Officials Divided in Debate on Invading Haiti." The *New York Times*, A1.

Sciolino, E. (1994, Sept. 13). "Invasion of Haiti Would Be Limited, Clinton Aides Say." The *New York Times*, A13.

Sciolino, E., H. French and D. Jehl (1994, Apr. 29). "Failure on Haiti: How U.S. Hopes Faded." The *New York Times*, A1.

Scowcroft, B. and E. Melby (1994, June 1). "Invade Haiti: A Sure Way to Make a Bad Policy Worse." The *New York Times*, A21.

Semb, A. (2000). "The New Practice of UN-Authorized Interventions: A Slippery Slope of Forcible Interference?" *Journal of Peace Research*, 37, 469–88.

Shacochsis, B. (1999). *The Immaculate Invasion*. New York: Viking Press.

Shamsie, Y. and A. Thompson (2006). "Introduction." In Y. Shamsie and A. Thompson (Eds.). *Haiti: Hope for a Fragile State*. Waterloo, ON: Wilfrid Laurier University Press, 1–12.

Sharkey, J. (1993, Dec.). "When Pictures Drive Foreign Policy." *American Journalism Review*, 15, 14–19. Retrieved March 11, 2006, from http://www.ajr.org/Article.asp?id=1579.

Shattuck, J. (1996). "Human Rights and Humanitarian Crises: Policy-making and the Media." In R. Rotberg and T. Weiss (Eds.). *From Massacres to*

Genocide: The Media, Public Policy and Humanitarian Intervention. Washington, DC: The Brookings Institution, 169–78.

Shenon, P. (1999, May 6). "Accords Signed for Timor Autonomy Vote, Rights Lawyer Harassed." The *New York Times,* A4.

Shenon, P. (1999, Aug. 28). "U.S. Warns Indonesia Over Political Violence." The *New York Times,* A4.

Shenon, P. (1999, Sept. 10). "President Asserts Jakarta Must Act or Admit Troops." The *New York Times,* A1.

Sherlock. P. (1996). "The Political Economy of the East Timor Conflict." *Asian Survey,* 36, 835–51.

Shiras, P. (1996). "Big Problems, Small Print: Guide to the Complexity of Humanitarian Emergencies." In R. Rotberg and T. Weiss (Eds.). *From Massacres to Genocide: The Media, Public Policy and Humanitarian Intervention.* Washington, DC: The Brookings Institution, 93–114.

Sidahmed, A. S. and A. Sidahmed (2005). *Sudan.* The Contemporary Middle East Series. London: Routledge-Curzon.

Simons, M. (1994, June 20). "France Says Allies Support Rwandan Plan." The *New York Times,* A7.

Simpson, C. (2002, Feb. 25). "Jonas Savimbi, UNITA's local boy." *BBC News.* Retrieved February 5, 2006, from http://news.bbc.co.uk/1/low/world/africa/264094.stm.

Smith, B. (1966). "Field Report: The Need for Humanitarian Intervention in Central Africa." Center for Human Rights and International Law, Washington College of Law, American University. Retrieved April 7, 2006, from http://www.wcl.american.edu/hrbrief.v3i3/rwanda33htm.

Smyth, F. (1994, Apr. 14). "French Guns, Rwandan Blood." The *New York Times,* A21.

Soderlund, W. (1970). "An Analysis of the Guerrilla Insurgency and *Coup D'État* as Techniques of Indirect Aggression." *International Studies Quarterly,* 14, 335–60.

Soderlund, W. (2003). *Mass Media and Foreign Policy: Post-Cold War Crises in the Caribbean.* Westport, CT: Praeger.

Soderlund, W. (2006). "U.S. Television News Framing of Haitian President, Jean-Bertrand Aristide, February 2004." *Journal of Haitian Studies,* 12, 78–111.

Spears, I. (1999). "Angola's Elusive Peace: The Collapse of the Lusaka Accord." *International Journal,* 54, 562–81.

Stairs, D. (1977–78). "Public Opinion and External Affairs: Reflection on the Domestication of Canadian Foreign Policy." *International Journal,* 33, 128–49.

Steel, R. (1999, Sept. 12). "East Timor Isn't Kosovo." The *New York Times,* IV19.

Stewart, I. (2002). *Ambushed: A War Reporter's Life on the Line.* Chapel Hill, NC: Algonquin Books of Chapel Hill.

Stockwell, J. (1978). *In Search of Enemies: A CIA Story.* New York: W. W. Norton.

Stotzky, I. (1997). *Silencing the Guns in Haiti: The Promise of Deliberative Democracy.* Chicago: University of Chicago Press.

Streiter, R. (2000). "Foreword." In J. Bock. *Sharpening Conflict Management: Religious Leadership and the Double-edged Sword.* Westport, CT: Praeger, xi–xxi.

Strobel, W. (1997). *Late-Breaking Foreign Policy: The News Media's Influence on Peace Operations.* Washington, DC: United States Institute of Peace Press.

Talbot, A. (2002, April 13). "The Angolan Civil War and US Foreign Policy." *World Socialist Web Site.* Retrieved February 5, 2006, from http://www.globalpolicy.org/empire/history/2002/0413angola.htm.

Talentino, A. (2005). *Military Intervention after the Cold War: The Evolution of Theory and Practice.* Athens, OH: Ohio University Press.

Talese, G. (1969). *The Kingdom and the Power.* New York: The World Publishing Company.

Tarr, S. B. (1993). "The ECOMOG Initiative in Liberia: A Liberian Perspective." *Issue: A Journal of Opinion,* XXI, 74–83.

Taylor, P. (1992, Aug. 3). "U.N. Chiefs Dispute With Council Boils Over." The *New York Times,* A1.

Taylor, J. (1999). *East Timor: The Price of Freedom.* London: Zed Books.

Thakur, R. (1994). "From Peacekeeping to Peace Enforcement: The UN Operation in Somalia." *The Journal of Modern African Studies,* 32, 369–410.

Thomasson, G. (1990, July 14). "Liberian Disaster: Made in the U.S.A." The *New York Times,* I21.

Thompson, A. (2006). "Haiti's Tenuous Human Rights Climate." In Y. Shamsie and A. Thompson (Eds.). *Haiti: Hope for a Fragile State.* Waterloo, ON: Wilfrid Laurier University Press, 51–69.

Tuck, C. (2000). "Every Car or Moving Object Gone." *The ECOMOG Intervention in Liberia,* 4. Retrieved March 23, 2006, from http://web.africa.ufl.edu/asq/v4/v4i1a1.htm.

(UN) United Nations. (1999). "The United Nations and East Timor: A Chronology." Retrieved August 24, 2006 from http.//www.un.org/peace/etimor.Untaetchrono.htm/.

(UN) United Nations. (2003a). United Nations Operation in Somalia II UNOSOM II (March 1993–March 1995). Retrieved July 17, 2006, from http:www.un.org/Depts.DPKO/missions/unosom2b.htm.

(UN) United Nations. (2003b). *Human Development Indicators 2003.* Retrieved September 22, 2006 from http://hdr.undp.org/reports/global/2003/indicators.indic_10_1_1.html.

(UN) United Nations. (2004, May 21). "United Nations Operations in Burundi." Retrieved June 25, 2006, from http://www.un.org/Dept/dpko/missions/onub/.

(UN) United Nations Security Council. (2005a). "Liberia." *Global Policy Forum*. Retrieved November 8, 2005, from http://www.globalpolicy.org/security/issues.liberindx.htm.

(UN) United Nations Security Council (2005b, Feb. 8). "Sudan Peace Agreement Signed 9 January Historic Opportunity, Security Council Told." Retrieved December 25, 2006, from www.un.org/News/Press/docs/2005/sc8306.doc.htm.

(UN) United Nations Integrated Mission in Timor-Leste. (2007, Jan. 4). "Fact Sheet on United Nations Integrated Mission in Timor-Leste." Retrieved on January 6, 2007, from http://www.unmiset.org/unmisetwebsite.nsf/6e7449fbabe9254a49256fle0020b424/05ccda24653e2c5d4.

Urquart, B. (1994, May 12). "Who Can Police the World?" The *New York Times Review of Books*, 29–33.

(U.S.) Department of Defense. (1994, Sept. 15). "Military Preparing for Haiti." The *New York Times*, A8.

Uvin, P. (1996). "Tragedy in Rwanda: The Political Ecology of Conflict." *Environment*, 38, 6–15, 29.

Uvin, P. (1998). *Aiding Violence: The Development Enterprise in Rwanda*. West Hartford, CT: Kumarian Press.

Vaccaro, J. M. (1996). "The Politics of Genocide: Peacekeeping and Disaster Relief in Rwanda." In W. Durch (Ed.). *UN Peacekeeping, American Politics, and the Uncivil Wars of the 1990s*. New York: St. Martin's Press, 367–407.

Vance, C. and D. Hamburg (1996, Mar. 9). "Avoiding Anarchy in Burundi." The *New York Times*, I23.

Verney, P., D. Johnson, W. James, M. A. Salih, A. S. Sidahmed, S. M. Kuol, and A. S. Hassan (1995). *Sudan: Conflict and Minorities*. [International Report 95/3]. London: Minority Rights Group International.

von Hippel, K. (1995). "Democratization as Foreign Policy." *The World Today*, 11–14.

von Hippel, K. (2000). *Democracy by Force: US Military Intervention in the Post-Cold War World*. New York: Cambridge University Press.

Wagner, M. (1998). "All the Bourgmestre's Men: Making Sense of Genocide in Rwanda." *Africa Today*, 45, 25–35.

Wallensteen, P. and K. Axell (1994). "Conflict Resolution and the End of the Cold War." *Journal of Peace Research*, 31, 333–49.

Wallensteen, P. and M. Sollenberg (2000). "Armed Conflict, 1989–99." *Journal of Peace Research*, 37, 635–49.

Weiner, T. (1994, Apr. 27). "Clinton Forces Out U.S. Envoy to Haiti to Display Resolve." The *New York Times*, A1.

Weiss, T. (1999). *Military-civilian Interactions: Intervening in Humanitarian Crises*. Lanham, MD: Rowman and Littlefield.

Weiss T. and C. Collins (1996). *Humanitarian Challenges and Intervention: World Politics and the Dilemmas of Help*. Boulder, CO: Westview Press.

Weiss, T. and C. Collins (2000). *Humanitarian Challenges and Intervention.* 2nd ed. Boulder, CO: Westview Press.

Weinstein, W. (1972). "Tensions in Burundi." *Issues: A Journal of Opinion,* 2, 27–29.

Weinstein, W. and R. Schrire (1976). *Political Conflict and Ethnic Strategies: A Case Study of Burundi.* Syracuse, NY: Maxwell School of Citizenship and Public Affairs, Syracuse University.

Wharton, C. Jr. (1994, Apr. 9). "The Nightmare in Central Africa." The *New York Times,* A21.

Wheeler, D. (1969). "The Portuguese Army in Angola." *The Journal of Modern African Studies,* 7, 425–439.

Wheeler, D. (1971). "Black Mother and White Father." In D. Wheeler and R. Péllisier. *Angola.* New York: Praeger, 28–50.

Wheeler, N. and T. Dunne (2001). "East Timor and the New Humanitarian Interventionism." *International Affairs,* 77, 805–27. Retrieved September 22, 2006, from http://www.ingentaconnect.com/content/bpl/inta/2001/0000007700000004/art00220.

Wilentz, A. (1994, Mar. 24). "Haiti's Death Mask." The *New York Times,* A23.

Windrich, E. (1992). *The Cold War Guerrilla: Jonas Savimbi, the U.S. Media, and the Angolan War.* New York: Greenwood Press.

Windsor Star. (2004, Mar. 17). "France Accused of Genocide by Leader." *The Windsor Star,* B2.

Wines, M. (1990, July 31). "U.S. Condemns Killings." The *New York Times,* A2.

Wines, M. (1992, Dec. 5). "Bush Declares Goal in Somalia is to 'Save Thousands.'" The *New York Times,* I1.

Wines, M. (1992, Dec. 6). "Aides Say U.S. Role in Somalia Gives Bush a Way to Exit in Glory." The *New York Times,* I14.

Wippman, D. (1993). "Enforcing Peace: ECOWAS and the Liberian Civil War." In L. F. Damroach (Ed.). *Enforcing Restraint: Collective Intervention in Internal Conflicts.* New York: Council on Foreign Relations Press, 157–203.

Zartman, I. W. (1995). *Collapsed States: The Disintegration and Restoration of Legitimate Authority.* Boulder, CO: Lynne Rienner.

Zinoman, P. and N. Peluso (2002). "The Legacy of Violence in Indonesia." *Asian Survey,* 42, 545–49.

Index

 *Also from Kumarian Press...*

Conflict Resolution and Peacebuilding:

Zones of Peace
Edited by Landon Hancock and Christopher Mitchell

Nation-Building Unraveled? Aid, Peace and Justice in Afghanistan
Edited by Antonio Donini, Norah Niland and Karin Wermester

Transacting Transition: The Micropolitics of Democracy Assistance in the Former Yugoslavia
Edited by Keith Brown

New and Forthcoming:

The World Bank and the Gods of Lending
Steve Berkman

Mobilizing for Human Rights in Latin America
Edward Cleary

**Surrogates of the State:
NGOs, Development and Ujamaa in Tanzania**
Michael Jennings

How NGOs React: Globalization and Education Reform in the Caucasus, Central Asia and Mongolia
Edited by Iveta Silova and Gita Steiner-Khamsi

Visit Kumarian Press at **www.kpbooks.com** or call **toll-free** 800.232.0223 for a complete catalog.

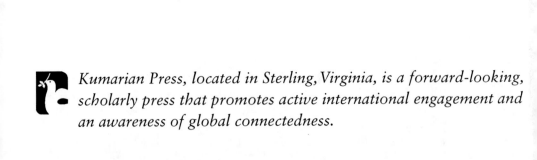

Kumarian Press, located in Sterling, Virginia, is a forward-looking, scholarly press that promotes active international engagement and an awareness of global connectedness.